T0318629

Managing Cultural Festivals

Tradition and Innovation in Europe

Edited by
Elisa Salvador and
Jesper Strandgaard Pedersen

Routledge
Taylor & Francis Group

LONDON AND NEW YORK

First published 2022
by Routledge
4 Park Square, Milton Park, Abingdon, Oxon OX14 4RN

and by Routledge
605 Third Avenue, New York, NY 10158

Routledge is an imprint of the Taylor & Francis Group, an informa business

British Library Cataloguing-in-Publication Data
A catalogue record for this book is available from the British Library

Library of Congress Cataloging-in-Publication Data
Names: Salvador, Elisa, 1977- editor. | Pedersen, Jesper S. (Jesper Strandgaard), 1959-
Title: Managing cultural festivals : tradition and innovation in Europe / Edited by Elisa Salvador and Jesper Strandgaard Pedersen.
Description: Abingdon, Oxon ; New York, NY : Routledge, 2022. | Series: Routledge research in the creative and cultural industries | Includes bibliographical references and index.
Subjects: LCSH: Festivals—Europe—Management. | Festivals—Europe—Planning. | Europe—Social life and customs.
Classification: LCC GT4842 .M36 2022 (print) | LCC GT4842 (ebook) | DDC 394.2694—dc23/eng/20211203
LC record available at https://lccn.loc.gov/2021048875
LC ebook record available at https://lccn.loc.gov/2021048876

ISBN: 978-0-367-64962-3 (hbk)
ISBN: 978-0-367-64960-9 (pbk)
ISBN: 978-1-003-12718-5 (ebk)

DOI: 10.4324/9781003127185

Typeset in Sabon
by codeMantra

Contents

Figures

Tables

Appendices

Boxes

Contributors

Pierre-Jean Benghozi is Research Director at the National Centre for Scientific Research (CNRS) and is Professor at the École Polytechnique (Paris) and GSEM (Geneva University). Since the early 1980s, Professor Benghozi has been developing pioneering research on information technology, telecommunications, media, and culture. His latest book deals with videogames as a cultural industry. He is Co-chair of AIMAC and is on the boards of several international editorial and scientific committees.

Ana Maria Botella Nicolás is a Professor of the Department of Didactics of Musical, Plastic and Corporal Expression of the Faculty of Education of the University of Valencia. She is a Doctor in Pedagogy at the University of Valencia and Graduate in Musicology and Teacher in Musical Education at the University of Oviedo. She has a professional degree in the specialty of piano and international Master in the same specialty. She is the author of more than a hundred publications in her area of specialization, music didactics. Her main lines of research are the didactics of listening, innovation, and interdisciplinarity in teacher training and the renewal of teaching methodologies.

Elena Castro-Martínez is a tenured scientist at the Spanish Council for Scientific Research (CSIC), working at INGENIO-CSIC, Universitat Politècnica de València, Valencia, Spain. She researches on knowledge transfer and exchange processes between universities and social agents, focusing on humanities and social sciences, and on innovation in culture.

María Devesa (PhD) is an Associate Professor at the University of Valladolid. Her research interests focus on cultural festivals and events, the economic impact of culture, demand studies, and tourism economics. She has published articles in various international indexed journals.

Ignacio Fernández-de-Lucio is a Professor *ad honorem* at INGENIO-CSIC, Universitat Politècnica de València, Valencia, Spain. He developed an extensive career as a Manager of science and knowledge transfer in public research centres. Since 1999, he has been conducting research on the relationship between science and innovation.

Luca Giustiniano (PhD) is Professor of Organization Studies at Luiss University (Rome, Italy) and is Director of the Centre for Research in Leadership, Innovation, and Organisation (CLIO). His research interests are focused on organization design. He has been Visiting Scholar at the Viktoria Institute (Sweden), the Sauder School of Business (Canada), the Interdisciplinary Centre for Organizational Architecture (Denmark), the Nova SBE (Portugal), the Waseda Institute for Advanced Study (Japan), and the University of Ljubljana (Slovenia). His papers have appeared in the *Journal of Management, Management and Organization Review, British Journal of Management, Computers in Human Behavior, Management Learning*, and *European Management Review.*

Kerem Gurses is an Associate Professor at the International School of Commerce and Digital Economy at La Salle (Ramon Llull University). Dr. Kerem Gurses holds a PhD in Management from IESE Business School and an MBA from the Illinois Institute of Technology. His research focuses on the corporate political strategies of organizations, and how organizations deal with regulation. He has published his research in distinguished journals such as the *Academy of Management Journal* and the *European Management Review.* Dr. Kerem Gurses has also done consulting and project work for the food, car, and aerospace industries.

Rosa Isusi-Fagoaga holds a PhD in musicology and a Conservatory higher degree in music. She is a Professor of music didactics at the Faculty of Education at the University of Valencia. Her research interests are social and cultural innovation in Higher Education and the transfer and dissemination of musical heritage.

Keiko Kawamata is Professor of Marketing, School of Cultural and Creative Studies, Aoyama Gakuin University, Japan. Her research interests lie in culture and marketing. She is the co-author of 'The Process of Development and the Evolution of Japanese Pop Culture Event: Case of World Cosplay Summit (Nagoya, Japan)', Proceedings: the EURAM 2020 Conference, December 2020.

Dorottya Eva Kiss has a multidisciplinary background and works at the crossroads of art, sciences, and 'human sustainability'. She holds a BA Cultural Sciences and a BA Performing Arts (Dance) and two MAs: Cultural Economics & Entrepreneurship and Arts & Cultural Sciences. Kiss ran her own dance theatre company for 12+ years, is a lecturer at Erasmus University and a licensed NLP MA Practitioner, and a certified business, social/EI consultant.

Arjo Klamer is Em Professor of cultural economics at Erasmus University. He is actively involved in a value-based approach in economics and currently works on the development of a programme in the humane economy. He authored *Doing the Right Thing* (2017) and currently works on a book entitled *A Sense of Purpose*.

Giovanni Masino is Full Professor of Organizational Behavior at the Department of Economics and Management, University of Ferrara, where he is currently Pro-Chancellor for work orientation and Director of the Ferrara Master School. He published several books and scientific articles in international academic journals on topics such as organizational change, work organization, leadership, proactivity and job crafting, decision making, and motivation in the workplace. He has been Visiting Scholar at the University of North Carolina at Chapel Hill (USA) and the University of Toulouse (France).

Carmelo Mazza obtained his PhD from IESE Business school, Barcelona (Spain). His research primarily focuses on institutional change and how managerial concepts and practices are diffused and institutionalized in different industries. Recent research focuses on the rise of new institutions and how they are supported/challenged by the external environment. His research is published in a number of international journals, books, and other academic outlets. Along with the academic experience, he has been involved in several consulting projects on new regulations and institutional transformation, and during the last five years, he has been acting as CEO of a small company in Malta.

Toshihiko Miura is Professor of Marketing, Faculty of Commerce, Chuo University, Tokyo, Japan. His research interests lie in global marketing and global consumer behaviour. He is the author of numerous books including *Why are Japanese Consumers Tough? Japanese and Contemporary characteristics of Consumers and Marketing in Japan* (Yuhikaku Publishing, 2013, in Japan).

Andrea Morelli is Researcher in cultural economics at Santagata Foundation and Symbola Foundation, Consultant at Foundation for Culture Torino, and Researcher Affiliate at OMERO Interdepartmental Research Centre on Urban and Event Studies at the University of Turin. He holds a master's degree in Economics of Culture at the University of Turin.

Shoetsuro Nakagawa is Associate Professor of Marketing and Consumer Behavior, School of Economics, Seijo University, Japan. His research interests lie in consumer psychology and digital marketing, with a particular interest in the psychological mechanism of consumers' choice of a specific digital platform.

Josef Pallas is Professor at the Department of Business Studies, Uppsala University, Uppsala, Sweden. His research focuses on organization and governance of public sector organizations in general and universities, governmental agencies, and municipalities in particular. He is interested in dynamics, consequences, and interplay of governing ideas connected to public appraisal and evaluation, media and news production, communication, as well as those associated with professionalism and collegiality.

Ludmilla Petrova is Researcher and Educator of cultural economics with a PhD from Erasmus University. She is Co-Founder of the Center for Research and Education in Arts and Economics (CREARE), where she works on the implementation of the Value-Based Approach Evaluation of cultural and social programmes and organisations across Europe.

Viktoriya Pisotska is a PhD Candidate in Management at Luiss University (Rome, Italy) and a Visiting PhD Fellow at the Copenhagen Business School, Department of Organization. Her research areas are Creative Industries, Organization Theory, Entrepreneurial Agency, and Project Organising. Her research focuses on how different competing demands can be managed in the context of Cultural and Creative Industries.

Elena Raviola is Torsten and Wanja Söderberg Professor in Design Management at the Academy of Art and Design, University of Gothenburg. Her research explores how digitalization transforms the organization of professional work, especially in the cultural and creative industries. She has conducted extensive field studies in European news organizations.

Albert Recasens is a Researcher at the Institute for Culture and Society of Universidad de Navarra (Spain) and the Director of the ensemble La Grande Chapelle and the record company Lauda Música. Throughout his career, he has combined artistic direction, record production, management of cultural events, and musicological research.

Ana Roitvan (MSc) is a Production Manager of the Segovia International Puppet Festival, *Titirimundi*. Likewise, she is an experienced Event Manager and Volunteer Coordinator at a number of different festivals.

Elisa Salvador (HDR, University of Paris 13; PhD, University of Turin) has worked on innovation policy for the Italian National Research Council (CNR) and was awarded CNR's Promotion of Research 2005 prize. She has collaborated with the Polytechnic of Turin and with the ESCP-Europe Business School; she taught at Iéseg School of Management; and she worked as a Researcher at Ecole Polytechnique, Paris investigating R&D and innovation in the cultural and creative industries. Currently, she is a Professor at ESSCA School of Management, where she coordinates the master's course in Managing Creativity and Innovation.

Iben Stjerne is an Assistant Professor in the Department of Organization at Copenhagen Business School, Denmark. Her primary research focus sits at the intersection of temporality, transient forms of organizing, and human resource management.

Giovanna Segre is Associate Professor in Economic Policy at the University of Turin, where she currently serves as Deputy Director of the Biennial

Master in Economics of Environment, Culture and Territory, Deputy Director of the Master in Cultural property Protection in Crisis Response, Vice President of the Interdepartmental Research Center for Urban studies, and Member of the Academic Board of the PhD in Technologies for Cultural Heritage. She is also a Research Associate of IRCrES-CNR and a Member of the Scientific Committee of the Santagata Foundation for the Economics of Culture. Her research interests and publications focus on economics of culture, cultural heritage, creative industries, and welfare economics.

Marianna Sigala is Professor at the University of Piraeus, Greece. She previously hold the position of the Professor of Tourism and the Director of the Centre for Tourism & Leisure Management at the University of South Australia (2015–2021). She has also been an academic staff at the University of Strathclyde and Westminster University (UK), and the University of the Aegean (Greece). Her academic credentials are combined with her professional experience in the tourism industry. Her interests include services and experience management, Information and Communication Technologies (ICT) in tourism and hospitality, as well as wine tourism. She is a widely published and multi-awarded authority: nine books, numerous papers in academic journals, and (keynote) presentations in international conferences. She has a long record of leadership and participation in international research projects funded by various entities such as the E.U., the Council of Europe and the Department of Foreign Affairs and Trade, Australia. She is a past President of EuroCHRIE and a past member of the executive board of ICHRIE and IFITT. She currently serves at the executive board of CAUTHE. She is the co-editor of the *Journal of Service Theory & Practice*, and the Editor-In-Chief of the *Journal of Hospitality & Tourism Management*. In 2016, she has been awarded the prestigious EuroCHRIE Presidents' Award for her lifetime contributions and achievements to tourism and hospitality education. Since 2020, Professor Sigala is also appointed as Research Fellow of CAUTHE.

Jean-Paul Simon is an Independent Researcher and Consultant specialised in media/telecom law regulation and strategy. He is a frequent speaker on telecommunications and media in Asia, Europe, and the USA. He holds a PhD in Philosophy (1975) and is a graduate (MBA) from the Ecole des Hautes Etudes Commerciales (HEC) (MBA, econometrics, 1971). He has written several books and articles on communications and public policy.

Jesper Strandgaard Pedersen, PhD, is Professor at Copenhagen Business School, where he serves as Director of Imagine. Creative Industries and Institutions Research Centre, and as Chairman of SCANCOR. His research focuses on organizational and institutional change, and on how managerial concepts and practices are produced, diffused, assessed, and institutionalized across a range of cultural-creative and knowledge-intensive settings. Recent research focuses on cultural intermediaries and evaluative practices in the fields of film, festivals, and food, and is published in, 'The Negotiation of Values in the Creative Industries. Fairs, Festivals and Competitive Events' (2011), Cambridge University Press, and in 'Technology and Creativity. Production, Mediation and Evaluation in the Digital Age' (2020), Palgrave, Macmillan.

Silviya Svejenova is a Professor in Leadership & Innovation in the Department of Organization at Copenhagen Business School, Denmark. Her research focuses on multimodal and temporal aspects of creativity, innovation, space, and place.

Norio Tajima is Professor of Marketing, Faculty of Commerce, Takushoku University. He specialises in marketing and consumer behaviour. His research interests cover diffusion of innovations and consumer behaviour related to Japanese pop culture. He is the Co-Author of *Marketing with Culture as a Competitive Edge* (Chuokeizai-sha, 2020, in Japanese).

Caterina Valenti is Junior Fellow of Santagata Foundation for the Economics of Culture with a master's degree in Economics of Culture at the University of Turin. Since 2019, she has been collaborating in the management, organization, and communication of University of Turin's Masters, including the international Masters "Cultural Property Protection in Crisis Response" and "World Heritage and Cultural Projects for Development".

Luca Zan, Bologna University, is involved in the management of arts/heritage organizations, within an international comparative perspective, and with fieldwork in China, Turkey, Peru, Ecuador, and Europe. He is Author/Co-Author of *Managerial Rhetoric and Arts Organizations*, 2006; *The Management of Cultural Heritage in China*, 2008; *Managing Cultural Heritage*, 2016; and *Heritage Sites in Contemporary China*, 2018. He is also active in management/accounting history, managing practice in protoindustrial settings, and management and accounting in historical perspectives. He is involved in international teaching in Arts Management: till 2020, he was Director of GIOCA, Unibo; Adjunct faculty MAM, CMU, Pittsburgh; and Adjunct faculty at CAFA, Beijing.

Preface and Acknowledgments

The inspiration for this book originated during the two-day international workshop on *"Cultural Festivals' Organization and Management: new Challenges in the Digital Age?"*, 26–27 November 2019, University of Valencia (Spain), organized by Elisa Salvador (ESSCA School of Management, France), Elena Castro-Martínez (INGENIO-CSIC, Universitat Politècnica de València, Valencia, Spain), Ana Maria Botella Nicolás, and Rosa Isusi Fagoaga (University of Valencia, Spain). The program of the workshop is available at: https://cfest.webs.upv.es/ The Workshop was organized under the label of The International Association of Arts and Cultural Management (AIMAC).

Like many other people around the world, we (Elisa Salvador and Jesper Strandgaard Pedersen), the co-editors of this edited volume, have been confronted with distant working and digital communication due to the Covid-19 pandemic that profoundly impacted the entire world. We have had to deal with all matters related to the construction of the book without having the possibility to discuss the matters of the book face to face in person along the journey from the emerging idea till the manuscript submission. We did our best to assure the completion of the book in the shortest possible time so as to provide current research and findings on cultural festivals to readers of the volume. To be able to achieve this, the editors would like to thank all the contributors of the book for their reactivity and respect of strict deadlines.

We are also grateful to the two anonymous reviewers as well as Routledge for enabling this volume. A special thanks to Terry Clague, senior publisher Routledge books, for the enthusiasm shown since the beginning about the idea of this edited volume and the constant help and encouragement.

Elisa Salvador and Jesper Strandgaard Pedersen

Foreword

Cultural Festivals – Quos Vadis in Research and Practice

Marianna Sigala

Festivals before and after COVID-19: the topicality and urgency of their study

Festivals have become a critical part of the fabric of our global society. During the last two decades, various figures have reflected the flourishing of festivals as an important social practice, business activity, and a (geo)-political/diplomatic strategy (Richards, 2017): the number of festivals taking place internationally; the numerous participants or tourists traveling to attend a festival; the plethora of educational offerings specialising on festivals/events management; the various local, regional, national, and supra-national governmental and non-governmental organisations developing policies and strategies to make their places eventful; and the mushrooming publications and research within academic and industry circles investigating various issues related to festivals. The festivalization (Frey, 2000) of our daily social, professional, and political life is not surprising when considering the important role and impact that festivals have on the economy, society, the physical environment, and our political life (e.g. Page & Connell, 2012). As the COVID-19 pandemic halted many festival activities, many have also learnt in the hard way how important festivals are on the (economic, social, psychological, and physical) well-being of people, artists, communities, and livelihoods alike.

This book aims to discuss the challenges and future directions related to the management and the research of the until now fast-growing festivals industry and specifically, cultural festivals. The focus of the book is very topical and important, since the COVID-19 pandemic did not only disrupt the operations of this industry, but it is fast changing and shaping new behaviours, attitudes, and operational settings, which all ultimately challenge the future and nature of the festivals (Davies, 2021). For many, the COVID-19 crisis is also seen as a transformational opportunity allowing us to rethink, re-sett, and re-shape the next normal of the tourism and events industry (Sigala, 2021).

The development of this book was conceptualised and based on research papers presented at the two-day international workshop on "Cultural Festivals' Organization and Management: new Challenges in the Digital Age?", 26–27 November 2019, University of Valencia (Spain), organized by Elisa Salvador (ESSCA School of Management, France), Elena Castro-Martínez (INGENIO-CSIC, Universitat Politècnica de València, Valencia, Spain), Ana Maria Botella Nicolás, and Rosa Isusi Fagoaga (University of Valencia, Spain). The Workshop was organized under the label of The International Association of Arts and Cultural Management (AIMAC).

Thus, the book chapters do not explicitly address the coronavirus crisis, since they are generally based on research that was designed and conducted before the pandemic hit. However, many of the chapter authors have managed to nicely re-consider and discuss their study findings within the light of the new setting created by the pandemic. In addition, even if the studies were developed before COVID-19, many of the issues that the chapters debate are still very contemporary and topical in this post COVID-19 era. This is because the COVID-19 crisis (Sigala, 2020) has made more evident and transparent many pre-existing challenges and issues related to festivals, as well as it has intensified and magnified the need and the urgency to act and address these issues.

The following sections identify and debate how the COVID-19 pandemic is intensifying the presence and the urgency of four major pre-existing issues challenging the festival industry. The sections also discuss how the book chapters contribute to deepen our current understanding and further explore these issues by discussing issues combining a theoretical underpinning and practical evidence. The studies presented in the book chapters collected findings from a wide range of genres of cultural festivals (e.g. music, cartoon, food, dance, film, book) taking place in various European countries (e.g. Spain, Italy, France, Sweden, Denmark, the Netherlands). Although the book represents insights and views coming only from one continent and 'western' culture, the book chapters provide in-depth critical discussions that have implications at a global scale. In addition, the book's perspective and field findings can be used as a good basis and 'benchmark' to enrich and complement the findings coming from other international studies and cultural perspectives. Finally, in concluding these sections, I also share some thoughts and directions on how we should be advancing our research and practice within the festival sector so that we can all try to help to (re)-build it back better.

Festivals and sustainability

There has always been a controversy about why and how much to fund and support the festivals (e.g. discussions about hosting festivals and/or governmental policies aiming to support festivals for (economic) growth). The debates are always centred around the impacts of festivals (whether their positive impacts outweigh the negative) as well as the sustainability of these impacts (e.g. long-term impacts and legacies of festivals). However, measuring the festivals' impacts for answering such questions (about whether and how to fund festivals and how to manage them to achieve sustainable and long-term benefits) is not a straightforward and easy process, because: there is a multi-dimensionality of impacts and many impacts cannot be quantified (e.g. social cohesion, community pride, and identify building; cultural preservation; noise/physical pollution; social discrimination); even if impacts can be quantified, their materialisation is not always guaranteed (e.g. translation of place/destination branding on tourists' future visitation and spending depends on many other uncontrollable factors than the festival itself); festivals have impacts on various stakeholders, who frequently have different and sometimes conflicting interests, agendas, perspectives, and priorities (e.g. festivals can generate tourists' spending and create jobs, but traveling for festivals also generates carbon emissions and may commoditise local culture).

The COVID-19 crisis and its repercussions have made everyone to recalibrate social values and personal priorities, to re-think his/her personal and work lifestyle and the latter's impact on issues like well-being and sustainability. People are becoming more environmentally aware and sensitive, and increasingly give more importance on solidarity, equality, corporate responsibility, and fairness. Health and safety values have prevailed in relation to the previous prevalence of economic values and the unquestionable mindset and assumption that development can only come through economic growth. Economies have slowed down and a new setting is being developed whereby health and safety become important with an economic price. People's decisions, leisure styles, and travel options are also found to be significantly influenced by the ongoing health and safety risks. The pandemic also changes the people's attitudes and consumption behaviour towards festivals: people start questioning whether it is worthwhile travelling for attending a festival or supporting a festival that commodifies local traditions and communities' values. Under this COVID-19 context, the urgency and need to address the festivals' sustainability, social responsibility, and their role in contributing to people's and communities' well-being are magnified.

The third section of the book consolidates five chapters focusing on the socio-cultural impacts of festivals. These book chapters develop and apply theoretical frameworks that highlight the need to measure the multi-dimensionality of the festivals' impacts. In doing so, the book chapters consider and provide some answers on how to address many of the above-mentioned 'problems' when measuring and managing the festivals' sustainability. For example, the book chapters provide answers to questions like: what type of festival impacts to measure and why these impacts matter? What indicators can be used to quantify these impacts? From whose perspective to measure festivals' impacts? By doing this, the chapters can assist festival managers to measure their success and (re)-direct their management practices to run sustainable festivals. The importance of measuring and knowing what to measure are widely known, i.e., you can only manage what you measure; and you become what you measure.

However, as many (e.g. Mair & Smith, 2021) have argued, events and sustainability should not be only about running sustainable events, because this gives a narrow research orientation and purpose for the industry to exist and operate. On the contrary, one should also think how to design and run festivals that can also contribute to the sustainability of the places hosting them as well as to the betterment and uplifting of the well-being of the festival participants, communities, and other stakeholders. COVID-19 tourism-related research also highlights the opportunity that the crisis has given us to re-set and re-imagine a better tourism and events industry. In this vein, scholars are urged to conduct more transformative research challenging and expanding current mindsets and assumptions (Sigala, 2020).

Even before COVID-19, a new genre of festivals (called transformational festivals) had emerged aiming to help participants and host communities to achieve self-development, improvement, and transformation. However, instead of thinking of transformational festivals as a separate and isolated type of festivals, it has become apparent that we need to make every festival transformative by embedding aspects and goals of transformation into its whole conceptualisation and implementation (e.g. design, program, operations, and impacts). Further research is required to better understand how to design, embed, and measure transformative goals and impacts into festivals. The book includes one chapter that can contribute towards this dialogue and our further investigations on how to embed and measure transformational goals and impacts into festivals. Arjo Klamer, Ludmilla Petrova, and Dorottya Eva Kiss co-authored a chapter that developed and applied a 'quality evaluator' to measure the impact of a cultural festival in the Netherlands; their assessment method and measurement indicators adopt a value-based approach in order to consider the changes in values that a festival generates to its audience or visitors in four spheres: the personal (e.g. meaningful work, autonomy, good and responsible citizen, and human being); social (e.g. good family, good friendships, good communities, collegiality); societal (e.g. justice, liberty, democracy, social cohesion, diversity, a sustainable environment, human rights); and the transcendental sphere (e.g. beauty, truth, meaning, faith). This is an interesting approach identifying 'spheres' of transformation and types of values contributing to well-being. Such values can help researchers and professionals alike to re-imagine and reform a 'better' future of festivals. The question however that still remains and needs to be answered is: what do we mean by 'better', as 'better' is a very relative and subjective world. Without defining 'better' and achieving universal stakeholders' consensus about its meaning and measurement, we would not be able to draft a plan and commit resources to achieve it.

Festivals and information & communication technologies (ICT)

ICT is the lifeblood of festivals. ICT support and enable festivals to happen in an efficient and effective way. ICT advances also disrupt and transform the industry by enabling innovation and change (Sigala, 2018a, 2018b). The COVID-19 crisis has further reinforced this critical role that ICT play in festivals. The COVID-19 has also accelerated and magnified many ICT-induced changes, innovations, and transformations within the festival sector. This is because during the COVID-19:

–   ICT have been instrumental and necessary in supporting festival operators, artists, communities, and organisations to maintain business continuity, revenue streams, and (virtual) presence as well as engagement and communication with their audience
–   ICT supported and enabled various innovations for necessity
–   ICT adoption has been accelerated; all actors from both the demand and supply side of the festival sector increased their adoption and use of ICT during the lockdowns and the continuous restrictions on mobility and festival operations
–   ICT have been instrumental for the re-opening and re-start of the festival sector, for example, use of applications to manage the size and location/flow of crowds; monitor contact tracing; provide touchless services and experiences (e.g. mobile payments, mobile ticketing)
–   ICT are argued to help the re-setting of the industry to build back better and become more 'sustainable'. For example, there is increased interest in ICT applications that support recycling and reduction of carbon emissions (e.g. micro-mobility solutions offered to festival goers to reduce traffic and emissions); and influence consumers' sustainable behaviour (i.e. monitoring and measuring healthy eating, and sustainable lifestyles)
–   ICT innovations and applications foster numerous changes on both the demand and supply of festivals. For example, ICT are shaping new consumption models, profiles, and behaviours of festival audiences; and they enable new types of e-festivals and new business models of festivals that change industry structure, offerings, and operations

Although there are numerous examples showing how ICT have fostered innovation, survival, change, and transformation within the festival sector during the COVID-19 crisis, these can be grouped into the following categories:

–   *Development and use of new distributions channels:* many festival operators were thinking and wanted to use social media, internet, and/or mobile channels to distribute and communicate their content/

performances for longtime before COVID-19; when the crisis started, some of them managed to do it even within limited time and resources. Many festival stakeholders developed their Facebook, LinkedIn, You-Tube, Instagram, or TikTok profile and have started using these channels to disseminate their offerings

– *New market development:* festival stakeholders were able to develop new markets (e.g. audience of online streaming festivals) or penetrate new markets by reaching them digitally, as they were never able to travel to attend the festival (e.g. people with disabilities, people living in remote places)

– *Customer relationship marketing:* many festival stakeholders use online channels not only to distribute digital offerings but also to engage and communicate with their audiences, build, and maintain their festival community during the lockdown or inactive festival periods

– *Digitisation of offerings/experiences:* creation of online festivals, online performances, virtual tours, virtual exhibitions, AR, VR, XR extended reality, and livestreaming

– *Human resource management:* although remote working may seem as the major ICT application supporting HRM, many festivals have taken the opportunity to also exploit ICT for employee training and personal development, employee support, online recruitment, and online auditions

– *Partner engagement:* online engagement and collaboration with festival stakeholders and partners

– *Technologies for contactless/touchless services:* the following ICT have become a 'necessity": customer flow management, social distancing tools for monitoring crowds and people movement, mobile payments, and ticketing

– *Market intelligence for market prediction and personalisation:* as more and more festival operations, customers, and stakeholders go online (and so, their online activity leaves a digital footprint), big data has become an important organisation resource that organisations need to collect, analyse, and interpret in order to take data-informed and timely operational and strategic decisions such as: to better understand and predict festival consumer behaviour; to measure and manage operational and business risks; and to monitor competitors' practices.

Various chapters of this book have studied and discuss technology-related issues for the festival sector. The major questions asked by these chapters include to what extent are the festival operators ready and/or have already adopted ICT? and how the way they use the ICT has or not changed and/or innovate their business model and operations? Although the ICT have substantially disrupted but also helped cultural sectors (such as the music, book, and film industries) to innovate and transform, evidence provided by the book chapters shows that operators in the cultural festivals are slow, reluctant, and not fully ready to embrace and use ICT. This is quite surprising, as ICT advances have already started to generate major and fast pacing changes into the festivals' marketplace and context. Chapter findings also show that the festivals demonstrate a low level of ICT-induced innovation. This is because most of the ICT applications adopted by the sector reflect a simple digitisation of their current administration, and operational and marketing practices (e.g. e-ticketing, e-marketing, mobile check-ins) rather than a creative use of ICT to support radical innovations and transformations of their business model (e.g. to develop virtual offerings and online festivals, adopt various pricing models for digital offerings such as festivals-as-a-service or subscription payments, use ICT to interact with live audiences in new ways).

Future research is required to better understand what 'constraints' and/or limits the festival sector to embrace the full potential of the digital revolution. Understanding and addressing this issue is important, as festivals cannot 'escape' from the digital revolutions, and cannot pretend that it does not exist and/or it does not change the festivals' environment. In their book chapter, Elisa Salvador, Elena Castro-Martinez, and Pierre-Jean Benghozi argued that the specific nature and offering of the festivals (a living production and the ability to experience in person a live performance) inhibits and keeps the industry back in using ICT in creative ways to transform their business models and offerings. However, the fact that festivals do represent a major experiential offering should not been seen as an obstacle in thinking and implementing ways in which the ICT can enable new genres of interactive experiences. Due to COVID-19, people were obliged to use and become familiar and experts with new ways of interactions in many spheres in their personal, family, and work life. This prolonged use of new interactive experiences has made people better understand the benefits but also the limitations and risks of such interactions, while it has created new habits, behaviours, preferences, and expectations for many aspects of life, services, and even cultural consumption. Consumers are not expected to forget their newly adopted and formed work, social, entertainment, and cultural consumption styles and go back to their 'old' habits when COVID-19 is over. Even the new socio-cultural, political, and legal framework may not allow going back. It is predicted that digital experiences (blurring and mixing the digital and physical dimensions of experiences) would dominate and be expected or preferred in the next normal of our personal, social, work, and leisure life. In this vein, it is the right timing for festivals practitioners and researchers to think and contribute on how festivals should be shaping and also be shaped by this new setting of digital experiences.

Some festival operators may still decide not to digitize their operations, offerings, and business models for various reasons. However, this does not mean that they can escape from the digital revolution and its implications; in fact, they cannot afford to be oblivious and inactive to the repercussions of the digital era. Two book chapters give good evidence and arguments for this. The chapter contributed by Ana Maria Botella Nicolás, Rosa Isusi-Fagoaga, and Elena Castro-Martinez shows that online educational concerts is probably the online way to appeal and attract the new generation that is born and grows up with the new ICTs. Unless if festivals use ICT to attract and educate/build this new market segment, they may end up with no audience in the near future. In their chapter, Josef Pallas and Elena Raviola provide another example highlighting the repercussions of the digital era. Even if festival operators do not want to build an online presence to network and 'discuss' online, other 'stakeholders' will do and they will also most likely talk about the former. Discussions on social media can critically influence the image, reputation, the identity, the community, and attendance and many other aspects of festivals. The chapter contributed by Pallas and Raviola highlights how a book festival addressed and managed online discussions that politized the identity and purpose of the festival. The chapter explains how the festival 'used' the social media to convert the threat of the online discussions to a transformational opportunity helping the book festival to evolve its 'purpose' and impact on the society; by embracing the social media, the book festival transformed itself from a marketplace aggregating book publishers to a place supporting and fostering political dialogues and social change.

Overall, ICT will continue to advance and influence every aspect of life. Hence, it is important to understand how festivals can follow but also lead this ICT evolution towards the 'betterment' of the industry; and how festivals can be influenced but also influence the ways in which ICT support and enable transformation and innovation. Research and practice should adopt an attitude and mindset towards ICT and festivals that reflects a more synergetic and symbiotic inter-relation between these two rather than a competitive, defensive, and/or offensive stance.

Festivals and marketplace: inter-relations, dynamics, and co-evolution

Cultural festivals are a time-bound performance providing a snap-shot representation of a constantly evolving feature, that is the contemporary and/or past socio-cultural features of a community and its place. Culture is a living organism that is constantly evolving through its enactment, re-enactment, and continuous performativity. Cultural festivals should also follow socio-cultural trends and fashions. In addition, cultural festivals may also trigger and foster social change as well as generate new socio-cultural fashions. This is because, by supporting and fuelling dialogues and other social practices, festivals can also act as field configuring events (FCEs) that encapsulate and shape the development of professions, technologies, markets, and industries (Lampel & Meyer, 2008). Cultural festivals and their (socio-cultural, political, and economic) marketplace co-evolve together by shaping and being shaped by each other. This perplex, reciprocal, and dynamic inter-relation between (cultural) festivals and the marketplace has always been at the research focus of many scholars aiming to understand and unravel the inter-complexities and dynamics defining and evolving this relationship. Festival professionals are also interested in understanding this relation, as they are daily challenged to manage it, balance conflicting powers, and use dynamics to ensure the 'success' of their festivals. Nowadays, COVID-19 has accelerated change in every actor and aspect of the marketplace system and so made this inter-relation more fluid, dynamic, and sensitive than ever before. COVID-19 increased the frequency and scale of change, and new changes are being introduced before previous ones being adopted, tested, crystalized, and/or institutionalized. For example, during COVID-19, we have seen the emergence and even one-off performance of various types of cultural festivals: street performances; neighbourhood festivals; opera concerts attended and co-created by locals being lockdown in their home balconies; drive-in concerts; and film screenings. Being performed under the pressure of a 'necessity' and as the only available option, these cultural festivals may never appear again or even been institutionalized. However, they have certainly influenced and re-shaped people's conceptualization, expectations, and understanding of cultural festivals. The influence of these localized, small-scale community and real-time co-produced occasions may even shape the future of cultural festivals and help drive more sustainability in the sector.

Overall, festival researchers and professionals alike are asked to operate, manage, and/or shape change in uncharted waters, when nothing is normal and whereby change is not any more the only constant. Under this context, there is an ever-increased need for researchers and professionals to be able to understand what is change, how it is happening, and how to study, manage, shape, and create it. Two chapters in this book provide some interesting theoretical lenses and approaches to help researchers and professionals to study, understand, manage, and shape change; this can also help us in our efforts to re-image and re-set festivals in the next normal. In their chapter, Josef Pallas and Elena Raviola explain the concept of field configuring events (FCEs) and how festivals can trigger and foster social change as FCEs. The authors also highlight the role of technologies in change and stress the need of managing change through both traditional and digital channels. In their chapter, Norio Tajima, Keiko Kawamata, Shoetsuro Nakagawa, and Toshihiko Miura show how a cultural festival was used to institutionalize a new 'culture'/market. The authors adopted an institutional approach to unravel how the festival legitimized and established a new cultural festival/market by using mega-marketing strategies (Humphreys, 2010) in order to build the cultural-cognitive, normative, and regulative conditions required to legitimatize the new market. This represents an interesting approach to understand and lead change when everything is un-normal, fluid, and under continuous shaping processes and forces. This approach is also in line with wider arguments in the management literature claiming that innovative organizations willing to adopt, survive, and thrive should not adopt a learning the market but a learning with the market approach (Sigala, 2016); in other words, it is not enough for organizations to simply identify and respond to market changes (pro-actively or re-actively), but they should primarily aim to co-learn and co-evolve with markets (i.e. shape and be shaped by market dynamics). In this vein, future research studies should be directed on what learning with the market means, and what market capabilities festival professionals should build and develop to interpret, interact, exchange, shape, and be shaped with cultural markets and actors. Identifying and building such dynamic capabilities in the festival sector can be a vital asset of the industry to create and shape festival futures.

Festivals, innovation, and creativity

The previous sections nicely explained the importance of innovation in the festival sector, and how urgent this has become due to COVID-19 crisis. Innovation is fostered and required not only because of sustainability requirements, technological advances, marketplace forces, and the need for resilience and adaptability. As a living entity, cultural festivals should have innovation into their core essence and purpose of existence. Innovation requires leadership and creativity, which are also important capabilities that researchers and professionals should nurture and exercise in the sector.

The book includes a whole section featuring four chapters discussing innovation within the cultural festival sector. The chapters focus on how to manage the two polarities, that is, tradition and innovation, that have for long been considered as obstacles of innovation. In some way, the management of this polarity also resembles the debates in the cultural (heritage) literature in terms of what is authenticity (e.g. Chhabra, 2021). Studies in this field can provide further light into the challenge on how to manage innovation in cultural festivals. Cultural festivals need to learn and break away from the past but also the shadow and destiny of the global future. Overall, the book chapters debate the following various issues that are important addressing when thinking about innovation and cultural festivals:

- The nature of cultural festivals and the impact of their distinctive features on innovation
- The types, processes, and actors of innovation involved in cultural festivals
- The dynamic relation between tradition and innovation and the role of festival identity

Conclusions

The book is being written (and probably read) while things are still uncertain, flex, and under rapid stress and change. I hope the COVID-19 pandemic will be an opportunity for us to re-set and re-consider the way we view, consume, co-create, manage, and study cultural festivals. I hope you will enjoy reading the book and that it will inspire you in various ways to create festival futures.

References

Chhabra, D. (2021). *Authenticity and Authentication of Heritage.* Routledge.

Davies, K. (2021). Festivals post Covid-19. *Leisure Sciences,* 43(1–2), 184–186.

Frey B. (2000). The rise and fall of festivals: Reflections on the Salzburg Festival. Working Paper No. 48. Institute for Empirical Research in Economics, Zurich.

Humphreys, A. (2010). Megamarketing: The creation of markets as a social process. *Journal of Marketing,* 74(20), 1–19.

Lampel, J., & Meyer, A. D. (2008). Field-configuring events as structuring mechanisms: How conferences, ceremonies, and trade shows constitute new technologies, industries, and markets. *Journal of Management Studies,* 45(6), 1025–1035.

Mair, J., & Smith, A. (2021). Events and sustainability: Why making events more sustainable is not enough. *Journal of Sustainable Tourism,* 29(11–12), 1739–1755. doi: 10.1080/09669582.2021.1942480.

Page, S. & Connell J. (2012). *The Routledge Handbook of Events.* Routledge.

Richards, G. (2017). Emerging models of the eventful city. *Event Management,* 21(5), 533–543.

Sigala, M. (2016). Learning with the market: A market approach and framework for developing social entrepreneurship in tourism and hospitality. *International Journal of Contemporary Hospitality Management,* 28(6), 1245–1286.

Sigala, M. (2018a). Festivals and social media: A co-created transformation of festivals goers and operators. In Mair, J. (Ed.) *Handbook of Festivals* (pp. 163–172). Routledge.

Sigala, M. (2018b). Social media and the transformation of the festival industry: A typology of festivals and the formation of new markets. In Mair, J. (Ed.) *Handbook of Festivals* (pp. 102–110). Routledge.

Sigala, M. (2020). Tourism and COVID-19: Impacts and implications for advancing and resetting industry and research. *Journal of Business Research,* 117, 312–321.

Sigala, M. (2021). Re-thinking of tourism and hospitality education when nothing is normal: restart, recover or rebuild. *Journal of Hospitality & Tourism Research.* doi:10.1177/10963480211012058.

Introduction

Managing Cultural Festivals: Context, Challenges and New Avenues of Research

Elisa Salvador and Jesper Strandgaard Pedersen

Since the late 1990s, cultural and creative sectors and industries have received increasing attention from scholars, practitioners and politicians as driving forces in the 21st-century economies. These sectors and industries are seen as sources for economic growth (Pine and Gilmore, 1999; Caves, 2000; Throsby, 2001) urban development (Jakob, 2013), branding for cities or local territories (Ooi and Strandgaard Pedersen, 2010, 2017; Scott, 2010), drivers for creativity (Lampel, Lant and Shamsie, 2000; Jones, Svejenova, Strandgaard Pedersen and Townley, 2016), as well as sources for social cohesion and solidarity (Higgs, Cunningham and Bakhshi, 2008).

The cultural and creative sectors and industries were among the first ones to be profoundly affected and challenged by the Internet revolution and information and communication technology diffusion, with consequent disruptions and transformations in value chain structure and business models (Salvador, Simon and Benghozi, 2019; Strandgaard Pedersen, Khaire and Slavich, 2020; Salvador and Benghozi, 2021). The strategies they are adopting in the digital age are inspiring. According to Benghozi, Salvador and Simon (2021), two main new strategies, not forcedly classifiable according to traditional theories, are emerging. The first one is a static but flexible strategy: flexibility and ambidexterity for absorbing the shocks of changing environments are its main characteristics. This strategy aims at overcoming organizational inertia through slow and cautious steps, not always in line with the rapidity of changes in the digital age. The second one is the dynamic and liquid strategy: this is a proactive and more than agile strategy, characterized by quick movements, rapid adaptations and constant changes to be in tune with the new configurations that are emerging externally (Benghozi, Salvador and Simon, 2021).

In this context, Cultural Festivals seen as 'events linked to cultural activities' are one of the most diffused examples of living production in all the fields of cultural and creative sectors and industries (Luonila and Johansson, 2016). And, as noted by Frey (2000) and Bennett, Taylor and Woodward (2014), the world, and in particular Europe, has over the years witnessed 'festivalization' (or 'festivalomania') as a fast-growing phenomenon, which

DOI: 10.4324/9781003127185-1

is manifested in the rapid increase in the number of festivals and their institutionalization (Mulder, Hitters and Rutten 2020).

Festivals are seen as increasingly important ways of organizing and distributing culture and, as events, they are seen as playing important roles in constituting, configuring, valorizing and maintaining local culture and heritage as well as global industries and fields (Lampel and Meyer, 2008; Moeran and Strandgaard Pedersen, 2011). In recent years, festivals attracted an increased attention from academic scholars as well as from practitioners and politicians exactly because of their proliferation and remarkable increase in number as noted by researchers from a variety of fields (e.g. Salvador, Castro-Martinez and Benghozi, Chapter 9; Rüling and Strandgaard Pedersen, 2010; Del Barrio, Devesa and Herrero 2012; Baez-Montenegro and Devesa-Fernandez, 2017). Nevertheless, the significance of festivals has for long been largely overlooked by scholars (cf. Pallas and Raviola, Chapter 7 on 'mediatization'; and Castro-Martinez, Recasens and Fernández-de-Lucio, Chapter 4 on 'innovation' as another example) and festival research still remains in an early stage – except maybe for tourism and marketing research dedicated to festival impact on host cities and regions (e.g. Getz and Andersson, 2009).

Last but not least, the recent COVID-19 pandemic – still in progress – that disrupted the organization and management of everyday life of people around the world as well as of economies strongly impacted also the performing arts' sector, including concerts, arts' events and festivals. Several festivals switched to an online edition in 2020 (and some also in 2021), and others simply cancelled and postponed the 2020 edition and rescheduled for a 2021 edition in the respect of the sanitary protocols for facing the pandemic. Nonetheless, there are also many small festivals that risk disappearing because of the financial consequences due to the COVID-19 crisis (cf. Simon, Chapter 13).

This edited volume also aims at renewing the attention on a niche field, *cultural festivals*, which is so important for valorizing cultural traditions and local heritage visibility as well as social well-being (cf. Segre, Morelli and Valenti, Chapter 5; Devesa and Roitvan, Chapter 10). Following the disruptive consequences of the COVID-19 pandemic, this fragile sector deserves more attention from public authorities and stakeholders at local, as well as regional, national and European level with suitable and dedicated plans for recovery and valorization of cultural festivals.

Cultural festivals: definition and state of the art

Festivals provide a rich and fascinating setting for research on organization and management (Rüling and Strandgaard Pedersen, 2010). Traditionally, organization and management theory has been based on the premise that organizations were or ought to be organized as permanent entities (Lundin and Söderholm, 1995). In their seminal article 'A Theory of the Temporary

Organization', Lundin and Söderholm (1995) present their thoughts on what marks a different type of organization, namely a temporary organization, creating a starting point for later research agendas on temporary organizations (e.g. Engwall, 2003; Stjerne and Svejenova, 2016; Sydow and Braun, 2018). When viewed as temporal organizations, Cultural Festivals are typically characterized by a couple of features. First, festivals often operate at the interface between permanent and temporary organizing, which leads to the emergence of various tensions with regard to status, coordination and temporal structures (Geraldi, Stjerne and Oehmen, 2020), to mention just some of the tensions, and their organizing change with regard to form and size during the year. Second, festivals differ with regard to their type and duration. Some festivals are one-off events, whereas other festivals are repetitive events and with a duration lasting from a few hours to several days or even weeks (Lampel and Meyer, 2008; Braun and Lampel, 2020). Similar observations on festivals as temporary organizations are also made by Abfalter, Stadler and Muller (2012: 6), stating,

"Festivals are an extreme example of seasonal organizations, the main season being ephemeral, reduced to a period of days or weeks when all staff members come together, business activity takes place, and services and experiences are delivered".

As a result, a multiplicity of perspectives is being brought to the study of festivals and arts' events. To embrace a range of these perspectives, we have settled for a broad and encompassing definition of Cultural Festivals. Rephrasing Allix's (1922) definition of fairs, in this edited volume, we define a Cultural Festival as,

> An event linked to cultural activities in the form of a temporary township, superimposed at intervals upon a permanent place (town or city), which in important, though not regularly defined, social, traditional and symbolic ways, contributes to the local or global (cultural) needs of a particular entity (e.g. industry, city, region, nation) and its group of members

Starting from this definition of Cultural Festivals, we focus primarily on Cultural Festivals in Europe. Historically, culture has played a pivotal role in European tradition as well as at EU level and it is part of a central pillar of its actions, not only for fostering cooperation among member states (cf. Tajima, Kawamata, Nakagawa and Miura, Chapter 12) but also for valorizing cultural heritage, national identity and tradition (Littoz-Monnet, 2007; Benghozi and Salvador, 2019).

Cultural festivals: present and future challenges

Getz (2008) states in the opening paragraphs of his review that events, such as Cultural Festivals, have many partners and proponents and many important societal and economic roles to play. Thus, situated at the crossroads of multiple institutions, interests and agendas, Cultural Festivals is a multifaceted phenomenon involving various stakeholders, interests and discourses prompting these events to cater for different and sometimes conflicting demands (Ooi and Strandgaard Pedersen, 2010; cf. Mazza and Strandgaard Pedersen, Chapter 3). Being situated at the crossroads of these different institutions, demands and interests, Cultural Festivals face several challenges. Given the growing number of festivals, the event organizers take part in a competition for attention, time and space as well as for attracting public and private funding for their festival. Thus, establishing and maintaining such an event on industry and audience agendas and anchoring it in the festivals' landscape is an important strategic task and challenge for festival organizers.

Thanks to an increased use of digital technologies for registration, ticketing, access control and so forth, festival organizers have access to detailed data about participants and they may start developing new organizational practices to exploit these data and allow festival organizations to optimize sessions, for example, regarding space and seats. Yet, one cannot take for granted that digital technologies, *per se,* have a beneficial or disruptive effect on all types of events. For example, traditional tools used for minor festivals organization and management, because of specific event peculiarities linked to the local territory and to the unique experience they provide to visitors, which cannot easily be replaced by digital tools. On the one hand, these festivals obtain customer loyalty and increase the number of visitors more through "word of mouth" than through digital channels and they look for new audiences also through educational programs involving students (cf. Salvador, 2020; Botella-Nicolas, Isusi-Fagoaga and Castro-Martinez, Chapter 8). Nonetheless, on the other hand, a festival's setting and its organization is a tricky matter (cf. Zan and Masino, Chapter 6). Such events are characterized by various temporalities (Geraldi, Stjerne and Oehmen, 2020; cf. Stjerne and Svejenova, Chapter 2) and a project focus that requires professional execution together with a motivated workforce under intensive short-term collaborations and the leadership of one or a few persons (Abfalter, Stadler and Muller, 2012). A related and additional domain of inquiry concerns the management of human resources and organizational knowledge within and across festival organizations. Festival organizations are often marked by fluctuating membership, temporary collaboration together with extensive use of and high turnover of volunteers (cf. Salvador, Castro-Martinez, Benghozi, Chapter 9). Dealing with such human resource issues, the transfer of knowledge, as well as sustaining the experience, and maintaining the identity of the festival collaborators become other fundamental issues to deal with and handle for the festival organizers (Strandgaard Pedersen and Mazza, 2011). From celebrating tradition and heritage, festivals are these years facing challenges concerning how to embrace and deploy innovative solutions, in particular digital technologies. Consequently, one may wonder what the influence and impact of the digital revolution on the organization and management of Cultural Festivals will be (cf. for example, Pisotska, Gurses and Giustiniano, Chapter 1). This matter is even more urgent following the massive digitalization of activities due to the COVID-19 pandemic.

Several important questions concerning the management and organization of such events follow from the proliferation of Cultural Festivals as well as the impact of the COVID-19 pandemic. An important question at stake is to understand what nowadays lays the foundation for the potential success or failure of Cultural Festivals. Is it their economic model, their management and organization, the nature of their offer, the services and experiences that they propose or their links to the various local stakeholders and city facilities and structures? Other important questions are, how can they generate and balance the funding from public authorities, private sponsors and ticket sales from audiences? Where and how can they find and develop new and future audiences? How can they measure and document the value and impact of the festival? How can they organize for this? All these are pertinent questions for cultural festivals in the 21st century. For example, Klamer, Petrova and Kiss (Chapter 11) propose a "quality evaluator" to evaluate and provide feedbacks about a cultural festival. Other chapters in this edited volume advance interesting solutions and/or describe Cultural Festivals' case-studies around Europe that provide some answers to the above questions.

The volume

This book is intended to provide an overview and insight of Cultural Festivals in Europe and how they have faced the challenges, taking insights from an international range of expected high-level scholarly contributors. Individual chapters highlight and analyze challenges in the creative sector around the organization, management and economics of Cultural Festivals. The book provides a comprehensive overview of scholarly research in this area, setting the scene for future research agendas. The focus in this volume is on tradition *vs* innovation in Cultural Festivals' organization and management, taking into account the consequences of the digital age revolution, as well as the value and impacts of these events. Matters related to educational programs and new audience development, as well as challenges related to sustainability solutions, are also included.

More specifically, the edited volume includes 13 chapters, and it is organized into three main sections. Part I is titled "Cultural Festivals Organization and Management: between Tradition and Innovation", while Part II is focused on "Challenges of Cultural Festivals in the Digital Age". Finally, Part III is concerned with "Value and Impacts of Cultural Festivals at Local and Regional Level".

A summary and introduction to individual chapters included in each section is provided here below.

Part I "Cultural Festivals Organization and Management: between Tradition and Innovation"

The volume begins with the chapter by Viktoriya Pisotska, Kerem Gurses and Luca Giustiniano (Chapter 1), who focus on the famous Venice Biennale and its Venice International Film Festival (Italy) through a qualitative analysis. They investigate how the tension between tradition and innovation is managed in one the oldest, most traditional and innovative cultural institutions, and the key role of organizational identity is highlighted in their chapter.

Then, in the following chapter, Iben Sandal Stjerne and Silviya Svejenova (Chapter 2) focus on food events as an example of cultural events. Through examining the temporal dynamics at these events in relation to tradition and innovation, they address the question 'How are traditions revived and ideas for the future revealed at food events?' Their study is focused on a temporal analysis of the Chefs' Manifesto food event.

Carmelo Mazza and Jesper Strandgaard Pedersen (Chapter 3) study the creation, transformation and maintenance of 'FestambienteSud', located in Monte Sant'Angelo in southern Italy. Hosting two UNESCO World Heritage List (WHL) sites, the festival with its many different stakeholders and agendas offers a setting to study how management of arts, culture, heritage and tourism may collide with economics and politics. The study is concerned with the institutional and organizational complexities and dilemmas rising from such a pluralistic setting and how they can be managed.

This section ends with a chapter by Elena Castro-Martínez, Albert Recasens and Ignacio Fernández-de-Lucio (Chapter 4). These authors develop a survey for looking at types of innovation and strategies employed by festival managers in Spanish early music festivals, as well as the benefits that these festivals derive from these innovations, helping them to carry out their main traditional mission of disseminating musical heritage.

Part II "Challenges of Cultural Festivals in the Digital Age"

This section begins with a chapter analyzing an Italian classical music festival, *"MITO SettembreMusica"*, written by Giovanna Segre, Andrea Morelli and Caterina Valenti (Chapter 5). The authors focus on the audience of a recent edition of this festival thanks to a sample of 2,800 questionnaires with the purpose to better understand the characteristics of the demand for classical music and the composition of its public in live events.

Then, in the following chapter, Luca Zan and Giovanni Masino (Chapter 2) analyze the Ferrara Buskers' Festival in Italy, which is one of the leading festivals of street artists in the world. The authors provide a historical analysis of this event, summarizing the main characteristics of three phases of the festival's history. In their analysis, they present and discuss the various views and sensemaking processes of the performing artists concerning busker identity and what it means to be a busker.

Josef Pallas and Elena Raviola for their part, in Chapter 7, focus on the case of the Swedish Gothenburg Book Fair, exploring the processes by which cultural fairs can become symbols of larger societal debates. Pallas and Raviola highlight how the management of Gothenburg book fair address and manage the online discussions that politicize the purpose and identity of the festival. They also address potential consequences of this evolution on cultural activities and original mission of cultural fairs and festivals.

Finally, in Chapter 8, Ana Maria Botella Nicolás, Rosa Isusi-Fagoaga and Elena Castro-Martinez focus on the musical and educational perspective of cultural festivals. They present an explorative study about music festivals in Spain and an analysis of Early Music Festivals in particular. The aim is to understand the link between tradition and innovation and their special focus on educational programs and didactic concerts.

Part III "Value and Impacts of Cultural Festivals at Local and Regional Level"

Elisa Salvador, Elena Castro-Martinez and Pierre-Jean Benghozi (Chapter 9) look at festivals related to less popular sectors such as publishing: they investigate and compare two case-studies of comics' festivals in France and Spain. The aim of their analysis is to identify the nature of the dynamics and strategies at work in order to highlight in which extent these small festivals clear up the structuration of a multi-faced economic model specifically linked to the characteristics of the sector.

María Devesa and Ana Roitvan (Chapter 10) explore the social and cultural impact of the Segovia International Puppet Festival (*Titirimundi*), the main puppet festival in Spain and one of the leading festivals of its kind in Europe. They propose a specific set of indicators to measure the sociocultural impact of arts festivals and they offer both a theoretical reflection on how to measure such effect and a practical application on the selected case-study.

Arjo Klamer, Ludmilla Petrova and Dorottya Eva Kiss (Chapter 11) propose a quality evaluator (QE) that they designed to evaluate the realization of cultural and social values and qualities of a cultural festival and its organization. The QE is intended to provide feedbacks for improvement. The authors apply the QE to the case-study of the performing arts Rotterdam Unlimited Festival.

Norio Tajima, Keiko Kawamata, Shoetsuro Nakagawa and Toshihiko Miura (Chapter 12) examine how Japanese pop culture events (JPCEs) have influenced the acceptance of the Japanese pop culture (JPC) in Europe, and especially in France. They focus on the Japan Expo, held in Paris since 2000, and they use the mega-marketing framework to analyze the development of JPCEs as a social legitimation process of JPC.

Concluding the volume, Jean-Paul Simon (Chapter 13) focuses on music festivals taking a closer look at a sample of these festivals in France, Italy, Spain and the UK. He analyzes data about music festivals, documenting the trend, and takes a closer view at some of the current assumptions about these festivals in Europe. He offers an overview of the economics of music festivals, and he concludes with questions about the economic impact of music festivals, and beyond the economic dimension, he stresses the multi-dimensional nature of music festivals.

As stated in the opening of this introduction, apart from some early scholarly contributions, the significance of festivals has for long been largely overlooked by scholars and festival research still remains in a fairly early stage. With this volume, it is our intention to contribute to mending part of this gap. Of course, this is just a starting point – we hope that other researchers will continue along our path and will deepen the investigations about Cultural Festivals.

References

Abfalter, D., Stadler, R., and Muller, J. (2012). The organization of knowledge sharing at the Colorado music festival. *International Journal of Arts Management*, 14(3), 4–15.

Allix, A. (1922). The geography of fairs: Illustrated by old world examples. *Geographical Review*, 12(4), 532–569.

Baez-Montenegro, A., and Devesa-Fernandez, M. (2017). Motivation, satisfaction and loyalty in the case of a film festival: Differences between local and non-local participants. *Journal of Cultural Economics*, 41, 173–195.

Benghozi, P.-J., and Salvador, E. (2019). The place of the cultural and creative industries in the EU policy orientation: The point of view of communications from the European commission. 15th International Conference on Arts and Cultural Management, AIMAC 2019, Ca' Foscari University of Venice, Italy, June 23–26.

Benghozi P.-J., Salvador E., Simon J.-P. (2021), "Strategies in the cultural and creative industries: static but flexible vs dynamic and liquid. The emergence of a new model in the digital age", *Revue d'Economie Industrielle*, n. 174(2): 117–157.

Bennett, A., Taylor, J., and Woodward, I. (2014). *The Festivalization of Culture*. Burlington, VT: Ashgate.

Braun, T. and Lampel, J. (2020), "Introduction: Tensions and Paradoxes in Temporary Organising: Mapping the Field". In Braun, T. and Lampel, J. (Eds.) *Tensions and paradoxes in temporary organizing (Research in the Sociology of Organizations, Vol. 67)*, (1–13). Emerald Publishing Limited, Bingley. https://doi.org/10.1108/S0733-558X20200000067006

Caves, R. (2000). *Creative Industries: Contracts between Art and Commerce*. Cambridge, MA: Harvard University Press.

Del Barrio, M.J., Devesa, M., and Herrero, L.C. (2012). Evaluating intangible cultural heritage: The case of cultural festivals. *City, Culture and Society*, 3, 235–244.

Engwall, M. (2003). No project is an island: Linking projects to history and context. *Research Policy*, 32(5), 789–808.

Frey, B.S. (2000). The rise and fall of festivals – Reflections on the Salzburg festival. *SSRN Electronic Journal*. https://ideas.repec.org/p/zur/iewwpx/048.html

Geraldi, J., Stjerne, I., and Oehmen, J. (2020). Acting in time: Temporal work enacting tensions at the interface between temporary and permanent organizations. In Braun, T. and J. Lampel (Eds.), *Tensions and Paradoxes in Temporary Organizing. (Research in Sociology of Organizations Vol. 67)*, 81–103. Emerald Group Publishing. https://doi.org/10.1108/S0733-558X20200000067010

Getz, D. (2008). Event tourism: Definition, evolution, and research. *Tourism Management*, 29, 403–428.

Getz, D., and Andersson, T.D. (2009). Editorial to the special issue on festival management. *Scandinavian Journal of Hospitality and Tourism*, 9(2/3), 109–111.

Higgs P., Cunningham, S., and Bakhshi, H. (2008). *Beyond the Creative Industries: Mapping the Creative Economy in the United Kingdom*. London, UK: NESTA.

Jakob, D. (2013). The eventification of place: Urban development and experience consumption in Berlin and New York City. *European Urban and Regional Studies*, 20(4), 447–459.

Jones, C., Svejenova, S., Strandgaard Pedersen, J., and Townley, B. (2016). Introduction to the Special Issue: Misfits, mavericks and mainstreams – Drivers of innovation in creative industries. Special issue of *Organization Studies*, 37(6), 751–768.

Lampel, J., Lant, T.K., and Shamsie, J. (2000). Balancing acts: Learning from organizing practices in cultural industries. *Organization Science*, 11, 263–269.

Lampel, J., and Meyer, A.D. (2008). Field-configuring events as structuring mechanisms: How conferences, ceremonies, and trade shows constitute new technologies, industries, and markets. *Journal of Management Studies*, 45(6), 1025–1035.

Littoz-Monnet, A. (2007). *The European Union and Culture: Between Economic Regulation and European Cultural Policy*. Manchester: Manchester University Press.

Lundin, R.A., and Söderholm, A. (1995). A theory of the temporary organization. *Scandinavian Journal of Management*, 11(4), 437–455.

Luonila, M., and Johansson, T. (2016). Reasons for networking in institutionalized music productions: Case studies of an opera house and a music festival. *International Journal of Arts Management*, 18(3), 50–66.

Moeran, B., and Strandgaard Pedersen, J. (Eds.) (2011). *Negotiating Values in the Creative Industries: Fairs, Festivals and Competitive Events*. Cambridge: Cambridge University Press.

Mulder M., Hitters, E., and Rutten, P. (2020). The impact of festivalization on the Dutch live music action field. *Creative Industries Journal*. DOI: 10.1080/17510694.2020.1815396

Ooi, C.-S., and Strandgaard Pedersen, J. (2010). City branding and film festivals: Re-evaluating stakeholder's relations. *Place Branding and Public Diplomacy*, 6(4), 316–332.

Ooi, C.-S., and Strandgaard Pedersen, J. (2017): In search of nordicity – How new nordic cuisine shaped destination branding in Copenhagen. *Journal of Gastronomy and Tourism*, 2, 217–231.

Pine, J.B. and Gilmore, J.H. (1999). *The Experience Economy*. Boston, MA: Harvard Business School Press.

Rüling, C.C., and Strandgaard Pedersen, J. (2010). Film festival research from an organizational studies perspective. *Scandinavian Journal of Management*, 26(3): 318–323.

Salvador, E., Simon, J.-P., and Benghozi, P.-J. (2019). Facing disruption: The cinema value chain in the digital age. *International Journal of Arts Management*, 22(1), 25–40.

Salvador, E. (2020). Cultural festivals: State of the art and new avenues of research. *EconomistsTalkArt.org Blog*, 7 January, https://economiststalkart. org/2020/01/07/cultural-festivals-state-of-the-art-and-new-avenues-of-research/

Salvador, E., and Benghozi, P.-J. (Winter 2021). The digital strategies of publishing houses: A matter of book content? *International Journal of Arts Management*, 23(2), 56–74.

Scott, A.J. (2010). Cultural economy and the creative field of the city. *Geografiska Annaler: Series B, Human Geography*, 92(2), 115–130.

Stjerne, I.S., and Svejenova, S.V. (2016). Connecting temporary and permanent organizing: Tensions and boundary work in sequential film projects. *Organization Studies*, 37, 1771–1792.

Strandgaard Pedersen, J., and Mazza, C. (2011). International film festivals: For the benefit of whom? *Culture Unbound: Journal of Current Cultural Research*, 3, 139–165.

Strandgaard Pedersen, J., Khaire, M., and Slavich, B. (eds.) (2020). *Technology and Creativity: Production, Mediation and Evaluation in the Digital Age*. Basingstoke: Palgrave Macmillan Publishers Ltd., pp. 1–291.

Sydow, J., and Braun, T. (2018). Projects as temporary organizations: An agenda for further theorizing the interorganizational dimension. *International Journal of Project Management*, 36(1), 4–11.

Throsby, D. (2001). *Economics and Culture*. Cambridge: Cambridge University Press.

Part I

Cultural Festivals Organization and Management

Between Tradition and Innovation

1 The Tradition of Being Innovative

The Case of the Venice Biennale and Its Venice International Film Festival

Viktoriya Pisotska, Kerem Gurses and Luca Giustiniano

> *Change and innovation constitute our stability and tradition.*
> (Interview, Director General of the
> Venice Biennale, 2019)

Introduction

Film Festivals play an important role in the global film industry (Rüling, 2009). Every year, more than 3,500 film festivals are held around the world and their number is constantly increasing. The birth of film festivals started as a European phenomenon in an effort to regenerate the post-war European economy and the growth thereof is often explained by the cities' attempts to differentiate themselves in a highly competitive, increasingly global marketplace (Quinn, 2005). Despite film festivals' proliferation, their significance has been largely overlooked (Moeran and Strandgaard Pedersen, 2011) and their research is "still in its infant stage" (Rüling and Strandgaard Pedersen, 2010, p. 319).

Prior to 1932, the concept of film festivals did not exist (Cowie, 2018). That year reports the foundation of the oldest – and one of the most prestigious – film festivals in the world, the Venice International Film Festival (VIFF), later followed by the Moscow International Film Festival (1935) and Cannes (1939). The aim of the VIFF was to raise awareness and promote international cinema in all its forms as art, entertainment and as an industry in the spirit of freedom and dialogue.[1] Aesthetic experimentation, spirit of research and openness are just some of the fundamental values of the VIFF, reflecting the values of the Biennale[2] under which it operates. On the one hand, the Venice Biennale has become a recognisable cultural institution as a result of its innovative ideas and changes; on the other hand, it has managed to survive wars, protests and many external influences endangering both its stability and existence. This chapter aims to explore how one of the oldest and most innovative cultural institutions and its VIFF deal with the competing demands of innovation and tradition.

DOI: 10.4324/9781003127185-3

The Venice Biennale is a public, cultural institution governed by private law which is allowed to operate according to entrepreneurial principles. Operating at the interface between what is "temporary" and what is "permanent" does, however, lead to unavoidable tensions, the management of which is still under-researched (Bakker et al., 2016; DeFilippi and Sydow, 2016; Stjerne and Svejenova, 2016). Recently, several scholars (e.g., Erdogan, Rondi and De Massis, 2020; Sasaki et al., 2020) have argued that organisational identity and founders' imprinting values can influence the organisational approach to innovation and tradition. The chapter therefore addresses the following question:

RQ1: How do cultural festivals and their parent cultural institutions deal with the tension between tradition and innovation and what is the role of organisational identity in managing this tension?

Furthermore, in addition to how the VIFF deals with the tension between tradition and innovation, other tensions may arise in a cultural festival embedded in a more permanent flow of organising. Henceforth, we ask:

RQ2: What other tensions can potentially arise in a cultural festival embedded in a more permanent parent institution?

Research methods

The chapter adopts an exploratory case study approach (Yin, 2015), examining the VIFF – an annual event in the cinema sector embedded in the permanent organisation of the Venice Biennale. The VIFF can be considered an extreme case of outstanding success: it is the oldest film festival in the world and one of the most prestigious in the arena of international film festivals. The festival has undergone many adversities and hardships throughout its existence; nevertheless, it has been successful in managing various competing demands, innovation and tradition included. The VIFF (i.e., the temporary part) also constitutes a perfect setting as it facilitates the examination of the tensions arising in the interplay with the Biennale Foundation (i.e., the permanent part).

Data collection

In our methodological framework, we employed: (i) participant observation of the 76th edition of the VIFF, including many informal conversations with Biennale employees and photo-ethnographic observation; (ii) several semi-structured interviews with lead organisational members (i.e., Director General, Deputy Director) and an in-depth narrative interview with the President of the Biennale and (iii) archival sources such as corporate documents, newsletters and media coverage. Different data sources contributed to the triangulation of our results and enhanced the internal validity of our book chapter.

Theoretical background

Nature of film festivals

Film festivals have been examined from a micro-social perspective in relation to individual decision-making, interactional dynamics and how these generate value and creative judgements (Moeran and Strandgaard Pedersen, 2011; Jones and Maoret, 2018); from a macro perspective, festivals' institutional role in creative fields remains a topic of interest (Schüssler, Rüling and Wittneben, 2014; Schüßler and Sydow, 2015).

From an institutional standpoint, film festivals constitute repetitive field-configuring and maintaining events. As such, they "set standards, define categories, contribute to the ongoing reassessment of creative activities" (Delacour and Leca, 2011) and shape the development of professions, technologies, markets and industries (Lampel and Meyer, 2008; Rüling, 2009; Rüling and Strandgaard Pedersen, 2010).

Film festivals are temporary, spatially and socially bounded organisations, relying upon mechanisms of inclusion and exclusion. The International Federation of Film Producers Associations (FIAPF) decides the criteria upon which to grant its accreditation to international film festivals seen as events bringing together films of the world and taking place over a limited period of time in a specific city (Mezias et al., 2011).

Film festivals are not just events, or a nexus of multiple events (Rüling and Strandgaard Pedersen, 2010), but they can be considered as projects, being "organized at a specific place for a specific period of time and then replicated in subsequent editions over time" (Uriarte et al., 2019, p. 319).

Film festivals can also fit the notion of project networks to some extent. DeFillippi and Sydow (2016) define project networks as a set of relationships, where: (1) no single actor may act as a legitimate authority for the network as a whole; (2) no definite criteria by which the boundary of the network may be identified and controlled and (3) there are temporarily limited and dynamically changing projects. In fact, film project membership is dynamic and often embedded in a more durable network of relations between permanent organisations and institutions. In addition, no film project is an island; its management is influenced by the shadow of past projects, in addition to future project opportunities (Engwall, 2003). The literature reflects contrasting views about the existence of a single legitimate authority in film festivals. Whereas Delacour and Leca (2011) argue that creative fields are characterised by a structure of power in which dominant actors impose, structure and stabilise their visions in the fields, both Rüling and Strandgaard Pedersen (2010) and Peranson (2008) claim the dependence of film festivals on multiple stakeholders' relations and different interest groups. In the context of the Venice Biennale, there is a central permanent organisation represented by the Foundation of the Biennale.

Previous research has investigated the long-established association between cities and cultural festivals (Quinn, 2005; Ooi and Strandgaard Pedersen, 2010), the latter contributing to local development by generating income, supporting existing and nascent businesses (Mitchell and Wall, 1986; O'Sullivan and Jackson, 2002), attracting tourists and improving the host city's image (Getz, 1991, 2008; Grappi and Montanari, 2011). Acknowledging the societal and economic importance of festivals and following the definition proposed by Salvador and Strandgaard Pedersen (2020, p. 1), which is itself based on Allix's (1922) definition of fairs, a film festival is

> a temporary township, superimposed at intervals upon a permanent place (town or city), which in important, though not regularly defined, social and symbolic ways, contributes to the local or global needs of a particular entity (e.g., industry, city, region, nation) and its group of members.

This book chapter explores the case of VIFF, a temporary festival organisation, which is embedded in the permanent Biennale Foundation, a context which remains scarcely researched (Uriarte et al., 2019).

Innovation and tradition

The embeddedness of temporary systems in more permanent ones leads to the emergence of "tensions, contradictions, synergies" such as stability and change, or tradition and innovation (Bakker et al., 2016; DeFillippi and Sydow, 2016), intensified by multiple institutional logics, such as art and commerce (Rüling and Strandgaard Pedersen, 2010; Uriarte et al., 2019).

Alternatively, the tension between tradition and innovation can be considered tension between stability and change (e.g., Erdogan, Rondi and De Massis, 2020; Suddaby and Jaskiewicz, 2020). If, on the one hand, tradition requires stability, on the other hand innovation requires change. The existing literature suggests that FCEs, film festivals included, are catalysts of institutional and organisational changes (Anand and Watson, 2004; Wilshusen and MacDonald, 2017). However, although traditions often appear to be old and invariant, they can be quite recent and invented in response to current circumstances (Hobsbawm and Range, 1983). In other words, traditions also have an inherently dynamic nature, an aspect that will be subsequently explored. Assuming that tradition is related to stability, several scholars have suggested that change is ontologically inseparable from the concept of stability, meaning it is impossible to describe one without the other (Schad et al., 2016). Scholars adhering to duality theories highlight the relationship between stability and change rather than stressing their contradictions, defining them as self-enabling and necessary for organisations to function effectively (e.g., Farjoun, 2010).

Other studies (e.g., Vrontis, Bresciani and Giacosa, 2016; Erdogan, Rondi and De Massis, 2020) have stressed the importance of both change and stability, or innovation and tradition, in achieving competitive advantages and organisational survival. For instance, Vrontis, Bresciani and Giacosa (2016), by exploring the case of an Italian family wine business, highlight the role of the territory in combining innovation and tradition and, therefore, achieve and maintain a sustainable competitive advantage. Furthermore, Erdogan, Rondi and De Massis (2020) stress the role of imprinting by previous generations in influencing a company's approach to tradition and innovation. The authors propose four strategies to manage the tradition and innovation paradox in family firms: (1) protecting the heritage – by combining a segregation approach to innovation (i.e., a separation between iconic products and new products and processes) with a preservation approach to tradition (i.e., a continuous commitment to the founder's values, beliefs and craftsmanship); (2) maintaining the essence – by combining an integration approach to innovation (i.e., a reinterpretation of traditional products) and a preservation approach to tradition; (3) restoring the legacy – by blending an integration approach to innovation and the revival approach to tradition (i.e., when some traditional elements have faded over time and there is regret about the loss) and (4) embracing nostalgia – by combining a segregation approach to innovation with a revival approach to tradition. Thus, Erdogan, Rondi and De Massis (2020) propose the construction of temporal symbiosis to indicate an organisation's capability to simultaneously adopt retrospective and prospective approaches to using its resources to concurrently achieve tradition and innovation.

The concept of traditions has recently reappeared in research concerning organisational identity (Ravasi and Schultz, 2006; Ravasi, Rindova and Stigliani, 2019) and organisational institutionalism (Dacin and Dacin, 2008). Several organisational identity scholars have argued that organisational identity can be viewed as a narrative construction (Chreim, 2005) and that "history is periodically reconstructed to promote a desired identity" (Ravasi, Rindova and Stigliani, 2019, p. 1524). Ravasi, Rindova and Stigliani (2019), by exploring four corporate museums, report three distinct modes of how organisations can engage with history and identity, namely (1) identity stewardship; (2) identity evangelising and (3) heritage mining. Identity stewardship implies the seeking of distinctiveness and the usage of historical artefacts able to track past trajectories and continue them in future. Identity evangelising means the implementation of a selective focus on artefacts associated with remarkable past accomplishments used to support present claims about the core values of the organisation. In a heritage mining mode, there is a flexible use of the past; organisational members use artefacts to enhance the appeal of new offerings by symbolically connecting them to memories and cultural symbolism. Additionally, Ravasi, Rindova and Stigliani (2019) illuminate the process through which members use material memory and traditions to reconstruct history and identity.

Such a manipulative use of the past had already been stressed in 1983 by two eminent historians: Eric John Hobsbawm and Terence Osborn Range. They coined the term "invented tradition", arguing that the past is often perpetually evoked and systematically reconstructed as a central part of the nation-building process and other similar processes. By arguing that traditions are often responses to novel situations, the authors identify the inherently dynamic nature of tradition (Beiner, 2001).

Sasaki et al. (2020) explored how long-lived Japanese firms attempt to reconcile change initiatives with traditional values left by past leaders. The authors suggest that guidelines and values – *ka-kun* in Japanese firms – can be viewed as strategic identity statements conveying the vision, mission, values and philosophy of the organisation, thus responding to the question of "who we are as an organisation". Consequently, the revision of identity statements offers an opportunity to connect the past, present and future (Hatch, Schultz and Skov, 2015; Sasaki et al., 2020). Furthermore, Sasaki et al. (2020) identify three strategies, namely (1) elaborating (i.e., focusing on several values from historical identity statements, and articulating their implications for the current context); (2) recovering (i.e., the formulation of a new identity statement based on the retrieval and re-use of past self-referred discourse and/or historical references) and (3) decoupling (the co-existence of a historical identity statement alongside a contemporary one aiming to provide guidance in a changing environment), to address the tension between tradition and innovation. The aforementioned strategies are associated with a different degree of change and innovation: recovery accommodating relatively small changes and decoupling fitting larger ones. Organisational identity, partly incorporated in strategic identity statements, is considered to be a vital factor in preserving traditional values and providing opportunities for change.

What can be identified from the existing literature is that the relationship between tradition and innovation is symbiotic. Traditions can be quite dynamic themselves (Hobsbawm and Range, 1983). Tradition and innovation feed and nurture each other, each providing the conditions necessary for the other to continue to exist (e.g., Vrontis, Bresciani and Giacosa, 2016; Erdogan, Rondi and De Massis, 2020). Organisational identity and founders' imprinting values can have an impact on organisational approaches to innovation and tradition (Erdogan, Rondi and De Massis, 2020; Sasaki et al., 2020); however, history and traditions can also influence the formation of organisational identity and provide opportunities to innovate (Ravasi, Rindova and Stigliani, 2019). Despite growing researcher interest in organisational identity, "the potential implications of organizational identity for the management of innovation" and, more extensively, for the relationship between tradition and innovation, remain underexplored (Anthony and Tripsas, 2016, p. 417). Our primary goal in this chapter is therefore to explore the role of organisational identity in managing this relationship. Furthermore, we responded to the invitation issued by many recent studies on organisational paradoxes (e.g., Schad et al., 2016; Cunha et al., 2017; Cunha and Putman, 2019) to produce more research on the dynamics and relationships between tensions. By acknowledging that the context matters (e.g., Erdogan, Rondi and De Massis, 2020; Sasaki et al., 2020), we explore the relationship between tradition and innovation and other tensions arising in the context of the VIFF, embedded in the more permanent organisation of the Venice Biennale.

Evolution of the Venice Biennale and its film festival

The Venice Biennale was founded in 1893 in Venice, Italy. Two years later, the Biennale held its first Exhibition of Contemporary Art, which attracted over 180,000 visitors and instantly became one of the most globally significant art exhibitions. The exhibition was characterised by its pure artistic and aesthetic nature. The Deputy Director recalled: *"When the Biennale was born it was the first art exhibition at the time when other exhibitions were commercial"*. Over the years, the Biennale Art Exhibition has welcomed artists such as Gustav Klimt (1899), Picasso (1910), Van Gogh (1920), Dali (1948), Miró (1948), Pollock (1950) and many others.

In the 1930s, the Venice Biennale was transformed into an autonomous body, passing its control from the Municipality of Venice to the Italian national government. Thanks to its increased funding and the efforts of President Count Giuseppe Volpi di Misurata, new cultural sectors were created, and the Biennale took on a multidisciplinary nature. In 1930, the Theatre sector was introduced, followed by the Cinema (1932) and the Music (1934) sectors.

The VIFF, at that time called the International Exhibition of Cinematographic Art, was the world's first large film festival; it originated in 1932, almost 40 years after the first public screening by the Lumiére brothers. The Venice Film Festival was then followed by the Moscow International Film Festival in 1935 and the Cannes International Film Festival in 1939. The latter was created in opposition to the VIFF due to its preference of Italian and German firms at times of fascism. Other major film festivals – Locarno International Film Festival and Berlin International Film Festival – were founded in 1946 and 1951, respectively.

In 1932, the VIFF did not end with an official award ceremony. Only participation diplomas were awarded to producer and category associations, intervening governments and individual film houses. From 1935 onwards, the VIFF became an annual event.

The activity of the Biennale was suspended during the war period: from 1943 to 1947 for the art, music and theatre exhibitions and from 1943 to 1945 for the film festival.

In 1968, a student protest took place. Crowds were protesting against a "Fascist and bourgeois" festival and sought a change in a statute from 1938. A few days before the opening, "an alliance of directors protesting the festival as an institution withdrew their films from the VIFF" (Cowie, 2018, p. 91). The student protest initiated a period of institutional changes resulting in a new Statute – "New Regulations of the autonomous Body 'La Biennale di Venezia'" – in 1973. The Biennale became a "democratically organised institution of culture", aimed at guaranteeing "full freedom of ideas and forms of expression" and at organising "international shows regarding the documentation, knowledge, criticism, research and investigation into the field of the arts" (article 1). An open and project-based foundation was provided, allowing for a working methodology based on experimentation, which openly acknowledged the requests of the 1968 protest.[3] A democratic board was established, comprising representatives from the Government, the most important local organisations, major trade unions and a staff representative.

The 1980s and 1990s were years of reform for the VIFF. Its Artistic Directors at that time – Marco Müller and Alberto Barbera – worked hard to maintain the festival's prestige. The President of the Biennale Paolo Baratta was pushing for more autonomy of the festival. As a result, in 1998 a new statute was approved transforming the Biennale from a semi-state body into an autonomous, entrepreneurial, private-law entity. The Venice Biennale was thus given the name of "Società di Cultura la Biennale di Venezia". New management and governance systems were subsequently implemented. In 2004, the Biennale received even more autonomy with the revision of the statute, changing its name to the Biennale Foundation – "Fondazione della Biennale di Venezia".

Today, the Venice Biennale is active in six cultural sectors: Arts (1895), Architecture (1980), Cinema (1932), Dance (1999), Music (1930) and Theatre (1934) in collaboration with the Historical Archive of the Venice Biennale (ASAC). The Biennale exhibitions and festivals enhance their reputation every year, continuing to attract an impressive number of visitors. In 2019, the Biennale Art Exhibition welcomed 593,616 visitors. The audience attendance at VIFF screenings reached 105,000 in the same year.[4] Its objective is to highlight, as vividly as possible, film works that bear witness to the progress of cinema as a means of artistic, scientific or education expression.[5]

Findings

The primary focus of our chapter is to explore how the Venice Biennale and its VIFF deal with the tension between tradition and innovation. However, we also uncovered other tensions within the Venice Biennale. We start the first section of our findings by unveiling these tensions and revealing how they are intertwined. Then we focus on the tension between tradition and innovation and show the role that organisational identity plays in managing this tension. Finally, we examine the relationship between tradition and innovation through the temporality lenses of past, present and future.

Tensions within the Venice Biennale

The Venice Biennale is a cultural public institution governed by private law allowing it to operate according to entrepreneurial criteria. The statute of 1998, revised in 2004, states the mission of the Biennale: "*to promote the study, research and documentation in the field of contemporary arts on a national and international level through stable activities, events, experiments, projects*".

At least three main tensions can be noted in the Biennale: (1) public versus private/entrepreneurial, in combination with art versus commerce; (2) permanent versus temporary and (3) stability versus change or tradition versus innovation.

Private-public tension

The tension between private and public is related to the fact that the Biennale is a Foundation, a public entity, albeit one with "*a legal personality under private law and is governed by the civil code and by the provisions implementing the code*" (Article 2, Statute 2004, n. 1). This implies that despite being a cultural public institution, the Biennale functions under private law in order to achieve organisational efficiency. In other words, this duality between public and private, which allows for organisational efficiency and entrepreneurial management, facilitates the artistic and innovative aspects of the Biennale. The tension between art and commerce can be partly considered as a sub-tension between public and private. On the one hand, the mission of the Biennale is to promote research in the field of contemporary arts; this is substantiated by the selection criteria based on quality and artistic contribution. On the other hand, the Biennale necessitates economic resources in order to keep functioning. The Director General reported:

> Economic resources to invest in projects are not infinite. We must constantly talk, understand how to help the Artistic Director do what he wants to do efficiently and effectively without spending resources and in some cases say, 'Sorry but unfortunately for this there are no resources; or we find them from third parties or unfortunately this thing cannot be done'.

Despite the importance of economic resources, lead organisational members of the Biennale do not perceive the tension between art and commerce as real:

> *Business has nothing to do here. There is an institution that invests economic resources of which a large part is generated by its own actions rather than by public funds…My only economic interest is to ensure that things are done well and to ensure that there is no imbalance.*
> (Interview, Director General, 2019)

This implies that the commercial aspect exists only for the sake of supporting the artistic aspect of the Biennale. Article 3 (n.3) of the Statute 1998, revised in 2004, reads: "*La Biennale can carry out commercial and other ancillary activities, in accordance with the institutional purposes. In any case, the distribution of profits, which must be destined for institutional purposes, is not permitted*".

Permanent and temporary organising tension

The second tension is between permanent and temporary organising: some organisational structures and agents are permanent, while others are temporary, and this can be due to various motives. The permanency exists to guarantee the continuity and stability of the organisation, while the temporariness can be due to the cost optimisation or specificity of profiles and events. In terms of organisational structure, the six cultural sectors of the Biennale are permanent but they operate through temporary annual or biennial festivals and exhibitions:

> *The sectors are absolutely permanent, they have stable organisational procedures.*
>
> (Interview, Deputy Director, 2019)

In terms of organisational agents, some are employed on a temporary basis, while some are employed for a longer period of time. For instance, organisational managers, the Director General included, are employed for a relatively extensive period of time to "*guarantee the autonomy of operations and to possess all the necessary professional skills to make the machine work*" (Interview, Deputy Director, 2019).

Stability and change tension

The third tension is between stability and change or tradition and innovation. The Biennale has existed for more than 120 years preserving its history and traditional values. Despite different historical vicissitudes (e.g., Second World War, student protests in the 1970s), since the beginning the Biennale has established itself as one of the most innovative cultural institutions in the world. We will focus on this tension in more detail in the next section.

The three tensions seem to be co-dependent. As explained by the President of the Biennale, being a public institution implies the need "*to provide 'something more' than what the market offers, the avoidance of pursuing ends which are non-artistic, economic or politically propagandistic*". Governance by private law entails the entrepreneurial orientation of the Biennale in the sense that it allows efficient and effective management, which is vital in guaranteeing the continuity and stability of the organisation. Simultaneously, stability (and traditions) is related to the permanency of some organisational structures and organisational members of the Biennale. Organisational stability would not be possible if the organisation did not follow its mission consisting of promoting research in the field of contemporary arts and, therefore, requiring constant change and innovation. This change is possible through the temporality of some specific profiles, such as Artistic Directors, selectors and programmers. In other words, different tensions are intertwined and complementary. This complementarity and interdependence of tensions led to the discovery that the word "tension" was misleading and had to be reconsidered. Subsequently, the Director General and the Deputy Director expressed some adversity towards the notion of "tension" and suggested using expressions such as "solicitations" and "complementary poles".

> *I think "tension" is a wrong term. More than tensions, these are solicitations, two poles that require each other to function.*
> (Interview, Deputy Director, 2019)

Tradition and innovation as part of the Venice Biennale identity

In relation to the dichotomy between tradition and innovation, the Director General stated that research and experimentation were in the DNA of the Biennale and constituted the essence of the organisation, its exhibitions and festivals.

> *The essence is promoting research in contemporary arts at an international level in Venice. It is our DNA! To do this, we need to be open to the world...we should not be conservative.*
> (Interview, Director General, 2019)

The Director General added "*change and innovation constitute our stability and tradition*".

It appears that tradition and innovation nurture each other and the identity plays a critical role in that. The realisation of the importance of organisational identity in managing tradition and innovation led to the exploration of the most central, distinctive and endurable features of the Biennale. We discovered that the key traits of the Biennale, also reflecting the values of its exhibitions and festivals, are experimentation, innovation and the supremacy of art; autonomy; the centrality of festivals and exhibitions and the importance of the city of Venice.

The first central trait forming the identity of the Venice Biennale is, thus, experimentation and innovation. The mission of the Biennale is expressed in article 3 of the Statute 1998:

> The Biennale is not for profit and has the aim, ensuring full freedom of ideas and forms of expression, to promote study, research and

documentation in the field of contemporary arts at national and international level through stable research activities, as well as events, experiments and projects.

In 2018, during the 75th VIFF, the President declared:

> *The Festival presents a profusion of works by great auteurs, and is marked by a further new opening up to genres, as part of its commitment to tracing works of high quality and vitality without preconceived classifications.*
>
> (Press release, President, 2018)

In 2019, in the opening speech of the 76th VIFF, the President stated:

> *A festival can promote quality without prejudice of genre. It can foster new talents, keep up the interest in formal research and experimentation, and on the other hand maintain the commitment of cinema to tackling fundamental questions relating to the human condition, to society and politics, in its various genres.*
>
> (Press release, President, 2019)

The historian Peter Cowie summarised the spirit of experimentation and innovation of the Biennale with the term of aesthetic experimentation that *"must, for la Biennale, always be discovered and put on display"* (Cowie, 2018, p. 22).

The autonomy of Artistic Directors in their artistic choices and autonomy of organisational management from any political influence constitute another essential trait of the Venice Biennale. In 2017, on the occasion of the 74th VIFF, the President declared:

> *We have always remained faithful to the principle of our independence and to the quality of the choices we make. Almost paradoxically, we continue to be a reference point for works which may not be destined for resounding box office success but which represent artistic and poetic moments worthy of attention and recognition. This is one of the essential functions of a festival that intends to maintain the world's esteem.*
>
> (Archival document, President, 2017)

Additionally, the centrality of exhibitions and festivals comprise a central trait of the Venice Biennale. Since its inception, the Venice Biennale was conceived as a cultural institution operating through festivals and exhibitions. Its first iteration was the Exhibition of Contemporary Art, followed by the exhibitions of other cultural sectors of the Biennale. In virtue of their temporariness and changing mandate of their Curators and Artistic Directors, exhibitions and festivals facilitate constant innovation.

In addition, the city of Venice is a central, distinctive and endurable trait characterising the Venice Biennale. During an event dedicated to Europe's audio-visual bridge between the USA, China and Japan, the Director General of the National Association of Audio-Visual and Multimedia film industries (ANICA) stated:

> *Venice has a sensational history, it is a film festival that Italian institutions wanted to be independent from the government. Venice is a point of reference for Europe; Venice is a history, continuity, innovation, productive transformation ever seen.*
>
> (Participant Observation, Director General of ANICA, 2019)

The embeddedness of the Venice Biennale in the city of Venice is so important that there is a certain overlap of identities: that of the city with that of the cultural institution of the Venice Biennale. Many locations, which are closed throughout the year, only open for the Venice Film Festival (e.g., Hotel des Bains and Palazzo Casino). The installation and embellishment of locations happen a few days before the beginning of the festival. The management of space follows the criteria of inclusion and exclusion. The exclusivity of certain areas, balanced by free access to others, increases the organisational reputation and reinforces the organisational identity of the Venice Biennale.

The identity of the Biennale helps to go beyond the vision of contradictions and complexities, embracing them and making them an inseparable part of organisational life. In 2019, on the occasion of the 76th VIFF, the President stressed how certain fundamental values, among which are quality, independence and openness, ensured the stability of the organisation, despite how everything around it was changing.

> *We planned and shaped a new reality, following a constant line and a few simple principles, while everything around us was changing...If our project has been rooted in a faith of certain basic values, among them quality, independence and courage, the pegging of the festival to La Biennale has proved decisive in favouring its pursuance with the indispensable continuity and coherence.*
>
> (Press release, President, 2019)

In sum, the identity of the Biennale drives the relationship between tradition and innovation. Through this identity, incorporating features of research, experimentation and innovation, tradition becomes innovation itself because innovation is a traditional value of the Biennale.

Tradition and innovation look through the lenses of past, present and future

We often tend to associate tradition with the past and innovation with the future. Let us consider how lead organisational members perceive the concept of time, reflective of the relationship between tradition and innovation.

In 2017, during the 74th VIFF, the Artistic Director announced that proposed films represented a look into the future, confirming the importance of being innovative.

> *Rather than a snapshot of the present, or a souvenir selfie of our contemporary cinema, the films we propose are in some way a perception of the future (...) like a forward sprint, as we scrutinise the horizon to spot "what's next".*
>
> (Press release, Artistic Director, 2017)

However, the present time and its most pressing themes are also important for the Biennale. In 2018, the President in his opening speech for the 75th VIFF announced:

> *The selection reflects a great faith in the movie as a medium and in its capacity to tackle themes of the present, themes that history and the human condition offer for our consideration.*
>
> (Press release, President, 2018)

The idea of the present, past and future was well argued by the Artistic Director during the 75th VIFF opening speech:

> *To consider cinema a collection of events, of processes, helps us to better grasp it, comprehend it, describe it (...). If we stop believing in a before and an after, in keeping with a linear and progressive logic, we realise that it is useless to compare the cinema of the past with the most recent cinema (or even better, with tomorrow's). It is useless to refuse to accept the changes brought about by technological transformations, the digital revolution or changes in the market.*
>
> (Press release, Artistic Director, 2018)

He suggests that it is useless to compare the past with the present or the future, implying that the relationship between tradition and innovation is somewhat blurred. Thus, it makes more sense to embrace them and consider cinema as a process in continuous development. This perception of cinema has an impact on how the Biennale (and its festivals) manage the relationship between tradition and innovation.

The Artistic Director stressed the importance of embracing complexities and contradictions, refusing the notion of past, present and future and, therefore, embracing tradition and innovation as if they were part of the same process:

> *We must take account of the events which are chaotically milling around: we are often tempted to downplay this confusion, to address it with the tranquilising expression "transition period". (...) What if*

it were more important to (...) grasp its fertile contradictions and irreducible complexities, instead of establishing temporary hierarchies? To proceed by inclusion instead of dogmatic distinctions, to broaden our gaze instead of only focusing selectively, to go beyond the limits instead of raising barriers? Without renouncing quality, or better, without ceasing to constantly question what it is and where it resides today, in this present which they tell us doesn't exist, in a universe which is no longer the past and not yet the future.

(Press release, Artistic Director, 2018)

In 2020, during the 77th VIFF, the President once again stressed the relationship between the past and the future:

The International Film Festival, along with all the other disciplines that make up the Venice Biennale, is a fundamental event ... above all for its enrichment of our fund of knowledge and the way that it allows us to make comparisons with the past and speculate about contents, languages and new technologies in the arts over the coming decades.

(Press release, President, 2020)

In simple words, the VIFF is a fertile ground of connection between the past, present and future, and tradition and innovation.

Discussion and conclusion

This book chapter illustrates the case of the Venice Biennale and its VIFF, the oldest film festival in the world. The primary focus of this chapter was to explore how cultural festivals embedded within more permanent organising deal with the tension between tradition and innovation. The chapter explores the ability of the VIFF to adapt to changes while maintaining its stability and its capacity to be at the forefront of innovation while remaining faithful to its traditional values.

We show how both innovation and tradition are part of the Biennale's identity. The identity of the Biennale, also reflecting the identity of its cultural festivals and exhibitions, includes traits such as openness, experimentation and innovation, the temporary organising of cultural festivals and exhibitions and the importance of the city of Venice. Our findings suggest that organisational identity is crucial to guarantee the continuation of the successful relationship between tradition and innovation as part of the Venice Biennale because innovation constitutes its essence and traditional value. Although our aim was not to explore the relationship between tradition and innovation through the lens of institutional theory, some parallels have been found. The studies of multiple institutional logics – competing "guidelines on how to interpret and function in social situations" (Greenwood et al., 2011, p. 318) – have started stressing the role of organisational identity in responding to institutional complexity, which occurs when an organisation confronts incompatible prescriptions from multiple institutional logics. In particular, Kodeih and Greenwood (2014) claim that several competing demands can be seen as an opportunity by an organisation and the responses to them can be shaped not only by current identity – what an organisation is – but also by an aspired identity – what an organisation wishes to become.

Our book chapter is in line with Chreim's (2005) claims that identity narratives often reflect values in the institutional environment and in "today's business world innovations are celebrated and the ability to change has become a value in itself" (p. 588). By showing how tradition and innovation are inextricably linked through the organisational identity of the Biennale, we support the theorising of those scholars claiming that innovation can be advanced by tradition (De Massis et al., 2016; Vrontis, Bresciani and Giacosa, 2016; Erdogan, Rondi and De Massis, 2020).

Extant research has stressed that history and traditions can be periodically reconstructed to promote a desired identity (Gioia, Schultz and Corley, 2000; Gioia, Corley and Fabbri, 2002; Ravasi, Rindova and Stigliani, 2019). The Venice Biennale has undergone various changes over its history, such as World War II, student protests and several reforms. The approval of new legislative decrees offered an opportunity if not to reconstruct then to reinforce and adapt the identity of the Biennale to these changes. The most impactful reform occurred in 1998. The 1998 statute, revised in 2004, brought about fundamental changes to the organisation, management and governance of the Biennale. It confirmed its public and cultural nature and, by introducing the management under private law, it allowed for more flexibility, autonomy and innovation. The change in the statute can be considered as a change in the strategic identity statement (Sasaki et al., 2020) as it conveys the vision, mission, values and philosophy of the organisation. In the case of the Biennale, it also offered an opportunity to connect the past, present and future (Hatch, Schultz and Skov, 2015; Sasaki et al., 2020).

Our case study reveals how the relationship between tradition and innovation could be seen through the lenses of temporality – the ongoing relationship between past, present and future (Schultz and Hernes, 2013). The lead organisational members of the Biennale refuse the hierarchy of time – they look forward, preserving the past and remaining faithful to the present by reporting current issues and progress in society. We could say that they use the process-time (Reinecke and Ansari, 2017; Holt and Johnsen, 2019), characterising time as nonlinear, qualitatively determined and endogenous to events and processes (Chia, 2002). In the same way that time is considered to be fluid and uncategorised, the relationship between tradition and innovation is constantly moving, in which two polarities coexist and nurture each other. The lead organisational members of the Biennale use their past strategically, embracing the rhetorical history, to maintain its identity and successfully manage its key stakeholders (Suddaby et al., 2010;

Suddaby and Jaskiewicz, 2020). Our book chapter partly contributes to the literature on temporality, which is still in its infancy (Ravasi, Rindova and Stigliani, 2019), by recommending researchers use the lens of temporality to examine tradition and innovation and by stressing the role of temporality as an important but understudied aspect of organisational identity (Schultz, 2016; Schultz and Hernes, 2020).

Although we mainly focus on the relationship between tradition and innovation, we also uncover other tensions potentially arising in a cultural festival embedded in a more permanent organising. Glynn (2000) has suggested that cultural institutions have identities composed of contradictory elements, such as artistic and utilitarian, because they contain a multitude of actors and perspectives. Our book chapter finds two types of tensions, in addition to stability versus change or tradition versus innovation, namely: public versus private, in combination with art versus commerce; permanency versus temporariness. These tensions are dynamic and persistent, not necessarily requiring a solution as they constitute significant polarities of organisational life. Each tension supports another. For instance, the tension between public and private is indispensable in its support of the tension between tradition and innovation. Being a cultural public institution but subject to private law allows the Biennale to be flexible and receptive of innovations, which ultimately constitutes the tradition value of the Biennale. By demonstrating how the tensions are nested and intertwined, we contribute to the literature on tensions and contradictions (e.g., Schad et al., 2016; Cunha et al., 2017; Cunha and Putman, 2019).

Ultimately, we advance the literature on festivals (e.g., Rüling and Strandgaard Pedersen, 2010; Moeran and Strandgaard Pedersen, 2011; Toraldo and Islam 2019; Toraldo, Islam and Mangia, 2019), and the project organising literature in general (Bakker et al., 2016; DeFilippi and Sydow, 2016; Stjerne and Svejenova, 2016), by exploring several tensions arising at the intersection between temporary and permanent organising and examining how these tensions can be managed through a strong and coherent organisational identity. Past research stresses the importance of cultural festivals for the city development (e.g., Grappi and Montanari, 2011). Consequently, we confirm these findings but also show the opposite direction of the development: the city of Venice with its infrastructure is an essential part of the Venice Biennale's identity and efficient existence.

Despite these contributions, this chapter has inevitable limitations; it is based on a single case study design. According to the conventional view, a single case can limit the generalisability of results. However, Flyvbjerg (2006) stresses that this view is misunderstood and argues that "formal generalization is considerably overrated as the main source of scientific progress" (p. 10). Nonetheless, we encourage future studies to conduct multiple case studies by exploring other cultural festivals to comprehend how they manage the relationship between tradition and innovation, conditions at the base of this successful combination and additional tensions arising in other cultural contexts. Although our chapter looks at the history of the Biennale and uses the data sources of the past, a processual approach was not the aim of our chapter. Future work can inspect the dynamic management of tradition and innovation over time.

In terms of practical value, we hope to provide a better understanding of how to improve the management of tensions in cultural organisations and their cultural festivals. With regard to the successful combination of tradition and innovation, we suggest that cultural festival organisers cultivate a strong organisational identity based on traits of art, experimentation, openness and innovation as the traditional values of their organisations. We also suggest that cultural festival organisers use their past and history to create an increased sense of belonging, identification and attachment of employees and visitors.

Notes

1 Source: https://www.labiennale.org/en/cinema/2020, accessed on December 29th, 2020.
2 The first biennial exhibition of Italian Art ("Esposizione biennale artistica nazionale") was established by the Venetian City Council in 1893. From the following year, a section was reserved for invited foreign artists. The first Biennale, "I Esposizione Internazionale d'Arte della Città di Venezia" (1st International Art Exhibition of the City of Venice) took place in 1895.
3 Source: https://www.on-curating.org/issue-46-reader/the-evolution-of-an-exhibition-model-venice-biennale-as-an-entity-in-time.html#.YLtJGpMzZpQ, accessed on June 5th, 2021.
4 Source: https://variety.com/2019/film/festivals/venice-audience-up-11-past-the-halfway-mark-gender-parity-in-accreditations-1203321562/, accessed on November 20th, 2020.
5 Source: Regulations of the VIFF.

References

Allix, A. (1922), "The geography of fairs: Illustrated by old-world examples", *Geographical Review*, Vol. 12 No. 4, pp. 532–569.
Anand, N., & Watson, M. R. (2004), "Tournament rituals in the evolution of fields: The case of the Grammy Awards", *Academy of Management Journal*, Vol. 47 No. 1, pp. 59–80.
Anthony, C., & Tripsas, M. (2016), "Organizational identity and innovation", In: Pratt, M. G., Schultz, M., Ashforth, M. E., Ravasi, D. (Eds.) *The Oxford handbook of organizational identity*, Oxford University Press, pp. 417–435.
Bakker, R.M., DeFillippi, R.J., Schwab, A., & Sydow, J. (2016), "Temporary organizing: Promises, processes, problems", *Organization Studies*, Vol. 37 No. 12, pp. 1703–1719.
Beiner, G. (2001), "The Invention of Tradition?" *History Review*, Vol. 12, pp. 1–10.
Chia, R. (2002), "Essai: Time, duration and simultaneity: Rethinking process and change in organizational analysis", *Organization Studies*, Vol. 23 No. 6, pp. 863–868.
Chreim, S. (2005), "The continuity–change duality in narrative texts of organizational identity", *Journal of Management Studies*, Vol. 42 No. 3, pp. 567–593.

Cowie, P. (2018), *Happy 75°. A brief introduction to the history of the Venice Film Festival*. La Biennale di Venezia.

Cunha, M., Giustiniano, L., Rego, A., & Clegg, S. (2017), "Mission impossible? The paradoxes of stretch goal setting", *Management Learning*, Vol. 48 No. 2, pp. 140–157.

Cunha, M. P. E., & Putnam, L. L. (2019), "Paradox theory and the paradox of success", *Strategic Organization*, Vol. 17 No. 1, pp. 95–106.

Dacin, M. T., & Dacin, P. A. (2008), "Traditions as institutionalized practice: Implications for deinstitutionalization", In: Greenwood, R., Oliver, C., Sahlin, K., & Suddaby, R. (Eds.) *The Sage handbook of organizational institutionalism*, Sage, pp. 327–352.

De Massis, A., Frattini, F., Kotlar, J., Petruzzelli, A. M., & Wright, M., Kotlar, J., & Messeni Petruzzelli, A. (2016), "Innovation through tradition: Lessons from innovative family businesses and directions for future research", *Academy of Management Perspectives*, Vol. 30 No. 1, pp. 93–116.

DeFilippi, R. J., & Sydow J. (2016), "Project networks: Governance choices and paradoxical tensions", *Project Management Journal*, Vol. 47 No. 5, pp. 1–12.

Delacour, H., & Leca, B. (2011), "A Salon's life. Field configuring event, power and contestation in a creative field", In: Moeran, B. & Strandgaard Pedersen, J. (Eds.) *Negotiating values in the creative industries: Fairs, festivals and other competitive events,* Cambridge University Press, pp. 36–58.

Engwall, M. (2003), "No project is an island: Linking projects to history and context", *Research Policy*, Vol. 32 No. 5, 789–808.

Erdogan, I., Rondi, E., & De Massis, A. (2020), "Managing the tradition and innovation paradox in family firms: A family imprinting perspective", *Entrepreneurship Theory and Practice*, Vol. 44 No. 1, pp. 20–54.

Farjoun, M. (2010), "Beyond dualism: Stability and change as a duality", *Academy Management Review*, Vol. 35 No. 2, pp. 202–225.

Flyvbjerg, B. (2006), "Five misunderstandings about case-study research", *Qualitative Inquiry*, Vol. 12 No. 2, pp. 219–245.

Getz, D. (1991), *Festivals, special events, and tourism*. Van Nostrand Reinhold.

Getz, D. (2008), "Event tourism: Definition, evolution, and research", *Tourism Management*, Vol. 29 No. 3, pp. 403–428.

Gioia, D. A., Corley, K. G., & Fabbri, T. (2002), "Revising the past (while thinking in the future perfect tense)", *Journal of Organizational Change Management*, Vol. 15 No. 6, pp. 622–634.

Gioia, D. A., Schultz, M., & Corley, K. G. (2000), "Organizational identity, image, and adaptive instability", *Academy of Management Review*, Vol. 25 No. 1, pp. 63–81.

Glynn, M. A. (2000), "When cymbals become symbols: Conflict over organizational identity within a symphony orchestra", *Organization Science*, Vol. 11 No. 3, pp. 285–298.

Grappi, S., & Montanari, F. (2011), "The role of social identification and hedonism in affecting tourist re-patronizing behaviours: The case of an Italian festival", *Tourism Management*, Vol. 32 No. 5, pp. 1128–1140.

Greenwood, R., Raynard, M., Kodeih, F., Micelotta, E. R., & Lounsbury, M. (2011), "Institutional complexity and organizational responses", *Academy of Management Annals*, Vol. 5 No. 1, pp. 317–371.

Hatch, M. J., Schultz, M., & Skov, A. M. (2015), "Organizational identity and culture in the context of managed change: Transformation in the Carlsberg Group, 2009–2013", *Academy of Management Discoveries*, Vol. 1 No. 1, pp. 58–90.

Hobsbawm, E. J. (1983), "Introduction: Inventing Traditions" In: Hobsbawm, E. J., & Ranger, T. O. (Eds.) *The invention of tradition. Past and present publications*, Cambridge University Press, pp. 1–13.

Holt, R., & Johnsen, R. (2019), "Time and organization studies", *Organization Studies*, Vol. 40 No. 10, pp. 1557–1572.

Jones, C., & Maoret, M. (2018), "Frontiers of creative industries: Exploring structural and categorical dynamics", In: Jones, C. & Maoret, M. (Eds.) *Frontiers of creative industries: Exploring structural and categorical dynamics*, Emerald Publishing Limited, pp. 1–16.

Kodeih, F., & Greenwood, R. (2014), "Responding to institutional complexity: The role of identity", *Organization Studies*, Vol. 35 No. 1, pp. 7–39.

Lampel, J., & Meyer, A. D. (2008), "Guest editors' introduction–Field configuring events as structuring mechanisms: How conferences, ceremonies and trade shows constitute new technologies, industries and markets", *Journal of Management Studies*, Vol. 45 No. 6, pp. 1025–1035.

Mezias, S. J., Strandgaard Pedersen, J., Ji-Hyun, K., Svejenova, S., & Mazza, C. (2011), "Transforming film product identities: The status effects of European premier film festivals, 1996–2005", In: Moeran, B. & Strandgaard Pedersen, J. (Eds.) *Negotiating values in the creative industries: Fairs, festivals and other competitive events*, Cambridge University Press, pp. 169–196.

Mitchell, C., & Wall, G. (1986), "Impacts of cultural festivals on Ontario communities", *Recreation Research Review*, Vol. 13 No. 1, pp. 28–37.

Ooi, C. S., & Pedersen, J. S. (2010), "City branding and film festivals: Re-evaluating stakeholder's relations", *Place Branding and Public Diplomacy*, Vol. 6 No. 4, 316–332.

O'Sullivan, D., & Jackson, M. J. (2002), "Festival tourism: A contributor to sustainable local economic development?" *Journal of Sustainable Tourism*, Vol. 10 No. 4, pp. 325–342.

Peranson, M. (2008), "First you get the power, then you get the money: two models of film festivals", *Cinéaste*, Vol. 33 No. 3, pp. 37–43.

Quinn, B. (2005), "Arts festivals and the city", *Urban Studies*, Vol. 42 No. 5–6, pp. 927–943.

Ravasi, D., Rindova, V., & Stigliani, I. (2019), "The stuff of legend: History, memory, and the temporality of organizational identity construction", *Academy of Management Journal*, Vol. 62 No. 5, pp. 1523–1555.

Ravasi, D., & Schultz, M. (2006), "Responding to organizational identity threats: Exploring the role of organizational culture", *Academy of Management Journal*, Vol. 49 No. 3, pp. 433–458.

Reinecke, J., & Ansari, S. (2017), "Time, temporality and process studies", In: Langley, A. & Tsoukas, H. (Eds.) *The Sage handbook of process organization studies*, Sage, pp. 402–416.

Rüling, C. C. (2009), "Festivals as field-configuring events: The Annecy international animated film festival and market", In: Iordanova, D., & Rhyne, R. (Eds.) *Film festival yearbook 1: The festival circuit,* St. Andrews St. Andrews Film Studies, pp. 49–66.

Rüling, C. C., & Strandgaard Pedersen, J. (2010), "Film festival research from an organizational studies perspective", *Scandinavian Journal of Management*, Vol. 26 No. 3, pp. 318–323.

Salvador, E., & Strandgaard Pedersen, J. (2020), "Managing cultural festivals between tradition and innovation", Call for Routledge book chapters.

Sasaki, I., Kotlar, J., Ravasi, D., & Vaara, E. (2020), "Dealing with revered past: Historical identity statements and strategic change in Japanese family firms", *Strategic Management Journal*, Vol. 41 No. 3, pp. 590–623.

Schad, J., Lewis, M. W., Raisch, S. & Smith, W. K. (2016), "Paradox research in management science: Looking back to move forward", *Academy of Management Annals*, Vol. 10 No. 1, pp. 5–64.

Schüßler, E., & Sydow., J. (2015), "Organizing events for configuring and maintaining creative fields", In: C. Jones, C., Lorenzen, M., & Sapsed, J. (Eds.) *Oxford handbook of creative industries*, Oxford University Press, pp. 284–300.

Schultz, M. (2016), "Organizational identity change and temporality", In: Pratt, M., Schultz, M., Ashforth, B. E., & Ravasi, D. (Eds.) *The Oxford handbook on organizational identity*, Oxford University Press, 93–105.

Schultz, M., & Hernes, T. (2013), "A temporal perspective on organizational identity", *Organization Science*, Vol. 24 No. 1, pp. 1–21.

Schultz, M., & Hernes, T. (2020), "Temporal interplay between strategy and identity: Punctuated, subsumed, and sustained modes", *Strategic Organization*, Vol. 18 No. 1, pp. 106–135.

Schüssler, E., Rüling, C. C., & Wittneben, B. B. (2014), "On melting summits: The limitations of field-configuring events as catalysts of change in transnational climate policy", *Academy of Management Journal*, Vol. 57 No. 1, pp. 140–171.

Stjerne, I. S., & Svejenova, S. (2016), "Connecting temporary and permanent organizing: Tensions and boundary work in sequential film projects", *Organization Studies*, Vol. 37 No. 12, pp. 1771–1792.

Suddaby, R., Foster, W. M. & Quinn Trank, C. (2010), "Rhetorical history as a source of competitive advantage", In: Joel, A.C., & Lampel, J. (Eds.) *The globalization of strategy research (Advances in strategic management)* (27), Emerald Group Publishing Limited, pp. 147–173.

Suddaby, R., & Jaskiewicz, P. (2020), "Managing traditions: A critical capability for family business success", *Family Business Review*, Vol. 33 No. 3, pp. 234–243.

Toraldo, M. L., & Islam, G. (2019), "Festival and organization studies", *Organization Studies*, Vol. 40 No. 3, pp. 309–322.

Toraldo, M. L., Islam, G., & Mangia, G. (2019), "Serving time: Volunteer work, liminality and the uses of meaningfulness at music festivals", *Journal of Management Studies*, Vol. 56 No. 3, pp. 617–654.

Uriarte, Y. T., DeFillippi, R., Riccaboni, M., & Catoni, M. L. (2019), "Projects, institutional logics and institutional work practices: The case of the Lucca Comics & Games Festival", *International Journal of Project Management*, Vol. 37 No. 2, pp. 318–330.

Vrontis, D., Bresciani, S., & Giacosa, E. (2016), "Tradition and innovation in Italian wine family businesses", *British Food Journal*, Vol. 118 No. 8, pp. 1883–1897.

Wilshusen, P. R., & MacDonald, K. I. (2017), "Fields of green: Corporate sustainability and the production of economistic environmental governance", *Environment and Planning A: Economy and Space*, Vol. 49 No. 8, pp. 1824–1845.

Yin, R. K. (2015), *Qualitative research from start to finish*, Guilford publications.

2 Food Events and the Temporality of Innovations

Iben Sandal Stjerne and Silviya Svejenova

Introduction

Cultural fairs, festivals, and other events have been considered of importance for the reenactment and negotiation of institutional arrangements in a particular field (Moeran and Strandgaard Pedersen 2011). They constitute inter-organizational "hotspots" for knowledge exchange and idea generation as well as reconnection with tradition (Schüssler, Rüling, and Wittneben 2014; Stjerne, Wenzel, and Svejenova, forthcoming). Food events, in particular, have become increasingly popular in recent years, ranging from locally anchored festivals that celebrate places, communities, and their traditions, such as "Copenhagen Cooking & Food Festival," to global virtual dialogues that explore big questions and seek novel responses to them, such as EAT and the Rockefeller Foundation's "Reimagining Food Systems," that span audiences across countries. Such events enable temporary encounters among diverse actors, such as food professionals, entrepreneurs, scientists, policy makers, and consumers, among others.

The temporary interactions at events have a novelty-generating capacity and a recognized potential to influence the trajectory of professions, technologies, and industries (Leca, Rüling, and Puthod 2015). They can also challenge and enable actors' rethinking of temporal structures, which "consist of recurring actions and events that are produced and reproduced reflexively [by them]" (Hernes and Schultz 2020, 3) by exposing them to a variety of other temporal structures. Yet, how exactly field-configuring events (Lampel and Meyer 2008) or, more broadly speaking, field-level events (Gross and Zilber 2020) that bring diverse actors together, contribute to connecting tradition and innovation remains an important, yet insufficiently addressed question (for some exceptions in relation to innovation, see Hjalager [2009] and Larson [2009]).

Thus, in this chapter, we ask: How are traditions revived and ideas for the future revealed at food events, and how does that dynamic contribute to the events' innovation potential? We address this question by taking on a temporality perspective, that is, moving from a chronological to a process view of time and acknowledging the importance of the continuously

DOI: 10.4324/9781003127185-4

negotiated present (Schultz and Hernes 2013), in which the shadows of different pasts and futures that actors bring together in their temporary encounters are connected and reinterpreted, gaining new meaning (Stjerne and Svejenova 2016; Stjerne, Wenzel, and Svejenova, forthcoming). Our theoretical ideas are inspired by and illustrated with insights from a launch event of the "Chefs' Manifesto Copenhagen Action Hub" that took place in Copenhagen in August 2018.

The Chefs' Manifesto—a novel global initiative supported by "a community of 700+ chefs participating from 77 countries, equipped with a simple set of actions to drive progress against the food issues that matter most to them" (SDG2 Advocacy Hub, 2021a)—was initiated by SDG2 Advocacy Hub (the UN's Sustainable Development Goal 2, which focuses on zero hunger) to connect debates on food systems' sustainability to the passion and meaning of food (Newnham, 2020). Chefs, together with food industry leaders, had developed the manifesto to push forward global efforts toward a better food future. Various launch events were set up in pivotal food cities around the world with the purpose to establish hubs that can mobilize local chefs and other actors and thereby accelerate and scale up the work toward a sustainable food future.

The Copenhagen event aimed at establishing a hub that could mobilize local chefs and other relevant actors in the Danish food industry to engage with "The Chefs' Manifesto." As in the case of other field-level events (Gross and Zilber 2020), the organizers had convened diverse actors of relevance to the "state of the art" of the culinary field in Copenhagen and Denmark, along with the leaders of the global initiative and some of the other Chefs' Manifesto Hubs organizers (e.g., London, New York). The dynamics we observed at the event can be understood through its embeddedness in the trajectories of both the global manifesto and movement and the local developments brought about by the New Nordic Cuisine's Manifesto and movement (for an overview, see: Byrkjeflot, Strandgaard Pedersen, and Svejenova 2013; Svejenova, Strandgaard Pedersen, and Byrkjeflot, forthcoming). Within the scope of this chapter, we selectively highlight three aspects of the temporal dynamics of this event in relation to tradition and innovation: the shadow of the global future, the shadow of the local past, and the "spark" of the present.

Our analysis of the temporal dynamics at the Copenhagen hub's launch event is based on a variety of sources, including: six semi-structured interviews with event participants and organizers; participant-observation at two action hub events (in Copenhagen and London); a two-day strategy workshop at the global SDG2 Advocacy Hub, followed by four online meetings; documents and podcasts from the SDG2 Action Hub's homepage on the Chefs' Manifesto. Data were collected in the period from August 2018, starting just a few days before the Chefs' Manifesto launch event in Copenhagen, and continued until December 2020, venturing over time across various other events related to the Chefs' Manifesto and its organizers.

During the ethnographic work, the first author not only interviewed but also interacted informally with key members at the events and meetings and social activities taking place afterwards. The intention with these interactions was to gain insights into how participants engaged with the past and evoked tradition(s), as well as their ideas and expectations for the future.

The chapter is structured as follows. First, we outline some relevant theoretical ideas on events' temporariness and temporality. Next, we provide a brief overview of the Chefs' Manifesto and the focal food event at the heart of this study—the launching of its Copenhagen Action Hub. This section is followed by a presentation of three different ways in which pasts are intended to be revived and ideas for the future explored at the Chefs' Manifesto launch event in Copenhagen. Finally, we discuss these insights and conclude with reflections on the relationship between events, innovation, and temporality, and suggest some directions for further research.

Events' temporariness and temporality

Events are "intentionally set-up temporally and spatially bounded social arenas at which diverse individuals from different organizations come together and interact with potential impacts on wider organizational fields" (Schüssler and Sydow 2015, 284). Temporary organizations, such as events, have been found to contribute to innovation not only in their parent organizations (Engwall 2003; Johansson, Löfström, and Ohlsson 2007) but also in fields (Ford and Randolph 1992; Sydow, Lindkvist, and DeFillippi 2004; Stjerne and Svejenova 2016). Their organizational uniqueness lies in their temporary nature as well as in their distinctive temporality.

They can be understood as "short-lived hotspots" and "temporary clusters" of intense exchanges (Maskell, Bathelt, and Malmberg 2006). Traditionally, they have been a place-specific and time-specific coming together of actors (Maskell, Bathelt, and Malmberg 2006). An event's *place specificity*—physicality and the respective "actors' interpretations, representations, and identifications" (Gieryn 2000, 467)—is determined by its local embeddedness and in certain contexts can influence the event's unfolding (Schüssler, Grabher, and Müller-Seitz 2015). An event's *time specificity* is defined in its planning, yet it is transcended by differentiated and nested temporalities that get enacted at the event, as well as the legacy of the event (Schüssler et al. 2015).

Within events' time specificity, rules can be temporarily suspended to allow for play (Mainemelis and Ronson 2006) and timelessness, or the feeling of transcending time and self, can emerge by immersing "in a captivating present-moment activity" (Mainemelis 2001, 548) in that, "being able to temporarily step outside of normal life — while keeping one's senses alert — is indeed like being reborn" (Ackerman 1999, 31). This, in turn, opens up possibilities for creativity and flow, and enables the emergence of new ideas.

Further, events can attach themselves to and detach from other temporary and permanent organizations (Sahlin-Andersson 2002; Stjerne and Svejenova 2016; Tukainen and Granqvist 2016), which can extend their limited temporal scope (Manning and Sydow 2007) and enable transitions beyond the temporal scope of the project (Sydow and Staber 2002). As actors bring their diverse temporal orientations to these events, resolving tensions of conflicting temporal orientations (Reinecke and Ansari 2015) and creating shared temporal frames and narratives among actors with disparate pasts (Hernes 2014) are essential for commitment to action (Granqvist and Gustafson 2016; Stjerne, Wenzel, and Svejenova forthcoming). At the same time, event participants' exposure to a variety of temporal structures requires searching for optimal distinctiveness (Alvarez et al. 2005; Pedersen and Dobbin 2006; Anteby and Molnar 2012), seeking shared ground, while preserving differences, which makes it possible for actors to create meaning and collectively derive new ideas at an event (Schüsler et al. 2015).

Below, we first introduce the Chefs' Manifesto and then overview the focal event for this study: the launch of the Copenhagen hub.

The Chefs' Manifesto and the launch of the Copenhagen hub

Activities related to the Chefs' Manifesto are coordinated and led by SDG2 Advocacy Hub. These activities seek to propel a global movement toward sustainability in the food industry, with chefs as "powerful advocates for a better food future—motivating people to make changes in their kitchens and communities and empowering them to call on governments and companies to also play their part" and influencing "what we grow, what we put on our plates and how we think and talk about food" (SDG action campaign's homepage, 2018).

The development of the Chefs' Manifesto's eight action points was initiated on November 3, 2017, in Milan, Italy, where chefs from around the world gathered together with representatives from various companies such as Unilever, Oxfam US, Global Citizen, and the World Food Programme to discuss next steps toward eradicating global hunger (SDG2 Advocacy Hub, 2021a). Working toward the UN's 17 Sustainable Development Goals (SDGs), in particular SDG2 "Zero hunger," was broad in ambition and connected actors from diverse fields, such as nutrition, agriculture, poverty, and biodiversity. As the bringing together of these diverse fields and interests into a global advocacy hub constituted a highly political arena, there was a need to connect the debates within it to the passion and meaning of food (Newnham, 2020). Chefs, together with food industry leaders, developed the manifesto with the agenda to push forward the prospects for a better food future through collective action. The idea, attributed to the SDG2 Advocacy Hub leader Paul Newnham, was to identify and involve chefs as catalysts for change in different local communities across the globe in order to achieve SDG2 by 2030.

When Paul Newnham started talking to chefs around the globe, he found that while "a lot of chefs [were] doing really cool stuff ... everyone was doing their [own] thing, which they were good at but it wasn't necessarily well connected" (Newnham, 2020). To connect these distributed efforts toward a shared sustainability agenda, those involved in the SDG2 Advocacy Hub started thinking about creating a framework that can bring together these individual initiatives. The Chefs' Manifesto singled out the following eight thematic areas that chefs were most interested in tackling, underpinned by an action plan with practical suggestions as to how chefs can contribute to the SDGs (SDG2 Advocacy Hub 2021b):

1   Ingredients grown with respect for the earth and its oceans
2   Protection of biodiversity and improved animal welfare
3   Investment in livelihoods
4   Value natural resources and reduce waste
5   Celebration of local and seasonal food
6   A focus on plant-based ingredients
7   Education on food safety and healthy diets
8   Nutritious food that is accessible and affordable for all.

The intention behind creating a global Chefs' Manifesto "written by chefs for chefs" was to develop a global general framework that would connect sustainability-conscious chefs across the globe and their manifold local initiatives:

> Often people come up with solutions and they say this solution first to this part of the world and they want everyone to join them in solving this. The reality is that the solutions we need are actually going to be very different ... so what works in London is going to be very different to what works in Bristol, to what works in New Delhi, into Lima or in Beijing.
>
> (Newnham, 2020)

To embed the Chefs' Manifesto in local communities and organize chefs around ideas for a societal impact, launch events were organized in food cities around the world, such as New York (June 2017), Milan (September 2017), London (June 2018), and Copenhagen (August 2018), among others. These launch events were expected to connect local chefs and "recruit" and motivate them to work with the manifesto in their daily practice, pushing forward an agenda for change toward zero hunger, which was also intended to improve local food, livelihood, health, and biodiversity challenges. These local action hubs would operate as virtual spaces that would connect chefs and foodies to kick-start local action on food sustainability, whereas having hubs across the globe would expand the reach and impact of the envisioned global movement.

The Chefs' Manifesto launch event in Copenhagen gathered some 30 chefs, chef students, entrepreneurs, food techies, food innovation professionals, and a few scholars at the Copenhagen Hospitality College in the city's district of Valby. The online invitation to the three-day event highlighted that the goal was to gather

> chefs from across Denmark, the Nordic region and beyond to cook and explore food sustainability at the launch of the Copenhagen Action Hub for the Chefs' Manifesto … [exploring how the] … manifesto [can] inspire and empower chefs to contribute to a better food future.
>
> (Copenhagen Cooking, 2018)

The event sought to inspire new directions in the Danish food industry by introducing a diverse set of convened local actors to the global initiative. It aimed at engaging these participants in coming up with novel ideas that can mobilize change that could spread and translate the Chefs' Manifesto to the local food community in Copenhagen. The idea was to create a local action hub that would function as "a nerve center where chefs return to again and again" (Field notes, event day 1).

The event was planned, organized, and led by renowned Danish chef Kamilla Seidler, who had recently returned to Copenhagen after six years' work in Bolivia. There, she had spearheaded the development of Gustu, a now-recognized restaurant with an added agenda of initiating culinary revolution in Bolivia and a social program for educating youth from financially challenged families into the chef profession. In light of her success in mobilizing change in Bolivia, she had been invited to partake in developing the Chefs' Manifesto together with 15 other chefs from all over the world. She has also become the driving force for the establishment of the Copenhagen Action Hub and its launch event. Each local hub intended to establish a network of chefs that would participate primarily in local activities that through the global homepage for the Chefs' Manifesto would then connect and promote global knowledge and change. The Copenhagen event's agenda sought local anchoring of the rather broad global Chefs' Manifesto, connecting it with the distinctive Copenhagen (and Danish) past, present, and future food trajectories. Below, we highlight three main aspects of the temporal dynamics at the launch event, which we argue influenced its innovation potential.

Temporal dynamics at the event

The following aspects inform the temporal dynamics at the launch event of the Copenhagen Action Hub (see Table 2.1 for an overview). The first is "The shadow of the global future," which was primarily revealed through

Table 2.1 Temporal dynamics unfolding at the launch event

Aspects of the temporal dynamics	Sub-event	Ways of mobilizing temporal shadows	Connecting tradition and innovation
The shadow of the global future	Introduction to the Chefs' Manifesto and reflections from launch and network events in London, New York, and Stockholm	"Collapsing future" and "Better food future." In the former way of mobilizing, the emphasis is on how current practices lead to a doomsday scenario wherein the food system would break, and in the latter, it is on how the change of actions would pave the way to a more sustainable food future.	Participants struggled to fully comprehend the grand narrative of the Chefs' Manifesto and how it connected to the local traditions and innovations.
The shadow of the local past	"How to Start a Local Food Movement" Discussion on food movements and conversation on the New Nordic Cuisine (NNC) Manifesto with its co-writers Claus Meyer and Jan Krag Jacobsen	"Learning from the past" and "Breaking away from the past." The former way of mobilizing seeks continuity through reinvigorating and enhancing the practices of NNC, whereas the latter implies showing how the Chefs' Manifesto diverts sufficiently from the past to legitimize its local relevance.	Participants explored how learnings from the NNC manifesto could help the Chefs' manifesto escalate change locally. No collective solution to this challenge emerged, as the novelty of the Chefs' Manifesto vis-a-vis the tradition established by NNC remained unclear.
The "spark" of the present	"Cooking the manifesto" Chefs cook together with fresh local ingredients and without recipes, using the eight action points of the Chefs' Manifesto as inspiration.	"Temporally suspending rules" and "Transcending time." The former way of mobilizing is through chefs' engagement in an improvisational cooking activity, whereas the latter is about getting deeply immersed in the present through the aesthetics of food.	Participants were energized by the hands-on experience with the Chefs' Manifesto and the playful connection to each other as well as to the food's materiality and aesthetics. This enabled new ideas to flow and temporarily anchored the new manifesto in the present.

the opening presentation by the Chefs' Manifesto leaders and the subsequent discussion. The second was "The shadow of the local past." It manifested itself in the conversation with the founders of the New Nordic Cuisine movement (and co-authors of its manifesto), which was initiated some 15 years earlier. The New Nordic Cuisine Manifesto had transformed the local culinary field and food culture, infusing them with both innovation and keen interest in reviving forgotten traditions. The third aspect was "The 'spark' of the present," which involved event participants "cooking the manifesto" together, without a recipe or a plan, playfully "materializing" its ideas by experimenting with local seasonal vegetables while preparing and serving food to others. Below, we elaborate on each of these three temporal aspects that constitute the temporal dynamic of the launch event and which influence its trajectory and potential for innovation.

The shadow of the global future

At the opening session, SDG2 Advocacy Hub leader Paul Newnham and renowned UK-based head chef Arthur Pots Dawson (leader of the London Action Hub for the Chefs' Manifesto), presented the manifesto as a new and much-needed vision for achieving a sustainable global food future. The two acted as advocates for the manifesto and related movement, seeking to align participants behind a shared understanding of a troublesome food future. In doing so, they formulated a collective global challenge triggered by the unsustainable global food system. Two main alternative scenarios and related horizons for the future were presented: a "collapsing future" and a "better food future." In the former, current practices lead to a doomsday scenario wherein the food system would break, and in the latter, the change of actions would pave the way to a more sustainable food future. The presentation and discussion geared toward guiding the attention of event participants to how past-present practices pave the way to a future collapse while inspiring hope for a "better food future" connected to acting responsibly in the present-future through the eight open-ended broad action points of the Chefs' Manifesto.

A feeling of hope for a better food future was created by evoking the Chefs' Manifesto statement "Act now," which pointed to the imminent need for change in practices to prevent the collapsing future becoming a reality. And while "act now" emphasized the significance and urgency of the present, the possible actions toward a "better food future" were only loosely defined. To make these actions comprehensible, they had to be made meaningful in the specific context, connecting with local "practices and ways of interpreting the 17 goals" (field notes, event day 1).

These stories were used not only to show the inherent challenges with the future of the food system but also to highlight how little an ordinary person knows about the food consumed and the need to start from the bottom and educate, getting people to be selective about what they eat, with the argument that chefs played a central role in enabling such awareness. The path to a better food future required new ideas, which chefs were in the powerful position to develop and implement, as educators, trendsetters, and motivators. The Chefs' Manifesto was presented as a novel approach, developed by chefs for chefs, to rebooting the broken food system, in which each and every participant in the room, from accomplished chefs to chef students, were referred to as important in the endeavor (field notes, event day 1). Thus, the manifesto's eight action points provided direction but also left enough room for local chefs' interpretation and initiative. That, in turn, opened up the possibility to connect the Chefs' Manifesto to and learn from the local past.

The shadow of the local past

The launch event also ventured back into some of the local (Copenhagen and Danish) culinary past's main reference points (particularly on the second day of the program). The past was brought to life at a round-table discussion on 'How to start a local food movement' with gastro-entrepreneur Claus Meyer and academic and communication professional Jan Krag Jacobsen, who had co-drafted the New Nordic Cuisine Manifesto that had launched the powerful movement for reforming Nordic cuisine and food. The Danish chefs participating in the event had been involved in this movement over the years and, thus, they could relate to the evoked past. Head chef Kamilla Seidler, the leader of the Copenhagen Action Hub, herself had been sent by Claus Meyer to Bolivia, to replicate learnings from New Nordic Cuisine in the shaping of the Bolivian culinary revival.

We identified two different ways in which the past and the New Nordic tradition were mobilized at the event, contributing to both "learning from the past" and "breaking away from the past." Meyer and Krag referred to the "lack of food quality" in traditional Danish cuisine and the utopian vision they had to disrupt and renew the food culture when creating the New Nordic Manifesto. The manifesto allowed to inspire a distributed action and movement, through which Copenhagen became an epicenter for culinary innovation. In the process, New Nordic Cuisine gained international fame for its freshness, simplicity, and purity, stemming from cooking with seasonal, local, soundly produced products, principles that were proclaimed in the New Nordic Cuisine Manifesto and showcased in the practices of Noma, which has topped the list of the world's best restaurants on several occasions. Additional initiatives related to the New Nordic Manifesto and movement sought to educate and support new chefs into these practices and to further engage the entire food production system from farm to fork. This also involved restaurants opening their own gardens as well as biodynamic farms appearing around Copenhagen driven by some of the leading figures from the local fine dining field.

Relating the Chefs' Manifesto to the New Nordic Cuisine Manifesto and movement was instrumental for opening up a debate on the local food future in relation to a prominent tradition from its recent past. The unfolding discussion focused on the efforts involved in creating a new style of cuisine as a break from the previously dominant French tradition, the challenges of handling big players and avoiding brands as well as the spread of the movement, which some considered successful in Copenhagen, but less so within the rest of Denmark. The scaling of the Chefs' Manifesto and what to do differently to the New Nordic Food movement became an important discussion point. Some suggested that the new manifesto had to spread throughout Denmark to actually make an impact, whereas others stated the need to involve the country's large food producers for the novel approach to scale up.

What the discussion of the past revealed was how much the New Nordic Cuisine statements, ambitions, and practices on sustainable cooking resonated with those put forward in the new manifesto. This created uncertainty as to the novelty of the latter and if/how it can provide distinctively different ways of working that could challenge in significant ways extant cooking practices. Further, the discussion raised the awareness of the challenges involved in amplifying the local efforts toward sustainable cooking. In addition to scaling-up and amplifying the efforts, the challenge with speed of innovation to ensure system change by 2030 was further recognized. This created a bridge from the local past to the concerns with the challenging global future, highlighting the need for reinvigorating and enhancing local practices while also "breaking away from the past" to explore and discover the meaning and relevance of the new Chefs' Manifesto in the present.

The "Spark" of the present

During the three-day event, there were cooking sessions in which the idea was to have a hands-on experience with the Chefs' Manifesto, i.e. to engage in "materializing" it. These sessions were referred to as "cooking the manifesto." They centered on the present exploration of what could creatively come from bringing together chefs from all over the world, without any concrete plan, just the eight action points of the manifesto as a guideline and some local ingredients selected according to the principles of the manifesto: for example, seasonal, local, representing biodiversity, grown with respect to the soil and environment. These sessions generated momentum for the Chefs' manifesto and revealed the energy of the present in two ways: by "temporally suspending rules" and working toward it without a plan, and by "transcending time" through the aesthetics of food in the engagement with fresh ingredients. That created a "spark" for creativity and a flow of new ideas by bringing participants closer together, through their culinary craft, in a way that neither the reflection on the global future, nor the revival of the local past and tradition were able to achieve.

In the first cooking session, the participants were to prepare a dinner for 210 guests at a local food festival "Harvest Feast," getting inspiration from the principles of the Chefs' Manifesto. ("Harvest Feast" is a yearly event where 1,500 people have dinner together, at a long table on the streets of Frederiksberg. Local chefs prepare the food with fresh ingredients, coming from small local farms.) The cooking session started with putting on aprons and non-slippery shoes and together participants opened the doors of a huge container full of organic vegetables grown at a local farm. The amount of unorganized and unknown vegetables was overwhelming, in particular to the student chefs who took part in the event. They were asked to cook without a detailed plan, leaving room to explore and "cook through the vision of the manifesto."

The free play and working with ingredients together allowed chefs to learn from each other and discuss as well as experiment with different techniques, sharing new ideas, wherein the curiosity and passionate engagement with the ingredients in cooking created a shared emotional bond and initiated a development of shared practices:

> You have to work with people who also have the passion for food ... You can see the people who love food, they always want to come and see and discuss, look when I do like that it will be better and so on ... It was just like [chef], he was so excited to show us all the things, like how to do things and do it properly, and even when presenting the food it needs to look nice, so it's the love in the food. It's not like we throw things out because we can use everything.
>
> (Chef student, interview)

The explorative and collaborative way of creating dishes and cooking with the ideas of the manifesto in mind to make a delicious three-course meal for 210 people, ensuring that everything served was delicious and prepared with love and care, added the shared emotional feeling among the participants.

Participants' energy was activated by the fresh local ingredients, coming directly from the farm, and the way of working with them together at the event. As explained by one of the chef students, "then, we just walked into that kitchen hives of boxes, herbs, etc. and I really had no clue what to do with that." Chef students felt initially overwhelmed by having so many vegetables that did not fit into an already existing recipe. Some of them asked the more experienced chefs what to do with the vegetables, and were given the freedom to experiment and "just do what you feel like." As one of the students explained, this extraordinary food experience left a huge impression on her and engaged her in a new way. At the time, she was unsure what to do with the manifesto, which she felt did not add a new framework itself, as she had already been working with sustainable food for years. Yet, the entire new exploratory way of engaging with fresh and new local vegetables had been a novel aesthetic sensation that had left a big impact:

> It was truly freaky and we talked about it that we are here students who know how to cook, and we were lost and we have never tried that before, but that was also part of it, and you could just see that it was high quality and vegetables were fresh and some we had never seen before, it was really [making a facial expression that states she is amazed] … it just did something, and there was a good energy around it and we had some delicious (raw) ingredients … And it's a huge impact you can make on students by that in only a few hours by bringing in such a Mecca of food.
>
> (Chef student, interview)

The spirit was high and inclusive. The cooking preparation—the three-course meal for the "Harvest Feast"—was not hurried. It allowed for people to stand round and talk a bit, as well as dare to try out new things in the kitchen and involve event participants who were not professional chefs. It was important that people had fun while cooking, suspending the rules of the usual time-pressured cooking practices in public kitchens and restaurants. A chef student explained that the passion when cooking together is about learning from each other, making it all come together, which requires slack time:

> We had to make lots of food, but we still had time to have fun and learn from each other and we used all the vegetables (zero waste), and people were just there to have a good time, there was no head chef to yell at you and no time limit.
>
> (Chef student, interview)

Event participants referred to the experience as "outstanding" and "energizing." In the words of a chef, the "[Chefs' Manifesto] is a story told about a chef that meets up with other chefs and they cook together," sharing the love of cooking (field notes, event day 1).

Thus, the 'spark' of the present came from the spontaneous interactions and fun, enabling connection between the participants and allowing them to explore narratives and create dishes related to the Chefs' Manifesto. Overall, "cooking the manifesto" was a memorable experience that focused the senses on the present and became a shared reference point for participants.

Discussion

In the previous section, we delineated and illustrated some particularities of the temporal dynamics at the launch event. These dynamics involve multi-temporality, that is, connecting multiple temporalities (Stjerne, Wenzel, and

Svejenova, forthcoming), such as: (1) mobilizing the present in a trajectory of ongoing pasts (and a strong local tradition shaped by New Nordic Cuisine) to ensure globally a "better food future" while preventing the scenario of "collapsing future"; (2) "learning from the past," yet "breaking away from the past" to create energy for the new global manifesto; and (3) developing a shared emotional bond through the "spark" of the present by "temporally suspending rules" and "transcending time" in a playful engagement with the fresh food aesthetics. Below, we elaborate on how these three aspects of the temporal dynamics offer a more nuanced understanding of how tradition and innovation unfold at events, focusing on timelessness, multi-temporality, and temporal bundling.

Timelessness. This study shows how the temporal dynamics at events is importantly influenced not only by the events' temporariness (Lampel and Meyer 2008; Schüssler et al. 2015) but, particularly, by suspending time and time-pressure rules and transcending time (Mainemelis 2001; Mainemelis and Ronson 2006; Geraldi, Stjerne, and Oehmen 2020). The temporal boundedness of events delimits, yet can also intensify the interactions, providing an opening for building trust and learning (Lampel 2001; Oliver and Montgomery 2008), as well as for playful experimentation (Mainemelis and Ronson 2006) in "out of time-moments in which one surrenders to the depth and intensity of immediate experience" (Mainemelis 2001, 563). Such sense of timelessness and deep emersion stems from the specific qualities not only of events but also of food, namely its biomateriality (Moser et al. 2021) and material temporality (Hernes, Feddersen, and Schultz 2021). As such, events can be understood as settings that catalyze timelessness and, in that, enable new ideas to flow.

Multi-temporality. The study also reveals how actors connect their multiple temporalities (Stjerne et al., forthcoming), i.e. their diverse repertoires of past experiences and ideas about the future, while experimenting in the present. Similar with the context of film projects (Stjerne and Svejenova 2016), innovation at food events emerges in micro-interactions, in which various actors draw on both shadows of future and past to legitimize novel ideas. In addition, as mentioned in the previous point, we note that innovative processes at events are also triggered by engagement with food's material temporality (Hernes, Feddersen, and Schultz 2021; Moser et al. 2021) that enables actors with diverse past references and traditions to experiment and improvise in the present and for the future.

We suggest that an event's innovation potential emerges in the interplay between futures and pasts as well as the engagement with the present at the event. While a shared global future can set a shared direction in which to engage beyond the scope of the event, the mobilization of pasts needs to connect in a way that offers a distinctiveness to the past while also drawing on its familiarity, enabling optimal distinctiveness (Alvarez et al. 2005; Pedersen and Dobbin 2006; Zuckerman 2016). More specifically, the temporal synergies at the event implied both learning from and breaking away from past while also issuing a need for change through projecting a "collapsing future" and presenting a better alternative of "a better food future" through the new Chefs' Manifesto. However, our findings show that while the Chefs' Manifesto succeeded in legitimizing the need for change, it failed to sufficiently tap into the local past of New Nordic Cuisine and did not provide concrete novel ways for practicing in the future, and hence lacked an optimal distinctiveness. Also, while events can be good at sparking energy, as they can enable timelessness (Mainemelis 2001) and focus energy into experimenting, which is a strong connector and motivator for change, but in itself does they do not allow to "keep the fire going" after they come to an end (Schüssler, Rüling, and Wittneben 2014) and may require other ways of sustaining the created connections among the actors and ensuring a continuity between traditions from the past and innovations projecting the future.

Temporal bundling. Based on our analysis of the launch event, we suggest that it could be insightful to consider complex events with further granularity, conceiving them conceptually as ecosystems of sub-events. Prior research has shown the unfolding of change across a series of field-configuring events, and the influence of occurrences external to the event series (Schüssler, Rüling, and Wittneben 2014). We look into the unfolding of microdynamics at one single event, which is in alignment with insights on the importance of the strength of ecosystems that support and provide resources for temporary organizations (Sydow and Stabher 2002). We show how the ecosystem of sub-events within one field-configuring event holds different temporal connections to past, present, and future, which collectively connect, interact, and unfold at the course of the event, thereby mobilizing or failing to mobilize change beyond the temporary scope of the event. Hence, we state that events should not be analyzed in a loop, but rather as sub-events that connect to various past-present-futures that bring forward the meaning, learning, and connections for change that the overarching event ends up mobilizing.

As affirmed by Engwall (2003), who studied the embeddedness of temporary organizations—tellingly titling his paper "No Project is an Island: Linking Projects to History and Context"—what makes projects successful is their connection to a permanent organization that established them. Similarly with temporary organizations that are part of an ecosystem of projects (Grabher 2002; Sydow and Stabher 2002), in this chapter, we argue that a given event can be understood as a part of an ecosystem of past, future, and concurrent events whose temporalities can be "bundled" together. The ecosystem in our context consists of a series of interconnected sub-events, each with its own temporal focus, such as voicing concerns about the global future, learning from the local past, and cooking together in the present. Taken together, in the span of the overall event, these sub-events could contribute to a temporal continuity between tradition and innovation in the present while also sparking energy for change. It is this temporal bundling that may reveal opportunities for innovation or, alternatively, hamper them, if the created connections with the past and extant traditions show the need for and the path to such innovation.

Conclusion

At the outset of this chapter, we asked how traditions are revived and ideas for the future revealed at food events that seek to mobilize for innovation. What we outlined and illustrated, in response to this question, were three distinctive temporal aspects (global future, local past, and the "spark" of the present) that get highlighted at different sub-events and, interwoven together, constitute the temporal dynamics at the food event, influencing its potential to connect tradition and innovation. Ensuring that certain sub-events enable timelessness that results in a "spark," could extend the temporal impact of the event even after its conclusion. While timelessness, multi-temporality, and temporal bundling can create energy for both continuity and innovation, sustaining that energy and momentum requires developing collectively ideas about a shared global future that can connect to the shadow of the local past. Further work is needed to unfold the complex, yet also fascinating connection between temporariness, temporality, and timelessness of and at events.

Acknowledgements

We gratefully acknowledge funding from the Velux Foundation (Velux Project #00021807 "The Temporality of Food Innovation").

References

Ackerman, D. 1999. *Deep Play.* New York: Vintage Books.

Alvarez, J. L., C. Mazza, J. Strandgaard Pedersen, and S. Svejenova. 2005. "Shielding Idiosyncrasy from Isomorphic Pressures: Towards Optimal Distinctiveness in European Filmmaking." *Organization* 12(6): 863–888.

Anteby, M., and V. Molnar. 2012. "Collective Memory Meets Organizational Identity: Remembering to Forget in a Firm's Rhetorical History." *Academy of Management Journal* 55(3): 515–540.

Byrkjeflot, H., J. Strandgaard Pedersen, and S. Svejenova. 2013. "From Label to Practice: The Process of Creating New Nordic Cuisine." *Journal of Culinary Science & Technology* 11(1): 36–55.

Copenhagen Cooking. 2018. Online event invitation. https://sdg2advocacyhub.org/chefs-manifesto/actions/copenhagen-action-hub-launch.

Engwall, M. 2003. "No Project Is an Island: Linking Projects to History and Context." *Research Policy* 32: 789–808.

Ford, R. C., and W. A. Randolph. 1992. "Cross-Functional Structures: A Review and Integration of Matrix Organization and Project Management." *Journal of Management* 18(2): 267–294.

Geraldi, J., I. Stjerne, and J. Oehmen. 2020. "Acting in Time: Temporal Work Enacting Tensions at the Interface between Temporary and Permanent Organisations". In *Tensions and Paradoxes in Temporary Organizing*, edited by Timo Braun and Joseph Lampel, 81–103. Emerald Publishing Limited.

Gieryn, T. F. 2000. "A Space for Place in Sociology." *Annual Review of Sociology* 26: 463–496.

Grabher, G. 2002. "Cool Projects, Boring Institutions: Temporary Collaboration in Social Context." *Regional Studies* 36(3): 205–214.

Granqvist, N., and R. Gustafsson. 2016. "Temporal Institutional Work." *Academy of Management Journal* 59(3): 1009–1035.

Gross, T., and T. B. Zilber. 2020. "Power Dynamics in Field-Level Events: A Narrative Approach." *Organization Studies* 41(10): 1369–1390.

Hernes, T. 2014. *A Process Theory of Organization*. Oxford: Oxford University Press.

Hernes, T., and M. Schultz. 2020. "Translating the Distant into the Present: How Actors Address Distant Past and Future Events Through Situated Activity." *Organization Theory* 1: 1–20.

Hernes, T., J. Feddersen, and M. Schultz. 2021. "Material Temporality: How Materiality 'Does' Time in Food Organizing." *Organization Studies* 42(2): 351–371.

Hjalager, A. M. 2009. "Cultural Tourism Innovation Systems: The Roskilde Festival." *Scandinavian Journal of Hospitality and Tourism* 9(2–3): 266–287.

Johansson, S., M. Löfström, and Ö. Ohlsson. 2007. "Separation or Integration? A Dilemma When Organizing Development Projects." *International Journal of Project Management* 25(5): 457–464.

Lampel, J. 2001. "The Core Competencies of Effective Project Execution: The Challenge of Diversity." *International Journal of Project Management* 19(8): 471–483.

Lampel, J., and A. D. Meyer. 2008. "Field-Configuring Events as Structuring Mechanisms: How Conferences, Ceremonies, and Trade Shows Constitute New Technologies, Industries, and Markets." *Journal of Management Studies* 45(6): 1025–1035.

Larson, M. 2009. "Festival Innovation: Complex and Dynamic Network Interaction." *Scandinavian Journal of Hospitality and Tourism* 9(2–3): 288–307.

Leca, B., C. C. Rüling, and D. Puthod. 2015. "Animated Times: Critical Transitions and the Maintenance of Field-Configuring Events." *Industry and Innovation* 22: 173–192.

Mainemelis, C. 2001. "When the Muse Takes It All: A Model for the Experience of Timelessness in Organizations." *Academy of Management Review* 26(4): 548–565.

Mainemelis, C., and S. Ronson. 2006. "Ideas Are Born in Fields of Play: Towards a Theory of Play and Creativity in Organizational Settings." *Research in Organizational Behavior* 27: 81–131.

Manning, S., and J. Sydow. 2007. "Transforming Creative Potential in Project Networks: How TV Movies Are Produced under Network-Based Control." *Critical Sociology* 33: 19– 42.

Maskell, P., H. Bathelt, and A. Malmberg. 2006. "Building Global Knowledge Pipelines: The Role of Temporary Clusters." *European Planning Studies* 14(8): 997–1013.

Moeran, B., and J. Strandgaard Pedersen. 2011. "Introduction." In *Negotiating Values in the Creative Industries: Fairs, Festivals and Competitive Events*, edited by B. Moeran and J. Strandgaard Pedersen, 1–35. Cambridge: Cambridge University Press.

Moser, C., J. Reinecke, F. den Hond, F., S. Svejenova, and G. Croidieu. 2021. "Biomateriality and Organizing: Towards an Organizational Perspective on Food." *Organization Studies* 42(2): 175–193.

Newnham, P. 2020. Chefs Manifesto Podcast, Episode 1 – Introduction & Conversation with Experts, Soundcloud, https://soundcloud.com/user-264172669/coming-soon-the-chefs-manifesto-podcast-series.

Oliver, A.L. and Montgomery, K., 2008. "Using Field-Configuring Events for Sense-Making: A Cognitive Network Approach." *Journal of Management Studies* 45(6): 1147–1167.

Pedersen, J. S., and F. Dobbin. 2006. "In Search of Identity and Legitimation: Bridging Organizational Culture and Neoinstitutionalism." *American Behavioral Scientist* 49(7): 897–907.

Reinecke, J., and S. Ansari. 2015. "When Times Collide: Temporal Brokerage at the Intersection of Markets and Developments." *Academy of Management Journal* 58(2): 618–648.

Sahlin-Andersson, K. 2002. "Project Management as Boundary Work: Dilemmas of Defining and Delimiting." In *Beyond Project Management: New Perspectives on the Temporary– Permanent Dilemma*, edited by K. Sahlin-Andersson and A. Söderholm, 241–260. Copenhagen: Liber – Copenhagen Business School Press.

Schultz, M., and T. Hernes. 2013. "A Temporal Perspective on Organizational Identity." *Organization Science* 24(1): 1–21.

Schüssler, E., G. Grabher, and G. Müller-Seitz. 2015. "Field-Configuring Events: Arenas for Innovation and Learning?" *Industry and Innovation* 22(3): 165–172.

Schüssler, E., C. C. Rüling, and B. B. Wittneben. 2014. "On Melting Summits: The Limitations of Field-Configuring Events as Catalysts of Change in Transnational Climate Policy." *Academy of Management Journal* 57(1): 140–171.

Schüssler, E., and J. Sydow. 2015. "Organizing Events for Configuring and Maintaining Creative Fields." In *Oxford Handbook of Creative Industries*, edited by Candace Jones, Mark Lorenzen, and Jonathan Sapsed, 284–300. Oxford: Oxford University Press.

SDG2 Advocacy Hub. 2021a. Chefs' Manifesto. www.sdg2advocacyhub.org/chefmanifesto.

SDG2 Advocacy Hub. 2021b. Resources. https://www.sdg2advocacyhub.org/resources.

SDG Action Campaign. 2018. Homepage. https://www.ifad.org/en/web/latest/-/story/a-chefs-manifesto-how-the-food-industry-can-deliver-a-better-future-for-food?p_l_back_url=%2Ffr%2Fweb%2Flatest%2Fstories%3Fmode%3Dsearch%26page%3D5%26delta%3D75%26start%3D3.

Stjerne, I. S., and S. Svejenova. 2016. "Connecting Temporary and Permanent Organizing: Tensions and Boundary Work in Sequential Film Projects." *Organization Studies* 37(12): 1771–1792.

Stjerne, I., M. Wenzel, and S. Svejenova. Forthcoming. "Commitment to Grand Challenges in Fluid Forms of Organizing: The Role of Narratives' Temporality." In *Organizing for Societal Grand Challenges*, edited by A. Gümüsay, E. Marti, H. Trittin, and C. Wickert. Research in the Sociology of Organizations.

Svejenova, S., J. Strandgaard Pedersen, and H. Byrkjeflot. Forthcoming. "From Innovation to Impact: Translating New Nordic Cuisine into a Nordic Food Model." In *The Making and Circulation of Nordic Models*, edited by H. Byrkjeflot, L. Mjøset, M. Mordhorst, and K. Petersen. London: Routledge.

Sydow, J., and U. Staber. 2002. "The Institutional Embeddedness of Project Networks: The Case of Content Production in German Television." *Regional Studies* 36(3): 215–227.

Sydow, J., L. Lindkvist, and R. DeFillippi. 2004. "Project-based Organizations, Embeddedness and Repositories of Knowledge." *Organization Studies* 25(9): 1475–1489.

Sydow, J., E. Schüssler, and G. Müller-Seitz. 2015. *Managing Inter-Organizational Relations: Debates and Cases*. London: Palgrave Macmillan International Higher Education.

Tukiainen, S., and N. Granqvist. 2016. "Temporary Organizing and Institutional Change." *Organization Studies* 37(12): 1819–1840.

Zuckerman, E. W. 2016. "Optimal Distinctiveness Revisited: An Integrative Framework for Understanding the Balance between Differentiation and Conformity in Individual and Organizational Identities." In *Oxford Handbook on Organizational Identity*, edited by M. G. Pratt, M. Schultz, B. Ashforth, and D. Ravasi, 183–199. Oxford: Oxford University Press.

3 From Festa to Festival

UNESCO Heritage and the (Invented) Tradition of a Cultural Festival

Carmelo Mazza and Jesper Strandgaard Pedersen

Introduction

The study is concerned with the institutional and organizational complexities rising from the management of culture, heritage, and tourism in the creation, transformation, and maintenance of a cultural festival. The town of Monte Sant'Angelo, located in the North of Apulia (Italy) and hosting two UNESCO World Heritage sites, and many different stakeholders and agendas, is a perfect, pluralistic setting to study how management of arts, culture, heritage, and tourism interact and may collide with economics and politics.

Festivals have over the previous decades been an object of analysis for several studies (Rüling and Strandgaard Pedersen, 2010; Moeran and Strandgaard Pedersen, 2011; Kredell, 2012; Andersson and Getz, 2014). From an institutional perspective, festivals have been interpreted as field configuring events (Lampel and Meyer, 2008) as well as institutions strengthening cultural images of cities (Strandgaard Pedersen and Mazza, 2011; Ooi and Strandgaard Pedersen, 2017). Several accounts of film festivals (Ooi and Strandgaard Pedersen, 2010; Mezias et al., 2011; Kredell, 2012; Mazza and Strandgaard Pedersen, 2017) show how the creation and maintenance of these institutions are strongly rooted in a web of institutional complexities, different logics and concerns, public and private actors, and different courses of action, which all deserve careful attention. Within the New Institutional approach to organizations, competing or multiple institutional logics have been largely referred as triggers for these clashes (Greenwood et al., 2011; Thornton, Ocasio, and Lounsbury, 2012). Varieties of strategic action by the professional groups, leading to different types of institutional work (Lawrence and Suddaby, 2006; Lawrence, Suddaby, and Leca, 2009), have been also referred to as a key factor explaining such conflicts.

Art and Management has never been an oxymoron per se. Large artistic accomplishments have always included an increasing dose of management as acknowledged in the emergence of great multi-disciplinary artistic schools like, for instance, Futurism (Calvesi, 1975) and Russian

DOI: 10.4324/9781003127185-5

Avant-garde (Argan, 2002). Similar evidence can be noted in the creative production (Eikhof and Haunschild, 2007) and in the emergence of creative entrepreneurs like Sergey Pavlovic Djaghilev for the rise of Russian ballet in the early 20th century (Sjeng, 2009; Sgourev, 2015). More recently, studies on the rise and institutionalization of cultural organizations have shown the interplay between artistic values and managerial performance in the cultural economy at large (DeFillippi, Grabner, and Jones, 2007), and in the organization of well acknowledged festivals (Mezias et al., 2011) as well as in the institutionalization of new film festivals (Strandgaard Pedersen and Mazza, 2011). The whole idea of festivals as field configuring events builds on the assumption that management is not decoupled from the artistic value of cultural events (Lampel and Meyer, 2008; Rüling, 2011). However, art and management may sometimes collide. Contexts, actors, situated conditions, and territorial peculiarities shape the patterns and processes of relation between art and management. Furthermore, the narration by key actors and actual accomplishments provides a further twist to this.

One of the aims of the chapter is to provide a thick description of the creation and maintenance of an institution. We study a context where weak ties among cultural organizations, local administration and other local actors prevail: The town of Monte Sant'Angelo, hosting two UNESCO World Heritage List (WHL) sites, studying the rise of FestambienteSud, the most important cultural event in Monte Sant'Angelo over the last two decades. We study Monte Sant'Angelo as the arena where relations among existing institutional actors within the cultural field meet, are reconfigured and new institutional actors emerge, get institutionalized and become a tradition. We focus on the institutional complexities and institutional works paving the way to the emergence of a novel cultural organization that in a few years became the champion of a new cultural project and events in WHL site. It is the case of the rise and transformation of a local festival, *FestambienteSud*, organized by the nationwide, green organization Legambiente, turning into it the key cultural event of the territory. The case is an in-depth ethnographic, longitudinal study relying upon multiple sources and data gathering techniques. They included 15 formal face-to-face interviews (lasting approximately 90 min), archival research, non-participant observations of the festival in the editions from 2008 onwards, informal exchanges by email and social network chats. Interviews have been conducted with key resources like FestambienteSud's Artistic Director and his closest collaborators, including the Director of Civil Theatre Festival within FestambienteSud, and local administrators. Our research interest lies in *understanding how the creation and maintenance of an institution takes place in a context marked by a complexity caused by multiple stakeholders with varied logics and concerns*. The chapter is structured as follows. First, the theoretical framework, based on the New institutional approach to organizations, is presented. Second, the research setting and the development of the festival is outlined. Third, our analysis is presented of the development and the way art and management have played out. Finally, a discussion and concluding remarks section concludes the chapter.

Theoretical framework

Friedland and Alford (1991) first introduced the concept of institutional logics as a notion to explain the inconsistent beliefs and practices inherent in the institutions of modern, western societies. Logics are seen as socially shared and intrinsically held beliefs and values that shape reasoning and provide criteria for legitimacy and approval in all levels of society (Friedland and Alford, 1991). However, as institutional environments are regularly fragmented with conflicting demands and multiple logics, this gives rise to institutional complexity. Kraatz and Block (2008: 243) refer to this setting as institutional pluralism, which describes "the situation faced by an organization that operates within multiple institutional spheres". In order to gain and maintain legitimacy, organizations positioned within such spheres must respond to distinct and often conflicting demands. As new actors enter the field, they bring new ideas and practices with them, and may consequently provoke reprioritization or change of institutional logics (Lok, 2010). Thus, institutional complexity is in constant flux, as "over the longer term, institutional complexity unfold, unravels and re-forms, creating different circumstances to which organizations must respond" (Greenwood, 2011: 319).

As Czarniawska (2000) implicitly suggested, institutions can be seen as suspended in a network of actors and action. Building on the application of network theory in organizational theory (Padgett and Powell, 2012), networks of actors and action are key elements to understand the emergence and settling of institutions (Christensen et al., 1997). This approach is widely shared by the scholars describing the institutional work required to create and maintain institutions Lawrence and Suddaby, 2006; Lawrence, Suddaby and Leca, 2009). Logics and actors define and design the context where institutions emerge and persist (Battilana, Leca, and Boxenbaum, 2009), and institutional entrepreneurship and various forms of institutional work carries the agentic microlevel signs of the processes of institutionalization and maintenance (Battilana and D'Aunno, 2009).

The research setting: FestambienteSud's festival in Monte S. Angelo and its development

Monte S. Angelo (MSA) is a town in the North of Apulia (Italy) almost at the same latitude of Roma, 242 km^2 large, at 796 m. altitude on the Manfredonia gulf. MSA hosts 12,158 inhabitants (source: Documento Unico di Programmazione Comune di Monte Sant'Angelo, 2019). The presence of non-Italian communities is limited to 1.3% of population; the largest non-Italian nationality group is from Romania accounting for 40% of the non-Italian MSA inhabitants. Over the last 20 years, Monte Sant'Angelo has experienced a significant decrease in numbers of inhabitants with a drop of about 15%. Such demographic changes are affecting many towns and villages in the South of Italy. Today MSA has fewer inhabitants than it had upon the unification of Italy in 1861.

Box 3.1 The history of Monte San Angelo

The history of Monte S. Angelo (MSA) is tightly related to Roman Catholic religion. According to the religious tradition, May 8th 490 A.C. Saint Michael's epiphany took place in a cave of MSA. The Bishop of Siponto, a town near MSA, who eye-witnessed the epiphany, immediately ordered to build a church on the cave. Becoming an important religious center during the Longobard age, a sanctuary was built above the cave of the epiphany during the 13th century attracting pilgrims travelling from Mont Saint Michel, in France, to Monte S. Angelo. In 1656, Saint Michael is reported to have appeared again in the same cave stopping the plague in MSA. After the unification of Italy (1861), MSA also became well known for entrepreneurial activities related to logging of timber. After World War II, MSA reached the highest number of inhabitants (22,800) turning MSA into a leading city in the Northern Apulia area, especially known for intellectual and artistic initiatives. By then, MSA hosted a secondary school in humanities ("Liceo Classico"), two cinema halls and a theatre. Several students went to universities in the North of Italy, returning to MSA bringing new experiences and worldviews. However, the agriculture-based economy soon entered into a progressive crisis only balanced in the 1970s by the opening of a chemical plant owned by ENI (the State-owned company) in the territory of MSA. The crisis of the Italian chemical industry in the early 1990s led to the economic stagnation of the town. MSA's young people studying in the Northern universities have progressively given up returning to MSA, and a general impoverishment of the cultural life has been characterizing the last decades. In this context, attention was paid to religious and cultural tourism as potential key resource to face the economic crisis.

In 2004, in this context, FestambienteSud festival was launched under the auspices of the local club of Legambiente, the main environmentalist association in Italy. There was no cultural festival in the area even though cultural activities were flourishing in Salento (South of Apulia) based on the local traditional music, Taranta. Festambiente is the trademark of the festivals organized by Legambiente, starting from the national event in Grosseto (Tuscany). It combines two different signs: (i) "Festa", meaning "party", claiming the idea of a festival involving citizens mainly for free, (ii) "Ambiente", meaning "environment", linking with the environmental concern that characterizes the Legambiente association's activity. MSA's festival included (iii) "Sud", meaning "South", displaying the aim to bridge the festival within the wide debate on the conditions of the South of Italy as a whole, above and beyond the local MSA dimension. MSA's festival "sub-title" has since the first edition been "Eco-festival delle questioni meridionali", meaning an ecologic festival addressing Southern development issues. It underlines the implicit political claim of FestambienteSud: the link between the green engagements and the solutions to the ever-lasting economic and social underdevelopment of the Southern part of Italy. "Eco-festival" was the subtitle of Legambiente's national event too, among the first to promote sustainability by plastic-free initiatives and broad environmental concerns.

FestambienteSud has offered about 700 events in 15 years with approximately 500,000 participants (both for free and ticket-based). Events have covered all the artistic expressions; music, for the "festa" meaning, and theatre have received a specific attention. Since the first four-day edition at the end of July, FestambienteSud has hosted a great musical concert to attract mass audience. At the same time, since 2006, FestambienteSud has hosted a theatre festival, called "Teatro Civile Festival", which brought many important theatrical pieces to MSA from the avant-garde scene in Italy. Interestingly, this theatre festival was not sharing the "festa" meaning, rather addressing a highly intellectual niche. Nevertheless, "Teatro Civile Festival" is rooted into the cultural initiatives funded by the Apulia Region. Both FestambienteSud and Teatro Civile Festival have been funded by the Apulia regional Government, initially with up to 50% of overall funds.

FestambienteSud changed over the years. From the data, we identified four main stages of evolution in the transformation of FestambienteSud: (i) foundational imprinting, (ii) the rise of the cultural event, (iii) the transformation of the festival into a big event, and (iv) the crisis and the festival beyond MSA. The following sections will outline more detailed each of these stages to identify and document the actors and agency at play in the various stages of the development of the festival.

Stage 1: Foundational imprinting

> Everything started in 2004 with a conference on the revitalization of MSA's old center which ended up defining the new social periphery of the town.
>
> (Interview 1)

FestambienteSud was born around the issue of how to raise the interest for the central area of MSA, which was out of the tourist flows. Saint Michael sanctuary is, in fact, at the end of the central area and tourist flows were located between the coach parking in the highest part of the town and the sanctuary. There was a problem on how to push tourists towards the old center. Similar problems were faced in other areas of Apulia by encouraging to locate commerce in the old towns. However, in MSA, this seems to meet increasing resistance by the local shop owners. The initial input of the festival organizers was to try to locate FestambienteSud initiatives in the old town to revigorate it. This strategy shaped the logic of the festival's first editions in several ways.

First, it shaped the relation with local administration and local shop owners. FestambienteSud was not bringing people to the usual areas of MSA. Consequently, new commerce activities and special arrangements to allow concerts and wide gatherings in the old town area were required.

Second, it shaped the relation with people. The audience of the events was not only asked to join the "festa" but also to re-enact an area of the town. This was also interpreted by people as a way to increase the asset value within the old town quarter and attract foreign investments like in many corners of Italy, namely Tuscany and South of Apulia. Regrettably, the economic crisis hit the town before the arrival of foreign investors.

Third, it shaped the choices about the content of the Festival.

> The first edition was focused on agriculture and food; this has been an ongoing interest of FestambienteSud, along with research on artistic languages like theatre and dance.
>
> (Interview 2)

The claim of the edition was "Pane, Olio e Meridione" (Bread, Olive oil and the South), resonating the most popular and well-known products of Apulia – bread and olive oil – and a very popular Italian movie of the fifties – "Pane, Amore e Fantasia". The claim announced debates, food tasting, music, and shows under the auspices of local administration, the Province, the Regional Government, the "Comunità Montana del Gargano" and the Chamber of Commerce. In this context, Legambiente was only providing the brand with no further support beyond the MSA club. Popular themes were needed to build this "pact" with the audience. An elite approach was seen to be unable to turn the old town into a popular space again. So elite initiatives, like "Teatro Civile", had to be balanced by street music and food and dance initiatives. The first editions of FestambienteSud were characterized by this cultural offer.

Finally, it was considered important to ground the festival as a cultural and political happening rather than one of the thousands summer "sagras"[1] hosted by almost all the towns of Italy.

> FestambienteSud should become the cultural event in MSA; to do this it should go beyond local demand and address a social, if not political,

role. Of course, it could not be expressed this way at the beginning; however, this was our aim since day one.

(Interview 1)

Distinctive organizational features of the festival were free offer, the location within the center of MSA (called "Junno"), the extensive use of young volunteers for logistic and administrative assistance, and the sparse relation with local administrations. These features have marked the institutional setting of FestambienteSud since its first edition.

Stage 2: The festival as a cultural event

In 2005, Nichi Vendola, a former communist supported by leftist parties, was quite surprisingly elected the head of the Regional Government of Apulia. The new administration soon started an ambitious program to encourage and strengthen cultural initiatives in the Region, selecting events to promote and further develop.

FestambienteSud, benefiting from the link between Legambiente and the new Regional administration, began to expand its scope. The first step was to acquire funds for the organization of Teatro Civile Festival. On one side, this increased the regional funds available to the entire FestambienteSud covering two thirds of the overall budget and thus balancing the shortage of private funds. On the other side, it allowed for a shift in the content of the festival.

> We had to set a new pact with MSA proposing them alternative languages and show - not only popular contents but also an intellectual challenge. We were asking people to assume a different standing towards culture; and MSA followed us!
>
> (Interview 2)

The Teatro Civile Festival became the symbol of this shift. The theatre had been already present in the first two editions of FestambienteSud. Now, the effort was to go beyond the traditional narrative theatre to explore other languages.

> We aim at disrupting the typical narrative theatre to propose something new, also as a space to promote and reflect what Legambiente was doing within FestambienteSud. The attempt clashed with the usual way of looking at theatre in MSA, strongly related to popular comedies mostly in dialect.
>
> (Interview 4)

A dilemma had to be managed within FestambienteSud regarding the coexistence of a popular offer and the attraction of a highly specialized niche of theatre. The way to solve this dilemma was constituted by an attempt to turn Teatro Civile Festival into one of the key events nationwide in the niche of avant-garde, outside the conventional theatre offer. The Regional Government was the partner of this attempt by providing funds and by supporting the initiative in communication terms. Teatro Civile became the intellectual avant-garde of FestambienteSud. After 2007, the organization managed to obtain a location in the old town for theatre – a beautiful old cloister of a monastery, the "Chiostro delle Clarisse". At the same time, the tolerance towards FestambienteSud was tested regarding the specialized niche but the audience gradually became more and more curious about what was offered.

> I still remember some tough reactions during one mise-en-scene. After a scene of explicit and obscene language I heard many people leaving the Chiostro delle Clarisse complaining out loud. Nevertheless, the day after we were sold out with the daily piece. It is a question of education; we started from scratch, but we had to resist any attempt to get closer to the average audience taste.
>
> (Interview 4)

At the same time, the popular side of FestambienteSud hosted free music concerts attracting young people from all over the Region. The festival moved from four days to an entire week. Local commerce, primarily hotels and restaurants, started noticing the difference of that week compared to the rest of the summer.

> We were disrupting the "business as usual" of restaurants and hotels. These weird actors, actresses and musicians wanted to eat very late at night and kitchens were used to close at 23.00. Nevertheless, they learnt to live with these new timing during that week.
>
> They said: it is better to have those crazy guys than nobody. In this way they share the project understanding it was good for the whole MSA.
>
> (Interview 5)

At the same time, FestambienteSud grew and addressed more complex cultural demands. During the festival, more events provoked reflections on 'green' and environmental issues and on the general issues of culture and environmental protection as asset for economic expansion. The festival itself became a way to respond UNESCO requests to meet WHL standards. As a matter of fact, as an Interviewee sustained,

> … environment and ecology were just a labeling provocation; in the South, environment means everything, from affirmation of legality to protection of old churches. So we are at the cross-roads of everything required by UNESCO.
>
> (Interview 2)

FestambienteSud was a resource for the application to UNESCO WHL by the town of MSA but also a threat for the local administration. Ongoing relations and support by the Regional Government and distance from the traditional cultural offer, that was usually supported by the local administration, put FestambienteSud organizers in an uncomfortable condition. For years, the local administration avoided to show up to the various events during the festival – to a certain extent, the festival was seen as an enemy. However, the Regional Government support and the enduring success, based upon the attractiveness of the cultural events, overcame the resistance of the local administration towards the institutionalization of the festival.

> As long as the festival has a strong tie with the people of MSA, administrative initiatives could do it no harm.
>
> (Interview 1)

Stage 3: The festival as a major event

In 2012, FestambienteSud was an institutionalized festival in the North of the Apulia area. Ongoing support from the Regional Government and increasing visibility made it one of the five leading cultural events of North Apulia building the 5FSS (Five Festivals Sud System) consortium along with "Suoni in cava", "Orsaramusica", "Carpino folk festival" and "Festival d'arte itinerante Apuliae". In 2012, the festival offered events for ten days and three weekends, covering almost the entire month of July. Moreover, in 2011, the Festival had added a winter edition, during the Christmas holidays, which was repeated in 2012. FestambienteSud's budget almost tripled, reaching 200,000 € with nearly 90% funded by local Town administration, the Province and the Regional Government. Presence of corporate funds was reduced and dropped over time due to the economic crisis and weakness of the local entrepreneurial fabric.

Thus, the four-day festival in the small town of Gargano had become a ten-day event gathering people from all over Italy as marketing investment was oriented to the Italian audience. There is no evidence of a growth of tourists' presence from abroad. Was it nevertheless too much to handle?

> The real question to address now is if a big festival is too much for MSA or there are still rooms for growing. Indeed, we need to know if it is too much not for MSA people but for the institutional context, sponsors, local administrations we can attract.
>
> (Interview 1)

To be able to expand, FestambienteSud had to undertake a process of institutional transformation. First, budget constraints could not be solved by public funds only. Lacking opportunity for important sponsorships due to the economic crisis, a pay-per-view model was implemented. By opening FestambienteSud to ticketing, "Festa" definitely turned into "Festival" aligning with the features characterizing cultural events. On one side, this increased attractiveness. On the other side, the old "almost sagra" nature of FestambienteSud vanished into becoming a media event success. The goal was to raise the ratio of funds from ticketing to 40% by keeping a tight relation between the festival and MSA.

Second, FestambienteSud aimed at pursuing excellence in everything it represented. In this sense, Teatro Civile, which could not go outside the intellectual niche, would have to turn into a top event nationwide in its specific niche. If it did not happen, Teatro Civile would remain linked to the availability of the Regional Government funds. Expected changes at the political level could harm it.

> Teatro Civile festival needs to become a top event in the national theatre landscape in the following three years. It has been already a miracle to create a theatre festival in a place with no theatre group. Now we need another miracle; it would be a pity if Teatro Civile does not survive.
>
> (Interview 4)

Third, content-wise FestambienteSud would have to call for the participation of guest stars. By keeping the "green" political emphasis, the ties with MSA had to be strengthened by the presence of well-known guests, who otherwise would have never appeared in MSA.

> Ties with MSA come from high quality of guests focusing on what people request. So we need top rock groups for young people, maître-a-penser for intellectuals, high quality musicians to play within the old town in free concerts. Legitimacy comes from that; people won't complain about prices or choices if quality cannot be disputed.
>
> (Interview 5)

Finally, location became an issue. Ticketing for top events could not be managed within the old town in a "Festa" setting. Moving the festival out of the old town to the Castle was a highly controversial move in 2011 and it continued in 2012. However, it proved to be consistent with the idea of adding mass attractiveness to the already structured festival. The Old town benefitted from the increased amount of tourism attracted by FestambienteSud and with an integrated tourist offer combining the cultural events, accommodation, and food tasting experience.

This evolution put FestambienteSud as the engine of the 5FSS, supported by the Region of Apulia as a key annual cultural festival. This increased FestambienteSud's ties towards the local administration and turned it into a key agent in the cultural policy of the entire North of Apulia.

In 2012 edition, this transformation reached the peak. On June 25, 2011, MSA received the UNESCO WHL inclusion. This piece of news allowed the festival organizers to speed up the implementation of novelties in the 2012 edition. The majority of events were based on ticketing. Big names of music, journalism and TV talk-shows were guests in MSA. The festival had been promoted throughout most of the country, including large railway stations in Milano and Roma. Tourist offers attracted people from all over the country with almost 10,000 tickets sold for several events. In 2012, the theme of FestambienteSud was, 'at the end of the world', referring to a Mayan prophecy.

> We put all the effort to show that no-one could do better in MSA. We are running fast to offer an event, which is in line with a UNESCO site. Others could criticize tickets, but people attended all the events, almost always sold out. And still, we have free events of high quality in the old town with theatre and dance. This was intended to be a No-U-Turn festival. They might kill FestambientSud but they could not do any better. People are with us. People now know where quality is. The festival will survive. Hopefully....
>
> (Interview 1)

By 'No-U-Turn' the informant means to organize such a huge and successful FestambienteSud festival that where it would be almost impossible not to fund it in the future. The festival expanded with a Winter edition during the Christmas holidays, (FestambienteSud Winter) dedicated to concerts. FestambienteSud became Legambiente's national festival for the South of Italy, the main event organized by Legambiente second to the national festival in Tuscany.

The 2013–2014 editions of the festival followed the same path of the 2012 grandeur. One of the most famous Italian progressive rock groups of the 1970s, the "Area", acted as the musical director of the festivals, bringing to MSA a high profiled, jazz-based, musical offer. In 2014, FestambienteSud for the first time went outside of MSA with some premieres that took place in Dublin and in the other UNESCO WHL sites in Apulia (Alberobello and Andria-Castel del Monte). Moreover, FestambienteSud included a summer school of Philosophy and a summer school of Jazz Music:

> FestambienteSud is now an international festival in terms of both guests and contents. We have also become a festival exporting culture: in fact, together with Area we have produced "Terra" an original musical piece dedicated to Lampedusa. In the last ten years, FestambienteSud hosted about 3.000 panelists and artists, 130 concerts, 120 theatrical pieces and over 200 meetings and seminars.
>
> (Interview of FestambienteSud
> Director reported on the website of the 2014 festival edition)

The press conference for FestambienteSud 2014 received very positive feedback from the Chamber of Commerce and the Local Administration of MSA. They remarked the level of excellence reached by the festival celebrating FestambienteSud as the key cultural event in the territory. FestambienteSud's institutional strategy managed to overtake the initial doubts and resistance from other institutional actors and became taken for granted even as a festival role model, as reported below in the General Manager of Legambiente's celebration of the 10 years of FestambienteSud:

> A tiresome but extraordinary 10 years journey! FestambienteSud now represents one of the highest experiences of our associations. It is a place for social experiments and cohesion. 10 years ago, we needed a great effort but now we offer this festival to the local community. It is a great win, a social and cultural win. I hope that many other festival editions will follow and that FestambienteSud could become a role model of the festivals in our Country.
>
> (Interview with the General Manager of Legambiente General reported on the 2014 festival edition's website)

Stage 4: The festival beyond MSA

In 2015, the landscape of the festival significantly changed. FestambienteSud experienced a decline in size due to the reduction of funds from the Regional Government after a change in the leadership of the governing coalition in May 2015. The same year, the local administration of MSA was removed after an investigation by the Internal Affair, and the Ministry hypothesizing organized crime's influence on the local administration. During these years, funds to FestambienteSud (and all the cultural initiatives at MSA) were lowered. The election in 2017 did not change the overall stance towards the Festival. FestambienteSud's Director's attempt to be appointed to the town council failed and the winning coalition did not prove supportive towards the festival. Funds from the local administration went down to less than € 5,000 a year, after having reached more than € 30,000 in early 2010.

The lack of support from the local administration and the cutbacks of Regional funds convinced FestambienteSud to move out of MSA looking for more attractive venues in the same area of Apulia. In 2018 and 2019, MSA hosted about 50% of the events, the remaining events being moved to larger towns like Vieste. Even though FestambienteSud kept strong ties with the territory, now the territory did not only mean MSA but spread throughout the entire Gargano area (the area where MSA is located). At the same time, attempts to imitate the festival were launched in 2017 under the auspices of the local administration of MSA. Allocating a significant budget during 2018–2019, (about € 150,000), a new festival called "Michael" was held in May every year focusing on the history and rituals of Saint Michael. The

MSA local administration and the Regional Government also promoted a film festival dedicated to pilgrimages, benefiting from a higher budget than FestambienteSud. Despite this competition, reduction of funds and size, FestambienteSud remained the key cultural event in MSA.

FestambienteSud 2015 partially reflected this new context since the festival organization reorganized before those events took place. A focus on agriculture, in the 2015 edition, reminded of the first festival editions emphasizing food and local territory. The number of events was slightly lowered even though the quality of the concerts remained high thanks to the new director of the musical events, the world-class jazz trumpeter Paolo Fresu.

From 2016 to 2019, the change in the institutional context affected the festival. The size of FestambienteSud in terms of number of events and variety of offers decreased. In fact, in 2017, the festival lasted only three days in August (rather than July), and three days in December. Music was again the only core, while Teatro Civile was discontinued due to lack of funding. The limited support from the local administration of MSA forced the festival organizers to look beyond MSA to find feasible venues. The overall economic crisis moved the festival back to the prevalence of "for free" events. Key events moved out of MSA, involving both other larger towns and specific locations. Like in 2017, when a concert took place in the Foresta Umbra, the Ancient and Primeval Beech Forest, to celebrate the second WHL site in MSA. This was the first time an event was hosted in the Foresta Umbra. FestambienteSud progressively aimed at becoming the festival for the territory, and not only for MSA, with an emphasis on urban regeneration that goes beyond any specific geographical context.

In 2018 and 2019, FestambienteSud received increasing economic support from the local administration of the town of Vieste, one of the top Apulian destinations for summer mass tourism about 50 km from MSA. The focus of the initial events in Vieste was on addressing the problems of the South of Italy. A large discussion took place on the social network debating whether FestambienteSud was moving out of MSA for good. This was seen as a severe transformation of the festival. The festival management was from MSA, the festival Director was involved in the political life of MSA and most of the volunteers were recruited in MSA. Consequently, the festival was perceived as an event belonging to MSA. Sharing the festival with other locations was seen by the MSA audience like the end of the FestambienteSud as they knew it.

At the same time, increasing distance between the festival organizers and the local administration of MSA justified the need to look for alternative venues even though some events remained in MSA. However, the original emphasis on the center of MSA seemed to disappear from the festival picture.

In 2019, the 20-year anniversary of the Legambiente club in MSA and the 15-year anniversary of FestambienteSud were celebrated. During the event, the strategy to make the festival look beyond MSA and beyond Apulia was confirmed by the festival Director, who stressed the impact of funding issues on the definition of the new strategy.

Analysis – The evolution of FestambienteSud

In this section, we outline the evolution of FestambienteSud by identifying the main aspects of each of the stages identified above. First, in Table 3.1, we identify the *key players* in each stage. We consider both organizational and institutional actors in the field. Not all of actors were considered key players in each stage: we distinguish "key players" as directly shaping the festival at each stage, from "followers", who adapt to the festival form without having a major role in defining it. In Table 3.1, we account for this variety based on the case study.

Second, in Table 3.2, below, we focus on the issues shaping the courses of action undertaken by the actors that seem key to understand the process of creation and maintenance. First, we identify the *main theme* covered by the festival in each stage, based on the titles and themes of the festivals. Second, we consider the *institutional relations* to the institutional context, identifying in each stage the institutional partners and those distancing from the festival. Third, we consider the *space* and the spatial choices made by the festival organization, the area of MSA and the territory involved in

Table 3.1 Key players and followers during the four stages

	Stage 1 Foundational imprinting	*Stage 2 The festival as a cultural event*	*Stage 3 The festival as a major event*	*Stage 4 The festival beyond MSA*
Key players	Festival organizers MSA local administration	Festival organizers Regional Government	Festival organizers Regional Government Legambiente Agency for tourist promotion of Apulia	Festival organizers Local administrations of other Gargano towns
Followers	Legambiente	MSA local administration Legambiente Local restaurants and hotels Other MSA cultural associations	Local (regional) media Chamber of Commerce Other MSA cultural associations	MSA local administration Regional Government Local restaurants and hotels Other MSA cultural associations

the festival. Fourth, we look at the *artistic offer* by outlining the emphasis on elitist or popular cultural offer. Fifth, we point out the *business and finance* perspective, outlining the importance of ticketing versus institutional funding by local/regional Governments. Sixth, we consider the *size and duration* of the festival (in terms of days and number of events). Seventh, we consider the *scope* of the festival, that is to say the extent to which it looks at the territory only or it is open to wider topics. In Table 3.2, we summarize four stages in FestambienteSud's development.

This synthesis allows us to identify what changed and what remained unchanged during the evolution of FestambienteSud. Interestingly, the festival kept the same management throughout the years, including the Director; nevertheless, strategy seemed to change in every stage with few elements

Table 3.2 FestambienteSud: main developments during the four stages

	Stage 1 Foundational imprinting	Stage 2 The festival as a cultural event	Stage 3 The festival as a major event	Stage 4 The festival beyond MSA
Main theme	Local food and tradition	The South and its strengths	Culture and social cohesion	Regeneration (urban and social)
Institutional relations	Positive with local administration	Positive with the regional govt Negative with local administration	Positive with regional govt and economic institutions Indifferent with the local administration	Indifferent with regional govt and economic institutions Negative with local administration
Space	Focus on the center of MSA	Combination of MSA center and the periphery	The focus is on the entire MSA	Spread outside MSA and reach the rest of Gargano
Artistic offer	Popular	Combination of popular and intellectual	Intellectual key events with marginal popular events	Popular
Business and Finance	Institutional funding (local govt)	Institutional funding (regional govt) Event ticketing	Institutional funding Event ticketing Tourist packages	Institutional funding (plurality of institutions) Only limited ticketing
Size and duration	Minor (about 4 days)	Minor to major (up to 7 days)	Major (up to 12 days)	Minor to major (4 days in MSA and 2 outside MSA) outside)
Scope	MSA territory	MSA territory	MSA territory and closer towns	The entire Gargano

untouched. The name and symbol of the festival remained the same as well as the title (*Eco-festival delle questioni meridionali*) and the focus on the South of Italy and its problems.

Tables 3.1 and 3.2 identify who engage with whom (the actors) and for what purpose (the agenda and issue) and in what context (the space). The story of FestambienteSud shows how the pursuit of festival survival was key to explain most of the institutional moves by the festival organizers. However, other actors (like the MSA local administration) appear at times to do the minimum to allow the festival to survive. So, over time, the context and dynamics are not the same for the various actors and this institutional complexity brings along different strategies in different stages.

Discussion and conclusion

Cultural events and management are highly interlinked. The study of the FestambienteSud shows that the microfoundations of this link could be studied in the interaction of institutional logics, actors, and courses of action. The interactions take place in a *milieu,* which is marked by institutional pluralism and complexity at the crossroads of several logics and worldviews. In the case of FestambienteSud, the crossroad was populated by political dynamics among public administrations, different events within the main festival, expectations of the audience, marketing attempts and, finally, the application for UNESCO WHL.

The evidence supports the arguments raised by Friedland and Alford (1991) and Seo and Creed (2002) on how institutional contradictions may create rooms for processes of institutional creation. Since its birth, FestambienteSud was crossing several contradictions. First, it was a cultural event whose content was deliberately outside the traditional culture represented in MSA. Second, events were now located in the old town where cultural events were not used to be hosted, in order to force people to populate the old town again. Third, FestambienteSud was promoted by an association, Legambiente, whose political reference was not represented in MSA local administration.

The institutional logics and related values and concerns behind these contradictions were manifold. On the one side, a logic of environmental concern pervaded the event conflicting with the idea of culture as politically neutral entertainment. On the other side, the emergence of a market logic in the later years challenged the existing notion of a for-free-festival. Finally, the institutional logic of mass culture provided organizers with the argument to adopt more market-based approach, namely tourist marketing and ticketing. Rather than being factors of paralysis, these contradictions provided the arguments to build a new festival, and to provide the anchoring rhetoric for FestambienteSud to continue every year, each time against and beyond the local political debate.

As for creative and innovative accomplishments, studies have found identity emerge from the way institutionalization balances contradictions and complexity (Alvarez et al., 2005; Strandgaard Pedersen and Dobbin, 2006). In a similar vein, institutional logics provided FestambienteSud with contradictions and complexity affirming its identity – that is to say, who are we? and who do we want to be? (Albert and Whetten, 1985). The inclusion of FestambienteSud and UNESCO WHL, rather than clashing, was found to reinforce each other even if many local politicians argued that the interaction was very complex at the beginning. However, the gap between festival organizers and local administration was not bridged in the end.

FestambienteSud was also found to be an accelerator of network formation. First of all, networks emerge from the same cultural events organization. This was a remarkable and new result for the North of Apulia. The idea of a consortium among cultural events was not common at all and the formation of 5FSS was a critical step to sustain institutional maintenance of FestambienteSud. Then, the web of relations with the Regional Government was of great interest. In fact, this was not a relation with the Government; rather, it was the relation with the various institutions created by the Apulia Region to deal with the promotion of culture. This gradually created a network of actors supporting the local cultural events and activated all the interested stakeholders.

Network of actors, as Czarniawska (2000) suggests, play the role of enabling action; in so doing they strengthen the process of institutional creation and maintenance. The case of FestambienteSud provides some evidence of this. The creation of FestambienteSud as an institution was definitely an outcome of the formation of a network of actors (Legambiente, the organizers, the local administration, etc.) informed by the same institutional values about the relevance of culture for the development of the small MSA town. Interestingly, the audience of the festival also represents an actor in this network. The emphasis given by interviewees to the ties with MSA or the "pact" with the audience reveals how the audience was a key actor in the network sustaining the creation of FestambienteSud as an institution. Thus, the presence of a strong network of actors was a key factor for the maintenance of FestambienteSud as an institution. It was reported to be the key role played by the Regional Government as a funding institution but also as a provider of a platform where cultural institutions find support and legitimacy. The role played by the Regional Government towards the different festivals was not that of a simple fundraiser. Regional Government established a platform made up of several ways of supporting the creation and maintenance of cultural institutions ranging from funds to legitimacy. In a conventional institutional framework, the survival and maintenance of FestambienteSud would be tightly linked to the legitimacy coming from the initiatives of the Regional Government. However, our findings suggest that legitimacy derives from the activities carried out by several actors linked to or created by the Regional Governments. Along with regulatory and practice-based platforms, the Apulia Region created a set of actors enforcing their policies as a new strategy of institutional work as suggested by Battilana and D'Aunno (2009). Thus, FestambienteSud moved from being supported by this network to be part of the network itself reinforcing the creation and maintenance of other cultural events in the North of Apulia area.

Finally, courses of action tend to create the social fabric, which all the institutions are made of (DiMaggio, 1988), setting the 'how' and 'where' of processes of institutional creation and maintenance. FestambienteSud was the result of a complex web of actions. The first action is organizers' efforts to enact a vision where MSA could host a cultural event along the lines of large cultural events in the country. The second action is the Regional Government and Legambiente's action to diffuse culture and green political views. FestambienteSud used a "green approach" in a quite open way, encompassing almost all the social tensions during these difficult years behind the "green environmentalist" label.

Courses of action establish symbols and crystallize meanings and social habits. They are at the core of the process leading to the invention of tradition as accounted for by Hobsbawm and Ranger (1983, 1992). Initiatives like the concert and theatre in the old town, the ticketing, the progressive expansion towards the Castle area, are actions, which ended up creating the tradition that *"during the last week of July something happens in MSA"*. Tradition and persistence are required to facilitate institutional taken-for-grantedness. When FestambienteSud became a tradition, it became very difficult to disrupt it in a small-town context. In this sense, following Hobsbawm and Ranger's (1983, 1992) interpretation, that tradition does not mean stability but persistence through a high degree of taken-for-grantedness. Courses of action are themselves a result of the network of actors and the enacted institutional logics and concerns in a way that is difficult to untangle. It can be argued that FestambienteSud's creation and maintenance as an institution has largely depended upon the ability of the main organizers to survive institutional contradictions and derive further opportunities for survival and expansion. As White (1993) holds, to unblock fresh action, new identities and conflicts are needed.

In the four fragmented stages of the festival life, organizers have been able to shape FestambienteSud's identity by simultaneously sending a message of continuity. The change from "Festa" to festival, the opening to commercial ticketing, the coverage of popular themes and niche intellectual offer have all allowed the festival to cope with institutional pressures and keep the claim of high artistic quality. Persistence through constant change has been the label, if any, of the organizers' institutional strategy. It can be argued that this is consistent with Battilana and D'Aunno's (2009) categorization of action for creation and maintenance of institutions and with most of the conclusions drawn by recent research on institutional work (Lawrence, Suddaby, and Leca, 2009).

An aim of this chapter was to provide a thick description of the creation and maintenance of an institution. We have attempted to account for a process of creation and maintenance of an institution in a particular context. Creation and maintenance have been analyzed through the lenses of institutional logics, actors, and courses of action. It can be metaphorically represented as a 'dance' because nothing remains stable over time in spite of institutionalized conventions and scripts for action. Logics are conflicting and competing over time. Actors form, destroy and re-form networks enabling concepts and courses of action to legitimize and develop or de-institutionalize and be discarded. Courses of action are undertaken and left aside according to fluid development of logics, networks of actors and expectations. In this liquid field, FestambienteSud negotiates identity and survival in each edition; and art and management try to find their own balance for the organization of each festival edition.

The interplay among institutional logics about cultural events in MSA has shaped the changes o FestambienteSud. At the same time, changes in the network of actors have been reflected in changes of the festival organization and in audience expectations. Finally, courses of action find different anchors in logics and actors' networks and are interpreted accordingly. Therefore, as held by Lawrence, Suddaby and Leca (2009), creating and maintaining institutions is not often the outcome of a conscious process of planning; rather, it is achieved by a constant process of fine-tuning to emerging contexts, shaped by the process and actors themselves.

Since June 2011, Monte S. Angelo has been in UNESCO World Heritage List and represents an example of how culture can be an opportunity for social and economic change, in spite of the fact that the gap between festival organizers and local administration was never quite bridged.

Note

1 "Sagra" means a peculiar mixture of festivals, local parties, and territory promotion events centered on the food characterizing a specific area. Italy is full of sagra of chestnuts, sagra of bread, sagra of wine, sagra of truffle, intended to promote very small towns during summer months. It is very rare that "sagra" gets any media coverage beyond the local area where they take place.

References

Albert, S. and D.A. Whetten (1985). Organizational identity. *Research in Organizational Behavior*, 7: 263–295.

Alvarez J.L. and S. Svejenova (2005) *Sharing Executive Power: Roles and Relationships at the Top*. Cambridge: Cambridge University Press.

Alvarez J.L., C. Mazza, J.S. Pedersen, and S. Svejenova. (2005). Shielding idiosyncrasy from isomorphic pressures: Towards optimal distinctiveness in European filmmaking. *Organization*, 12: 863–888.

Andersson, T.D. and D. Getz (2009). Festival management. Special Issue of *Scandinavian Journal of Hospitality and Tourism*, 9(2/3): 109–348. Routledge. Taylor & Francis Group.

Argan, G.C. (2002). *L'arte moderna 1770–1970*. Milano: Edizioni Sansoni.

Battilana, J. and T. D'Aunno (2009) Institutional work and the paradox of embedded agency. In T. Lawrence, R. Suddaby and B. Leca (eds.) *Institutional Work: Actors and Agency in Institutional Studies of Organizations*, 31–58. Cambridge: Cambridge University Press.

Battilana, J., B. Leca, and E. Boxenbaum (2009). How actors change institutions: Towards a theory of institutional entrepreneurship. *Academy of Management Annals*, 3(1): 65–107.

Calvesi, M. (1975). *Il Futurismo: la fusione della vita nell'arte*. Nuova ed. Milano: Fabbri.

Christensen, S., P. Karnøe, J. Strandgaard Pedersen and F. Dobbin (eds.) (1997). Action in institutions. *American Behavioral Scientist*, Special issue, 40(4): 389–538. Sage Periodicals Press.

Czarniawska, B. (2000). *A City Reframed. Managing Warsaw in the 90s*. Reading UK: Harwood Academic Publishers.

DeFillippi, R., G. Grabner, and C. Jones (2007). Introduction to paradoxes of creativity: Managerial and organizational challenges in the cultural economy. *Journal of Organizational Behavior*, 28: 511–521.

DiMaggio, P. (1988). Interest and agency in institutional theory. In L. Zucker (ed.) *Institutional Patterns and Culture*, 3–22. Cambridge, MA: Ballinger Publishing Company.

Eikhof, E.R. and A. Haunschild (2007). For art's sake! Artistic and economic logics in creative production. *Journal of Organizational Behavior*, 28: 523–538.

Friedland, R. and R.R. Alford (1991). Bringing society back in: Symbols, practices, and institutional contradictions. In W.W. Powell and P.J. DiMaggio (eds.) *The New Institutionalism in Organizational Analysis*, 232–266. Chicago, IL: University of Chicago Press.

Greenwood, R., M. Raynard, F. Kodeih, E.R. Micelotta and M. Lounsbury (2011). Institutional complexity and organizational responses. *The Academy of Management Annals*, 5(1): 317–371.

Hobsbawm, E. and T. Ranger (1983; 1992). *The Invention of Tradition*. Cambridge: Cambridge University Press.

Kraatz, M.S. and E.S. Block (2008). Organizational implications of institutional pluralism. In R. Greenwood, C. Oliver, R. Suddaby and K. Sahlin-Andersson (eds.) *The Sage Handbook of Organizational Institutionalism*, 243–275. London: Sage.

Kredell, B. (2012). T.O. live with Film: The Toronto international film festival and municipal cultural policy in contemporary Toronto. *Canadian Journal of Film Studies*, 21(1): 21–37.

Lampel, J. and A.D. Meyer (2008). Field-configuring events as structuring mechanisms: How conferences, ceremonies, and trade shows constitute new technologies, industries, and markets. *Journal of Management Studies*, 45: 1025–1035.

Lawrence, T., and R. Suddaby (2006). Institutions and institutional work. In S.R. Clegg, C. Hardy, T.B. Lawrence, and W.R. Nord (eds.) *Handbook of Organization Studies*, 2nd Edition, 215–254. London: Sage.

Lawrence, T., R. Suddaby and B. Leca (2009). *Institutional Work: Actors and Agency in Institutional Studies of Organizations*, 31–58. Cambridge: Cambridge University Press.

Lok, J. (2010). Institutional logics as identity projects. *Academy of Management Journal*, 53(6): 1305–1335.

Mazza, C. and J. Strandgaard Pedersen (2017). Organizational adaptation and inverse trajectories: Two cities and their film festivals. In G. Kruecken, C. Mazza, R. Meyer and P. Walgenbach (eds.) Chapter 11 in *"New Themes in Institutional Analysis: Topics and Issues from European Research"*, 282–304. Cheltenham UK; Northampton, MA, USA: Edward Elgar.

Mezias, S, J.S. Pedersen, K. Ji-Hyun, S. Svejenova, and C. Mazza (2011). Transforming film product identities: The status effects of European premier film festivals 1996–2005. In B. Moeran and J. S. Pedersen (eds.) *Negotiating Values in the Creative Industries: Fairs, Festivals and Competitive Events*, 169–196. Cambridge: Cambridge University Press.

Ooi, C-S. and J. Strandgaard Pedersen (2010). City Branding and film festivals: Re-evaluating stakeholder's relations. *Place Branding and Public Diplomacy*, 6(4): 316–332.

Ooi, C-S. and J. Strandgaard Pedersen (2017). In search of Nordicity – How new Nordic cuisine shaped destination branding in Copenhagen. *Journal of Gastronomy and Tourism*, 2: 217–231.

Padgett, J.F. and W.W. Powell (2012). *The Emergence of Organizations and Markets*. Princeton, N.J: Princeton University Press.

Rüling, C.C. (2011). Field-configuring events: Institutionalization and maintenance in an animation film festival. In B. Moeran, and J.S. Pedersen (eds.) *Negotiating Values in the Creative Industries: Fairs, Festivals and Competitive Events*, 169–196. Cambridge: Cambridge University Press.

Rüling, C.C. and J. Strandgaard Pedersen (2010). Film festival research from an organizational studies perspective. *Scandinavian Journal of Management*, 26(3): 318–323.

Seo, M. and W.E.D. Creed (2002). Institutional contradictions, praxis, and institutional change: A dialectical perspective. *Academy of Management Review*, 27(2): 222–247.

Sgourev, S.V. (2015). Brokerage as catalysis: How Diaghilev's Ballets Russes escalated modernism. *Organization Studies*, 36(3): 343–361.

Sjeng, S. (2009). *Diaghilev: A Life*. Oxford: Profile Books.

Strandgaard Pedersen, J. and F. Dobbin (2006). In search of identity and legitimation – Bridging organizational culture and neoinstitutionalism. *American Behavioral Scientist*. Special issue, 49(7) March: 897–907.

Strandgaard Pedersen, J. and C. Mazza, (2011). International film festivals: For the benefit of whom? *Culture Unbound: Journal of Current Cultural Research*, 3: 139–165.

Thornton, P.H., W. Ocasio, and M. Lounsbury (2012). *The Institutional Logics Perspective: A New Approach to Culture, Structure and Processes*. Oxford: Oxford University Press.

White, H. (1993). *Identity and Control*. Princeton, NJ: Princeton University Press.

4 Innovation in Early Music Festivals

Domains, Strategies and Outcomes

Elena Castro-Martínez, Albert Recasens and Ignacio Fernández-de-Lucio

Introduction and objectives

Innovation has been described as a strategic activity involving companies and, more recently, administrations and other social entities (OECD-EUROSTAT, 2018), which contributes to both competitiveness and to social progress in areas such as employment, the environment and health. This justifies the interests of governments in promoting them. In 1934, the economist Joseph Alois Schumpeter laid the foundations for an understanding of the effects of innovation on the development of companies and the economic systems in which they operate (Schumpeter, 1934). However, it was not until the early 1990s (OECD, 1992) that the study of innovation and innovation processes began to be promoted. This triggered the development of innovation policies in OECD member countries and the realization that innovation could provide various kinds of benefits to innovative companies and have highly relevant social effects. Early innovation studies focused on industry, but gradually extended to include other sectors, including the cultural sector.

From an innovation perspective, the cultural sector is complex. First, it combines manufacturing (graphic arts, musical instruments) with different kinds of services (publishing, cinematography, video and television programmes, sound recording, libraries and museums, artistic creations, the performing arts). Second, it includes a range of different sized companies, public entities, private non-profit institutions and individual artists, and other service professionals such as restorers and cultural guides. Third, the cultural sector depends heavily on public resources, either through ownership of entities that are part of the sector (e.g., museums, theatres, concert halls, libraries, archives, festivals, etc.) or because many of the sector's private actors (musicians, music festivals, etc.), rely on public aid to conduct their activities (Baumol and Bowen, 1965).

A case study of knowledge transfer and exchange in the field of musicology (Castro-Martínez, Recasens and Jiménez-Sáez, 2013) shows the importance of innovation for early music festivals and the dissemination of

DOI: 10.4324/9781003127185-6

previously unknown musical heritage. The absence of studies on innovations in early music festivals prompted a deeper and broader study, designed to contribute to a better understanding of both innovation and its relationship with musicology research in the context of early music festivals. The aim of this chapter is to describe the in-depth analysis developed to learn about innovation in a very traditional type of festivals (those dedicated to early music) and identify the types of innovation implemented, the strategies employed by festival managers to create these innovations, as well as the benefits that early music festivals derive from these innovation efforts, helping them to carry out their main traditional mission (dissemination of musical heritage). To do it, a survey on innovation activities, strategies and the results derived from these activities in early music festivals was developed in collaboration with early music festival directors. To ensure robust and comparable results, the 58 member festivals of the European network of early music festivals (REMA – Réseau Européen de Musique Ancienne), the only early music network in Europe, were surveyed and answered by more than 40% of the respondents.

Literature review

Several authors (Miles and Green, 2008; Stoneman, 2010) have suggested that, due to its differences with industrial and other services innovation, the innovation process related to the creative industries requires particular and detailed investigation. Innovation in the cultural sector has been analysed in terms of specific subsectors, such as art restoration (Lazzeretti, 2003), music (Wilson and Stokes, 2005; Castro-Martínez, Recasens and Jiménez-Saez, 2013), archaeology companies (Parga-Dans, Castro-Martínez and Fernández de Lucio, 2012), book publishing (Benghozi and Salvador, 2016) and museums (Li and Ghirardi, 2019).

Several studies examine the interactions and innovation networks in different sectors (e.g., Asheim et al., 2007; Martin, 2013) and differentiate among the different sources of knowledge for innovation depending on the respective sector's knowledge base (analytical, synthetic and symbolic). These works focus on one of the so-called 'symbolic sectors', as a cultural sector, and conclude that since the activities in these sectors are often developed within a project framework, interactions differ from project to project. It is suggested that this generates intensive activity, which, in principle, involves local actors or actors from the same region with the same cultural affinities (Martin, 2013). However, in a study of the video game industry (Chaminade, Martin and McKeever, 2021), the authors suggest that knowledge exchange networks are both regional and global, although they serve different purposes and use different mechanisms.

A particular creative industry case is cultural festivals (music, cinema, etc.), which are classified as events and, due to their singularity, are analysed from the perspectives of their management (Getz, 2008), the degree of uncertainty (Rüling and Strandgaard Pedersen, 2010) and their social impact (Del Barrio, Devesa and Herrero, 2012). The professionalization of events, particularly cultural events such as arts festivals, began in the mid-20th century. The literature includes several case studies of innovations related to festivals, focusing on different genres (Mackellar, 2006; Hjalager, 2009), using different approaches (Orosa-Paleo and Wijnberg, 2008; Larson, 2009) and aimed at different objectives (Carlsen et al., 2010). Arts festivals have some common characteristics, including the need for management of a highly artistic product that is time-bound and has a well-defined purpose (Rolfe, 1992). Mackellar (2006) uses Schumpeter's (1942) categories of product, process, organization, marketing, services and social aspects to examine innovations related to a regional festival held in Australia. MacKellar (2006) analyses the actors involved according to their actor type (social/business) and their mutual interactions, and shows that the breadth and depth of the resulting innovations are the result of network interactions and the strength (frequency and duration) of these exchanges.

Orosa-Paleo and Wijnberg (2008) proposed a new approach to determine the innovativeness of a specific festival held in the Netherlands, based on calculating a referent innovativeness index according to the number of new performers, and a classification innovativeness index related to the number of different musical genres included in the festival. The authors compared the values of these indices for the same festival held in two consecutive years. They identified differences indicating whether the innovativeness of the festival had increased or decreased from one year to the next.

Hjalager (2009) uses an innovation system approach to perform a detailed analysis of the different actors involved in a contemporary music festival, held in Denmark (Roskilde Festival), and the direct and indirect relationships established among the actors. She identifies different types of innovations that emerged during the development of the festival and several spin-offs that were created around the festival which offer different types of products and services.

Larson (2009) conducted a case study of three festivals held in Sweden. He considers festivals as inter-organizational networks, in which the different stakeholders (festival organizers, audience, host city, sector, restaurants, volunteers, the media) contribute to the development of advances in various product, process, marketing, organization and social aspects. He found that the importance given to innovativeness varied across festival organizers and that other stakeholders involved in the complex festival organization network play relevant roles in the innovation process. As festival organization becomes more professional, other planned, more institutionalized processes emerge, including market research which provides information to assess audiences' experiences and develop new products.

Carlsen et al. (2010) analyse innovation and failure management strategies in the context of three cultural festivals in the UK, Norway and Sweden. They examine the value chain and identify the stakeholders and various elements that contribute to festival success or failure. The authors conclude that partners and networks are essential for innovativeness and that failures can occur simultaneously with the introduction of innovations. They suggest that festival managers should try to identify success and failure cycles in order to prevent future failures.

One area where the identification of innovation is particularly complex is the arts. In this field, it is difficult to separate the originality of a performance from its innovativeness. For instance, Castañer and Campos (2002) claim that the generally accepted definition of innovation (the first offer by a company of a new or differentiated product or service) does not apply to the arts sector and that an artistic innovation can take the form of the programming of a work that is new to the field (Castañer and Campos, 2002, p. 32). Gohoungodji (2020) analyses three Canadian music festivals and suggests that artistic innovation is a process that involves numerous stakeholders, who sometimes collaborate over the production of a new artistic good, for example, related to staging. However, he also provides a detailed list of the different types of innovations that may emerge in this setting. Drawing on work on the innovation strategies implemented in festivals, Calvo-Soraluce and Viñals-Blanco (2014) studied the effect of social media on innovation. They found that social media can contribute to new product development and marketing and can transform the festival experience. In a review of the literature on innovation in music industry processes, Saragih, Simatupang and Sunitiyoso (2018) show the importance of interactions with various types of stakeholders in co-innovation and open and collaborative innovation processes, but do not delve into the diversity of possible strategies. Along similar lines, a study of knowledge transfer and exchange processes in an early music context (Castro-Martínez, Recasens and Jiménez-Sáez, 2013) shows that early music festivals are relevant as promoters of content innovations, which arise from the interactions among diverse stakeholders (musicologists, early music performers, producers and specialized and exigent audiences).

All of the above works are based on case studies and focus mostly on contemporary pop/urban music festivals. However, they add to our understanding of the different aspects of innovation in the context of festivals (domains, types, interactions, actors and other stakeholders, barriers).

This chapter focuses on early music festivals, which have some organizational, production and commercial aspects in common with other music festivals, but which have some specific aspects, such as links to heritage sites and relationships with music education and musicology research centres.

Context

The term 'early music' is generally used to describe music composed before 1800, although it can refer, also, to how this music is performed. It led to what is known as the 'Early Music Movement' (Butt, 2002). Musicology research goes beyond the publication of results in books and journals and includes the transfer of new knowledge to music performers. The revival of early music has resulted in the organization of specialized festivals, currently numbering more than 300, mainly in Europe, and the existence of a specialized circuit. The success of these events has had a significant impact on music programming, with early music becoming increasingly more relevant. Alongside the integration of early music in mainstream music cycles, the sector has undergone a process of professionalization through the integration of organizational, funding and marketing systems from other sectors.

The different artistic ensemble models can be distinguished by type (from chamber groups and consorts, to choirs and orchestras); composition (regular members, guest soloists, ad hoc participation of different performers); function (occasional, stable administrative facility, reduced office) and funding (public/private, travel or production aid, structural grants from related institutions). There seems to be significant variability between ensembles from southern or peripheral Europe and those from countries with strong cultural policies (François, 2005). Early music festivals almost inevitably involve musicians from several different countries, which leads to intensive mobility of musicians across different continents.

The entities involved in the organization of early music festivals in Europe coalesced to form REMA, the European Early Music Network. REMA currently includes 122 active organizations, based in 22 European countries, involved in the production of early music festivals and concert series. REMA membership includes festivals (76), ensembles, orchestras, professionals and some festival networks (European Festivals Association and Nordic Early Music Federation, Irish Early Music Network). France accounts for the highest number members (25), followed by Italy (18), Belgium (9) and Germany, Spain and the UK (7). REMA works with other European cultural platforms to promote networking activity, publication of research and performance of joint projects.

Conceptual framework and methodology

The study analyses three aspects related to innovation processes: first, innovation types, second, the strategies and stakeholders involved in achieving them and, third, the benefits deriving from the innovative effort.

The innovation types are based on those defined by Schumpeter (1942), which underpin innovation surveys (OECD-EUROSTAT, 2005), but extending the conventional set of business domains (production, marketing, organization) to include services related specifically to the creative industries. Miles and Green (2008) used the term 'hidden innovation' to describe innovations that, in their opinion, were excluded from current measures of innovation and were linked, in particular, to the cultural industries. They proposed a conceptual creative industries innovation framework to allow a precise and structured view of the various cultural industry areas where innovation is likely to emerge. Their conceptual framework has been applied in work on managing cultural innovation and cultural policy (Brandellero and Kloosterman, 2010; Jaw, Chen and Chen, 2012).

Miles and Green's (2008, pp. 65–67) conceptual framework categorizes creative industry innovations according to five main culture-related process domains: general management and funding activities; production and pre-production; communication; product and user experience. They identify 15 potential innovation sites within these five domains and their corresponding interfaces: (1) general administrative activities and financial management; (2) business model; (3) value chain location and positioning; (4) communication with suppliers and partners; (5) internal communication; (6) back-office/backstage production processes; (7) transactions; (8) marketing and customer relationship management; (9) product content; (10) performance and production processes; (11) product format; (12) product delivery; (13) user/product interface; (14) user interactions and (15) user capabilities.

In relation to strategies, the innovation literature suggests that innovators implement one or a combination of three basic strategies (Vega-Jurado et al., 2008): innovation based on their own resources and capabilities ('making'); innovation enabled by acquiring or renting knowledge, equipment or materials from a third party ('buying') and innovation facilitated by cooperation with some other entity ('cooperating'). All three strategies and their respective stakeholders are included in the model developed to analyse innovation in festivals.

The outcomes or benefits of innovation can be grouped into four areas (OECD-EUROSTAT, 2005, p. 79): competition, demand and markets; production and delivery; workplace organization and other (relations, economy, society) which can be adapted to the cultural industries value chain.

Since we considered that the concepts and terms related to innovation might be unfamiliar to festival managers, the initial questionnaire that was developed for this study contained an exhaustive list of potential innovations in each area, the strategies and actors involved and the possible expected benefits. The draft questionnaire was discussed with the directors of three internationally recognized early music festivals in Spain and was revised based on their suggestions. The resulting draft was discussed with members of the REMA executive committee, whose suggestions related to other possible innovations helped to refine it further. The proposed project was presented at a REMA general meeting (June 2013) where we asked REMA members for their agreement to participate in the survey.

The questionnaire asked about innovation areas, strategies and benefits and was organized in several sections, as follows:

1   General data on the festival: name, web site, start year, calendar of events, periodicity, mailing address and contact person.

2   Information related to the most recent festival (number of concerts, budget and funding sources, personnel), links between the festival and other initiatives in the region/town, membership of festival networks and participation in their activities.

3   Context: availability of financial resources, spaces, personnel and other information and services required for the festival organization.

4   Innovation types in main domains and their interfaces (see detail in Appendix 1).

5   Innovation strategies and the stakeholders involved, according to the taxonomy proposed by Vega-Jurado et al. (2008).

6   The results of innovative activities and the kinds of benefits obtained.

In the sections that asked about innovation types, respondents were given a list of possible innovations and could indicate all that applied. Questions about proposed innovations referred to the previous three years and respondents could choose among three answers: (1) YES, (2) NO and (3) Introduced before the reference period. There was space to add other innovations not included in the list provided; none of the respondents added any. In the section on benefits, the proposed list was based on the benefits identified in the OECD-EUROSTAT Oslo Manual (2005), adapted to festivals. The analysis was based on counting the numbers of times the proposed alternatives were chosen.

The survey was administered online in two rounds – in September 2013 and January 2015. The preliminary results (2013) were presented at a REMA annual meeting held in autumn 2014. The second round of the survey received more responses – some from festivals that had not responded to the first round and some which modified previous responses and corrected errors.

Results and discussion

General information

From the 58 festival organizers in 19 countries who were invited to respond to the questionnaire, 28 directors from 12 countries agreed to participate, but 4 failed to complete the innovation section and were dropped from the analysis. We achieved a response rate of over 40% was obtained which included a wide representation of countries. All the festival directors involved authorized use of individualized data. Appendix 2 provides a list of the festivals that provided completed questionnaires.

The festivals exhibit several differences related to their longevity (birth-dates ranging from 1920 to 2010), budget (ranging from €42,000 to €2.5 million) and number of concerts (ranging from 6 to 150). In terms of funding, on average, 65% of total revenue comes from regional and local public entities, 17% from ticket sales and the remainder from a mix of cultural associations, private sponsors and festival merchandising (recordings), pro-grammes and advertising. All of the festivals were held annually – in spring (26%), summer (37%) or autumn (26%) (some festivals also programme concerts for the winter months) – and lasted around a week to ten days. Cer-tain festivals are specific to particular cities and, although a few are held in European capitals (Copenhagen, Stockholm, Ljubljana), most are located in smaller cities and towns – often with an important historical heritage. Most concerts are held in historic buildings (churches or palaces), which offer more suitable acoustics for early music, which was conceived for such spaces. However, some festivals prefer modern music halls that allow larger seating capacity (higher income). Some festivals are multi-site, that is, they include concerts held in different locations in a given geographical area; for example, the Utrecht festival involves over 20 cities in the Netherlands and Belgium and the Úbeda and Baeza Festival includes concerts held in both of these towns and another eight nearby small towns.

The festivals are organized as non-profit cultural charities (42%), non-profit non-governmental organizations (NGO) (29%), private entities (17%) and public entities (13%). Festival managers reported that organizing bodies had remained the same for several years and no other organizational innovations were identified. The organizational structures of these festivals tend to be limited; they involve full-time annual employment of one to five employees (mean 1.5) and part-time employment of between one and seven employees per year (mean 1.8 and mode 1). During the time that the festival runs, another 1–40 individuals are employed (mean 7). Two of the festivals (Haute Jura and Ribeauville) have no paid staff; they are run solely by vol-unteers who have been members of the organizing cultural charity for more than 40 years. Similar to popular music festivals, volunteers are recruited to work at early music festivals directly via the web, posters and job boards or through local entities such as cultural associations, universities and city halls. Although volunteers are important for the development of the festi-vals, they are not as numerous as in popular music festivals (mean for early music festivals is around 15).

Regarding funding sources, most festivals are funded from a variety of sources: ticket sales, local, regional and national grants, cultural associa-tions, private sponsors, advertising, sales of recordings of previous concerts and sales of other cultural products, with large differences among festivals in the proportions of each of these sources of revenue. Only four reported a single source (public funding). None of the festivals reported using crowd-funding and none stated that they had included a new source of funding in recent years; no innovations in funding mechanisms were identified.

Given the importance of context for the development of innovations, fes-tival organizers were asked about the availability of appropriate conditions, professionals, knowledge and the services required to organize the festival. Most organizers responded that there was good availability of all these aspects and many claimed to have sufficient musicology research resources, which is a singular aspect of early music festivals. Only one festival, Gregynog, which is held in 'a remote rural area of Wales' (according to the respondent), reported difficulties related to getting access to large musical instruments and availability of specialists in the local area to tune old instrument; the organizers were required to hire in this expertise – usually from London.

Innovation areas

We grouped the identified innovations in two broad groups: (a) pre-production, production and product; and (b) commercialization, communication and marketing.

Production, pre-production and product

Most festivals are themed: the theme or motto might commemorate the birth or death of a composer or poet, or be related to a local historical event, and is intended to increase the attractiveness of the festival to the public. Less than half of the festivals considered sponsors' interests or local preferences, which is evidence of their considerable autonomy.

For most festivals, the participation of new and foreign artists was not an innovation, nor was the performance of music never performed in modern times or new approaches to the interpretation of well-known compositions, or the re-reading of known pieces because such offerings are part of their essence and the interests of their most loyal audience. This highlights the importance of links with universities and musicology research centres and relations with other early music festivals and cultural entities. Regarding contents, some directors stressed the need for the programmes to contain works and performers well known to the loyal audience year after year, i.e. to combine innovation with tradition, as this loyal audience expects their familiar or favourite pieces as well as known interpreters.

Some festivals organize parallel activities that provide opportunities for young musicians or are used to present awards. To increase their audiences, many (67%) of festivals provide educational concerts or performances aimed specifically at children, dance shows and other forms of artistic expression. They also offer lectures, discussions and films about the lives of contemporary composers, musical instrument workshops and courses for new performers. These parallel activities are aimed at providing audiences with a better understanding of early music and the range of activities is designed to attract a more diverse audience.

A few festivals referred to staging innovations, related to the use of lighting, audiovisual resources or props or sensory experiences to submerge the audience in the atmosphere of the period, the context or the ceremony for which the piece was conceived; 50%–60% of festivals have never introduced such innovations and perform the concerts in a traditional way and in the same venues year after year, usually churches and other buildings that constitute the historical heritage of the cities in which they are held. However, more than 60% of festivals had offered concerts in new venues in the previous three years, including newly restored or newly discovered historical or artistic spaces and 'contemporary' spaces such as science museums, gardens, shopping malls or bars and natural areas that might attract younger audiences. Also, a few festivals had organized concerts at unusual times (midnight or in the morning), in conjunction with special shows, for example, outdoor shows for children, or innovative use of the physical space such as mats rather than conventional audience seating.

New product formats include live simultaneous broadcasting of concerts outside the concert venue. Two festivals project shows on screens outside the venue or in cinemas, 5 had installed screens in historic or artistic buildings with adequate acoustic conditions to allow a satisfactory experience, 11 festivals offer live broadcasting on the radio and 12 festivals provide live streaming on the web. The live streaming had been confined to particular days, for example, 21 March, which is the European Day of Early Music, and involved only selected parts of past concerts. Half of the festivals offered digital products (CDs, DVDs) related to their past concerts; none offered MP3 formats. Product format innovations fall into the product delivery and user interface category and are highly dependent on the festival budget. Artists are paid according to the media employed to distribute their performances; in other words, they receive royalty payments if the concert is recorded for sale or public dissemination. All but one of the respondents indicated that budgetary constraints were a determinant of programme contents and said, also, that the media rarely paid copyright application fees.

To complement the festival concerts and, thus, enrich their content, festivals have introduced new parallel activities, such as meetings with the artists, conferences, dinners, talks, workshops, awards ceremonies and presentations of new recordings. The first two were the most frequent; the others apply to only a few festivals.

Due to the small numbers of recordings available from niche local or national producers, more than half of the festivals allowed different record companies to sell their recordings in festival shops to allow festival audiences to buy recordings by artists they are interested in, although recorded elsewhere. This was considered to make a significant contribution to the dissemination of early music.

Commercialization, communication and marketing

Commercialization, communication and marketing innovations were identified in terms of ticket prices, discounts and sales outlets, and the mechanisms used to interact with audiences and to publicize the festival's activities.

Innovations in ticket pricing for regular audiences included packages providing entry to several concerts or the whole festival, packages combining festival concerts with other cultural activities and packages that include concerts in other festivals and hotel accommodation. Most festivals offered the first two types (66%), but only a few offered deals that included other activities or other festivals and hotel accommodation which imply coordination with other entities. The small numbers of staff involved in early music festivals makes such coordination difficult and consequently sales are carried out by traditional mechanisms.

Most festivals offer special rates for young people aged under 18 and for students. Only a few offered discounts for pensioners, unemployed people, large families, groups, education centres or groups at risk of exclusion. Regarding ticket sales and cancellations, none of the respondents reported development of smartphone apps for ticket sales and cancellations were possible only in three festivals.

Nine festivals reported some type of customer loyalty schemes based on identification systems for regular customers, 11 declared no loyalty scheme and 4 did not answer. The benefits of the schemes that were offered were advance booking, reserved seating, discounted tickets and a newsletter providing details of forthcoming events.

Fewer than half of the festivals provide advance information on planned activities or advance ticket sales, via email. Most festivals interact with users via phone, email and Facebook; a few use social media, such as Twitter, SMS or MMS, or online forums or blogs. The scarce use of many of these means is again due to the need for additional specialized staff which are unaffordable for these festivals.

Ten festivals had conducted audience satisfaction surveys to identify potential improvements. The York festival had been administering such surveys since 1986; the others since 2005. Some conducted annual surveys, others conducted them every two or three years.

Most festivals engage in a range of intensive activities to publicize their festival programmes (via the festival website, a local website, local press, radio and TV channels, journals, classical music radio stations). However, early music is poorly represented on national general-interest TV channels and classical music TV shows, confirming that it remains a minority genre. Finally, very few festivals offer smartphone information applications.

The results of our survey show that almost all the festivals had introduced some commercial or communication innovations, the most radical related to very large festivals (Utrecht and Göttingen) and very small festivals with limited budgets (Úbeda and Baeza, the International Bach chamber music festival, the Copenhagen Renaissance Music Festival, the Wunderkammer and the Day of Early Music in Alden Biesen). It seems that the capacity to innovate in these areas depends not just on financial capabilities but also and perhaps more so on the creativity and commitment of managers and volunteers.

Innovation strategies

The festivals identified the strategies used to achieve the innovations described above, specifically, making, using their own means (64%), buying from companies (10%) and cooperating with other entities (27%). In contrast to innovation in other sectors, buying is not the main strategy except in the case of technological communication innovations.

The respondents identified 26 types of stakeholders, including festival associations belonging to REMA, artists, research centres, music schools, local and regional governments (tourism and cultural actors), sponsors, materials and equipment suppliers, volunteers and general and specialized music media. Depending on the type of innovation, the festivals interacted with all of these stakeholders.

Some innovations are related to festival content (new artists, revivals, new approaches to the performance of well-known works) and are based mostly on own resources, although some were achieved in collaboration with early music festival networks, artists, research centres and music schools. Several festivals had links to local research institutes and music schools. Collaborations with early music networks and artists, universities and music schools involve international and local actors, which is in line with the findings in Martin and Moodysson (2011) for moving media (TV production, digital arts and design, development of computer games software, etc.).

Innovations in production and staging, such as use of audiovisual material, new sound designs, new lighting or unconventional venues, tend to be in collaboration with equipment suppliers and local authorities. Introducing festival audiences to a different experience often involves other local culture and tourism actors.

Marketing and communication innovations tend to involve universities and music schools, local and specialized media and volunteers with social media skills.

Innovation outcomes

Festival managers identified the following as possible benefits of the innovations implemented: larger and more diversified audiences, increased ticket sales/revenue, new festival sponsors, larger amounts of sponsorship, increased involvement of local and new stakeholders in the development of the festival, reduced production and organization costs and improved prestige and enhanced public image of the festival.

In the case of almost all the festivals, innovative efforts resulted in larger and more diversified audiences and, therefore, higher ticket revenue and greater visibility and prestige. A small number of festivals had achieved reduced costs or gained new sponsors.

The questionnaire asked which of the suggested benefits had been achieved and their importance (high, moderate, low). The responses showed that the benefits were considered to be mostly moderate (46%) or high (35%).

Greater visibility and prestige increase the profits from early music festivals. Larger and more diversified audiences guarantee the future of early music festivals, despite their niche status. The innovations introduced are allowing early music festivals to be seen as important cultural events, with significant impact on their host cities and regions, and as relevant platforms for international cultural cooperation.

Conclusions

This study contributes to current knowledge on innovation in the creative industries by shedding light on innovation types, strategies and benefits in the context of early music festivals, a sort of cultural festival, which usually take place in historical places, aimed at generally local and specialized audiences. This is the first in-depth study of innovation in this context and has provided the expected better understanding of the areas of innovation, strategies and outcomes achieved in this kind of cultural festivals. Methodologically, the study demonstrates the importance of identifying these activities to allow festival managers to appreciate their capacity for innovation.

Preliminary work with festival directors to identify potential innovation areas and possible innovations, allowed the design of a questionnaire that helped directors to conceptualize, reflect and structure their innovative activities, which they had been doing intuitively, and could be applied to other cultural festivals.

Based on our sample, early music festivals develop different types of innovations and also use different innovation strategies, most notably cooperation with other stakeholders. In terms of product and production, the festivals combine innovation with tradition, as most loyal audiences are familiar with early music and, along with interesting novelties in content, performance or staging, they expect to hear their familiar or favourite pieces. Regarding the outcomes of the innovative effort, festival directors were aware that their innovations had led to improvements, the most intangible being increased prestige and the most tangible being bigger and more diversified audiences. However, they were aware, also, that these innovations had not translated into reduced production or organizational costs or involvement of new stakeholders or sponsors.

Almost all respondents had introduced some of the possible innovations identified for each innovation area, but there were differences among them. Innovative capacity related to these festivals does not depend on budget or the numbers of people involved as staff or volunteers; both the largest festivals and those with very small budgets reported high numbers of innovations. It seems that innovations depend on the creativity and amount of effort expended by the individuals involved in the festival organization, but this is an aspect that was not addressed in the questionnaire and would require further research.

The results of this study show that content related product innovations (e.g., premieres of recently discovered compositions or pieces not performed in modern times), depend heavily on musicology research and music performances, that is, on research in the humanities, and the festivals' links to musicology research and interpretation schools. This is similar to Pavitt's (1984) science-based sectors, which depend on new knowledge, and complements the findings in Zukauskaite (2012) that universities contribute to innovation through joint competence building, changes to market concepts and new social corporate responsibility actions.

This study has two main limitations. On the one hand, the sample of respondents, although representative of the population studied, is small. On the other, festival managers were unable to specify whether their innovative activities had been aimed only at their respective event or included all early music festivals. This is not surprising since they have not previously been asked to reflect in detail on this dimension of their activities. It would be interesting to know to what extent the innovations identified had occurred in other types of classical music festivals and, especially, whether those innovations not identified for early music festivals (general administrative activities and financial management, business model, value chain location and positioning, communication with suppliers and partners, internal communication and transactions) applied to other cultural festivals.

Acknowledgements

The authors are grateful to the European Early Music Network (REMA) and the festival organizers who agreed to respond to the questionnaire. We are especially grateful to Peter Pontvik and Helena de Winter, chairman and executive secretary of REMA when the survey was conducted, who enthusiastically involved themselves in the project. We acknowledge helpful contributions on questionnaire design and piloting from the directors of three Spanish early music festivals: Esperanza Asiain (Estella), Javier Marín (Úbeda y Baeza) and Alberto Martín (Pórtico de Zamora).

The authors would like to thank two anonymous reviewers for their constructive comments.

A preliminary version of this article was presented and discussed at the 15th International Conference on Arts and Cultural Management (AIMAC), held in Ca' Foscari University of Venice, Italy, June 23–26, 2019.

References

Asheim, B., Coenen, L., Moodysson, J. and Vang, J. (2007) 'Constructing knowledge-based regional advantage: Implications for regional innovation policy', *Int. J. Entrepreneurship and Innovation Management*, 7(2–5), pp. 140–155.

Baumol, W. and Bowen, W. (1965) 'On the performing arts: The anatomy of their problems', *The American Economic Review, Papers and Proceedings*, 55, pp. 495–502.

Benghozi, P.-J. and Salvador, E. (2016) 'How and where the R&D takes place in creative industries? Digital investment strategies of the book publishing sector', *Technology Analysis & Strategic Management*, 28(5), pp. 568–582. https://doi.org/10.1080/09537325.2015.1122184

Brandellero, A.M.C. and Kloosterman, R.C. (2010) 'Keeping the market at bay: Exploring the loci of innovation in the cultural industries', *Creative Industries Journal*, 3(1), pp. 61–77. https://doi.org/10.1386/cij.3.1.61_1

Butt, J. (2002) *Playing with History: The Historical Approach to Musical Performance*. Cambridge-New York: Cambridge University Press. https://doi.org/10.1017/CBO9780511613555

Calvo-Soraluce, J. and Viñals-Blanco, A. (2014) 'Stimulating attendees' leisure experience at music festivals: Innovative strategies and managerial processes', *Global Journal of Management and Business Research: F Real Estate Event & Tourism Management*, 14(2), pp. 38–52.

Carlsen, J., Andersson, T.D., Ali-Knight, J., Jaefer, K. and Taylor, R. (2010) 'Festival management innovation and failure', *International Journal of Event and Festival Management*, 1(2), pp. 120–131. https://doi.org/10.1108/17852951011056900

Castañer, X., and Campos, L. (2002) 'The determinants of artistic innovation: Bringing in the role of organizations', *Journal of Cultural Economics*, 26, pp. 29–52. https://doi.org/10.1023/A:1013386413465

Castro-Martínez, E., Recasens, A. and Jiménez-Sáez, F. (2013) 'Innovation systems in motion: An early music case', *Management Decision*, 51(6), pp. 1276–1292. https://doi.org/10.1108/MD-11-2011-0433

Chaminade, C., Martin, R. and McKeever, J. (2021) 'When regional meets global: Exploring the nature of global innovation networks in the video game industry in Southern Sweden', *Entrepreneurship & Regional Development*, 33(1–2), pp. 131–146. https://doi.org/10.1080/08985626.2020.1736184

Del Barrio, M.J., Devesa, M. and Herrero, L.C. (2012) 'Evaluating intangible cultural heritage: The case of cultural festivals', *City, Culture and Society*, 3(4), pp. 235–244. https://doi.org/10.1016/j.ccs.2012.09.002

François, P. (2005) *Le monde de la musique ancienne. Sociologie économique d'une innovation esthétique*. Paris: Economica.

Getz, D. (2008) 'Event tourism: Definition, evolution, and research', *Tourism Management*, 29(3), pp. 403–428. https://doi.org/10.1016/j.tourman.2007.07.017

Gohoungodji, P. (2020) 'How do artists innovate on scene? Understand the implementation of artistic innovation through three Canadian music festivals', *International Journal of Strategic Management*, 20(1), pp. 67–78. https://dx.doi.org/10.18374/IJSM-20-1.7

Hjalager, A-M. (2009) 'Cultural tourism innovation systems. The Roskilde festival', *Scandinavian Journal of Hospitality and Tourism*, 9(2–3), pp. 266–287. https://doi.org/10.1080/15022250903034406

Jaw, Y-L. Chen, Ch-L. and Chen, S. (2012) 'Managing innovation in the creative industries – A cultural production', *Innovation: Management, Policy & Practice*, 14(2), pp. 256–275. https://doi.org/10.5172/impp.2012.14.2.256

Larson, M. (2009) 'Festival innovation: Complex and dynamic network interaction', *Scandinavian Journal of Hospitality and Tourism*, 9(2–3), pp. 288–307. https://doi.org/10.1080/15022250903175506

Lazzeretti, L. (2003) 'City of art as a high culture local system and cultural districtualization processes: The cluster of art restoration in Florence', *International*

Journal of Urban and Regional Research, 27(3), pp. 635–648. https://doi.org/10.1111/1468-2427.00470

Li, C. and Ghirardi, S. (2019) 'The role of collaboration in innovation at cultural and creative organisations. The case of the museum', *Museum Management and Curatorship*, 34(3), pp. 273–289. https://doi.org/10.1080/09647775.2018.1520142

Mackellar, J. (2006) 'An integrated view of innovation emerging from a regional festival', *International Journal of Event Management Research*, 2(1), pp. 37–47.

Martin, R. and Moodysson, J. (2011) 'Innovation in symbolic industries: The geography and organization of knowledge sourcing', *European Planning Studies*, 19(7), pp. 1183–1203. https://doi.org/10.1080/09654313.2011.573131

Martin, R. (2013) 'Differentiated knowledge bases and the nature of innovation networks', *European Planning Studies*, 21(9), pp. 1418–1436. https://doi.org/10.1080/09654313.2012.755836

Miles, I. and Green, L. (2008) *Hidden Innovation in the Creative Industries.* http://www.nesta.org.uk/publications (accessed 10 September 2020).

OECD (1992) *Technology and the Economy. The Key Relationships.* Paris: OCDE.

OECD-EUROSTAT (2005) *Oslo Manual. Guidelines for Collecting, Reporting and Using Data on Innovation, 3rd, The Measurement of Scientific, Technological and Innovation Activities.* Paris/Luxemburg: OECD Publishing/Eurostat.

OECD-EUROSTAT (2018) *Oslo Manual 2018: Guidelines for Collecting, Reporting and Using Data on Innovation, 4ª ed., The Measurement of Scientific, Technological and Innovation Activities,* Paris/Luxemburg: OECD Publishing/Eurostat.

Orosa-Paleo, I. and Wijnberg, N.M. (2008) 'Organizational output innovativeness: A theoretical exploration, illustrated by a case of a popular music festival', *Creativity and Innovation Management*, 17(1), pp. 3–13. https://doi.org/10.1111/j.1467-8691.2007.00463.x

Parga-Dans, E., Castro-Martínez, E. and Fernández de Lucio, I. (2012) 'La arqueología comercial en España: ¿un sistema sectorial de innovación?', *Cuadernos de Gestión*, 12(1), pp. 139–156.

Pavitt, K. (1984) 'Sectoral patterns of technical change', *Research Policy*, 13(6), pp. 343–373. https://doi.org/10.1016/0048-7333(84)90018-0

Rolfe, H. (1992) *Arts Festivals in the UK.* London: Policy Studies Institute.

Rüling, C.C. and Strandgaard Pedersen, J. (2010) 'Film festival research from an organizational studies perspective', *Scandinavian Journal of Management*, 26(3), pp. 318–323. https://doi.org/10.1016/j.scaman.2010.06.006

Saragih, H.S., Simatupang, T.M. and Sunitiyoso, Y. (2018) 'Multi-actor innovation in the music industry: A state-of-the-art review', *International Journal of Innovation Science*, 10(4), pp. 430–453. https://doi.org/10.1108/IJIS-07-2017-0065

Schumpeter, J.A. (1934) *The Theory of Economic Development.* Cambridge, MA: Harvard University Press.

Schumpeter, J. (1942) *Capitalism, Socialism and Democracy.* New York: Harper.

Stoneman, P. (2010) *Soft Innovation: Changes in Product Aesthetics and Aesthetic Products.* New York: Oxford University Press Inc. https://doi.org/10.1002/9781118739044.ch4

Vega-Jurado, J., Gutiérrez-Gracia, A., Fernández de Lucio, I. and Manjarrés-Henríquez, L. (2008) 'The effect of external and internal factors on firms' product innovation', *Research Policy*, 37(4), pp. 616–632. https://doi.org/10.1016/j.respol.2008.01.001

Wilson, N.C. and Stokes, D. (2005) 'Managing creativity and innovation. The challenge for cultural entrepreneurs', *Journal of Small Business and Enterprise Development*, 12(3), pp. 366–378. https://doi.org/10.1108/14626000510612286

Zukauskaite, E. (2012) 'Innovation in cultural industries: The role of university links', *Innovation*, 14(3), pp. 404–415. https://doi.org/10.5172/impp.2012.14.3.404

Appendix 4.1

Innovations proposed in the questionnaire

For all questions, the possible answers were: Yes (implemented in the last three years), No and Yes, but it was already available or had been done before.

1 Organization and funding:

1.1 *Legal status:* Public entity, Private entity, Non-profit cultural association, Non-profit Non-Governmental Organization, Public-private consortium, Other (specify)

1.2 *Funding sources:* Tickets, Public sponsors (Local, Regional, National, European Union, Cultural associations, Private sponsors, Advertising, Crowdfunding, Other resources)

2 Pre-production, production and product

2.1 *Content of product:* New performers, Established foreign performers, Premiere of pieces of music not performed in modern times, New approaches to the performance of known musical compositions, Re-reading of known pieces of music, New staging, New contextualization (atmosphere of the time, visual projections during the concert, religious choreographed piece of music and in other context, etc.), Educational concerts, Presentation of the program/instruments, Dance and other forms of artistic expression, Others (specify)

2.2 *Performance and production processes:*

2.2.1 New illumination, New sound, Use of audio-visuals, Others (specify)

2.2.2 *Are the concerts offered online or in an alternative place?* New spaces, On line (streaming), Cinemas, Screens in alternative places, Others (specify)

2.3 *Product format and delivery of product*

2.3.1 *Offer of digital products associated with past or present concerts:* CD, DVD, MP3/FLAC, Radio, TV, Dissemination through YouTube, Vimeo or other managers of audiovisual contents, Own channel of radio or TV, Others (specify)

2.3.2 *Collaboration with record companies or distributors to sell CD or DVD during the festival*

2.3.3 *Parallel activities:* Meetings with artists, Conferences, Midday meals, Colloquiums, Awards for the artists, Workshops, Presentations of CD, Others

3 Commercialization, communication and advertising

3.1 *Prices and bookings:* Ticket packages for several concerts, Ticket packages for the whole festival, Combined ticket packages for concerts and other cultural activities, Combined ticket packages for other festivals, Tourist packages (Ticket + hotel packages or similar), Others (specify). Special rates: Under the age of 18 years, Students, Pensioners, Unemployed, Large families, Groups, Educational centres, Groups at risk of exclusion, Others (specify). Audience loyalty system.

3.2 *Sales points:* Points of sale in advance, Telephone, Internet, Smartphone app, Option to cancel, Others (specify)

3.3 *Mechanisms to facilitate user-festival organizer interactions:* e-mail, Facebook, Twitter, SMS or MMS, Internet forum, Blog, Others (specify). Audience satisfaction survey.

3.4 *Festival advertisement media:* Festival website, Web of the City Hall, Local press, Local radio stations, Local TV channels, National press, National radio stations, National TV channels, Press agencies, Specialized music journals, Radio (classical music programs), TV (classical music shows), Facebook, Twitter, Smartphone apps, Newsletter.

Appendix 4.2
Responding early music festivals

Name	Country	Starting date	Type of entity	No. of concerts
Musica vzw-Impulscentrum Domein Dommelhof	BE	1973	NGO	37
Muziekcentrum De Bijloke (Gent)	BE	2000	Public	150
Händel Festival de Halle	DE	1920	NGO	46
International Händel Festival Göttingen	DE	1922	Private	40
Copenhagen Renaissance Music Festival	DK	2006	Private	15
Musica Antigua Aranjuez	ES	1994	Private	8
Festival de Música Antigua de Úbeda y Baeza	ES	1997	Public	28
Semana de Música Antigua de Estella	ES	1967	Public	15
BRQ Vantaa	FI	2010	NGO	13
Festival D'Ambronay	FR	1980	Cultural Charity	30
Festival de Musique Ancienne de Ribeauvillé	FR	1984	Cultural Charity	9
Festival de Musique de Haut Jura	FR	1978	Cultural Charity	10
Grandezze & Meraviglie, Festival Musicale Estense	IT	1998	Cultural Charity	16
Pavia Barocca	IT	2000	Cultural Charity	23
Festival Antiqua (Bolzano)	IT	1991	NGO	7
Festival Echi Lontani	IT	1994	NGO	21
Wunderkammer	IT	2006	NGO	12
Festival Monteverdi	IT	1983	Private	10
International Bach chamber music festival	LV	2001	Cultural Charity	6
Utrecht Early Music Festival	NL	1981	Cultural Charity	146
À Volta do Barroco	PT	2006	NGO	8
Stockholm Early Music Festival	SE	2002	Cultural Charity	15
Gregynog Festival	UK	1933	Cultural Charity	17
York Early Music Festival	UK	1977	Cultural Charity	21

Source: Own elaboration from the survey about innovation in REMA early music festivals.
Note: In type of entity, NGO means Non-profit Non-Governmental Organization.

Part II

Challenges of Cultural Festivals in the Digital Age

5 A Classical Music Festival and Its Audience

The Case of MITO Settembre Musica

Giovanna Segre, Andrea Morelli and Caterina Valenti

Introduction

Over the last few decades, the attention of scholars, cultural managers, and policymakers has grown around the choices, expectations, and consumption habits of the cultural consumers (Peterson, 1992; Peterson and Simkus, 1992; Peterson and Kern, 1996; Holbrook et al., 2002; Kutz-Gerro and Sullivan, 2006). Part of this interest is related to a negative trend affecting the demand for some cultural activities, visible, in particular, in the classical music and opera sector, where a continuous decline in concert hall attendance is accompanied by a growing estrangement of young audiences (Rizkallah, 2009; Pitts et al., 2013; Saayman and Saayman, 2016). Scholars have tried to address the issue of declining cultural consumptions in the field of classical music studying the orchestras with the aim of providing, not only a general description of the audience, but also some suggestions for orchestras' organization, and for the adoption of marketing and audience development strategies (Kolb, 2000; Wolf, 2006; Roose, 2008). The alienation of the young public, in particular, can be traced partly back to the lack of space given to classical music by the mass media, which leads to a lack of attentive listening skills among younger spectators, and partly to the psychological and social barriers they perceive concerning this world, which they see as expensive, formal, and stiff (Arenella and Segre, 2019). However, fully investigating the causes that have led to the declining presence of spectators in concert seasons, and to the decreasing interest in classical music in general, is not easy, also due to the lack of empirical data on classical music audiences.

In Italy, a country exceptionally rich in history and heritage of classical music, the availability of data on audience and cultural consumption in the classical music sector is, nevertheless, weak, and specific studies are rare. ISTAT (2019) data allow a partial description of the Italian consumer of classical music; however, not enough detailed and complete information is offered. From the ISTAT survey, we know that only 9% of the Italian population aged 6 and more attends classical music concerts, that women's frequency of attendance is higher than men's frequency, and that the

DOI: 10.4324/9781003127185-8

audience of classical music concerts is mostly composed of elderly people. The available data confirm how classical music in Italy appears to be a shrinking sector, that survives thanks to a truly loyal audience, but struggles to attract new public, especially among the younger population.

With the purpose to better understand the characteristics of the demand for classical music and the composition of its public in live events, this chapter analyses the 42nd edition, held in Turin and Milan in September 2019, of the festival *"MITO SettembreMusica"*, one of the most successful Italian events for classical music. The festival has a long history characterized by strong elements of discontinuity and innovation and represents a successful example of integration between tradition and innovation. The opportunity to study the audience of a classical music festival is remarkable since a festival not only represents an important venue for classical music concerts' passionate but it is also a special occasion for a different audience to approach the classical music. We found compelling studying the audience of a recent edition of the festival, and provide a description of the main characteristics of its public, prior to the COVID-19 pandemic. The analysis is developed with the aim of highlighting some peculiar strategic choices of this cultural event, which has evolved during its 42 years by introducing innovations both in the cultural offer and in its general positioning within the city. It is a festival that has at the core the purpose of disseminating the culture of the classical music to residents, tearing down the perceived barriers for the consumers, and actively operating on the link between classical music and the well-being of individuals. In Section 2, we present the main features of the festival. In Section 3, the results of the analysis of the festival's audience, conducted on the original data collected from a sample of 2,800 questionnaires, are examined focusing on the demographic characteristics and on the cultural consumption activities. A special focus is dedicated to the classical music festivals' newcomers, presented in Section 3.3. In Section 4, some insights from the concerts in unconventional venues in Turin are considered, based on the analysis of a subset of questionnaires. Section 5 concludes the chapter.

MITO SettembreMusica

The festival was founded in 1978 under the name *"SettembreMusica"* (music in September) on the initiative of the Councillor for Culture of the Municipality of Turin, with the explicit aim of bringing, for the first time in the city of Turin, cultured music outside concert halls and involving also a totally new audience. This ambition was pursued along three strategic factors.

1   *The classical music conceived as a broad cultural offer.* Since its beginning, in this classical music festival, classical music was seen both in relation with other genre, and in relation with other cultural and

creative sectors. Ballet was included, as it is actually often the case in music festivals, but also the collaboration with audio-visual and book producers took place. The musical programmes, which largely focused on classical music with numerous symphonic and chamber concerts, gave also space to jazz, rock and pop concerts, songwriters, and ethnic music with performances dedicated to foreign music traditions belonging to many different countries in the world. The festival is conceived as a musical journey with national and international cultured music as a navigator. Furthermore, the musical offer was often enriched by specific projects conceived and realized exclusively for the festival and including other cultural and creative sectors. For 26 editions, from 1985 to 2011, a series of events dedicated to the main contemporary composers was accompanied by the publication of monographic books in collaboration with important Italian publishers, thus testifying a vision of the festival as a wide cultural event involving its audience in a cross-cultural experience. Recently, a digital archive, available to all on the open access repository "Byterfly", was created to make available all the materials produced since the festival's first edition (i.e., concerts' hall booklets, every edition's general programme, and the photographic archive). This huge open access archive provides a detailed window on the history of this well-established experience in the world of classical music, valuable both for enthusiasts and just curious classical music consumers. This attitude towards innovation and cultural sector cross-fertilization remains a distinctive factor of the festival, which, in the Italian panorama, is considered a real promoter of innovation within the very traditional sector of classical music. The inclusion in the programme of different music genre was progressively reduced, and an increasing curatorial effort was concentrated on the core activity of classical music. In 2012, a new festival, collecting the experience made in Turin around the jazz performances, was organized under the name "Turin Jazz Festival". But this is another story.

2 *The choice of conventional and unconventional venues.* The concerts are organized in many different venues, including more typical locations such as theatres and concert halls, but also churches, squares, social centres, courtyards, private palaces and villas, museums, exhibition spaces, bookstores, libraries, and clubs. During the festival, a special program called "Musical Moments" was launched in Turin, in order to bring concerts also in hospitals, prisons, and retirement homes. Furthermore, the location of the concerts is carefully distributed between the city historic centre and the suburbs, thus inviting citizens to rediscover some distinguishing places of the city. A programme of more than 80 concerts in unconventional locations, but accessible to all, demonstrating how good music can overcome physical and cultural barriers and aiming at reaching people who do not usually attend musical performances in the traditional concert halls.

3   *The widening of the consumers' target.* The aim of the festival is clearly
to enlarge the public by involving cultural consumers usually not attracted by classical music. Applying the so-called "democratization"
model of cultural consumption, the festival is conceived for local public
and its cultural growth. The tourist market, therefore, is not considered
a priority. As a consequence, the price strategy was set to keep low the
level of prices and to provide several free concerts. Furthermore, the
festival pays specific attention to children and adolescents by organizing concerts and musical theatre performances every weekend during
the festival, with the awareness that music is a fundamental element
in accompanying the process of growth and education of the new generations. In any edition, the level of ticked sold and occupied places is
over 95% and in particular the events designed for the children and
adolescents and their families are always registering the ticket sold out.

The festival's growing success over time, and the continuous innovations
and improvements it includes, were enabled also by the fertile context offered by the city of Turin, which has fruitfully managed to free itself from
the strong industrial past, mainly linked to the car production. A new identity of the city was designed, where the cultural offer was a key factor and
a renewed cultural vitality was a strategic axis for development (see, among
others, Vanolo, 2008; Belligni and Ravazzi, 2013).

In 2007, the management of the festival was entrusted to the Turin Foundation for Culture (*Fondazione per la Cultura Torino*), a non-profit organization participated by the Municipality of Turin, which promotes and
implements many of the major cultural events and activities taking place in
the city.[1] The Foundation manages all the operational and organizational
phases of the cultural events, starting from the choice of the artistic contents, then collecting the funds and resources for the feasibility of the event,
which is executed by directly engaging the required artists and professionals, and finally curating the communication plans for the promotion.

In 2007 also began the joint management with the city of Milan through
the Musical Afternoon Foundation (*Fondazione I Pomeriggi Musicali*), a
non-profit organization promoted by the Lombardy Region, the Municipality of Milan, the Province of Milan, and private entities, recognized by
the Italian Government as an official concert-orchestral institution. Mainly
dedicated to the management of its orchestra and, since 2001, also to the
direct management of the public theatre Del Verme founded in 1866 in the
historic centre of Milan. The name was changed accordingly in "*MITO
SettembreMusica*", where "*MI*" indicates the name of the city of Milan,
and "*TO*" the name of the city of Turin.[2] Since then, the co-organized festival stands as a vanguard in the processes of integration between the two
major cities of northern Italy and as an example of cultural vitality. This
strategic alliance has given rise to one of the most important European festivals with an average of 206 concerts and 3,000 artists per edition, during

around 20 days. The strong public character of the initiative, also due to the fact that the festival is organized by two important non-profit bodies under the control of the local government is manifested in the desire to address precisely the city and its citizens not only in terms of entertainment but also for educational, cultural, and social purposes.

For the majority of the festival's editions, the artistic direction was assigned to Roman Vlad, composer, musicologist, and pianist, and Enzo Restagno, renowned critic and musicologist, who jointly managed and implemented the artistic aspects until 2006, when Enzo Restagno took over the entire responsibility until 2015. Since 2016, the artistic director has been Nicola Campogrande, who is not only a music critic and renowned academic but also one of the most interesting contemporary Italian composers, and, in the same year, the festival became thematic and solely dedicated to classical music, offering its audience three or more concerts a day with the participation of artists and ensembles of international stature.

The audience of a classical music festival

The 2019 edition of MITO was complemented by a research on its audience. The research was commissioned by the Turin Foundation for Culture[3] to the University of Turin, and was based on a sample of 2,800 questionnaires designed and analysed by the authors with the main purpose of detecting relevant characteristics of the MITO audience.

The possibility to study in deep the audience of a classical music festival can contribute to shed light on the promising innovations that the classical music live concerts sector could include in order to enlarge and rejuvenate its audience. Classical music festivals and traditional concerts seasons, although they both revolve around classical music, have in fact the potential to attract different kind of public. In addition to the audience who steadily attend the classical music concerts, during a festival various audience's segments are involved, mainly because a festival concentrates the programs in a defined period of time, offers more than one performance a day, and benefits from an intensive communication before and during the event.

Moreover, festivals are often perceived as a great moment of social engagement which can benefit in particular local residents. Although important festivals attract in particular tourists and visitors, cultural events are increasingly designed to involve and impact local communities. This is the mission of MITO. Each year, the festival offers a program characterized by a distinctive leading theme, involves different international artists and orchestras having different backgrounds, and creates events ranging from the traditional classical music concert to the more innovative ones, in conventional and unconventional venues. The collected data are analysed with the aim to give some insights towards innovations for a traditional genre, such as classical music. Nevertheless, to renew the relationship with the audience, approaching new and/or younger spectators is actually crucial for any cultural events.

The audience of MITO was analysed by collecting information about the socio-demographic profile of the public attending the concerts and adding two perspectives to be further investigated: (i) the wider cultural consumptions activities of the public and (ii) the characteristics of the spectators attending the festival for the first time. The questionnaires were self-administrated, distributed by volunteers at the beginning of the concerts and collected shortly after the concerts' end. In the edition under investigation, 128 concerts were performed and attended by 74,000 spectators in Turin and Milan, from 3 to 19 September. The performances where the sample was collected, were identified based on a principle of maximum heterogeneity and differentiation to best capture the different characterizations of the festival's programming and audience. The position of the concerts (city centre and suburbs) and the price (paid and free) are the main variables for the stratified sampling plan adopted. The size and number of the strata were determined through an ex-ante evaluation of the expected attendance for each stratum and verified ex-post with the numbers of the effective attendance.

Gender and age

The results of the analysis (Table 5.1) highlight that the audience is mostly female (61.5%), and that the mean age is 55.3 years, with the largest subpopulation represented by the over 65 (32.3%). These figures are consistent with the gender and the age profiles of the typical Italian classical music consumer, as identified by the only updated and comprehensive study in

Table 5.1 Main characteristics of MITO audience (N = 2,800)

Variable	Frequency
Gender	
Female	61.2%
Male	38.8%
Age	
18 to 25	6.1%
26 to 35	7.6%
36 to 45	9.2%
46 to 55	19.1%
56 to 65	25.2%
Over 65	32.8%

Source: Own elaborations.

Italy, conducted by the Osservatorio dello Spettacolo dell'Emilia-Romagna on a sample of six concerts in 2008 and 2015, performed in the Emilia Romagna region. Similarly, Arenella and Segre (2019), in a study on the classical music audience in Turin, especially focused on the disaffection of young generations, highlighted the presence and discussed the effect of the high proportion of over 65 consumers.

The audience of MITO is characterized by being mainly local (Table 5.2), since 90% of the audience in Turin and 87% of the audience in Milan has a domicile in the city. Only less than 1.5% of the respondents are foreigners. This result confirms the significant meaning reached by this high-level cultural event for the local community. A strategy and positioning of the festival successfully achieved.

Cultural consumptions

These results are clearly a reflection of a population of enthusiasts composed of strong cultural consumers with a good liking for the consumption of classical music concerts, as we should expect interviewing a classical music festival's audience. The average of concerts attended by interviewed is around 5.8 per year and 18.6% of them declared to attend more than 12 concerts per year and 14.1% between 7 and 12. At the other end of the scale, just 10% of the people said they had not attended any classical music concerts in the last year. These data are particularly interesting especially in the light of those regarding the cultural participation in Piedmont, according to which the majority of residents (90%) do not have attended any classical music performance in the last year (ISTAT, 2019).

Our results allow a further understanding of the preferred cultural consumption activities of the classical music audience (Table 5.3). MITO participants are, as well as being classical music fans, major readers (declaring to read more than 12 books per year), cinema enthusiasts (stating to have seen more than 12 movies in the last year) and, finally, strong museum visitors (claiming to have made more than 12 visits in museums). They appear, however, not very interested in jazz and rock/pop concerts and dance performances.

Table 5.2 MITO: An international festival conceived for the local audience (N = 2,800)

Audience provenance	*MITO in Turin*	*MITO in Milan*
City	70.41%	66.31%
Metropolitan area of the city	20.24%	20.74%
Region	4.65%	6.87%
Other Italian regions	3.38%	4.62%
Foreign	1.32%	1.45%
Total	*100%*	*100%*

Source: Own elaborations.

Table 5.3 Cultural consumption activities of MITO audience (*N* = 2,800)

Cultural sectors	Frequency of attendance					
	None	From 1 to 3	From 4 to 6	From 7 to 12	More than 12	Total
Classical music concerts	9.5%	36.2%	21.6%	14.1%	18.6%	100%
Jazz music concerts	50.8%	35.0%	8.3%	3.7%	2.2%	100%
Rock/pop music concerts	56.5%	30.6%	8.2%	2.9%	1.8%	100%
Dance performances	53.5%	36.4%	6.7%	2.5%	1.0%	100%
Theatre performances	20.2%	40.7%	20.7%	11.4%	7.0%	100%
Cinemas	10.8%	23.0%	22.6%	18.7%	25.0%	100%
Museum visits	6.3%	25.7%	28.3%	20.6%	19.1%	100%
Books read	5.3%	17.6%	21.3%	19.0%	36.9%	100%

Source: Own elaborations.

The classical music festival newcomers

MITO is a festival dedicated to classical music. As such, it experiences some of the effects related to the barriers typically influencing the consumption pattern in this sector (Rizkallah, 2009; Pitts et al., 2013; Saayman and Saayman, 2016), where a general decrease in the concert hall audiences is accompanied by an increasing estrangement of young consumers.

Unlike this general trend reported by most of the scholars, it is interesting to note that our focus on the new audiences, attending the MITO festival for the first time, shows (Table 5.4, Newcomers' column) that the age distribution involves the young consumers in a significant proportion. Newcomers' audience is more evenly distributed among the various age groups than the "loyal" audiences (Table 5.4, Loyalists' column, which includes all the audience who attended more than one edition of the festival). In other words, comparing the two distributions by age groups, it emerges that the festival attracted a younger audience than the loyal ones. The presence of young people up to the age of 25 (14.9%) is more than four times that of those who said they had been attending the festival for more than two editions, and just as positive trends are found among young adults aged between 26 and 35 (14.5%) and among spectators who said they were aged between 36 and 45 (12.0%). The average age of the newcomers thus drops from 57 years of the loyalists to 48 years. In the light of these data, if the trend would remain the same over the years, and this situation will be accompanied by an audience development strategy enabling the festival to retain the newcomers, we can certainly expect to see a rejuvenation of the general audience of MITO.

Table 5.4 Newcomers and loyalists age differences
(N = 2,800)

Age groups	Newcomers (N = 647)	Loyalists (N = 2,153)
From 18 to 25	13.7%	3.9%
From 26 to 35	13.5%	5.9%
From 36 to 45	11.5%	8.5%
From 46 to 55	19.3%	18.9%
From 56 to 65	20.8%	26.6%
Over 65	21.3%	36.3%
Total	100%	100%

Source: Own elaborations.

Table 5.5 Newcomers' and loyalists' classical music
concerts participation (N = 2,800)

Number of concerts	Newcomers (N = 647)	Loyalists (N = 2,153)
None	23.0%	5.6%
From 1 to 3	45.9%	33.4%
From 4 to 6	16.3%	23.1%
From 7 to 12	6.5%	16.3%
Over 12	8.3%	21.6%
Total	100%	100%

Source: Own elaborations.

A further analysis was aimed at investigating whether the public is made by newcomers or loyalists concerning the attendance frequency to classical music concerts. In other terms, this study wants to discover whether the audience attracted by the festival is a regular consumer of live classical music or whether the participation becomes an opportunity to approach this musical genre, attesting the formative role of the festival towards new audiences.

The results presented in Table 5.5 highlight how most of the newcomers have the profile of "weak" consumers, declaring in 50% of the cases that they attended between 1 and 3 concerts, and only 6.9% attended more than 12 concerts in the last year, compared to 20.3% of the loyalists. The traditional audience shows a rather high attendance rate, with only 5.6% declaring that they had not attended any classical music concert in the last year. On the other hand, the preference for listening to live classical music of the spectators attending the festival for the first time proves to be more moderate, rising to 21.6%. These newcomers are undoubtedly a new audience both for MITO and for classical music concerts, an audience "in training" which represents about 4% of the total number of questionnaires collected. Therefore, even if the socio-demographic data of MITO audience reflects the common trend of classical music consumptions, these data suggest that the strategy of democratization and audience development put in place by the festival seem to show a possible path to overcome some of the most likely consumption barriers perceived.

Another element differentiating the two groups is the information channels used to find out about the festival. The 48.5% of newcomers declared that they learned about the festival thanks to the word of mouth by friends and family, revealing the essentiality of the socio-relationship component for this category of visitors. These data fit perfectly with the fact that, when it comes to newcomers compared to the loyalists, fewer respondents say they attended the shows alone (6%), while more have attended with friends (38.9%) or family (25.3%). Looking at this information, we may say that the best ambassador of the festival is its own audience, confirming its good capacity to build loyalty and, more importantly, engage the public. This is a direction in which the festival can continue to work if it aims at retaining as many newcomers as possible and to rejuvenate its audience.

Some insight from the concerts in unconventional venues

One of the characteristic features of the MITO festival in Turin was the enrichment of the traditional programme with concerts specifically organized in non-conventional places such as hospitals, psychiatric communities, prisons, retirement homes and care facilities. The program lasts 8 days and consists of more than 80 concerts in which artists and organizers meet in different places and situations, from the more reserved and sensitive to exclusion ones, to the more inclusive ones, both in the frame of a less-known Turin. Introduced in 2009, this set of concerts is organized with the involvement of the students of the Turin music academy and it is conceived as an itinerant performance covering a network of care and social services and offering "music moments", as they call these concerts, in unconventional situations and locations, demonstrating how classical music can overcome physical barriers as well as cultural. Since these particular concerts are not open to the general public but played only for the residents of these facilities that live in situations of confidentiality or exclusion, no data were available, unlike concerts.

The part of the programme dedicated to unconventional venues has two complementary souls; the concerts held in care facilities, and the concerts organized in unusual venues for classical music located in suburban areas of the city. This set of activities is presented under the name of "*MITO per la Città*" (MITO for the City) and it represents a social and geographic extension of MITO's traditional roots. The social value of classical music is conveyed by working on the link between music and the well-being of individuals. Studies on the subject (MacDonald, 2013) report on the significative and beneficial effects of listening to music and show that music is a distinct communication channel that can influence everyone's emotions (Hargreaves, Miell, and MacDonald, 2012) proving to be an excellent tool in managing, for example, stress, anxiety, and distress through its capability of distracting and engaging listeners in a multitude of cognitive and emotional ways (Sloboda and O'Neill, 2001; DeNora, 2010; Saarikallio, 2011; Mitchell and MacDonald, 2012).

The concerts performed in the peripheral areas of the city, in particular, represent an audience development strategy, designed by the organizers with the aim of bringing to classical music concerts those who do not usually attend the traditional concert halls. We can define this as an attempt of democratising classical music, which is mistakenly seen as an elitist cultural art form. Cultural democratization (Dubois, 2016) refers to all those activities, strategies, and, more generally, policies aiming at providing access and at disseminating cultural resources, usually scarce and insufficient. Studies on the sector of classical music have found that it is often perceived, especially when it comes to young people, as an expensive activity, too formal, austere and performed in a language difficult to understand and appreciate without prior knowledge of cultured music (Kolb 2000; Dobson, 2010; Arenella and Segre, 2019). In other words, people seem to experience high barriers of entry that prevent them from discovering this art form. MITO for the city is an attempt to spread an art form that is not scarce in relation to quantity but perceived by the majority as understandable and appreciable by only a few. Therefore, we could include this programme in the group of democratization strategies since it has at its core the purpose of disseminating access to classical music, tearing down the perceived barriers of entry.

In our study, we analysed this side programme with the intention to investigate any potential differences between the audience of the performances in the centre and in the suburbs. A total of 15 performances in Turin were carefully identified (out of the 57 events in Turin) in order to reflect the distribution of the events in the centre and out of the centre, and 2,041 questionnaires were collected. Table 5.6 presents the results of the analysis applied to the Turin case and allows the comparison of the main variables investigated in order to compare the audience in the two types of venues (city centre and periphery).

Not surprisingly, the venues located in the city centre attract more public from outside the Piedmont region (11.4%) than the venues located in the peripheries (6.7%). In the peripherical venues, more than 77% of the audience is local. These venues attract more men than in the central ones, and the composition of the audience is slightly younger as far as under 35 are concerned. Over 65 are, however, a bigger group in the periphery. The differences between the audience in the centre and in the periphery concerning the level of education distribution, highlight the presence of a higher percentage of the public with a high school degree in periphery and a higher percentage of the public with a university degree in the centre.

Table 5.6 Audience differences between city centre and peripheral areas in Turin (N = 2,041).

Variable	City centre (N = 1,390)	Peripheries (N = 651)
Domicile		
Turin	67.1%	77.4%
Metropolitan area	21.4%	17.7%
Other Piemonte	5.6%	2.6%
Other Italy	4.2%	1.5%
Abroad	1.6%	0.8%
Gender		
Female	61.5%	54.8%
Male	38.4%	45.1%
Age		
Up to 25	5.6%	6.9%
From 26 to 35	7.3%	9.2%
From 36 to 45	10.0%	8.7%
From 46 to 55	19.5%	16.2%
From 56 to 65	25.1%	22.7%
Over 65	32.3%	36.1%
Education		
Middle school	7.3%	8.2%
High school	34.8%	41.5%
University. Bachelor degree	43.5%	38.0%
University, Master degree	14.4%	12.3%

Source: Own elaborations.

In 2019, in Turin, the 42nd edition of the festival was performed. The festival is renowned, and more than 20% of its audience participated in it for more than 14 editions. Table 5.7 analyses the loyalty of the public and highlights similar levels for venues in the centre and in the periphery. The main share (33.1%) is represented by those who have been attending the festival for 2–4 editions in the periphery, followed by participants who took part in the festival for 5–13 editions, both in the centre and in the periphery. About 20% of the audience is represented by visitors at their first experience, validating the good ability of this cultural manifestation to engage a new audience, which is under 35 years of age in 40% of cases.

In other words, the survey shows that around 80% of MITO spectators have been following the festival for several years and continue to attend its live performances, whether in the case of the central or in the peripheral venues. It may be of interest to underline that the substantial share of the audience belonging to the class who participated to MITO between 2 and 4 editions, can be the effect of the fact that a relevant share of those who meet MITO for the first time remain somehow faithful in the following years.

Table 5.7 MITO participation loyalty, differences between city centre and peripheral areas in Turin (N = 2,041)

Number of MITO edition	City centre (N = 1,390)	Peripheries (N = 651)
First time	20.4%	19.9%
Between 2 and 4	26.8%	33.1%
Between 5 and 13	28.6%	26.1%
Over 14	24.2%	20.9%
Total	*100%*	*100%*

Source: Own elaborations.

Conclusion

Classical music is the protagonist of the festival MITO. This traditional cultural expression is performed within a programme that explores some forms of innovation. In the field of classical music, the possibility of experiencing innovations in live concerts is of particular relevance, given the intrinsic natural adherence to cultural conventions of this kind of performance. Classical music festivals can then represent an important occasion to implement strategies of audience development dedicated to a younger and new audience. In addition to the typical public attending classical music concerts, during a festival, a wider audience could be involved, and new impacts could be generated on society.

The character of exceptionality of a festival, which concentrates a dense program in a defined period of time, in the case of MITO is further developed by including also unconventional venues located in the city's peripherical areas. The festival is, in fact, conceived basically for the local audience and combines the high quality of the musical performances, specially designed for the occasion, with a great opportunity to get closer to the classical music offered to a new public.

The need to add new research and evidence about the actual and potential public for orchestras is presented in Wolf (2006) and Rizkallah (2010), when the problems and challenges faced by classical music concerts are investigated. So, this chapter aims at contributing to collect evidence on the subject, also to support the identification and implementation by similar festivals of audience development strategies and actions capable to reverse the current negative trends faced by the classical music sector, as far as the demand is concerned.

Our results highlight that the festival expresses a good capacity to build loyalty and, somehow more importantly, is successful in engaging new public. The fraction of newcomers in his audience is quantitatively relevant, and it includes young people and represents therefore an important asset both to impact on society and to reach a rejuvenated audience. The ability to engage the younger public is crucial also for the long run economic sustainability of the festival as far as the tickets' revenues are concerned.

In a similar context, the study by Arenella and Segre (2019), applied to the successful experience of the Turin Philharmonic Orchestra, indicates three main directions to approach younger generations and thus maintain the long run viability of the orchestra: the introduction of new channels of communication with the adoption of new languages; the expansion of the offer through the contamination with other cultural sectors and with new technologies, and the deconstruction of stereotypes related to classical music venues and habits. MITO festival is another example, which, starting from Turin and merging later with Milan, testifies to the power of innovation in a traditional cultural sector where the centrality and the quality of classical music remains, in any case, full.

Another very important feature of MITO festival, which can be of interest to other similar festivals, is the attention paid to the integration of the citizens with the urban fabric of the city. MITO is an event pursuing both the aim of reaching people who do not usually attend musical performances in the traditional concert halls, and bringing people, who do usually attend musical performances in the traditional concert halls, to unusual locations in different parts of the city. MITO is, since many years, a musical journey with national and international cultured music as a navigator, where its old and new audience can move together and enjoy their city.

Notes

1 In 2019, the Turin Foundation for Culture directly organized in the city of Turin 10 important cultural festivals, managing a total of 750 events that altogether registered more than 150,000 presences.
2 In the following sections, we will refer to "MITO SettembreMusica" simply as MITO.
3 We would like to thank Nicola Campograande, Claudio Merlo, Laura Tori and the Secretary-General of the Turin Foundation for Culture, formerly Angela La Rotella and currently Alessandro Isaia, for the precious insights and fruitful collaboration.

References

Arenella, O. & Segre, G. (2019), Il pubblico della musica classica: innovare l'offerta per ampliare il consumo dei giovani, *Quaderni IRCrES*, 4(2), 3–18.

Belligni, S. & Ravazzi, S. (2013), Policy change without metamorphosis. The 1993–2011 urban regime in Turin, *Metropoles*, 12.

DeNora, T. (2010), Emotion as social emergence. Perspectives from music sociology, in P. N. Juslin, & J. A. Sloboda (Eds.), *Handbook of Music and Emotion: Theory, Research, Applications*, Oxford: Oxford University Press, pp. 159–183.

Dobson, M. C. (2010), New audiences for classical music: The experiences of non-attenders at live orchestral concerts, *Journal of New Music Research*, 39(2), pp. 111–124.

Dubois, V. (2016), 'The French model' and its 'crisis': Ambitions, ambiguities, and challenges of a cultural policy, *Debats. Journal on Culture, Power and Society*, 1, pp. 81–97.

Hargreaves, D. J., Miell, D., & MacDonald, R. A. R. (Eds.) (2012), *Musical Imaginations*. Oxford: Oxford University Press.

Holbrook, M. B., Weiss, M. J., & Habich, J. (2002), Disentangling effacement, omnivore, and distinction effects on the consumption of cultural activities: An illustration, *Marketing Letters*, 13(4), pp. 345–357.

Istat (2019), *Cultura e tempo libero*, Rome: Istat.

Kolb, B. M. (2000), You call this fun? Reactions of young first-time attendees to a classical concert, *MEIEA Journal*, 1(1), pp. 13–29.

MacDonald, R. A. (2013), Music, health, and well-being: A review, *International Journal of Qualitative Studies on Health and Well-Being*, 8(1), pp. 206–235.

Mitchell, L. A., & MacDonald, R. A. R. (2012), Music and pain evidence from experimental perspectives, in R. A. R. MacDonald, G. Kreutz, & L. A. Mitchell (Eds.), *Music, health and wellbeing*, Oxford: Oxford University Press, pp. 230–239.

Osservatorio Regionale dello Spettacolo "Emilia-Romagna" (2008), Indagine sul pubblico effettivo e sul pubblico della danza, della lirica e della musica jazz.

Osservatorio Regionale dello Spettacolo "Emilia-Romagna" (2015), Il pubblico della lirica in Emilia Romagna.

Peterson, R. A. (1992), Understanding audience segmentation: From elite and mass to Omnivore and Univore, *Poetics*, 21, pp. 243–258.

Peterson, R. A., & Simkus, A. (1992), How musical tastes mark occupational status groups, in M. Lamont & M. Fournier (Eds.), *Cultivating Differences: Symbolic Boundaries and the Making of Inequality*, Chicago, IL: The University of Chicago Press, pp. 152–186.

Peterson, R. A., & Kern, R. M. (1996), Changing highbrow taste: From snob to omnivore, *American Sociological Review*, 61, pp. 900–907.

Pitts, S. R., Dobson, M. C., Gee, K., & Spencer, C. P. (2013), Views of an audience: Understanding the orchestral concert experience from player and listener perspectives, *Journal of Audience & Reception Studies*, 10, pp. 65–95.

Rizkallah, E. G. (2009), A non-classical marketing approach for classical music performing organizations: An empirical perspective, *Journal of Business and Economic Research*, 7, pp. 111–124.

Roose, H. (2008), Many-voiced or unisono? An inquiry into motives for attendance and aesthetic dispositions of the audience attending classical concerts, *Acta Sociologica*, 51(3), pp. 237–253.

Saarikallio, S. (2011), Music as emotional self-regulation throughout adulthood, *Psychology of Music*, 39(3), pp. 307–327.

Saayman, M., & Saayman, A. (2016), Clustering attendees at the Philharmonic Orchestra's summer festival, *Leisure Studies*, 35(3), pp. 314–331.

Sloboda, J. A., & O'Neill, S. A. (2001), Emotions in everyday listening to music, in P. N. Juslin, & J. A. Sloboda (Eds.), *Music and Emotion: Theory and Research*, Oxford: Oxford University Press, pp. 415–430.

Sullivan, O., & Katz-Gerro, T. (2007), The omnivore thesis revisited: Voracious cultural consumers, *European Sociological Review*, 23(2), pp. 123–137.

Vanolo, A. (2008), The image of the creative city: Some reflections on urban branding in Turin, *Cities,* 25(6), pp. 370–382.

Wolf, T. (2006), *The Search for Shining Eyes: Audiences, Leadership and Change in the Symphony Orchestra Field*, Miami, FL: Knight Foundation.

6 Ferrara Buskers Festival (1998–2001)

Design, Emerging Meanings and Sense Making

Luca Zan and Giovanni Masino

Introduction

This is a strange chapter. Not so much because of the object of our analysis, the Ferrara Buskers' Festival (FBF from now on). It is the period of our investigation that requires some explanations.

Trying to take seriously the idea of participant observation, in 1999 the two of us applied to perform at the Festival as buskers with our duo, the Acoustic Travellers (mind the British spelling, if you want to find us on internet!). Being accepted (as 'credited musicians', see below), we performed there for two days, while the rest of the week we were looking around and observing the organization of the event as it was unfolding. The following year we went back to the Festival to conduct a study on it. Then, we published a preliminary paper in Italian (Masino and Zan, 2002), and prepared a case study in English.

Eventually, at the end of 2019, we contacted the organizers, to update the case. But then the format of the 2020 edition was completely different from the previous ones because of the Covid pandemic (no street music, only a few concerts were performed just to 'keep the name alive'); the 2021 edition will be similar to the 2020. So, while we are still in the process of updating our study with fresh data, we decided to write this chapter in order to document our original study, solely based on the data that we collected back then. In a sense, this is an historical paper: we describe the way things were perceived and reported to us in 1999/2000.

The FBF is a uniquely interesting case of a complex organization where the initial vision of the founders remained fundamentally the same over the years and yet many crucial aspects evolved quickly, leading to a dramatic and somewhat unforeseen success. The formula was completely new, so the organizers had to deal with a lot of uncertainty and, at the same time, with complex interactions between a variety of actors (artists, audience, local politicians and entrepreneurs, organizers), carriers of different meanings, interests and needs but, at the same time, sources of unforeseen opportunities. Our goal was to explore such a unique case, with a specific focus on performing artists, for a number of reasons. Certainly, artists represent the

DOI: 10.4324/9781003127185-9

main 'characters' of the FBF. However, far from being a uniform group, artists also constitute the main source of the overall diversity of roles and interpretations which over the years brought to the organizers both significant challenges and opportunities for change. In the end, our case aims to show that variety and ambiguity (of actors, relationships, meanings) can be seen as the 'raw material' that nurtures transformation, innovation and, eventually, success. The case was also interesting because the literature on Festivals was not even existing at the time of our study, with few exceptions (Roda, 1989; Frey, 2000). We could only refer to a broader managerial and organizational literature on strategic change, learning processes, emerging phenomena, sense making and identity (à la Mintzberg, Pettigrew, Normann, Weick), as in those years the arts management field was in its early development. While observing an unusual, complex case like the FBF, we could not help but notice the naïve approaches that proposed in unproblematic terms the logic of programming and the managerial rhetoric to arts organizations, starting from the buzz word 'mission' (Zan, 2006).

In the following years, a specific literature emerged on Festivals, in parallel with a "Festivalization process" (Roche, 2011), along a variety of perspectives, in addition to specific events (such as Santoro and Solaroli, 2013; Todd, 2014; Batchelor, 2015): urban regeneration (Sassatelli and Delanty, 2011), cultural tourism (Rollins et al., 2007), audience development (Pegg and Patterson, 2010), event management (Getz, 2009), stakeholders involvement (Bagiran and Kurgun, 2016), economic and social impacts (Bracalente et al., 2011), participatory processes and community involvement (Toraldo and Islam, 2017; for a review see Pareschi and Ponzoni, 2021). The latter is where we could (ex post) position our paper, providing a further example in this direction, working at a microlevel on sense making focused on one specific category of actors: the street artists themselves, in their variety and in the ambiguity of the underlying processes inside busking activities (Kaul, 2014; Macchiarella, 2015; Williams, 2016).

A few insights on methodology: our study was conducted through a classic approach of participant observation. Following a preliminary study of documents and extensive interviews with the organizers, with their explicit consent in 1999, we indeed participated to the FBF as artists, in order to have a good sense of the inner workings of the Festival, to closely interact with artists, organizers, audience and, in the end, to have an 'inside view' of what it means to be a performing artist at the FBF. We also conducted a number of semi-structured interviews in 2000 to several performing artists (about 20) in order to understand their experiences, personal histories, meanings, needs and motivations about busking and performing at the FBF. A few excerpts of such interviews will be provided below to clarify some of the most interesting findings. As we stated above, we are currently in the process of updating our case study with fresh data, but in this chapter, we only report our findings from our 2001 study.

FBF: a successful event

You could have expected anything from a city like Ferrara, with its rich artistic and historical heritage of rare beauty. Anything, except that it would host the greatest Festival of street artists in the world, with artists and spectators occupying the city for a week and transforming it into a stage with continuous performances from 6 PM till midnight. It is the greatest event of its kind in the world in terms of audience, about 800,000 visitors in one week. The event had strong impact on the media, with countless national news headlines and television programs talking about it.

In 2001, 177 groups (a total of 660 artists) from 21 countries were involved, totaling 1,044 performances for about 2,296 hours. "If the groups had performed one after the other, we would have had 96 days of non-stop performance", the Festival leaflet proudly claims. Besides the musicians, various other types of artists perform during the Festival (jugglers, fire-eaters, clowns, mime artist, etc.).

The Festival is appreciated by music enthusiasts and musicians. Many important names from the musical scene have visited it over the years, and some even performed in it as street artists. The Festival has become an important aggregation center for this kind of events around Italy and internationally.

Between planning and emergence

In 2001 (at the time of our research), the FBF was deeply rooted in the city. This is the outcome of a transformation process that lasted more than a decade. The original formula of the event has changed somewhat overtime (Roda, 1989; Benati and Pasqualini 1991). Let us briefly summarize the main characteristics of three phases of the Festival's history.

1st phase: the early days (1988–1993)

Following the 1st edition in 1988, where it was designed as a one-off event, the Festival was soon transformed into a permanent event. Since then, some of the essential characteristics are still unchanged:

- the Festival lasts one week with performances in the afternoon and in the evenings;
- it is not a competitive event, while it has a strong community spirit;
- the management of the Festival invites specific artists whose travel and hotel expenses are reimbursed, without any fees;
- the public does not pay any entrance fee, but donations to the artists are warmly welcomed;
- the performances take place in the city center, within the pedestrian area, and the location assigned to each artist is decided by the organization.

The goal of the organizers was to legitimize a form of minor art which was strongly linked to the anarchist myth of the underground movement, which has left deep signs in our culture, where there is still a place for the 'easy rider' or 'on the road' myths in some corner of our identity (Roda, 1989).

There was nothing similar anywhere else: there were places where buskers could perform, but not a 'buskers Festival'. The idea itself could be seen as "a contradiction in terms" (Walker, 1989): buskers usually perform individually on the street without any form of organization. This was Stefano Bottoni's vision, the Festival founder, who managed to involve the town administration in this experiment (Alvoni, 2001). "It was not a question of pressing a button but rather of setting everything in motion, convincing the administration to do something they had never done before". An important constellation of roles was then initiated, backed by the town council, among countless doubts and difficulties. A well-prepared team emerged, whose members were still all present in 2001, with a crucial role in the institutionalization of the Festival.

Success happened immediately, in the first year, helped by a series of contacts with the regional television which produced an incisive report that year. The event was repeated the second year, and the success was strengthened by the enthusiastic participation of Lucio Dalla, a famous Italian musician. At that moment, the organizers began to consider the event as permanent, even in relation to their individual professional careers.

The formula was refined in the following years. For example, in relation to performances, the organization evolved from an initial situation of total spontaneity to more structured forms of organization (e.g., with indications of the locations for musicians and artists and how they should rotate).

But there is another element that spontaneously arose, gradually acquiring a central role in the event: the presence of 'uninvited' musicians who joined the event and performed on the streets independently. These so-called 'aggregated artists' increased so much over time that the organization was forced to state that they would be accepted "only as long as there were available places to play".

2nd phase: consolidation (1994–2000)

A new phase started in 1994, when the new Ferrara Culture Councilor expressed the desire to regularly support the event. The introduction of a specific subsidy to the Festival in the municipal budget affirmed the permanent nature of the Festival. Moreover, the city spaces for artists' performances increased. Also, the formula was improved with the addition of significant changes:

- The Festival was enriched by a preview event and a follow-up event in neighboring cities, playing an important role in promoting the Festival.
- Given the growing pressure of spontaneous participants, in 1996 the category of 'credited' artists substituted the 'aggregated' category.

Thus, while the relevance of improvised performances was recognized, a need of some form of discipline in order to guarantee the smooth running of the performances was met. Musicians had to apply in advance, send a demo and, if accepted, they were assigned a specific location to play and their performance was precisely scheduled.

- More attention was given to the artists' socialization: in 1998, the 'Busker House' was opened, a catering area with a kitchen, a bar and 300 seats that can accommodate the nightly jam sessions. The 'Busker Card' (for shopping discounts) was also introduced.
- Catering services for the public were organized and coordinated, setting up covered eating areas and refreshment places, in agreement with restaurant and shop owners.
- In the meantime, a number of parallel artistic and cultural events were held.

These changes increased the complexity of the Festival's organization, but they resulted in new sources of financing and new sponsorships (these private contributions now cover 41% of the total costs, while the rest is provided by the municipality).

3rd phase: managing the success (2000 onward)

The 'current situation' – as perceived in 2001 – of the FBF is characterized by large numbers of visitors and relevant, but not too difficult, logistic problems. Without an entrance fee, it is difficult to measure audience, but the number provided on the web page in 2001 was around 800,000 in the whole week.

The original formula has been enriched with new facets: besides charity initiatives and the publication of a CD with musical excerpts from the invited artists, the most important novelty was the opening of the 'Buskergarden' in 2000. This is an open space near the city walls where artists perform until late at night, in a secluded setting where the noise is dramatically reduced. The Buskergarden has become so popular that in 2001 the area has been open for the whole month of August, with its own program, two stages, a bar, catering areas and structures for campers during the Festival week.

One of the main sources of the gradual but constant innovation was the need to solve problems, especially problems about keeping order. This is an actual obsession for the managers, clearly because of the growing number of people, events, sounds and noise and related issues. The need for social regulation proved to be one of the driving forces in the process of innovating and refining the Festival's formula, together with the pressures coming from those artists who burst autonomously into the scene and were not expected. In addition to the core of the initial intuition, one of the conditions for the development of the Festival lies in the ability to cope with these threats/opportunities (see Table 6.1 for an overview).

Table 6.1 Continuity and change at the Ferrara Buskers' Festival, 1988–2001

1st phase: the early days (1988–1993)	2nd phase: consolidation (1994–2000)	3rd phase: Managing the Success (2001)
<ul><li>1st edition (1988) as a one-off event</li><li>Transformed into a permanent event<ul><li>one week long, end of August</li><li>not a competitive</li><li>no entrance fee</li><li>the historical center of the city as stage</li><li>20 invited artists (reimbursement but no fee)</li></ul></li><li>Soon needs for disciplining:<ul><li>space allocation for preforming</li><li>accepting 'aggregated' (i.e. not invited) artists</li></ul></li></ul>	<ul><li>Officially supported by the Town: stable financial support</li><li>First collateral events: preview (Comacchio); a one-day tail in (S. Giovanni in P.)</li><li>The "credited artist" position is created (selection on bottom-up application, more than 200 groups a year)</li><li>The organizational complexity increases<ul><li>the Busker House (1998)</li><li>the Busker Card</li><li>catering services and bars for visitors</li><li>collateral events (exhibits, competitions, etc.)</li><li>new financial support by sponsors</li></ul></li></ul>	<ul><li>Large numbers of visitors 800,000</li><li>Enriching the original formula.<ul><li>charity initiatives</li><li>CD with excerpts from the invited artists</li><li>Buskers Garden: open whole August</li></ul></li><li>Perceived tensions:<ul><li>musicians vs non-musicians;</li><li>real buskers vs other buskers</li><li>logistics problems for too many people</li></ul></li><li>Relationship with the audience:<ul><li>from a music to an entertainment event?</li><li>impatient flipping among performances</li><li>no time for collective creation of performance?</li></ul></li></ul>

An organization with a variety of meanings

The Festival can be analyzed in terms of sense making processes by a constellation of actors, as each of them attributes different meanings to the experience. Indeed, we can identify a successful interaction between different groups (the public and its different segments; the local community, ranging from administrators to shop and restaurant owners; the founders, the organizers and the volunteers; the artists themselves, with their different motives), with their different though converging interests (in line with Ooi and Pedersen, 2010).

In other words, an element of interest is this strange type of organization:

- it responds to many expectations, almost a constellation of motives: so many different interests which almost magically converge;
- the rewards for the actors are articulated differently for each group: it is entertainment for the audience; it is business for restaurant owners and other commercial activities; it provides experience and sense of belonging to volunteers; it is praise and consensus for politicians; it is opportunity for the artists (a special focus of our research: see below).

There are few qualitative studies available regarding the consumer of street music (Roda, 1989; Benati and Pasqualini 1991). The Festival's success seems to highlight a sort of market inefficiency: it reveals the hidden demand for a different form of music consumption, as a general phenomenon. Audience takes a less passive, less structured, less 'televisual' role in enjoying music. While for a few people (probably specialists and enthusiasts) the decision to participate may depend on the type of music and performance, the general public of the Festival seems to look for novelties in terms of *different forms of musical consumption* rather than different *musical work*. What matters – deserving a deeper analysis in terms of sociology of musical consumption – is the format itself, the need to overcome a way of consuming music that is passive or too standardized, where the consumer sits or is forced to stay in one context/concert. Instead, at the Festival, consumers can go around, they can find a huge variety of performances, they can listen to what they want and they can choose continually among a large number of options and experiences. A sort of anticipation of the 'shuffle function' that is now common on our MP3 readers.

There are other hidden demands though, on the part of the literally hundreds of volunteers who are willing to participate, or the administrators and politicians who want to 'be there', or other economic actors, restaurant and shop owners, etc. The Festival acts as a sort of catalyst for some latent demands and offers: the various actors bring their contributions and obtain a reward for this 'cooperative game', in a win-win interaction.

Apart from a very small number of complaints from some citizens or shop owners about the noise (complaints that are challenged by their own associations), there are no negative results at a local level. This interaction satisfies everyone, in different ways. It is difficult to identify the 'losers' in this game. It is even difficult to think about who could be the competitors. We are actually dealing with a production/process of social value, of sociality, of social interaction and an activity of musical and art production and consumption, all at the same time.

We also think that the artists themselves should be included among the most important consumers of this event, with their heterogeneous, individual strategies of use and appropriation of the Festival. Perhaps, they share a common need: the need to be there, to participate. The strength of this category of actors has been fundamental in the process of designing or at least modelling the event, as we saw earlier. So, it is worth listening to these producers-consumers (the 'conducers').

Buskers or busking: a subtle issue?

There's no better way to learn about the crucial, multidimensional role that artists play within the Festival than letting them speak for themselves. In 2001, we interviewed a number of artists, and many interesting elements surfaced. We can only briefly summarize a few here, while trying to convey a sense of the multiple identities and motivations that emerge in such a complex, diverse and yet quite unified, cooperative context.

A surprising variety of actors

From an event called Ferrara Buskers Festival, you would expect precisely that: a festival of buskers. However, the definition of busker is not without controversies. What the public sees while walking around during the Festival seems quite homogeneous, at first sight. The artists play music, sing, dance, mime, juggle or all these things together. In front of the performers, ever-present, there is the 'hat' or any other container, for the listeners' donations. The public sees and enjoys street artists. But, is it really this simple? Quite the contrary. We asked a German musician who describes himself as a 'professional busker' complaining about the declining presence of people like him:

> Every year I see fewer professional buskers and more people who, for the occasion, go and play on the streets…Once you went to festivals even just to meet old friends from the street who you don't see during the year…now even here buskers are getting scarce.
>
> (RE)

The same artist, when asked what makes a busker a 'professional', replied:

> I work with a hat, otherwise I wouldn't be a busker! Organized events are something different and they are also part of a personal choice. Thirteen years ago, when I started, I did four years of 'clean street', I mean that I avoided all the organized festivals 'cause I wanted to get to know myself, I also wanted to know the people who stopped to see my show and I had to learn how to know the street. After this experience I understood that maybe it was the moment to go to a few festivals in some different situations.
>
> (RE)

The very place of origin or background of the 'professional busker' can be sometimes surprising, as in the following two groups:

> I studied architecture and as a hobby I did mime, now I do mime as my work and architecture as a hobby!…I've been doing it for 20 years… I've always lived by this and I feel very fortunate to be able to do it.
>
> (SA)

> I used to work in a bank and I was a university assistant lecturer… it's a choice that is the result of a series of steps and unrealized dreams and when you've got the possibility to realize them, well, off you go, immediately.
>
> (GC)

In short, 'real' buskers are street artists who earn a living only with donations in street performances: the participation on contract at organized
events like festivals, fairs, even private parties like weddings and others, is
not part of their activity.

On the other hand, the first artist mentioned above admitted that after a
period of complete refusal of contexts other than the street, his professional
career made him accept the participation at 'a few' festivals and 'some' different situations. The same artist adds:

> I'm not saying that only professional buskers should be able to work
> there, but as in all professions, there should be professional ethic!
> Sometimes it's not like that at festivals, because some people think they
> can come and perform on the street, using very loud amplification and
> with a very limited respect for the show that's going on nearby... I don't
> use any amplification, my respect for who's next to me is very deep and
> also spiritual.
>
> (RE)

Thus, the busker is not an artist only performing on the street, according
to a certain 'contractual form' (the implicit contract between the artist who
performs freely and the people who donate freely). Busking is more broadly
a specific 'way' of interpreting the artistic performance. It is not a street
concert, and there is no amplification; thus, it is not an invasive performance, busking should be respectful of the context in which it happens. It is
a performance that fits 'naturally' in the situation that the artists themselves
choose, where they have the possibility of being listened without becoming
a 'foreign body'. This is not an isolated opinion: the buskers who describe
themselves in a professional sense are ready to defend their old category's
identity, as seen above. However, testimonies like these are not many at the
FBF: more often the 'busking' experience is different, it is quite variegated,
not characterized in such a 'strong' way. Here is what three bands told us:

> I stopped working with a hat three years ago; now I work on contract
> and my performances number from 50 to70 a year, depending on the
> years.
>
> (JO)

> We feel we're buskers, too; let's say that what we earn yearly is 80%
> from busking, but not as much on a hat, no, we work with local admin-
> istrations and we do a lot of events all over Italy, we consider ourselves
> valid, professional buskers; the remaining 20% comes from theatres,
> halls, weddings, funerals, etc. Busking has grown also for this reason;
> professional performers have joined 'cause busking has become a kind
> of business.
>
> (GC)

I'm half a busker, I mean I'm a busker, but I don't busk for twelve months a year... I normally busk in the summertime. If they call me and they pay me then I go; otherwise I busk, it's publicity, image, I work 'with a hat' and the income is often good.

(RM)

Testimonies like these are numerous. It appears that most of the artists practice 'real busking' but also work on contract for specific events, addressing the issue of several subcultures/subgroups inside buskers generally defined. Indeed, they do not despise contractual obligations and actually they use busking as a way to promote themselves and get new contracts. There is no clear discontinuity: there are artists who busk only ('pure buskers') and accept to work on contracts occasionally and exceptionally, while there are others who busk when they have nothing else to do, and others who busk and work on contracts as well, depending on the time of the year.

While some of them openly recognize to be 'half buskers', admitting implicitly that busking is substantially different from a performance on contract, it is also interesting that others call themselves buskers even when they perform mainly on contract rather than with 'hat'. This last category, which we could call 'contractors', appears to be more numerous and more variegated than the 'pure' buskers. However, there are testimonies that make us think of another possible kind of artist. Let us listen, for example, to what a duo, a British and an American, who joined together to play in Ferrara, have to say:

When we play in our own groups, we don't busk... We busk only here, in Ferrara......It is nice to abandon all the other things - the drums, other things – and play a concert only with guitar and voice...it is nice to leave the electricity behind for a week...we haven't said even one time to the people to leave money... we never said anything. On the contrary, we said 'If you want, you can... but we don't have a product, we are not selling anything, we are just here for the music.... It is not for the money, absolutely not for the money this week.

(TW)

Another similar testimony comes from a South African band (this is also a 'temporary' band) who were asked whether they normally busk:

No, I am not a busker, I've come here to have a cultural experience. I am a musician. I perform a lot of concerts in South Africa... you know, South Africa really doesn't have a culture of busking. We come from a recent history of much struggle and I think in any situation like that, things like busking don't really exist. In our past, things like street traders weren't allowed. It was very restrictive.

(AB)

These are few but significant cases of professional musicians, not buskers. Some of them come from busking, others never busked before and find in Ferrara an ideal setting to do something substantially different from performing on stage or in a recording studio, even just for a short period of time.

The fact that the Festival's organizers keep inviting those musicians too, clearly 'non-buskers', emphasizes the importance of these artists for the Festival. This is relevant not only in terms of music quality offered by the Festival but also in order to affirm the Festival's own identity. At the same time, it underlines the importance of the potential mutual enrichment between the art of busking and the mainstream art.

Besides 'pure buskers', 'contractors' and 'non-busker musicians', a number of other characters, that we could call 'amateur musicians', fully participate at the FBF. These 'non-buskers/non-professional musicians' find in the Festival a prestigious institutional roof under which to find shelter and cultivate the desire to perform as a form of enjoyment without worrying about prejudices, biases or other 'social sanctions': a legitimizing process for all of them, though with different meanings for each.

To summarize, we can spot at least four types of artists: buskers who perform only 'with a hat'; buskers who perform on contract; professional musicians who do busking sometimes: amateurs.

A crucial element becomes clear: the notable variety of artistic and professional profiles that make up the FBF. While strolling along the narrow streets of Ferrara, you could think that all buskers are the same. This idea would be deceiving. Or even better said: it is correct, in a way, because 'the customer is always right': the fact that one does not realize the differences between the artists is intrinsically an interesting element of the context. On the other hand, it is clear that the variety of types of performers that we underlined above is much more relevant for the producers (the artists) than the listeners (we are using here very general economic categories, such as production and consumption, without reference to what is normally refereed to inside creative industries). We could say, overall, that FBF is a Festival of 'busking' rather than of 'buskers'. It is a Festival of artists from different backgrounds and origins, who meet for a week and share the experience of performing on the streets. It is a mixture of different personal stories, professions, skills. It is basically the meeting point of two different sensibilities. One is the sensibility of an artist (and art) *of* the street (a busker), that is, a performance that develops and breeds on the road, created and codified according to a specific language and functional to that way of communication. If that language were used in a different context (a stage, or a recording studio), it would not have the same communicative power. The other is the sensibility of musicians (or artists) who bring their art *onto* the street, but who are not buskers. Their art was born and bred somewhere else, and yet it is proposed within a street context not only to test the impact on the public (and on the other artists), in a setting which is devoid of conditioning and prejudices, therefore more genuine and free, but also to enrich their art with inspirations that only this kind of experience may generate. It is an actual learning process through which all artists benefit from the relationship not only with the public, but also with other artists, as they develop new sensibilities and transfer them into new artistic expressions.

Why busking? The artists' motivations

There is a basic trait, a sort of common ground shared by all buskers: that particular challenge, that particular relationship that develops between the artist and the public, when one's real worth is valued and assessed. This emerged from all the interviews and the following extract is emblematic:

> If you are a busker you stand on the street, and if you are good, people stop. You get the most honest opinion about your music. If I go to a bar and someone wants to have a beer, they have to listen to me whether they want it to or not. Especially if he has already ordered his beer. But on the street, you just stand there and play. And if people stop, that means that they like what you do. It is the most honest opinion you can get from someone.
>
> (GR)

Of course, many are the artists, thus many are the motivations. Perhaps, the strongest motivation, as emphasized by almost all artists, is the opportunity to meet other artists. Everybody agreed on this: buskers, professional performers, amateurs, musicians and non-musicians. Let us read what a professional musician from New York and an artist from South Africa have to say:

> Being from NY, I am not exposed to any of this because there something like the FBF doesn't exist, an occasion where musicians come from around the world and play together and share ideas and learn things from each other…and teach each other … I think that is what I like the most about it…our band is a good example of what happens in Ferrara, where you get a band of people where, if it wasn't for Ferrara, they would never meet.
>
> (TW)

> What I most enjoy is the sense of camaraderie. It is a very cosmopolitan, diverse group of people. The friendliness, the communication… it is really great. I have the feeling that it is more a question of relationships with colleagues, than the audience. I feel that in a sense it is more important and more specific.
>
> (AB)

These reports are emblematic of two aspects that all artists emphasize: the Festival is both a learning and a meeting opportunity. The first aspect emphasizes the cross-fertilization among the artists, a reciprocal enrichment, the exposure to different techniques, instruments, sensibilities and ways to make music. The second aspect has even broader consequences: the possibility not only to learn and teach but also to create new artistic identities in terms of groups or performances. The following testimony is very explicit:

> During these years we've caught up with the most different experiences, our band has just played with a group from Mongolia and other jazz players, this is really interesting... this is what happens every night at the Busker's House.
>
> (GC)

Professional artists mainly gain experience and inspiration which becomes useful in introducing some innovations in their music. The freedom guaranteed by the atmosphere of the FBF encourages experimentation.

It is not easy to understand to what extent the motivations just mentioned are specific to the FBF or common in similar events. Undoubtedly, every Festival can offer similar opportunities, but Ferrara has certainly a specific character because of its strong international personality, the atmosphere of freedom and openness, and the existence of structures such as the Busker House. These are characteristics that are not easily found anywhere else. One is the media's attention, which allows all participating artists to meet with entertainment operators, to acquire new work opportunities and, more generally, to get a reputational advantage. Another one is the beauty of the city and the magical atmosphere that the combination of its architecture and the music creates, as well as the variety of spaces available, in terms of size, light, acoustics, which seems to fill many different needs. Finally, the relationship that organizers are able to create with the artists is also important. Artists appreciate the management's attitude meant to maintain the not so easy balance between informality and its capacity to understand their needs and solve their problems quickly and successfully. Sometimes, this good relationship blossoms into a real friendship between the artist and the most prominent organizers, to the point that some artists have been employed in the organization.

Not only art and fascination: problems and critical aspects

The relationship between artists and the FBF is not, of course, without critical aspects. The majority of issues concerns transformations taking place at that time (2000), particularly the significant increase on the number of listeners and, more generally speaking, the size of the event.

The most problematic point is the way artists perceive their relationship with the public. Many artists are convinced that many listeners participate to the FBF because they are drawn to the Festival itself rather than to the artistic performances. In other words, the event is gradually losing its original meaning and becoming just a general entertainment event, where the artists simply are the soundtrack, not the main center of gravity.

> The public now come to enjoy themselves, not to appreciate the performances, anymore...in the turmoil they just walk around, and they don't even respect a well arranged, valuable performance... it might happen that someone behind you, while you're performing, speaks on the mobile and says: 'yes mum, I'm here, where the buffoons are'...after a while you can't stand it anymore and start thinking why am I doing this show for only 10 interested persons while the others couldn't care less whether you perform or not ... so what's the value of the FBF? Do people come for the performances or just to enjoy themselves?
>
> (RD)

This is how many artists feel, but not all of them. Some, in fact, appreciate the competence of the listeners, their capacity to appreciate busking as it rarely happens anywhere else and elevate it at the same level of dignity as other forms of more traditional and more widely recognized art. A juggler relates:

> Here it's like being in a theatre, where people come from far away to just see what we do...it's a nice public, experts by now, 'cause many have kept coming for years.
>
> (JO)

This is a controversial theme, however. It is reasonable to suppose that both opinions contain some truth. There is no doubt that the FBF has had a very important role in spreading a better awareness of the artistic value of busking among the public. But it is also true that many people in the audience have a limited awareness and they therefore see the Festival as a moment of recreation partially or fully detached from the value of its artistic proposal. This is clearly manifested by the behavior of some audiences:

> The public has changed a lot... I remember when, 20 years ago, I used to perform in full tranquility with no music and the people would watch for twenty or more minutes and look at even the smallest details... not anymore, your performances must be full of thrill otherwise they get impatient.
>
> (SA)

At times, it looks like a sort of TV watching, a distracted and impatient 'zapping' among several and diverse proposals, without really looking at them, almost like the real attraction is not the artist anymore, but the amusing context (Rosa, 2013, would refer to societal acceleration). This is clearly frustrating for the artists, for two reasons: first, because the public carelessly listens to 'bits and pieces' of the performances, not fully appreciating their artistic value. Second, because the public jumps from one artist to another without stopping long enough: therefore the 'mood' is lost, the typical busking process of 'collective creation' of the performance in which spectators play an active part is replaced by a sort of separation between the artist and the public, a distance that denies one of the essential characteristics of busking.

Another issue concerns the relationship between the Festival's identity and the artists' own artistic identity. The non-musicians (mimes, clowns, etc.) sometimes find it difficult to truly feel part of the Festival, because the media give full attention to the musicians only, or because the non-musicians cannot be 'invited' but only 'credited', or because of the locations chosen for the performances which, according to some, privilege the musicians. On the other hand, the pure buskers do not easily accept the fact of being a minority when compared to the artists who are partially or very different from them. However, their expressions of discomfort are marginal, to be interpreted as part of a variety that is the best trait of the FBF's tradition and as such, it necessarily generates some difference of views among different sensibilities, and yet they deserve to be taken into account as opportunities to reflect about possible future improvements of the event.

Final remarks

In this section, we will underline some of FBF's distinguishing features at the time of our research. We will also comment on what is still interesting in our narrative compared to the evolution of the literature that was going to emerge in the following period, either at a general level, on Festivals, and more specifically about busking. This will also allow us to spell out the title we choose for this chapter.

First, at the general level, this is an interesting case about decision making and strategic change, without the simplistic view which often characterizes the arts management literature and its passion for buzz words (starting from 'missions': for a critique see Zan, 2006). In our understanding, ambiguity is an essential part of the picture.

What we see in the FBF case is an intriguing combination between continuity and change: the original edition of the Festival left a sort of imprinting that is still visible now (one-week duration, non-competitive, international). Yet, at the same time, huge breakthroughs have also emerged: the transformation from one-off to a permanent event; the incorporation of the unplanned, unforeseen desire to participate by uninvited artists, later disciplined inside the category of 'credited artists', which account for about 80% of all performances; plus, the other initiatives (the Busker House, the Busker Garden) that were added over time. It is this interaction between what was planned and the emerging issues that makes the case so compelling at the general level, as a Festival.

Indeed, what is fascinating is the overall ambiguity which characterizes the event. Who the actors are, the different groups of 'constituents' and their inner articulation, with specific motivations and meanings: all of this was far from clear at the beginning of the story and was still so at time of our investigation. For instance, the audience composition has never been investigated, in terms of specific preferences, needs or even 'buying behavior' mechanisms. Even more so for the artists, that we interviewed extensively. The overall ambiguity, far from being an obstacle, seems to allow variety to emerge while facilitating adaptation. Such an ambiguity would have been frozen if we tried to identify the 'mission' of this event and to 'prove' a superficial understanding at once, forever, for everybody, anthropomorphically attributed to the Festival as if it was a person with its willingness and desires. Rather, sense making becomes a central perspective: for all actors, for us as analysts, and for the readers themselves.

Second, at a more specific level, our case can be related to the small but interesting literature on busking, providing a specific set of meanings that makes it different from other kinds of Festivals. Some of the elements that this literature discusses are surely present in our case, starting from its basic nature of "exchange of gifts" (Kaul, 2014: 40), within a context of interaction between the artist and the audience which takes place 'for free', to use the word of the magic song by Joni Mitchell. Both artists and audience find a specific form of interaction, in a sense archaic (when unstructured and live performance was the only way to enjoy music and arts), before the invention of recorded music, and the diffusion of "canned music" (Macchiarella, 2015: 13). Here, busking can help falsifying the mainstream musicological discourse, which tends to provide value to the music work in itself, in its musical canon, in isolation from the context of interaction, "separating the concept of value from the affirmation of music as a source of joy and becoming" (Williams, 2016: 147). Indeed, what emerges from our interviewees is the intense, focused interactions with the audience, the authentic challenge of conquering the listeners' attention and time, a sort of co-production of art and social energy within such interaction.[1]

While corroborating these basic aspects, some elements in the FBF case are still useful to better address the discussion. In our understanding, *busking* is a more general and interesting phenomenon than *buskers* themselves: real, 'full time' buskers are the exception; a lot of musicians (here at FBF and elsewhere) simply use busking as a form or format of performing. To the audience, this represents a disposition to be influenced by unknown arts/artist/genres, within a sort of 'shuffling' attitude (in general with busking the audience does not know who is there and what's next: at FBF only the invented artists are known in advance). Within this context, a variety of meanings are enacted by different artists, ranging from open rehearsal, experimentation, jam session, promotion, as described by our interviewees, while sharing a sense of belonging to a community of musicians, well beyond the organizational distinction between invited and credited artists. While in service companies it is usually possible to find cases of mixed roles, with the customer who often takes part in the process of distributing the service and takes on some characteristics of the producer (see the neologism 'prosumer' in the marketing literature), here the same participation phenomenon occurs in a special sense (still using the same general economic categories): it is the producer himself (the artist) who is also at the same time a customer, perhaps the most important customer, a user, the 'client' of the service offered, in a sort of self-production (for those who like puns, more than prosumer we could say in this case 'conducer', which also sounds better for musicians).

Third, the FBF is not simply a Festival, nor simply busking: it is busking at a Festival, providing a quite different context from the more usual busking outside an organized event. After having considered FBF as an event in general and after having looked inside busking activities in general and the relations amongst artist and between artists and audience, we need to take a deeper look at the specific context provided by the FBF.

The most significant difference is that, in an organized busking event, there is a pre-arranged structure (selection of artists, of locations, promotional initiatives, a 'prepared' audience, etc.). So, the social environment is not completely natural or spontaneous, it is in many ways pre-arranged, it is legitimized. This makes things a bit easier for the performers, as the challenge to attract listeners to their location is, in part, already taken care of. And that has little to do with the technical proficiency of the artist: Weingarten (2007), for example, documented an interesting experiment, in which one of the most famous violinists in the world, Joshua Bell, was asked to busk anonymously in Washington DC, playing master works in western music with his 3.5 million $ Stradivari. The outcome was that the attention received by this world class musician from the people passing by was extremely low. This is not a problem for the artists performing at the FBF: the audience is 'captive', in many ways, but at the same time it is not anchored to the single performer, as it happens, for example, in a theater. It is up to every listener to freely pick and choose who to listen to and for how long. So, notwithstanding such captivity, a sort of indirect competition between artists for the listeners' attention is nonetheless generated by the organized event setting.

Other elements, specific to the Festival, also emerge. The formula of the FBF attracts a very large number of people, which is at the same time rewarding and desirable for the artist but also problematic for the listeners and for the artists themselves, because of the noise, the distractions and the sheer difficulty for each listener to enjoy the show (and, even more, to interact with the artist) with too many people around. The idea of co-production between artists and audience, which is at the very core of busking, may be more difficult to be enacted here and, in some extreme circumstances, almost completely lost.

If some key elements of busking as we normally understand it are changed somehow, then what is that makes this context so attractive for all artists? Is there a common ground of their heterogeneous sense making processes that is specific to the FBF? Our answer is that if 'non-organized busking' is all about the relationship between the artist and the public, in 'Festival busking' the relevance of the relationship between artists seems to become crucial. We refer to relationships (personal, artistic, professional, etc.) that develop before and after every performance, which create opportunities for collaborations, new artistic inspiration, new job opportunities or just for sharing experiences and establishing new connections in personal networks.

These are the reasons why context matters so much. The pre-arranged structure of an event may change several key elements about the core idea of busking, but in the specific case of FBF the structure also creates opportunities for the construction of new meanings and new motivations, for all actors involved, particularly the artists. Indeed, it is a structure that clearly embraces and enables a significant level of variety (of actors, experiences) and, by consequence, of ambiguity, rather than suppressing or containing it. That is why we claim that artists may be seen as the most important 'customers' of the Festival. In a way, one could argue that the meanings attributed to the FBF's experience by both the audience and the artists evolved over time together with the FBF's organization itself. Indeed, a sort of institutionalization process seems to be happening, in which interplays between intentions, values, problems, solutions, meanings and motivations develop over time into a new evolving formula, one where the FBF is now somewhat different from its origin, and yet still deeply rooted in the most fundamental intuitions (and values) of the founders.

This is also the process within which we may observe the evolution of the sense making of the key actors, artists and listeners. The construction of meaning seems to be diverging, in both cases, from the initial 'center of gravity' of everybody's attention, the artistic performance. On the one hand, at its origin the event clearly attracted a lot of people searching for a format of music consumption that was more active and participative, different or even opposite from the traditional passive channels. The very success of the FBF generated a new context in which it is becoming questionable whether the FBF experience can be as participative as it used to be, because the large audience prevents, at least in several cases, a very close relationship between the artist and the listeners. However, the attractiveness of the FBF as a more generic ludic event is becoming more important, one in which not only listening to music, but also eating, drinking and being together become key elements of its appeal. On the other hand, for the artists, the relationships between artists are becoming increasingly relevant. Just like it seems that many music lovers are looking for more social forms of music consumption, maybe artists too are looking for a more social, more boundary-less (in terms of genre, culture, role specialization, etc.) form of music creation and inspiration, especially in this era of increasingly solitary, computerized, loop-based, home-located music producers. The FBF seems to provide, to artists, such an opportunity.

Overall, it seems that the FBF represents a very interesting, long term social experiment of sorts. Just like Joshua Bell put himself in an unusual, strange (for him and his music) context of music performance, and a quite surprising outcome resulted, similarly the FBF is putting an ancient, essential, 'naked' form of music performance and consumption into an unusual, organized (value-driven rather than strategy-driven) context, a strange mixture of elements that shouldn't go well together: the freedom of busking and the constraints of an organization, the intimacy of the performer-listener relationship and the mass appeal of the event. What is happening is yet to be fully understood, may be "the wheel's still in spin", but already we see developing an interesting story of organizational creativity and ambiguity, artistic cross-fertilization and development and production/consumption evolution.

As we warned at the beginning, this is a strange chapter, trying to tell a strange, unique story.

Note

1   While the Italian expression *musica dal vivo* is a translation of the English 'live music', Macchiarella reminds us of another expression that was once common in Italian, though difficult to translate: *musica dal vero* (approximately 'true/real music'), suggesting that only the interaction makes it 'true/real'.

References

Bagiran, D., and Kurgun, H. (2016), A research on social impacts of the Foça Rock Festival: The validity of the festival social impact attitude scale, *Current Issues in Tourism*, 19:9, pp. 930–948.

Batchelor, B. (2015), This beer festival has a theatre problem!": The evolution and rebranding of the Edmonton international fringe theatre festival, *Theatre Research in Canada*, 36, pp. 33–51.

Benati, G., and Pasqualini, L., 1991, *La città per suonare*, Spazio Libro.

Bracalente, B., Chirieleison, C., Cossignani, M., Ferrucci, L., Gigliotti, M., and Ranalli, M. G. (2011), The economic impact of cultural events: The Umbria Jazz music festival, *Tourism Economics*, 17:6, pp. 1235–1255.

Getz, D. (2009), Policy for sustainable and responsible festivals and events: Institutionalization of a new paradigm, *Journal of Policy Research in Tourism, Leisure and Events*, 1:1, pp. 61–78.

Kaul, A. (2014), Music on the edge: Busking at the cliffs of Moher and the commodification of a musical landscape, *Tourist Studies*, 14:1, pp. 30–47.

Macchiarella, I. (2015), Suoni osteggiati: note sulla busking music, *Medea*, I:1.

Masino, G., and Zan, L., (aprile 2002), Il Ferrara Buskers Festival: progettualità, emergenza e costellazione di significati, *Micro & Macro Marketing*, a. XI:1.

Ooi, C. S., and Pedersen, J. S. (2010), City Branding and film festivals, *Place Branding and Public Diplomacy*, 6, pp. 316–332.

Pareschi, L. and Ponzoni, N. (2021), A struggle of capitals over the identity and the cultural offering of Festivaletteratura, in Demartini, P., Marchegiani, L., Marchiori, M., and Schiuma, G. (Eds.), *Cultural Initiatives for Sustainable Development*, 249–270. Springer, Cham.

Pegg, S. and Patterson, I. (2010), Rethinking music festivals as a staged event: Gaining insights from understanding visitor motivations and the experiences they seek, *Journal of Convention & Event Tourism*, 11:2, pp. 85–99.

Roche, M. (2011), Festivalization, cosmopolitanism, and European culture. On the sociological significance of mega-events, in Giorgi, L., Sassatelli, M., and Delanty, G. (Eds.), *Festivals and the Cultural Public Sphere*, 124–142. Routledge, London.

Roda, R. (Ed.), (1989), *I musicisti di strada*. Interbooks, Padua.

Rollins, R.; Delamere, T. (2007), Measuring the social impact of festivals, *Annals of Tourism Research*, 34: 3, pp. 805–808.

Rosa, H. (2013), *Social Acceleration: A New Theory of Modernity*, Columbia University Press, New York.

Santoro, M., and Solaroli, M. (2013), Ecologia istituzionale di un festival: il caso Umbria Jazz, *Polis, Ricerche e studi su società e politica*, 1, pp. 81–124.

Sassatelli, M., and Delanty, G. (2011), Festivals in cities, cities in festivals, *European Arts Festivals*, https://www.academia.edu/9403566/_Festivals_in_cities_cities_in_festivals_with_G_Delanty_in_L_Giorgi_et_al_European_Art_Festivals_Strenthening_Cultural_Diversity_Brussels_OOPEC_2011

Todd, L. A. (2014) Developing brand relationship theory for festivals: A study of the Edinburgh Festival Fringe, in Yeoman, I. S., Robertson, M., McMahon-Beattie, U., Backer, E., and Smith, E. (Eds.), *The Future of Events and Festivals*, Routledge, London, pp. 157–176.

Toraldo, M. L., and Islam, G. (2019), Festival and organization studies, *Organization Studies*, 40:3, pp. 309–322.

Walker, T. (1989), La tradizione del musicista di strada, in Roda, R. (Ed.), *I musicisti di strada*. Interbooks, Padua.

Weingarten, G. (2007), Pearls before breakfast: Can one of the nation's great musicians cut through the fog of a D.C. rush hour? Let's find out, *Washington Post*, April 8th 2007.

Williams, J. (2016), Busking in musical thought: Value, affect, and becoming, *Journal of Musicological Research*, 35:2, pp. 142–155.

Zan, L. (2006), *Managerial Rhetoric and Arts Organizations*, Palgrave MacMillan, Basingstoke.

7 Becoming a Symbol and Losing Control

The Gothenburg Book Fair and the Alt-right Debate

Josef Pallas and Elena Raviola

Introduction

As the theme of this book suggests, there is a vast range of issues that make cultural festivals a societal phenomenon that both mirror and shape economic, cultural and political aspects of our life and our societies (Moeran and Strandgaard Pedersen 2011, Báez-Montenegro and Devesa-Fernández 2017). Being situated within a context of diverse academic disciplines such as cultural studies, anthropology, organizational and management studies, political science, development studies, tourism and event management as well as sustainable development and innovation studies, cultural festivals have shown that they can be seen as expressions and drivers of highly institutionalized social structures and processes (Toraldo and Islam 2019) that are in many contexts involved in shaping identities, structures, practices, products and destinies of individuals, organizations, communities, cities, industries, fields as well as countries and cultures (Jaeger and Mykletun 2013, Shay 2014, Perry et al. 2020).

In organizational research, cultural festivals have attracted attention as formative and innovative moments in the development of different cultural fields such as the book and publishing industry (Weber 2018), music (Meyer et al. 1998, Watson and Anand 2006), film (Rüling and Pedersen 2010, Mazza and Pedersen 2017) and art (Ekström 2019). Following the neo-institutional reasoning, cultural festivals are addressed as an example of *field-configuring events* (Leca, et al. 2015, Schüßler and Sydow 2015). Being defined as "temporary social organizations such as tradeshows, professional gatherings, technology contests, and business ceremonies field-configuring events (FCE) encapsulate and shape the development of professions, technologies, markets, and industries" (Lampel and Meyer 2008: 1026). FCEs are thereby located at the intersection of issues, interests, actors and their relations and are as such central in understanding social and societal change. FCEs create unique and specific moment(um)s in which fields are constructed and reconstructed by offering opportunities for information exchange and emergence and maintenance of collective cognitive structures such as discourses and (meta-) narratives.

DOI: 10.4324/9781003127185-10

In this chapter, we focus on a particular stream of literature exploring cultural festivals – as well as other field-configuring events such as fairs, exhibitions and conferences – as functioning not only as significant moments of formation of different cultural fields and industries (Mazza and Pedersen 2017), but also as arenas for medially enhanced processes that connect these cultural fields with the field of politics (Merkel 2013, Bennett 2016, Raviola et al. 2019). To be more specific, in this chapter, we focus on *how the use of social and traditional media transformed a specific field-level event (in our case the Gothenburg's Book Fair) from being a primarily cultural event to an event which has gained the characteristics of a political arena.*

The rest of the paper is structured as follows. In the next section, we address cultural festivals as field-configuring events. Here, we argue for understanding the development and transformation of cultural fields as closely connected the way FCEs are embedded and recreated within the context of working practices and values of the media. Introduction of our case and methodology precedes a section where we present how the Book Fair has become an arena for political controversy – mostly due to the use of social media. We finalize the chapter by point at different mechanisms through which the Book Fair has become the site of interactions, contestations and controversies that have had both political and medial underpinnings and implications.

Cultural festivals as field-configuring events

Whereas literature on FCEs has focused on events such as festivals, fairs and conferences as moments in time that have the capacity to change or stabilize (longitudinal) trajectories of specific fields (cf. Anand and Jones 2008, Mazza and Pedersen 2017), other type of research has directed its attention towards what happens inside these events to reveal some of the micro-dynamics of different fields (Gross and Zilber 2020). FCEs have in this context mostly been studied with focus on their role in organizing, governance and configuration of the *structural* properties of a given field. Several studies (Hardy and Maguire 2010, Rüling and Pedersen 2010, Gross and Zilber 2020) have also pointed to FCEs as being arenas for symbolical, narrative and discursive activities and struggles in which fields are defined and redefined – notably in relation to other related fields. It is in the context of the symbolical processes that a discussion on the media and FCEs is of particular interest.

However, there are only few studies that have explicitly explored the interplay between media and FCEs and the ways in which such an interplay influences the development of a particular field. These studies suggest three different aspects of the media-FCEs relationship. First of all, many FCEs – including cultural festivals – can be seen as media events in their own right (Dayan 2009). That is, they include transculturally binding elements that are widely communicated not only in and by mass media but also by the vast variety of social media platforms, which in turn are extensively dependent on media events for content (cf. Bolin 2009, Couldry et al. 2009). News media companies are active partners and sometimes even organizers of many fairs, festivals, conferences and exhibitions. The success of these events is then often measured in terms of media attention, news coverage, clicks, followers or agenda-setting capacities. Secondly, as the media landscape has dramatically changed over the last 30 years, so too has the ways in which FCEs are attended and organized. The digitalization of news production and the significant growth of social media have innovated and transformed many traditional interaction patterns within and around the FCEs (Mangematin et al. 2014). The effects of digitalization on cultural events has also been accelerated by the covid-19 pandemic. Salti (2020) for instance addressed the transformation of film festivals where face-to-face interactions have been replaced by virtual formats which challenges not only film festivals underlying modus operandi but also their environmental footprint. Thirdly, the links between different fields (e.g. political, cultural, economic) are being redefined as traditional and social media (including other types of digital fora) shape the debate and actions in the public space, not least by their role in covering and connecting major events in these fields with each other (Schüssler et al. 2014, Sigala 2018).

Being crossed by political and societal trends and diffused and proliferated by media and social media in particular means that FCEs, such as cultural festivals, become a center for heated discussions surrounding wider issues rather than the actual cultural production at their core. Thus, FCEs might become – more or less willingly – not only sites for gathering actors around the exchange of a product or service – like books, films, food, sport, etc. – but also a site for interaction between actors gathering around particularly contested issues of concern, and not necessarily around the actual or planned content of the FCE at hand (Vermeulen et al. 2016).

This chapter explores mainly the third aspect of media-FCE's relationship by focusing on the Gothenburg Book Fair in Sweden. During 2016 and 2017, the Book Fair became the center of a very lively debate on the appropriateness of letting an extreme right-wing publisher exhibit at the fair. The public controversy which took the case of the Gothenburg Book Fair as an occasion to discuss the limits of freedom of speech and the appropriate ways of handling the growing extreme-right movement in a democratic society, a discussion which was held alive for about 15 months. During this period, the Gothenburg Book Fair became a symbol for the larger national and international societal tensions around the extreme-right movement. And, as a symbol, the Book Fair was often used both rhetorically and practically as a platform to foster the debate (Grafström and Windell 2019). The available empirical material from this period shows that the Book Fair organizers had limited capacity of controlling the content of the public conversation going on during the fair, and to react to the hijacking of the conversation by the extreme right-wing publisher and alt-right social media users into the context of wider political debate (Raviola et al. 2019).

Our study

The material used in this chapter is from a qualitative study of the Gothenburg Book Fair that we studied during two years between Spring 2016 and Spring 2018. The research design was inspired by multi-sited ethnography (Marcus 1995) as a way to study complex processes taking place simultaneously in different social arenas and organizations.

The project was originally aimed at investigating the emergence of one piece of news from the simultaneous perspective of several actors. At the beginning of 2016, we decided to keep a watch on the Book Fair, betting on the fact that in due time some piece of news would emerge. About five weeks before the actual fair, overnight, the presence of an extreme right-wing publisher at the fair had caught the attention of traditional and social media and had become news: We thus started to follow a number of other actors, such as several newspapers, publishers exhibiting at the fair, journalists, social media, cultural workers, that were involved in the development of the news before, during and after the Book Fair. We continued to follow news, Twitter and the Book Fair organization's decisions throughout the year until the following Book Fair (2017) as well as a period of time following these events.

We generated field material in three main ways: interviews, observations and twitter (tweets). We conducted around 40 interviews with the main actors before, during and after the fairs. Observations of meetings, seminars and public debates around the news were also performed as to increase our understanding of work practices. Twitter posts were downloaded during the whole period before, during and after the fair, including hashtags related to the news and specific accounts that seemed particularly active. A total of 18832 Tweets were collected during the period 27th of May 2016 and the 31st of October 2017, encompassing two book fairs (22nd–25th of September 2016 and 28th of September–1st of October 2017) and the Twitter activity in-between, gathered around the hashtag #bokmässan (the book fair). Finally, Swedish press coverage was also gathered regarding the Book Fair.

The analysis of the interview and observation material was inspired by grounded theory, following three main parallel processes. First, the interview and observation material was initially coded openly to then be coded in an increasingly focused manner. Second, memos were written to keep track of theoretical development ideas and of analytical insights emerging in the coding process. Third, a narrative of the whole case and of specific episodes was reconstructed. For the purpose of this chapter, twitter material was treated as a support to the analysis of interviews and observations and only a partial analysis of this material is shown in this chapter.[1]

The Gothenburg Book Fair: the beginnings and its development

The four days of the Book Fair are comprised of literary events, poetry readings as well as discussions and debates where writers, scholars, Nobel Laureates, politicians and thinkers from around the world appeared in readings, talks and high-profile debates. With 100,000 annual visitors, it is purportedly the largest annual cultural event in Scandinavia. Every year, a specific theme permeates the entire fair. In 2016, the designated theme was "Freedom of expression" as a celebration of the 250th anniversary of legal guarantees for freedom of information and a free press in Sweden. In 1766, Swedish parliament abolished censorship of books and newspapers and required authorities to provide public access to all official records with the passing of 'His Majesty's Gracious Ordinance Relating to Freedom of Writing and of the Press'.

The Book Fair was first held in 1985 by Conny Jacobsson, who had been a teacher at the Library College, and Bertil Falck, who has been head of the administration for the Gothenburg library system and prior to that a salesman for a computer business and a policeman. Conny's and Bertil's idea was to create a meeting place for teachers and librarians to discuss and exchange ideas for their sector.

Despite the fact that neither Conny nor Bertil were public intellectuals with connections in the cultural world, they managed to create an event that grew through the years. Since the beginning, their ambition is to create the biggest cultural event in the Nordic countries. As Bertil and Conny thought about the librarians' need of learning, they organized a seminar program for the first year of the fair, and in fact initially thought about the event as a Library Conference. To this day, the seminar program is one of the most important elements of the Book Fair.

The seminar program is accompanied by an exhibition of publishers presenting and selling books and by an international rights center where publishing rights are exchanged, with a focus on Nordic literature. The Book Fair has grown impressively in numbers: "3700 items in the program and 2700 participants, and 800 exhibitors" (Interview, February 2016, Communication Manager). Also, about 1,200 journalists are present at the fair, where most of Swedish newspaper publishers have a stand and their own program.

Organizationally, the Book Fair was run by the company Book and Library which was independent until the mid-2000s when it got acquired by the Swedish Fair Group, which is the current owner. The personnel consists of about 15 employees, divided primarily into three functions: managing relations with exhibitors, creating and editing the seminar programs and communication. Running a fair through a profit-driven company is quite unusual when looking at the international landscape, as to many other European countries. Often, it is either a foundation or the ministry of culture or the publishers' association that is responsible for, or at least acts as a patron for the fair. These founders' belief was that the commercial viability of the fair would allow it to be free and survive political and economic changes. As a private commercial entity, its business model functions with revenues from the exhibitors renting their display space and the visiting public paying for entrance tickets.

Communication, and in particular press coverage, has always been important for the Book Fair, as Bertil acknowledged in an interview. Some of the employees at Book and Library recognized the Book Fair as a big communication event, where it is quite difficult to stand out and break through the noisy and abundant offers of seminars and debates (Communication manager, first interview, March 2016). The news that comes out of the Book Fair are usually related to well-known authors or celebrities visiting the fair, significant political propositions from state agencies like the Ministry of Culture, or the many journalists who conduct book interviews with well-known authors at the fair and who store material to keep it ready and available for later publications during the year. As the web-editor at Book and Library said during an interview in 2016, their ambition is to prolong the newsworthiness of the Book Fair throughout the year by,

> check[ing] a little what's happening around the world and follow the news or different anniversaries or theme days or things like that, and to link them to our seminar program of last or coming years.
>
> (Web-editor at Book and Library)

Thus, even before the events of 2016, the Book Fair was trying to go beyond its physical and time limits in terms of communication and become relevant throughout the whole year. Media coverage was, however, still mostly concentrated around the days of the actual fair and the efforts of publishing links to the seminar program had not yet produced great audience results. Despite these limits, the Book Fair has made moves to go beyond a strict focus on books and has moved towards becoming a wider platform for debate. As Ulf Roosvald, a journalist who wrote a book on the history of the Book Fair, noted, the Book and Library received the Knowledge Prize from the National Encyclopedia in 2007. The reason read as follows:

> Because the fair of Book and Library in Gothenburg has over more than 20 years developed into a unique meeting place for the distribution of knowledge. The fair has with its incredibly comprehensive seminar program, with its stimulating cultural milieu and with the help of an intensive media coverage managed to engage a big part of the Swedish people for knowledge and the written word.
>
> (Roosvald, 2009: 172)

The Book Fair has thus assumed a status beyond its function of creating a space for selling books and intellectual property rights and has contributed to shape the cultural field in Sweden as well as the rest of Scandinavia. As the motivation for the Knowledge Prize read, part of this development can be attributed to the extensive (and intensive, as the motivation put it) media coverage dedicated to the Book Fair.

The Gothenburg Book Fair 2016

A few weeks prior to the 2016 Book Fair, it was first made public that the right-wing weekly publication Nya Tider (New Times) was going to be one of the exhibitors at the fair. An article titled "Extreme right-wing newspaper exhibits at the Book Fair" was published on 17 August by the Swedish Book Retail Magazine (Svenska Bokhandel). The article read:

> New Times is a weekly newspaper on the very extreme right-wing, which according to the magazine Expo [an investigative magazine], has strong connection to the Nazi organization The Nordic Resistance Movement. In its presentation on the Book Fair website, New Times writes that they tell 'about what the system media [i.e. the established media] cover in the dark, lie about or distort'. The newspaper will now have a stand at Book and Library for the first time.
> - Our policy in general is that everybody needs to make their voice heard, independent from public opinion. It is the very essence of the freedom of expression. But we don't let the exhibitors use the platform in a way that goes against human rights and freedom, says Book and Library CEO Maria Källsson.
>
> (Lars Schmidt, Svensk Bokhandel, August 17, 2016)

The article was critical to the coming development of the Fair. As soon as it was published and shared on twitter that Wednesday, reactions grew strong and vocal on social media as well as on traditional media. As a reaction to this piece of news, the organizers of the fair got overwhelmed with upset reactions, both in private contacts with citizens and publishers but also from the public domain, through social media and the cultural supplements of established newspapers. Book and Library then made a new decision and rejected New Times´ participation just a couple of days after the first news was published. As the CEO later recalled in an interview, on that Friday afternoon, after a consultation with the top management of the Swedish Fair Group, they published a press release announcing the decision not to allow New Times to exhibit at the fair. This new decision sustained the discussions both on twitter and in established media. At the end of August, Book and Library made yet another press release. After the contract had been reviewed legally, no other solution had been found, so it was confirmed finally that New Times would be attending the Book Fair.

The public debate following these different rounds of decisions from the organizers of the Book Fair focused intensely on two main themes. One concerned what we could call the "organizational scrutiny" that focused on the critique of the organization Book and Library for not having clear routines and principles about who is and is not allowed to exhibit at their fair. The debate continued in a lively manner both in public and private arenas. Journalists wrote many opinion pieces and answered each other for weeks and twitter accounts tweeted actively under the hashtag #bokmassan. In this debate, the CEO of Book and Library was the most exposed figure representing the organization. In all her interviews, she was asked the rhetorical question of how this possibly could have happened. The public conversation also steered the internal organizational conversation at Book and Library towards these types of questions, although they did not respond actively to critique and other accusations directed towards them on Twitter as they were unsure of how to effectively use this platform.

The second theme in the public debate was the issue of how the extreme-right movement should be treated in a democratic society, and the appropriateness of allowing them to exhibit at the Book Fair 2016. This debated theme connected the Book Fair to a number of larger societal issues, like freedom of speech, the growing extreme-right movement, the status of the left wing in politics, the failure of the cultural elite, as well as democracy itself. As the head of the cultural newsroom of a national tabloid wrote:

> The fundamental idea of democracy - the autonomy of the people - is challenged by massive forces, but it is only freedom of expression issues that engage us. What words can be used? What can you draw? Who should be allowed to speak, and where? This is how both intolerance and martyrdom are created. Our times have a sad attitude towards the power of conversation to convince. The call to stop the uncomfortable view is heard more and more often. As a publicist, I am tormented by the left wobbling around the liberal freedoms and rights for which older generations of the left fought bloodily. These are rights that must be self-evident if we are ever given the chance to build a Swedish society on socialist principles. Throwing away these principles does not inspire confidence.[2]

And then she also brings into reason an explicit connection to the Swedish Democrats, a Swedish conservative party with cultural and historical connections with fascism and white nationalist movements, and to the difficulty of Swedish society and parliament to manage their presence. This connection is important especially in light of the fact that in 2010, the Swedish Democrats secured their first seats in Parliament and in 2018 the party received 17.6% of votes in the national election.

The Book Fair finally came and lasted as per usual 4 days, Thursday to Sunday, 22–25 September 2016. At the inauguration, the Swedish Minister of Culture and Democracy Alice Bah Khunke mentioned the importance of continuous work to safeguard freedom of speech and lamented that "we are not doing enough". In interviews with the press, she supported the decision to allow New Times to exhibit at the fair, as she promoted the necessity to be where the dark forces are to show that democracy is stronger and that we will not bend to their pressure. So, she also engaged in the public debate around democracy and the appropriateness of New Times exhibiting. After the inauguration, everything seemed to have started as usual. Thursday was the day for the industry and we walked around observing and conducting our interviews without hearing too much talk about New Times and its affairs. Twitter was too quite calm on this debate.

On Thursday evening however, after the closure of the Book Fair, the Swedish Public Service Television broadcasted a live-interview with New Times editor-in-chief Vavra Suk. This interview sparkled a lot of discussion both within established media and on twitter. The discussion revolved around freedom of expression and its limits. Many asked whether the editor-in-chief of a newspaper, with a proven connection to Nazi organizations and which thereby does not stand up for the principle of all humans being equal, should be treated like any other interlocutor and thereby be invited to a peer-to-peer conversation. Others defended the wide limits of the Swedish legislation on freedom of expression.

Media coverage in numbers

The intensity of the public debate around the Book Fair 2016 was also testified by the number of media items published and tweets circulated. Within traditional media, including press, web, TV and radio, 212 pieces of news were published concerning the Book Fair and New Times during the week after the initial article was published in 16 August 2016, this according to the Swedish media database Mediearkivet. Just the week before, there had been no news on this in the traditional media outlets. The discussion around the case of New Times however continued in the following weeks, summing up to 1,377 articles by the end of September. As a term of comparison, articles on the Book Fair published during the whole month of August were 309. During the week of the Book Fair, 2,340 news items were published by established media, of which 517 referred to New Times.

The number of unique tweets in the first week after 16th of August were 1,152, and the number of unique twitter accounts participating in the conversation were 149, generating an average number of tweets per account of 7.7. The main accounts driving the twitter debate in the same period however were roughly 9 (out of 149). These accounts were active in producing tweets and replying to others. The remaining 140 were simply forwarding information.

Aftermath of the 2016 fair: the internal work

After the Book Fair 2016, Book and Library engaged in a process aimed at internally discussing the issue of freedom of expression and the current crisis, as well as formally defining the principles for exhibition at the fair and Book and Library´s guiding values. This process was facilitated by a PR consultant. A former local journalist, whose role was to help the organization discuss and see the consequences of different options.

In December 2016, Book and Library presented the results of this process in a seminar at the Museum of Photography in Stockholm and published this on the Book Fair website.

As the communication director said in an interview with us, they decided to present their guidelines in Stockholm at a public seminar. Presenting their guidelines was done because of the intenseness of the media debate, and choosing to present this in Stockholm was thought to attract greater public attention than if they had done so in Gothenburg. At the seminar, the CEO of the Frankfurt Book Fair was invited as well as two journalists that were expected to lift the conversation to the general issue of Freedom of Expression.

In December 2016, then Book and Library announced in two different documents their basic values and the exhibition principles. The first values were values they, as an organization, stood for which would primarily inform the seminar program and other activities organized formally and officially by the Book Fair. They also settled around wider principles for the acceptance of applications and exhibitors' place at their fair. Here is how they formulated a condensed version their principles:

> **Where does the boundary go for whom is allowed to exhibit at the fair?**
> *We start from relevance, diversity and free opinion building. It is always the Book Fair that makes an overall assessment and make a decision on the best possible combination of exhibitors on a limited fair surface. A single exhibitor cannot plead our principles and with their support require a place on the floor of the fair. (www.bokmassan.se)*

As the communication director said in an interview, these principles are based on three pillars: breadth – "otherwise it is like a literature festival"; relevance in a wide sense and free opinion building, much like what the public libraries do. In deciding upon these three principles, Book and Library in Sweden discussed with international partners in the Book Fairs' network, Ferieros, whom the CEO of Book and Library met in October 2016, right after the Frankfurt Book Fair, the world's biggest Book Fair.

One particular issue that was discussed in the internal process of defining these principles was whether a belief in all people's equal value should be used as a yardstick for allowing or respectively not allowing organizations to exhibit. This would have implied that they would have needed to check and monitor every applicant organization. This would have been practically impossible.

The values of the organization Book and Library stand for were formulated as following:

> Our values are openness, free opinion building, diversity and respect for all people's equal value. These values guide our work in many ways, especially in our collaborations and activities at the Book Fair. We will not therefore accept that forces which stand for intolerance and hate win territory. We will use our tools and our arena to educate, disseminate facts and build opinion to counteract racism and xenophobia.
>
> (www.bokmassan.se)

In announcing these values and principles, Book and Library communicated that their operations and their responsibilities are two-folded. On the one hand, there is the ground floor, where the organizers offer an open arena for exhibition and rent out different spaces, without being responsible for the content that is exhibited. These principles are in accordance with Swedish law and were to put in place to guide the selection of the exhibitors, just like any public space. On the other hand, there is the first floor, where the seminars would be taking place according to a program put together by the Book Fair. In this space, they would be responsible for the selected content, just like a publisher for its publication.

Besides this work, Book and Library reviewed their exhibitors' contract and introduced new paragraphs in order to defend itself from potential damages from exhibitors. In particular, this new paragraph was added:

> The Supplier is entitled to terminate the Agreement with immediate effect if it can be assumed that a Representative of the Exhibitor or anyone else who, at the Exhibitor's invitation, will attend the Exhibitor's Stand during the Fair, has been charged with agitation against the crowd, unlawful threats or other similar crimes. The Supplier's right under this paragraph shall in no way limit the Supplier's rights as per paragraph 25.

The third part of Book and Library's reaction is to have a new procedure, like the involvement of an external partner investigating the nature of the applicant organization. As they did when New Times applied for a space at the fair, and Book and Library in turn engaged Expo. The goal was to check that the applicant respected their principles and did not have a pertinent criminal history. After this presentation, Book and Library were satisfied and thought the whole story could finally come to rest.

Spring and summer 2017: unexpected turns

In March 2017, however, a video was published that raised a lot of debate around the presence of New Times at the Book Fair. The video showed a person who calls himself a "citizen journalist" insistingly knocking at the door of a national tabloid's editor in chief and compelling him to open the door to answer questions. The video ends with the citizen journalist encouraging everybody to do the same against the cultural elite which keep the masses misinformed. In this video, the protagonist was accompanied by a woman that worked as a vice-chief editor at New Times.

A heated debate unfolded in the media with many suggesting Book and Library ought to revise their decision to accept New Times and instead take the chance to exclude them from the exhibition. Book and Library decided to send the video for a judicial examination by an external law firm in order to ascertain whether there were sufficient grounds to leave the contract. This examination resulted in a rejection that there was any direct relation between New Times and the video, as the vice-chief editor had participated as a private citizen and not as a publisher or a representative of the newspaper.

The decision to accept the extreme right-wing publisher in 2017, especially after the publication of such a contested video raised wide critique within the literature scene both in Sweden and internationally. Many national and international newspapers announced in June a boycott of 200 authors. In addition, a series of alternative events to the Book Fair were announced to be organized in the same city and at the same time as the Book Fair, the two biggest being: Bokmassa (The Mass of Books) and Scener och samtal (Scenes and conversations).

In August 2017, the Nordic Resistance Movement applied for permission to demonstrate on Saturday, 30 September, starting right in front of the Book Fair. Saturday is the busiest day for the Book Fair and approximately 30,000 people usually attend the fair. The police gave them permission to demonstrate but did not allow them to begin their demonstration at the entrance to the Book Fair and instead allowed to the group to depart from behind the building.

Book and Library at this point engaged actively and intensely in a dialogue with the police in an effort to caution them to the dangers this decision might have. They wanted them to change their decision. The media closely and intensively covered the issue and often referred directly to The Nordic Resistance Movement and New Times:

> Over the past year, the Nordic Resistance Movement has intensified its tactics of being present in the public space on symbolic dates and symbolic places. The demonstration in Stockholm last November in connection with the November pogrom, the May demonstration in Falun, the presence in Almedalen [a major Swedish political event] and now the application to demonstrate in Gothenburg on 30 September - the Book Fair and the big day of the Alternative Book Fair - are all signs of this.[3]

The Book Fair 2017: the extreme right steals the show

The Book Fair of 2017 finally came to being in the midst of all the protests and so did the alternative events. On the Saturday during the fair, the Nordic Resistance Movement gathered its members in a place close to the entrance of the fair, but were stopped and forced back by police. No clashes happened in the city. There were however 30% less visitors at the Book Fair than the previous year.

On 28th of November, about 2 months after the fair, Book and Library announced that the organization had decided to exclude New Times from next year's Book Fair because one single exhibitor had taken too much attention and time from the organization, thus making it difficult to focus on its core activities. A number of other decisions were announced to renew the Book Fair.

As shown above in the frequency diagram (Figure 7.1.), peaks in activity visibly occur in 2016 on the 20th of August ($N = 213$), the 22nd of September ($N = 645$) and the 25th of September ($N = 521$), and in 2017 for the 22nd of April ($N = 112$) and 29th of September ($N = 737$).

Discussion

The Book Fair was for long time an uncontroversial field-configuring event for the publishing field, an exchange field based in the publishing industry. As the Book Fair grew, it also started being associated with the wider field of culture and was marketed as "the biggest cultural event on the Nordics". This broadening of scope by the Book Fair also meant an intensification of societal and political trends and debates crossing and shaping the program of the fair. In 2016, when an extreme right-wing publisher was admitted to exhibit at the fair, the event became the center of an intense public, political and media debate on the boundaries of freedom of expression and on the opportunity for the Book Fair organizers to admit or expel this publisher. As the debate, which took place both on social and traditional media and was driven by journalists, public intellectuals and right-wing Twitter-users, has grown, the properties of the Book Fair as a media event have become increasingly salient. This attention has come to strengthen the status of the Book Fair in a direction where it was seen as an occasion to discuss and act upon wider trends in society and politics. And as such, the fair has become one of the events central for understanding and relating to the growing influence of the conservative party The Swedish Democrats and the right-wing movements in Swedish politics.

Our material is a witness to the transformation in which the Book Fair between 2016 and 2018 itself became not only an arena for but also a symbol of the wider societal development and of the questions surrounding freedom of expression, its boundaries in public space and possibilities to limit it in private arrangements. It can be argued that the debate around

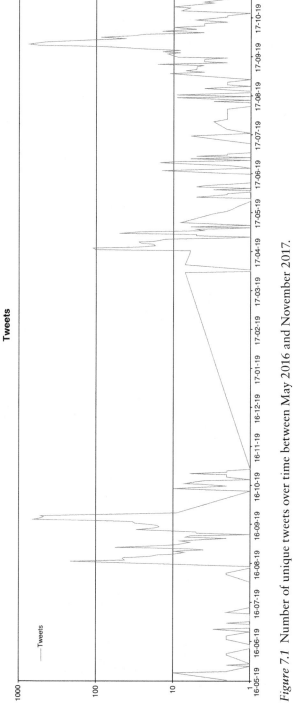

Figure 7.1 Number of unique tweets over time between May 2016 and November 2017.

New Times' participation at the fair and its connection to the alt-right's position in society in a sense 'hijacked' the Book Fair. The fair, by its attractiveness as a media event and by its contradictory decision making involving the New Times, has been forced to keep its doors wide open for other actors to politicize the until-then relatively downplayed and limited role of the fair in the field of politics. The fair has become the site of inter-actions, contestations and controversies that have both political and me-dial underpinnings and implications (Couldry et al. 2009, Zietsma et al. 2017). The effort by the organizers to regain control of the debate that threatened the image, reputation and status of the whole event as primar-ily a cultural event seems to have the opposite effect. The 'purification' of the fair by specifying and clarifying its core values and principles fol-lowed by the attempts to control the spin around the controversial video released by the Nordic Resistance Movement in 2017 misfired. The fair found itself in a situation where many people were dropping out and the Nordic Resistance Movement could carry out its manifestation and other activities reducing the chances of the Book Fair ever returning to its pre-New Times era.

What this case highlights, is how the intense involvement from media in a public controversy may have played a crucial role in transforming a field-level event from being a meeting place for actors within a spe-cific cultural industry to becoming a media event with potential to bring politics into the very core of the event (Hardy and Maguire 2010, Gross and Zilber 2020). Our illustration of how the debate hijacked by the alt-right's mobilization on social media, as well as by direct actions pushed the Gothenburg Book Fair into the field of politics points at three differ-ent mechanisms of such a transformation: temporally extending the field-level event; decentering the agency from the organizers to other centers of action and redefining the focus and eventually also the core of the event. How these mechanisms might play out in other contexts such as festivals, awards, conferences or carnivals – both individually and in parallel with other changes in the field of culture – calls for further empirical and the-oretical inquiry.

Notes

1 The material used for this chapter was originally gathered in co-operation with our colleagues Maria Grafström (Stockholm Center for Organizational Research), Jaan Grünberg (Uppsala University), Claes Thorén (University of Uppsala) and Karolina Windell (Stockholm Center for Organizational Re-search) as a part of a join project. The material was used with their consent.
2 Aftonbladet, 2016-08-23 (https://www.aftonbladet.se/kultur/a/p6lkaX/vanstern-maste-sluta-vingla).
3 Dagens Nyheter – 2017-08-18 (https://www.dn.se/arkiv/kultur/extremt-med-veten-taktik-varfor-far-nazister-tillstand-att-marschera-sa-centralt-i-svenska-stader/).

References

Anand, N. and B. C. Jones (2008). Tournament rituals, category dynamics, and field configuration: The case of the Booker Prize. *Journal of Management Studies*, 45(6): 1036–1060.

Báez-Montenegro, A. and M. Devesa-Fernández (2017). Motivation, satisfaction and loyalty in the case of a film festival: Differences between local and non-local participants. *Journal of Cultural Economics*, 41(2): 173–195.

Bennett, A. (2016). *The festivalization of culture*. Routledge. London.

Bolin, G. (2009). Media events, Eurovision and societal centers. In: Couldry, N. et al. (eds.) *Media events in a global age*. Routledge. London. Pp. 33–147.

Couldry, N. et al. (2009). *Media events in a global age*. Routledge. London.

Dayan, D. (2009). Beyond media events: Disenchantment, derailment, disruption. In: Couldry, N. et al. (eds.) *Media events in a global age*. Routledge. London. Pp. 35–43.

Ekström, K. M. (2019). *Museum marketization: Cultural institutions in the neoliberal era*. Routledge. London.

Grafström, M. and K. Windell (2019). *Självgenererande nyhetsjournalistik – när åsikter blir nyheter*. Stockholms centrum för forskning om offentlig sektor (SCORE). Stockholm.

Gross, T. and T. B. Zilber (2020). Power dynamics in field-level events: A narrative approach. *Organization Studies*, 41(10): 1369–1390.

Hardy, C. and S. Maguire (2010). Discourse, field-configuring events, and change in organizations and institutional fields: Narratives of DDT and the stockholm convention. *Academy of Management Journal*, 53(6): 1365–1392.

Jaeger, K. and R. J. Mykletun (2013). Festivals, identities, and belonging. *Event Management*, 17(3): 213–226.

Lampel, J. and A. D. Meyer (2008). Field-configuring events as structuring mechanisms: How conferences, ceremonies, and trade shows constitute new technologies, industries, and marketsguest editors introduction. *Journal of Management Studies*, 45(6): 1025–1035.

Leca, B. et al. (2015). Animated times: Critical transitions and the maintenance of field-configuring events. *Industry and Innovation*, 22(3): 173–192.

Mangematin, V. et al. (2014). *Disassembly and reassembly: An introduction to the Special Issue on digital technology and creative industries*. Elsevier. Amsterdam.

Marcus, G. E. (1995). Ethnography in/of the world system: The emergence of multi-sited ethnography. *Annual Review of Anthropology*, 24(1): 95–117.

Mazza, C. and J. S. Pedersen (2017). Chapter 11. Organizational adaptation and inverse trajectories: Two cities and their film festivals, (pp. 282–304). In Kruecken, G., Mazza, C., Meyer, R. & Walgenbach, P. (Eds.). *New themes in institutional analysis Topics and Issues from European Research*. Cheltenham UK; Northampton, MA, USA: Edward Elgar Publishing.

Merkel, U. (2013). *Power, politics and international events.: Socio-cultural analyses of festivals and spectacles*. Routledge. London.

Meyer, A. et al. (1998). The organization science Jazz festival: Improvisation as a metaphor for organizing. *Organization Science*, 9(5): 540–542.

Moeran, B. and J. Strandgaard Pedersen (2011). *Negotiating values in the creative industries: Fairs, festivals and competitive events*. Cambridge University Press. Cambridge.

Perry, B. et al. (2020). Cultural heritage entanglements: Festivals as integrative sites for sustainable urban development. *International Journal of Heritage Studies*, 26(6): 603–618.

Raviola, E. et al. (2019). Between market and culture: The case of the Gothenburg Book Fair. In: Ekström, K. (ed). *Museum marketization*, Routledge. Lonond. Pp. 61–77.

Roosvald, U. (2009). *Boken om Bokmässan*. Arena.

Rüling, C.-C. and J. S. Pedersen (2010). Film festival research from an organizational studies perspective. *Scandinavian Journal of Management*, 26(3): 318–323.

Schüssler, E. et al. (2014). On melting summits: The limitations of field-configuring events as catalysts of change in transnational climate policy. *Academy of Management Journal*, 57(1): 140–171.

Schüßler, E. and J. Sydow (2015). Organizing events for configuring and maintaining creative fields, (pp. 284–300). In Jones, C., Lorenzen, M. and Sapsed, J. (Eds.). *Oxford Handbook of Creative Industries*. Oxford Univeristy Press. Oxford.

Shay, A. (2014). *Choreographing identities: Folk dance, ethnicity and festival in the United States and Canada*. McFarland. Jefferson.

Sigala, M. (2018). Social media and the transformation of the festival industry: A typology of festivals and the formation of new markets, (pp. 102–110). In Mair, J. (Ed.) *The Routledge Handbook of Festivals*. Routledge. London.

Toraldo, M.-L. and G. Islam (2019). Festival and organization studies. *Organization Studies*, 40(3): 309–322.

Vermeulen, P., et al. (2016). Strategic responses to institutional complexity. *Strategic Organization*, 14(4): 277–286.

Watson, M. R. and N. Anand (2006). Award ceremony as an arbiter of commerce and canon in the popular music industry. *Popular Music*, 25(01): 41–56.

Weber, M. (2018). *Literary festivals and contemporary book culture*. Springer. New York.

Zietsma, C. et al. (2017). Field or fields? Building the scaffolding for cumulation of research on institutional fields. *Academy of Management Annals*, 11(1): 391–450.

8 Music Festivals and Educational Concerts in Spain

A Landscape between Tradition and Innovation

Ana Maria Botella Nicolás, Rosa Isusi-Fagoaga and Elena Castro-Martínez

Introduction

Studies on Cultural Festivals have been increasing in recent years and have primarily focused on the organisational, economic or media aspects (Del Barrio, Devesa & Herrero 2012; Rajaobelina, Dusseault & Ricard 2019). Furthermore, today's society and culture lives in a process of continuous transformation immersed in a constant technological and digital revolution that is continuously forced to innovate and adapt to new environments (Moreau 2015) and audiences (Aurier & Guintcheva 2015; Bollo, Da Milano, Garibaldi & Torch 2017).

In the digital era in which we live, this adaptation needs to link two necessary aspects such as creativity and technology (Strandgaard, Khaire & Slavich 2020).

Arts festivals as part of Cultural festivals are "condescended packages of artistic activity, with complex logistics, and a well-orchestrated funding system based on synergies between public subsidy, corporate sponsorship and own resources" (Klaic 2006).

The cultural festivals have been frequently studied from the point of view of management, sociology or anthropology (Getz 2010) to analyse their professional practice, their roles and impacts in society and culture and their relations with tourism. Also, there are some studies focused on popular music festivals (Snell 2005) or Opera (Luonila & Johansson 2016), but rarely from the musical or educational perspective, even having a direct and relevant impact on people, society, territory and culture (Robertson, Rogers & Leask 2009).

Among the different typologies that exist, we focus our attention in our speciality classical music festivals in turn contain various formats that are continuously evolving. The importance of classical music festivals was highlighted in the 2005 International Federation of Arts Council and Culture Agencies (IFACCA) Report d'Art No. 21, produced by the Budapest

DOI: 10.4324/9781003127185-11

Cultural Funding Observatory, which summarised the main purposes of festivals: the development of art forms, community audiences, tourism and economic regeneration, which means encouraging and expanding musicians, enhancing training, strengthening local or regional identity, attracting tourists, democratising access to culture. All this results in a favourable economic impact and improved social welfare.

These challenges suggest a series of questions on which we will reflect in the course of this paper: How can be these aims achieved? Would it be possible to achieve some of them by boosting educational programmes at festivals? How are the educational programmes at Spanish music festivals? How many of them offer it? What regulations have there been and are there in this respect? What is the place of technology in these festivals? And the autochthonous repertoire of Hispanic heritage?

Although the process of teaching and learning music usually takes place in formal, institutional contexts like schools, academies and universities, there are studies that show the transmission of music teaching and learning that takes place in a more informal environment, as music festivals (Snell 2005).

In Spain, as in other Western countries, there are a lot of cultural and music festivals. There is an interesting overview study with a case study conducted a little over a decade ago based on the National Institute of Performing Arts and Music data (Baltà & Hermosa 2007) and a study about culture and sustainable development that include an example of innovation at institutions and some proposal for new policies focused on Barcelona city and coordinated by J. Pascual (2009). The role played by festivals in the dissemination of works that are performed for the first time since their time has been analysed in the course of a study of early music production (Castro-Martínez, Recasens & Jiménez-Sáez 2013). There is also some study conducted from the point of view of the festival programmer (Sánchez-López 2016 & Sánchez-López 2018).

According to current data provided by the Music and Dance Documentation Center in the National Institute of Performing Arts and Music (IN-AEM), there are 594 music festivals in Spain, of which 45 are from early music, 41 from contemporary music, 9 are lyrical festivals, 16 from sacred music and 101 from jazz. The rest (more than 64%) are not classified or generic. Of the festivals as a whole, 404 have the international label and only 2 correspond to the specific area of education. Only 137 are promoted by a private institution (INAEM 2019). Although didactic programs and educational concerts are generalised in large auditoriums, these tend to focus on a repertoire of classical music and Romanticism with very few incorporating music prior to the 18th Century (Sánchez-López y Marín López 2009). However, this type of music, which is also known as historically informed music, also has its spaces, its audience and its festivals, usually linked to monumental cities or historical sites.

This chapter presents an explorative study that shows a landscape of music festivals in Spain and an analysis of Early Music Festivals in particular. The main objectives of this chapter are to contextualise Early Music Festivals and its educational concerts in the panorama of music festivals in Spain, focussing on the traditional and innovative aspects they present; to reflect some of the barriers and challenges they present and to make some proposals for the future to promote educational music activities.

In the absence of information on the educational programmes of Spanish music festivals, we have conducted our research of the analysis from the web pages and the Music and Dance Documentation Centre report to shed light on the current cultural situation in Spain, or at least to provide more up-to-date data reaching 2019 with a considerable sample.[1] We shall concentrate on music festivals to identify their characteristics and particularities, focusing on educational activities.

A landscape of music festivals and educational concerts in Spain: classical and early music

Main figures and characteristics

The *European Festivals Association* (EFA) has brought together music, dance, acting and multidisciplinary arts festivals since 1952. It currently includes 100 festivals and associations from 40 countries. This figure is very low in regard to the number of cultural events that are actually held. The Spanish Classic Music Festivals Association "*FestClásica*" is a full member. It was founded in 2007 with the goal of integrating the most important Music Festivals held in Spain in the early, classical and contemporary music disciplines. Thanks to these associations, the study "*Music Festivals, a changing world. An international comparison*" (2013), could be carried out, which shows the final results of a research project carried out over more than three years, jointly organised by Emmanuel Négrier (researcher at CNRS—France), Michel Guérin (Director of the Cultural Policy Observatory of the Wallonia-Brussels Federation), and Lluís Bonet (a professor at Barcelona University) (Négrier, Bonet & Guérin 2013).

Some artistic festivals are assigned the EFFE Label,[2] which is the European Seal of Quality for remarkable artistic festivals that prove their commitment to the field of arts, community participation and international openings. In the 2017–2018 season, 715 festivals were awarded this label. Nearly all disciplines can be found among these festivals, from circus to opera, including photography and folklore. In regard to music, a total of 25 Spanish festivals were awarded the label in 2017, including jazz, pop, rock, folk, electronic and early music, as well as classical music. In 2019, over 800 festivals in Europe were awarded this distinction.

Bonet and Cerreño (2013) state that it is not possible to understand the activity and evolution of festivals in Spain without first studying the role of townships and regional governments in the funding and management of these events. Spain is different from other countries in terms of the huge number of small festivals, i.e. the mean number of performances festival is 26, whereas in Europe it is 41. And, the mean audience is 18,300, whereas in Europe it is 23,700.

Classification and repertoire of Spanish music festivals

According to the data provided by the "*Centro de Documentación de Música y Danza*" [Music and Dance Documentation Centre], 594 festivals were held in Spain in 2019, of which 45 were early music, 41 contemporary music, 9 lyrical festival, 16 sacred music and 101 jazz festivals. The rest were not classified or were generic. Sixty-eight percent of the festivals are international, and only two were specifically declared as educational festivals. Only 23% were promoted by a private institution.

In the public Spanish Network of Theatres, Auditoriums, Circuits and Festivals, the data does not appear to be updated regularly either, since the most recent list of Fairs and Festivals dates back to 2017.

Methodology

The selection criteria we employed to select music festivals in Spain were as follows:[3]

a   Music festivals with more than two editions, i.e. held periodically
b   Events open to the public
c   Programming shows the specific music style
d   Geographically located in Spain
e   Time lag more than two days and less than one performing season
f   On-line access to information

Of the total 216 festivals held in Spain in our sample, 39 are specific early and Baroque music, but there are 58 which include a repertoire of early music, such as one of the most important festivals: the "*Quincena Musical*" in San Sebastián, which in 2019 reached its 80th edition and in 2017 was awarded the European EFFE label. Along with the above, the International Music and Dance Festival of Granada and the International Santander Festival are the ones that have had most editions. Table 8.1 shows a classification of classical music festivals, ordered by repertoire:

In order to carry out a detailed analysis of the educational programmes of the festivals, we propose classifying educational activities in festivals on the basis of the different target audience types, whether performers under tuition or the general public (see Table 8.2):

Table 8.1 Classical music festival classification by repertoire[4]

		Include repertoires of:			
2019 FESTIVALS	Festivals	Chamber music	Early music	Traditional music	Educational activities
Early and Baroque	39	39	39	4	22
Sound Art	7	2	0	0	6
Classical	55	47	0	2	20
Contemporary	14	14	0	0	7
Eclectic	19	16	9	3	6
Flamenco	7	0	0	0	0
Jazz	16	16	0	0	1
Lyrical	6	3	0	0	3
Mixed	43	43	43	4	20
Organ	10	6	6	1	2
Totals	n=216	186	97	14	87

Source: Own elaboration.

Table 8.2 Classification of educational activities in festivals

A. Active tuition targeting young performers
    a. Performing, composition or conducting course, etc.
    b. Master class or specialisation
    c. Group practical: orchestra, choir, chamber or management
B. Workshop for performers
C. Participative projects for performers
D. Receptive learning, targeting all types of public
    a. Educational concert
        Children and families
        Schools
        Concert for young people
        Social concert
    b. Prior conference
    c. Prior chats and dialogue
    d. Open rehearsals
D. Participative projects for performers
E. Programme notes

Source: Own elaboration.

Results and discussion

Educational activities

An analysis of the data in Table 8.3 shows that more than a 40% of festivals programme some kind of educational activity. If, for example, we keep to sound art festivals, understanding such as experimental, interdisciplinary

Table 8.3 Early music festivals with educational activities in 2019

Name of festival	City	Performance courses	Group practical	Workshops	Educational concerts	Prior conference	Chats, dialogue
FEMUBA—Albacete Baroque Music Festival	Albacete					YES	
Musicaloxa Organi Music Workshops and Cycle	Callosa d'en Sarrià	YES					
Sancti Iohannis Early Music Cycle	Sant Joan d'Alacant					YES	
Mare Musicum Early Music Festival	Roquetas de Mar	YES				YES	
Vélez Blanco Renaissance and Baroque Music Festival	Vélez Blanco	YES				YES	
Gijón Ancient Music Festival	Gijón	YES		YES		YES	YES
Abulensis, International Music Festival. Ávila	Ávila			YES		YES	
Tiana Antiga. Barcelona	Tiana					YES	
Peñíscola Ancient and Baroque International Music Festival	Peñíscola				YES		
Early Music Morella	Morella	YES	YES	YES	YES	YES	
Early Music Festival	Granada				YES	YES	
Castillo de Aracena Early Music Exhibition	Aracena	YES		YES			
Early Music Week	Artà				YES		YES
Úbeda & Baeza Early Music Festival	Úbeda & Baeza						YES
Molina Early Music Festival MOMUA	Molina de Segura	YES	YES		YES	YES	
Sierra Espuña International Early Music Festival	Aledo, Totana…		YES		YES		
Puerto de la Cruz Early and Baroque Music Festival	Puerto de la Cruz	YES				YES	
FEMAS Seville Early Music Festival	Seville					YES	
Early Music Festival	El Poblet		YES			YES	
"Gaspar Sanz" Guitar Festival	Calanda	YES				YES	
Valencia Early Music Festival	Valencia	YES					
Daroca Early Music Festival	Daroca	YES	YES				

Source: Own elaboration.

and contemporary art, this percentages reaches 85%, which is particularly significant given the promotion and projection that they require owing to their limited programme and wish to be better understood. If we choose the early music festivals cohort, this percentage is 56% (without mix and organ festivals):

Active tuition targeting young performers

From the first format of our classification, targeting young performers, we can find the example of the Daroca Early Music Festival and Course (Zaragoza), which in addition to specific instrument classes, also includes joint vocal and instrument classes. It reached its 41st edition in 2019, one of the longest ongoing festivals of its kind. The group practical sessions have included work on the following, according to the course leaflet:

> Fragments (scenes) of *"El robo de Proserpina y sentencia de Júpiter"*, an opera composed by Filippo Coppola (Maestro of the Chapel Royal of Naples) of a Spanish text by Manuel García Bustamante (Secretary of State and War of Viceroy Marquis of Los Vélez) and in accordance with the dramatic Spanish models. To a certain extent, it can be considered the first Spanish opera (entirely sung musical drama) of which a complete score has been conserved, with instrumental parts in addition to the voices and continuo.

All of this took place under the supervision of the harpsichord player and musicologist Luis Antonio González Marín, author of the critical edition of the work published by CSIC and of free on-line access. The Daroca Festival was the only venue for tuition on historical instruments in Spain for many years. In fact, early music studies were not officially taught until 2001 at the ESMUC in Barcelona (Higher School of Music of Catalonia) and at the MUSIKENE in San Sebastián (*Euskal Herriko goi-mailako musika ikastegia*/ Higher School of Music of the Basque Country). Previously, only a few higher music conservatories, such as the one in Seville, offered some specialities such as the viol or plucked string instruments. Therefore, this educational activity, parallel to recitals and concerts by the great performers of early music, had a major musical and cultural impact. Today, it is still an essential annual meeting point for specialist musicians.

Workshops for performers under tuition

The workshop, particularly at Jazz festivals, usually consists of training meetings on a specific style with specialists. After the theory class and dissertation, practical classes are held under the supervision of specialists. The difference between this and a Master Class is that it is performed in groups.

The *Abvlensis Festival. International Music Festival*, in its eighth year of ongoing homage to the composer Tomás Luis de Victoria, has joined the commemoration of the 5th Centenary of the first round the world tour by the Juan Sebastián Elcano, contextualising the figure of Victoria and her polyphony. Over two days, a children's workshop was held dedicated to the "*Seises*" choir, a choral society that Victoria was part of in Ávila cathedral in the 16th century.

Participative projects for performers under tuition

In the case of participative concerts, the most well-known is the Messiah by Georg Frienrich Häendel or Requiem by Wolgang Amadeus Mozart, both organised by the social funds of banks, but also other programmes such as *OCNE Adopt a Musician*[5] or *C@ntamos contigo*.[6] At early music festivals, the most similar thing is the group practical sessions that we mentioned earlier, although the participants are the students on the performance courses. We are unaware of any projects in which people external to the performance collaborate at an artistic event.

Receptive learning, targeting all types of audience

At educational concerts, the aim is to encourage active listening, to arouse curiosity and promote the learning of this type of art. It is increasingly more common for there to be a central festival and activity theme, within a given historical-social context. This allows different fields to be tangentially addressed, rather than being exclusively limited to the music itself, thus avoiding the isolation and ostracism commonly associated with classical music. Concerts of this type require some minimum inputs to be effective. The scenography may be minimal, but the lighting requires imagination and is absolutely essential. At the best auditoriums, there is an entire team including psychologists and pedagogues who are in charge of designing the educational projects, which must inevitably include the following items (Ortega 2009, p. 48).

a   Prior scenic plot and staging as the framework for the proposal
b   High performing quality by the performers
c   A coherent presentation and schedule between performances
d   An educational guide in conjunction with the concert, suited to the age of the attendees, and previously prepared by the teaching staff, where the artistic and educational goals are specified.

In addition to recognising music, the style and the composer or author through these experiences, the ultimate goal is for participants to enjoy the concert and to understand the protocols of auditoriums, getting used to them, thus doing away with the image and prejudices of elitism so closely associated with classical music. But particularly, to quote Aróstegui (2002, p. 3): "educational concerts are for music to be felt and lived rather than to be rationalised".

The *Peñíscola Festival*, one of the most remarkable, invited the researchers and multi-instrumentalists Emilio Villalba and Sara Marin to perform at the last edition:

> They have been working for more than eight years on concert work in Spain, Portugal and France, with performances combining music, theatre and narratives. In their career they have reconstructed over forty historical instruments with the help of lute-makers, converting their shows in a genuine sound museum on stage: violas, vihuelas, psalteries, hurdy-gurdies, clavicymbalums, organettos [...] With painstakingly designed staging and laborious reconstruction work and musical arrangements, their concerts include a selection of pieces ranging from Al Andalus music and traditional Sephardic cancioneros, to medieval codex music prior to reaching music from the Spanish Renaissance.
>
> (2019 festival programme, p. 11)

In line with the conference format is the case of the *Urdaibaiko Organoak—Joxe Mari Eguileor* Festival, which, although not a specific early music festival, is a good example to highlight transversal organ festivals in different ways, for the amount of its score literature and the relevance of its instrumental heritage. The festival is organised by the Bizkaia Council, and is held in different towns with historical organs. It has been one of the acclaimed tourist attractions for several years. The conference, or exhibition, is produced by the artistic director, Benantzi Bilbao, and features some of the most emblematic instruments. As an introduction, the workings of organs are briefly explained, and the attendees are allowed to view the inside of the "secret", i.e. the wooden box where the pipes are fitted, to see the inner pipes and all the bellows mechanisms. Afterwards, by performing some pieces, the singularity of the workings of this instrument are shown, using most of the register, and particularly the "artillery", a feature of Iberian organs.

Programme notes

Finally, showing and setting on record the importance of programme notes for concerts is considered important. It is an essential requirement, particularly when dealing with early music, that the programme notes on the musical performance properly explain the context of the work and its authors, emphasising what the artist actually wanted the audience to perceive. We highlight the exceptional case of the *Úbeda & Baeza Early Music Festival (FeMAUB)*, which this year reached its 24th edition, and which annually publishes its programme written by professionals, with data and details regarding the recovery of our musical heritage. The attending public therefore have the necessary tools to discover the authors and performed work, which is not at all common in concert halls. This festival was awarded the European EFFE label in 2017, and was recognised as the Best Cultural Institution of Andalusia.

Some barriers to solve

One of the main objectives of festival organisers and managers is to ensure proper, outreaching dissemination of their cultural products. In this sense, one of the great problems faced by classical music festivals is the lack of audience compared to other types of more contemporary music festivals. To some extent, this is due to the public's lack of knowledge on the kind of repertoire of past eras, which is not the case and is not questioned in the visual arts for example. Museums showing paintings from the past often have a regular public, even if they are not experts on the history of art. The public can visit a museum alone and see the works or take a hand guide to understand them better, but without musical knowledge, they have no access to the music, the intermediary (the performer) and the performance (the concert) are needed to foster people's knowledge and appreciation of the music.

Lack of public

In order to analyse the classical music festival panorama in Spain, looking at the significance of these concerts within culture is an interesting exercise, with the current attendance figures on the one hand, and on the other, the lack of attendance at classical concerts and the main reasons to explain this. The reason is that attendees, however frequent or sporadic, are already knowledgeable on classical music. If we consult the Cultural Statistics Yearbook (Ministry of Culture and Sport 2019, p. 225), it is striking to see the declining interest in classical music over a period spanning just four years, as can be seen in Table 8.4.

The main reason for not attending classical music concerts is the lack of interest. This percentage increased from 29.2% to 41.4% of the population in just four years. This trend is also observed in the rest of cultural activities. In a comparison with the 2009 data (Ministry of Culture and Sport 2009, p. 196), this figure was similar at 42.8%. In other words, in a 10-year period, the same trend in these values is maintained (see Table 8.5).

This is a fact that public creation has had very little or no repercussion on, if there has in fact been any investment in cultural incentives at all. The crisis of 2008 and subsequent years of alleged economic recovery have not helped to improve or increase any of these data. Apart from this point of view, it is important to highlight attendance at classical music concerts. The *SGAE Yearbook* (2019, p. 14) describes:

Table 8.4 Main reasons for not attending cultural events in percentage of total population (2015 and 2019)

	It is expensive		There is not much choice in my area		I prefer to listen to it on the radio / watch it on TV, video, Internet		Leaving home is difficult	
	2015	2019	2015	2019	2015	2019	2015	2019
Attending cultural events								
Theatre	19.0	14.7	14.0	15.2	1.3	1.7	7.4	5.3
Opera	13.4	9.9	10.3	9.8	1.2	1.5	6.0	4.0
Zarzuela	12.3	6.7	10.7	9.3	1.3	1.2	6.0	3.8
Ballet/Dance	13.8	9.8	11.4	10.5	1.3	1.8	6.4	4.5
Circus	15.0	8.2	13.6	13.6	1.1	1.3	6.4	3.8
Classical Music Concerts	14.3	10.7	11.1	10.7	2.1	2.8	6.8	4.6
Modern Music Concerts	21.3	17.8	14.7	14.8	2.7	3.2	8.1	5.8
Cinema	28.9	25.5	9.0	8.9	10.2	8.3	9.2	7.4
Bull Fights	8.1	4.8	6.6	6.1	1.8	1.1	4.6	2.6

	No time		No interest		Nobody to go with	
	2015	2019	2015	2019	2015	2019
Attending cultural events						
Theatre	23.4	25.4	22.5	27.6	3.0	2.4
Opera	21.4	18.0	33.5	47.7	2.2	1.8
Zarzuela	21.5	17.0	34.4	53.1	2.3	1.7
Ballet / Dance	22.1	20.8	31.8	43.4	2.4	1.8
Circus	22.9	18.5	30.2	46.2	2.8	2.4
Classical Music Concerts	23.4	20.4	**29.2**	**41.4**	2.7	2.1
Modern Music Concerts	24.7	26.8	18.0	22.9	3.1	2.3
Cinema	25.5	31.3	11.2	12.1	3.5	2.3
Bull Fights	15.9	12.7	39.5	61.2	2.1	1.3

Source: Own elaboration based on data from the Survey on Cultural Habits and Practices in Spain of the MCUD (Ministry of Culture and Sport).

The growing trend continues for the fourth year on the run, observing increases in the three indicators, despite which the values of 2008 have not been reached. Comparing the 2018 and 2008 results, there is a downturn of 11.7% in the number of concerts, 7.4% in attendance figures and 3.1% in proceeds. In 2018 there were 15,776 classical music concerts (…) of which, 64.1% were free, which is equivalent to 10,119 concerts, and the remaining 35.9% entailed entrance fees, i.e. 5657 concerts.

Table 8.5 People according to main reasons for not attending cultural events in percentage of total population in 2009

	It is expensive	There is not much choice	Prefer to watch/hear it on TV / video / radio /PC	Leaving home is difficult	No time	No interest	Nobody to go with
Theatre	14.6	16.0	2.2	4.6	20.8	32.5	2.4
Opera	10.1	10.7	1.5	3.7	15.4	49.2	2.0
Zarzuela	9.6	11.1	1.7	3.7	15.4	49.9	2.0
Ballet/Dance	10.2	12.1	1.8	3.8	16.7	46.3	2.2
Classical Music Concerts	10.9	13.0	2.1	4.7	17.7	**42.8**	1.9
Modern Music Concerts	15.6	17.8	3.0	5.4	22.6	27.9	1.9
Cinema	21.3	10.4	11.2	8.3	28.6	15.6	2.3

Source: Own elaboration based on data from the Survey on Cultural Habits and Practices in Spain of the MCUD (Ministry of Culture and Sport).

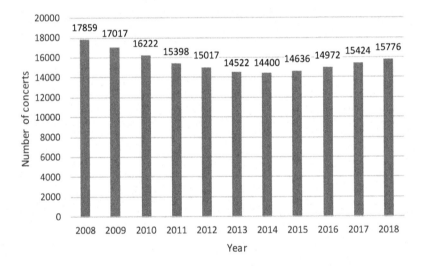

The General Society of Authors and Publishers of Spain makes no specific reference to early music. Owing to the structural characteristics (small groups of performers), we assume it is included in the chamber music figures. On analysing these statistics, we can conclude that 40% of the population does not take part in any classical music cultural activity, and that following the crisis, the choice at musical institutions has not recovered. It must also be pointed out that care should be taken with the data in the surveys. As Ariño (2018) points out, different procedures are used when compiling data making standard comparisons with other countries rather difficult. This researcher is convinced that

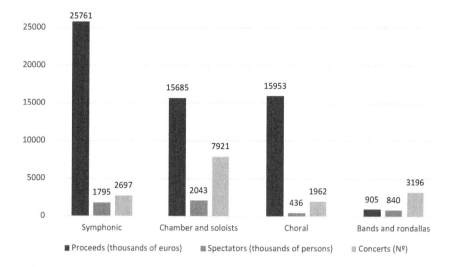

in participation outside the home, the public no longer conform to attending specific events, but now demand an involvement in significant experiences. Therefore, the people in charge of programming these events need to implement multi-product strategies [...] or multi-function events.

(Ariño 2018, pp. 44–45)

He also points out that increasing attendance at cultural events does not depend so much on reducing the price of tickets, but more about adapting to the concepts today's public demand. And, he particularly emphasises, among other significant issues, strong action during primary school education to encourage public attendance. In other words, committing to education in formal and informal contexts, both inside and outside the educational system.

Lack of educational programmes

Several music festivals, auditoriums and public orchestras programme educational concerts or functions. Nevertheless, more often than not these are not included in this database. Moreover, it is increasingly more common to find talks or conferences before concerts that exercise this illustrative function. In many cases, the educational programmes are run by staff of the auditoriums but not by education specialists. Nevertheless, these actions intending to be educational, are sometimes isolated cases providing no continuity afterwards, or, at the other end of the scale, are extremely successful when they are led by celebrities, such as the talks by the television presenter Ramon Gener at "*Les Arts*" in Valencia.

Main challenges

Some of the challenges that Festivals face in today's society are the creation of new audiences, the renewal of the repertoire, the increase of educational programmes and the use of digital technologies.

Create new audiences

One of the biggest challenges that cultural festivals face, and the most significant common denominator, is generating new audiences, who, for Javier Estrella, director of the Aranjuez Early Music Festival, is one of the main strategies to pursue. "People have to be given the chance to listen to different music" (cited in Bonet 2011, p. 37). In order to reach them (the audiences), gateways need to be provided, and psychological, social and educational barriers that sometimes prevent this must be broken down. A festival usually has more freedom to break down those barriers than an auditorium or other type of permanent venue, but the suitable bridges need to be designed for each type of potential audience.

Indeed, generating new audiences[7] entails three main dimensions: educational, artistic and marketing. In this document, we shall discuss the educational side of this subject.

Within the framework of the "4th Cultural and Citizenship Meeting" of 2008 by the Ministry of Culture and Sport, the White Book on Creating, Forming and Developing Culture Audiences[8] was published. The members of the music sector panel debated a number of proposals which are outlined as follows:

a   To boost the subject of music at primary and secondary schools, providing teachers with the necessary, interdisciplinary tools to be able to offer true, useful content in musical education at primary and secondary level.
b   To promote the feeling of propriety of classical music. To update the "census" of our cultural heritage, extending it to from classical culture to present day culture.
c   To improve the relationship between programmers and artists with teachers through periodical meetings in order to adapt content to the changing educational reality.
d   To implement a subject on musical information and critic in Master's courses on cultural management.
e   To create a transversal university training programme in generating audiences for professionals in all sectors linked to education and culture.

This declaration of intentions would really be suitable justification to implement educational programmes in each of the social segments. In fact, in 2019, the *Official Journal of the Basque Country*,[9] for example, published subsidies for projects and activities that had the aim of creating, securing and increasing cultural audiences in the Basque Country. These grants not only entailed creating resources but also the need for ideas and projects to encourage cultural practices.

Renew the repertoire

Early music festivals programme musical repertoires up to the 18th century, inclusive. The music is performed on instruments made as they were at that time, using methods based on historically documented information, although it would be rather Utopian to think that it is performed as it was in the past, attempts are made to be as true as possible to how music was created at that time, in other words, with an historical basis for artistic decision-making which has as its goal the re-creation of performances as close as possible to the composer's original conception (Lawson & Stowell 1999).

Programming unknown works for the public entails a certain risk for festivals, and in most of early music festivals, performances of known works are combined with "recovered" or recently transcribed works. That is why they work as events to recover musical heritage. This is particularly true at festivals that are linked to musicology research centres.

This brings us to tangentially review the offer of proposals by early music groups and one of their major achievements: recovery of musical heritage, which is what Ariño and Llopis (2017) called "*cultural patrimonisation*" as an instigator or motive of interest. This new outlook on tradition, i.e. contemporary cultural "*patrimonisation*" and the correlative upturn in cultural tourism, permits mobilising tangible and intangible assets as cultural heritage. This is believed to be one of the main innovations that the collective identifying traits have driven on the one hand, and on the other, directing tourism towards this type of consumption of cultural heritage. Along these lines, as yet we do not have any information on whether or not this is currently being implemented, but educational concerts could be a vehicle to improve knowledge about Spanish composers, by programming their works in concerts of this type, which would serve two purposes: promoting better musical culture in general, whilst at the same time disseminating autochthonous musical heritage of enormous wealth.

Increase the educational programmes

Ross (2012, p. 289), a The New Yorker critic, highlighted the isolation of art that the philosopher John Dewey published in 1934:

> The most unavoidable problem with contemporary music education is that many teachers have trained in the monastic culture of music conservatories, where technical command precludes all else, and any discussions on the social, political or spiritual significance of music is ignored.

The pleasure and delight of simply listening to music must be added to the above. Performance is strongly driven, but encouraging public attendance or audition is not, which in itself is paradoxical. In this sense, early music was a catalyst for concert formats, from the repertoire that was renewed to include work until the 18th century, the instruments that were reconstructed following the organology of the day, the costumes in line with the historical context, the concert halls in emblematic venues, moving to churches and castles, or the programmes that have included a wide, attractive explanation to contextualise the repertoire and its performance. All of this is done with the goal of being as true to the epoch as possible, and in turn to enhance a unique, comprehensive experience for the audience.

In the introduction, we saw the need for education in the creation of new audiences and in innovation on cultural practices. Parallel to concerts, festivals organise additional entertainment or specific educational activities for the attending public. We shall now move on to discuss them in an attempt to categorise and value them.

Use of digital technologies

Classical music festivals in Spain have hardly adapted to the use of digital technologies and, in general, remain stuck in tradition. Only a few smaller festivals, especially some Early Music Festivals, have adapted and are now streaming live concerts (e.g. *Capella de Ministrers* Group), especially after de COVID-19 pandemic. This pandemic has been a cultural shock (OCDE 2020), but at least in Spain, some non-governmental entities contribute to the diffusion of music using new technologies (e.g., the FBBVA).[10] There are also private channels that try to help the layman to better understand musical works[11] to which it is possible to subscribe.

Conclusions

Throughout these pages, we have outlined a current panorama of music festivals in Spain, focusing on didactic programmes of classical music festivals in general and Early Music Festivals in particular. Traditional and innovative aspects have been analysed and the barriers and challenges in today's society have been pointed out. The first results indicate that there is a considerable lack of didactics in Spanish festivals that are capable of proposing a real, applicable educational programme model that can form new audiences in today's society. Those responsible for these festivals are likely to receive advice from teaching professionals to optimise existing programs and launch new ones in order to train new audiences. It seems that festival organisers have become aware that in order to fill auditoriums, as in times gone by with the presence of people, festivals need to offer something different, something innovative, formative, that exceeds the immediate consumption of music over the Internet or digital devices and that favours the understanding and enjoyment of the sound phenomenon, especially when the style of music dates back to by-gone times.

Another aspect to take into account in Music Festivals, and especially in early Music Festivals, is the lack of attention to an autochthonous repertoire, i.e., of Hispanic heritage. This heritage brings together both Spanish and Latin American music. In some cases, the promotion of Hispanic heritage has proven to be an innovative and motivating aspect, not only for performers and programmers but also for the public. This contributes to the renewal of the repertoire, nowadays fundamentally based on the canon of Central European music of the 18th and 19th centuries. In the case of Early music festivals, for the performance of works from the past in modern times, collaboration between musicologists and performers is necessary. This work team also needs educators and pedagogues to present this material in an attractive way to the public in our society and indeed to create new audiences.

The people responsible for music festivals, especially Early Music Festivals, need to receive advice from teaching professionals to optimise existing programs and launch new ones in order to train new audiences. For that purpose, festivals must offer something different, something innovative, formative, that exceeds the immediate consumption of music over the Internet or digital devices and that favours the understanding and enjoyment of the sound phenomenon, especially when the style of music dates back to by-gone times.

The main conclusions indicate that there is a considerable lack of didactics in Spanish festivals, that propose an applicable and real educational programme model that can form new audiences. In this sense, another important challenge is to incorporate digital technologies into educational concerts, and not only in the dissemination of music. Those responsible for these festivals are likely to receive advice from teaching professionals to optimise existing programs and launch new ones in order to train new audiences in the Digital Age. It seems that festival organisers have become aware that in order to fill auditoriums, as in times gone by with the presence of people, festivals need to offer something different, something innovative, formative, that exceeds the immediate consumption of music over the Internet or digital devices and that favours the understanding and enjoyment of the sound phenomenon, especially when the style of music dates back to by-gone times.

In addition, some proposals have been made for an increase, which would contribute to the improvement of the educational programmes of the festivals and to creating new, necessary audiences. Attention was also drawn to the need to use digital technologies to adapt classical music festivals to the needs of today's society, essential during and probably also after the COVID-19 pandemic, but this is another subject for further study.

Some reflections and proposals for the enhancement and improvement of educational programmes

Including educational concerts in festivals is ultimately an initiative by the artistic programmer. But it is true, however, that this is promoted and incentivised through financial grants that are offered within the framework of cultural policies. In 2019, the Ministry of Culture published a set of programme support grants for lyrical, music and dance festivals, exhibitions, competitions and conferences for one hundred thousand euros, to a total of six million euros. These grants supporting festivals mainly value the cultural interest of the festival, the profile and scope of the project, the economic trajectory and viability, and also if commissioning composition is considered or musical premieres, if transitional musical genre is recovered, the number of national and international participants, their diversity from different regions, the number of editions, awards and recognition, and also the social impact. In other words, according to the Resolution by the National Performing Arts Institute, through which the dance, lyrical and music grants were published for 2019, in order to award the grants, the contribution of the projects or activities to the territorial rebalancing of the choice of dance, singing or music in Spain was valued, the number of potential target audiences, and the social profitability of the project and its possible impact on underprivileged groups or those at risk of social exclusion. Likewise, contribution of the project to the excellence in education or dissemination in the community was taken into account, and its role in generating and consolidating new audiences. In other words, 10% of the valuation criteria is for social impact, and therefore festivals are encouraged to promote educational concerts or activities that generate or consolidate new audiences.

On reviewing the grants prior to the economic crisis,[12] 2008 or 2009, the resolution added a specific chapter for the entities: Support for educational lyrical and music project programmes aimed at generating audiences and improving education in the sector. All these actions had to be justified by means of certificates by a duly accredited copyright manager, or by means of a certificate issued by the owners or managers of the theatres, auditoriums or institutions where the performances or projects were held. This means that INAEM has been supporting entities, and not only festivals to develop and promote educational programmes for ten years. In other words, there was full support for educational programmes, rather than a percentage of the total. A comparative study would be required to confirm that the results were as wanted in order to justify this variation, or that because of the crisis it was appropriate to give stability to the festivals and not the entities. But it is true that ultimately just five grants were approved for the overall amount of 36,000.00 Euros in 2008 and 2 in 2009 for 15,000.00 Euros. We do not know the specific weight of the final value for the festivals held in 2019.

Our proposal is to apply the 2009 criteria with specific amounts for educational projects, but for festivals, i.e. to specifically finance educational concerts, taking into account the following criteria:

a Performing quality of the artists
b Social, cultural and educational interest
c Budgetary balance
d Social profitability
e Recovery or creation of heritage
f Artistically innovative in format or technology
g Professional, interdisciplinary team.

This would establish some minimum guarantees for educational projects, which could be in-house production by each festival, or through contracting a company or musical group, providing that the minimum quality requirements are met. These public grants do not exempt festivals from the contribution they must make to generating new audiences through their budgets. Indeed, subsidies are support and resolutions are policies, although they can be continuously adapted. These educational projects are not exclusively educational concerts targeting young people or families, but they can be designed in different formats, as we have seen earlier, such as conferences, workshops and programme notes.

Finally, attention must be brought to the fact that one of the huge resources of festivals are the early music groups and the variety of programmes they offer. It is only fair to value the marvellous current status that several Spanish chamber music and soloists have owing to their international outreach and recognised prestige and work, some of whom have been awarded the National Music Prize (*Seville Baroque Orchestra, Hesperion XXI, Accademia del Piacere, La Ritirata, MUSIca AlcheMIca, Al Ayre Español*, among others) or international awards such as the *Orphée d'Or de la Académie du Disque Lyrique* in France (awarded by *La Grande Chapelle*).

Notes

1 List of samples consulted in our sampling: https://www.anamariabotellanicolas.com/2020/07/18/mapa-interactivo-festivales-de-musica-clasica-en-espana/
2 https://www.festivalfinder.eu/effe-label
3 We have not included programmes that are entirely a band or choir, because of their amateurish nature, although they are extremely necessary particularly because of their educational, social and entertaining function.
4 Website queries 2019 information. Classification: EARLY AND BAROQUE: Historical instruments / SOUND ART: Only sound art and new vanguard / CLASSICAL: Does not include historical instruments or contemporary music / CONTEMPORARY: Contemporary and current music / ECLECTIC: Includes Mixed, Sound Art, Jazz, Flamenco, Dance and other types / FLAMENCO: Only flamenco / JAZZ: Jazz Music / LYRICAL: Vocal recitals / MIXED: Early,

Baroque, classical, contemporary, chamber and choral music / ORGAN: Focussing on the organ.
5 http://ocne.mcu.es/explora/adopta-un-musico
6 http://ocne.mcu.es/programacion/historico/18–19/c-ntamos-contigo
7 At the faculty of Social and Human Sciences at Deusto University, there is a degree on: Expert in Audience Strategies https://socialesyhumanas.deusto.es/cs/Satellite/socialesyhumanas/es/instituto-estudios-ocio/formacion-permanente
8 https://culturayciudadania.culturaydeporte.gob.es/libro-blanco.html
9 https://www.euskadi.eus/ayuda_subvencion/2019/publicos/web01-tramite/es/
10 https://www.youtube.com/watch?v=hMXe6OF3phM
11 https://www.youtube.com/channel/UCa3DVlGH2_QhvwuWlPa6MDQ
12 For example: Official State Journal No. 50 of 27/02/2008, RESOLUTION of 8th February 2008 and Official State Journal No. 159 of 02/07/2009, Resolution of 18th June 2009, criteria on page 55496.

References

Aurier, P & Guintcheva, G 2015, 'The dynamics of emotions in movie consumption: A spectator-centred approach', *International Journal of Arts Management*, 17(2), pp. 5–18.

Ariño, A 2018, 'Perspectivas sobre la participación cultural en Europa', En VV.AA. *Observatorio Social de "la Caixa". Participación, cultural y bienestar. ¿Qué nos dicen los datos?* (pp. 43–46), Obra social "La Caixa".

Ariño, A & Llopis, R 2017, *Las prácticas culturales en la Comunidad Valenciana*. Valencia: Generalitat Valenciana. https://www.academia.edu/34925454/Las_prácticas_culturales_en_la_Comunidad_Valenciana

Aróstegui, J L 2002, *Una Educación Musical Postmoderna: Los Conciertos Didácticos*, Granada, LI Festival Internacional de Música y Danza de Granada.

Baltà, J & Hermosa, I 2007, 'Spain', in D. Ilczuk & D. Kulikowska (eds.), *Festival Jungle, Policy Desert? Festival Policies of Public Authorities in Europe. Comparative Report*. Warsaw. https://www.ics.ulisboa.pt/file/5117/download?token=oFLzaR-W

Bollo, A, Da Milano, C, Gariboldi, A & Torch, C 2017, *Final Report. Study on Audience Development - How to Place Audiences at the Centre of Cultural Organisations*. Brussels: European Commission. https://op.europa.eu/en/publication-detail/-/publication/cc36509d-19c6-11e7-808e-01aa75ed71a1

Bonet, L 2011, 'Tipologías y modelos de gestión de festivales', in L Bonet & H Schargorodsky, (dirs), *La gestión de festivales escénicos: conceptos, miradas y debates* (pp. 41–87), Gescènic, Barcelona.

Bonet, L & Carreño, T 2013, 'The context of music festivals in Spain', in E Négrier, L Bonet & M Guérin (eds.), *Music Festivals, a Changing World: An International Comparison* (pp. 182–192), Paris, Michel de Maule.

Castro-Martínez, E, Recasens, A & Jiménez-Sáez, F 2013, 'Innovation systems in motion: An early music case', *Management Decision*, 51(6), pp. 1276–1292.

Del Barrio, M J, Devesa, M & Herrero, L C 2012, 'Evaluating intangible cultural heritage: The case of cultural festivals', *City, Culture and Society, 3*, pp. 235–244.

Getz, D 2010, 'The nature and scope of festival studies', *International Journal of Event Management Research, 5*(1), pp. 1–47.

INAEM 2019, Instituto Nacional de las Artes Escénicas y de la Música. http://www.musicadanza.es/

Klaic, D 2006, 'Festival', *Lexicon, Performance Research*, 4(11), pp. 54–55.

Lawson, C & Stowell, R 1999, *The Historical Performance of Music*, Cambridge, Cambridge University Press.

Luonila M & Johansson T 2016, 'Reasons for networking in institutionalized music productions: Case studies of an opera house and a music festival', *International Journal of Arts Management, 18*(3), pp. 50–66.

Luonila, M, Suomi, K & Johansson, M 2016, 'Creating a stir: The role of word of mouth in reputation management in the context of festivals', *Scandinavian Journal of Hospitality and Tourism, 16*(4), pp. 461–483.

Ministerio de Cultura y Deporte 2009, *Anuario de estadísticas culturales*, Secretaría general técnica. https://es.calameo.com/read/0000753359ad1b60c932f.

Ministerio de Cultura y Deporte 2019, *Anuario de estadísticas culturales*, Secretaría general técnica. https://es.calameo.com/read/0000753351cd7416c7edb.

Moreau F 2013, 'The disruptive nature of digitization: The case of the recorded music industry', *The International Journal of Arts Management, 15*(2), pp. 18–31.

Négrier, E, Bonet, L, & Guérin, M (eds.) 2013, *Music Festivals, a Changing World: An International Comparison*, Paris, Michel de Maule.

OCDE 2020, *Culture Shock: COVID-19 and the Cultural and Creative Sector*. www.ocde.org

Ortega, M C 2009, '¿Qué es un concierto didáctico?', *Papeles del festival de música española de Cádiz, 4*, pp. 45–55.

Pascual, J (coord.) 2009, *Culture and Sustainable Development: Examples of Institutional Innovation and Proposal of a New Cultural Policy Profile*, Barcelona, Ajuntament. With the support of UNESCO.

Rajaobelina, L, Dusseault, P, & Ricard, L 2019, 'The mediating role of place attachment in experience and word of mouth: The case of music and film festivals', *International Journal of Arts Management, 21*(2), pp. 43–54.

Robertson, M, Rogers, P, & Leask, A 2009, 'Progressing socio-cultural impact evaluation for festivals', *Journal of Policy Research in Tourism, Leisure and Events, 1*(2), pp. 156–169.

Ross, A 2012, *Escucha esto*, Barcelona, Seix Barral.

Sánchez-López, V & Marín López, J 2009, 'Los conciertos didácticos del Festival de Música Antigua de Úbeda y Baeza: cinco años de experiencias educativas (2002–2006)', *Eufonía: Didáctica de la Música, 45*, pp. 117–123.

Sánchez-López, V 2016, 'Los conciertos didácticos desde la mirada del programador?', in M. Rodríguez López (ed.), *Didáctica de la música: de la investigación a la práctica* (pp. 77–92), Almería, Procompal.

Sánchez-López, V 2018, 'Programación musical y educación para la infancia: los proyectos educativos del Centro Cultural de Belén y la Fundación Calouste Gulbenkian de Lisboa', *Per Musi*, Belo Horizonte, UFMG, pp. 1–22.

Snell, K 2005, 'Music education through popular music festivals: A study of the OM Music Festival in Ontario, Canada', *Action, Criticism, and Theory for Music Education*, 4(2), pp. 1–35.

Strandgaard Pedersen, J, Khaire, M & Slavich, B (eds.) 2020, *Technology and Creativity: Production, Mediation and Evaluation in the Digital Age*, Palgrave Macmillan Publishers Ltd., Basingstoke.

Part III

Value and Impacts of Cultural Festivals at Local and Regional Level

9 (The Economics of) Cultural Festivals in the Digital Age

An Analysis of the Comics Publishing Industry

Elisa Salvador, Elena Castro-Martínez and Pierre-Jean Benghozi

Introduction

Festivals are one of the most diffused examples of living production in the cultural and creative industries (CCIs) (Frey, 1994; Caves, 2000; Luonila, Johansson, 2016). However, up to the 1990s "the *study of temporary events such as Festivals, markets, fairs and other ephemeral events*" was relatively limited[1] (Benghozi, Nénert, 1995: 66). In recent years, festivals have attracted increased attention and increased in number (del Barrio et al., 2012; Baez-Montenegro, Devesa-Fernandez, 2017). Moeran and Strandgaard Pedersen (2011) highlight that fairs, festivals, and competitive events are field-configuring events and enable ritualized industry practices. Several studies investigate various aspects related to the organization, management, and success of these events (cf. among others, del Barrio et al., 2012; Snowball, 2013; Vestrum, 2014; Wong et al., 2015; Dantas, Colbert, 2016; Baez-Montenegro, Devesa-Fernandez, 2017).

Since the earliest cultural economic and management studies, there have been several works that have focused on music and film festivals (cf. Section 1) which are the longest established festivals. They represent popular activities and are well-suited to public performances, events and shows to which these temporary events can be linked. However, few works look at festivals related to less popular sectors such as publishing. The aim of this contribution is to investigate these smaller events by conducting a case study of comics festivals to identify the nature of the dynamics and strategies at work. We consider their location, how the offers are structured and their strategic positioning in the publishing industry by examining the impact of two selected festivals organized in two small cities in France and Spain: the comics festivals in Angers[2] (France) and Avilés[3] (Spain). Detailed analysis of the characteristics of these selected festivals along their various editions, shows in which extent they clear up the structuration of a multi-faced economic model, and how they are linked specifically to the characteristics of the CCI sector.

DOI: 10.4324/9781003127185-13

On the one hand, festivals constitute specific forms of territorial economic energization. Whatever their size, they contribute to the attractiveness and identity of the place hosting them through the local anchoring of cultural activities. On the other hand, the organization of festivals around a variety of activities – in our case about comics – highlights the possibility of conceiving innovative formats linked to local cultural or craft traditions.

From a methodological point of view, we rely on an analysis of public documentation on the festivals (i.e. promotional material, festival programs, media, and press articles available on the Internet) which allows identification of their main characteristics. We systematically explored this content. We also conducted face-to-face interviews between July 2016 and April 2019 with the festival organizers to complement the framework by identifying perceptions, comments, and precise development strategies fulfilled in the event organization.

The chapter is structured as follows: Section 1 provides an overview of festivals as events presented in the management literature; Section 2 offers a brief description of the selected festivals in France and Spain and Section 3 provides a discussion and some concluding remarks.

The literature on festivals: a brief overview

There are several reasons for the economic revival and local/regional interest in festivals. First, they support tourism developments and contribute to the economic revival of towns and territories. Since the 1960s, hundreds of festivals take place in Provence (France) during the summer and there is a large stream of research in cultural economics which focuses on the impact of these events (see below). They are seen as providing opportunities for small cities to establish an identity and acquire a visibility that otherwise might be difficult. The recent explosion in festivals could be related also to their experiential nature which distinguishes them from the increasing digital diffusion of culture. According to Luonila and Johansson (2016: 53), Festivals *"promote celebration and a sense of community and produce experiences for a wide range of audiences"*. The presence of multiple festivals around the world with different cultural and creative focuses is well known. In 1994, Frey highlighted the rapid growth in the number of classical music and opera festivals. Frey (1986, 1994) was one of the first authors to investigate the festival phenomenon in depth. He focused on music festivals analyzing the economics and main characteristics of the Salzburg Festival. Also, several studies of cultural practices highlight a revival of amateur participation, a vibrant but often ignored aspect (Rajaobelina et al., 2019).

The motivations for cultural event and festival attendance have been the subject of several studies. For instance, Wong et al. (2015) focus on food festivals and highlighted the effects of quality, emotion, image, and satisfaction on loyalty to the event. Similarly, Baez-Montenegro and Devesa-Fernandez (2017) identify the factors that attract new festival visitors while retaining previous audiences. They focus on the case of a film festival and highlight the role of and relations among motivation, satisfaction, and loyalty.

Most research focuses on music, television, and film festivals. For example, Vestrum (2014) looks at music festivals and the embeddedness of community ventures within the local community. Luonila and Johansson (2016) examine the reasons for networking through the case study of an opera house and a music festival. Dantas and Colbert (2016) investigate the differentiating factors and longevity of the Festival de Lanaudière (Quebec), Canada's largest classical music festival. Vecco and Srakar (2017) estimated the effects of two Slovenian jazz music festivals on tourism inflows and the economic resilience of the host cities. Benghozi and Nénert (1995) analyze the Cannes film festival through a commercial and artistic logic: they were the first scholars to conduct a systematic analysis of the economics and the management of this international film event.

Food festivals also are important in rural and marginal areas and contribute to development, branding and local identity building. Local food is used to create a kind of "place branding" to enable the survival of rural localities (Blichfeldt and Halkier, 2014). Del Barrio et al.'s (2012) case study evaluates Spanish cultural festivals as examples of intangible cultural heritage. There are also several book festivals. Publishing is the oldest media and content industry subsector. The specific field of comic books (*bandes dessinées, BDs*, in French) attracts significant interest (Benghozi, Salvador, 2015, 2016) and has great potential in the overall book publishing industry (Salvador, Benghozi, 2021). Comic books are a sector that is recognized worldwide but systematic investigations of its business practices are scarce (Mayfield et al., 2001).

The contribution of festivals to local or regional development in terms of attracting tourists, their marketing impact and image building has been investigated by several scholars[4] (Frey, 1986, 1994) but few studies focus on the organization, structuring, and management of festivals and their nature and dynamics (Benghozi and Nénert, 1995).

The main characteristics of festivals include what Abfalter et al. (2012: 4) identify as *"temporality, virtuality and a project focus"*. In general, *"Festival organizations benefit from a highly committed and intrinsically motivated workforce, but they face the challenge of intensive short-term collaboration and the dominance of one or a few individuals"* (Abfalter et al., 2012: 5). Events such as festivals tend to be the subject of intense seasonal organization involving both permanent staff and short-term employees recruited for a cyclical event taking place in a fixed time period – generally the summer, and in a particular location (Abfalter et al., 2012: 6). Regular face-to-face meetings are complemented by e-mail exchanges to communicate among and share knowledge among event organizers (Abfalter et al., 2012). Reputation, image, brand (cf. the Cannes film festival in France, Benghozi, Nénert, 1995, or the Porispere music festival in Finland,

Suomi et al., 2020), seasonality and level of institutionalization (Luonila, Johansson, 2016) are key to the perception of the festival.

The institution of festivals in the context of CCIs such as the publishing industry is somewhat paradoxical. The attractiveness and *raison d'être* of festivals are underpinned by their eventful, spectacular, and unique character. This raises questions about why festivals should survive around productions that are easily available from bookshops or libraries.

The case of the music industry shows that their survival is based on the development of new economic models precisely based on the articulation between dematerialization on the one hand, strengthening of living events like Festivals and concerts on the other hand. Therefore, it is important to understand the dynamics of industries such as book publishing, and requires a better understanding of festival success factors, economic models, type of offer, services, and experience they provide and their links with various types of local actors. From a research perspective, it would seem interesting to analyze more specifically festivals where neither their size nor exclusivity is sufficient to explain the programming and the notoriety. This focus allows more precise identification of the structuring dynamics at work beyond the most obvious event spectacle dimensions.

The context is shaped strongly by the geographical and territorial anchoring of development models and the development of information and communication technologies (ICTs) has likely had an impact on festivals. They enable dematerialization of production and availability and consumption of cultural content and have had a disruptive effect on CCIs, value chains, sector organization, traditional business models, and role and importance of the various economic players. The digital revolution has had a disruptive effect on the traditional CCI model with the book publishing and the music and cinema industries the most affected (Benghozi et al., 2018; Salvador et al., 2019). The music sector was the first to experience disruption in the 1990s and shows that these technologies stimulate unprecedented hybridization dynamics based on the coupling of global and dematerialized online (e.g. offshore) markets with stronger local and physically anchored activities such as concerts. These hybridizations can be found also in other cultural industries including those always considered digital such as videogames. The videogame sectors in recent years has extended to include e-sports and performing arts alongside massive multiplayer gaming.

Whether and to what extent these digital technologies have also influenced the nature and ecosystem of festivals, and whether festivals have exploited these new resources to develop new business models and consolidate and expand their format, notoriety, and audiences are issues that need investigation. With the exception of the unprecedented period of the covid-19 pandemic which forced festivals to reinvent themselves to compensate for the containment and banning of public events, first observations of festivals show relatively limited appropriation of digital technologies. The technologies adopted seem to be focused mainly on improving preparation and support functions (remote relations, administration, ticketing) and communication (promotion, program information). Smaller festivals seem not to have been affected by digital innovations due, perhaps, to the local links and the unique experiences they promise which are not easily substituted by digital experiences. These festivals achieve customer loyalty and increased attendance via word-of-mouth (Rajaobelina et al., 2019). However, digital strategies have a place: they support various services for festivals which are often under-staffed and depend on large numbers of volunteers, and increase visibility, and thus festival success through use of social networks such as Facebook and Twitter.

However, during the period of the covid-19 pandemic, which severely affected all cultural events, both small and large festivals and cultural institutions have had to innovate. Many were obliged to cancel events, but some tried to provide the festival experience using digital means.[5]

The case of the two festivals in France and Spain

In this section, we provide a description of the characteristics of the cases including their focus and objectives and their organization and management. Table 9.1 summarizes some key elements of the selected festivals.

The comics festival in Angers, France

Main focus and objectives

The Angers comics festival is run by a non-profit organization (see Table 9.2) and has been held annually since 1999 during the first weekend of

Table 9.1 A snapshot of the two festivals

Festival	Year of creation	Period	Number of days	Number of visitors (latest editions)	Ticket price	Budget (on average)	Communication channels
Comics Festival in Angers, France	1999	December	2	>3,000	5 euros 1 day, 6 euros 2 days	60,000 euros	Radio, local press, comics' specialized websites, Facebook
Comics Festival in Avilés, Spain	1996	September	5	30,000–35,000	0 euros	27,500 euros	Radio, local press, comics' specialized websites, Facebook, Twitter

Source: Authors, based on websites and interviews.

December. It was aimed initially at promoting the comic culture in the local Maine-et-Loire area but received visibility at the national level as one of the first festivals dedicated to comics. This particular publishing sector has experienced phenomenal growth and success in recent years particularly among younger audiences. One of the novelties of this festival is that it provides an evidential and exclusive dimension which is not provided by comic book publications. The organizers focused on building a link between a traditional aspect of the culture of Angers – wine growing – and comic book authors. The first edition of the festival – "Vini BD 1re Cuvée"[6] – was held at the beginning of December 1999 in the Angers Congress Centre. Since then the festival has been advertised as the "Angers BD" (Angers Comics) but wine growers have always been present although in small numbers.

The location was chosen because Angers is a big town with good infrastructure and good tourist facilities, and the capabilities to organize a national event. It also has the most comics' shops in France and is home to comics artists. The aim was to promote local comics authors and the city of Angers. The municipality of Angers, the Pays de la Loire region and local sponsors (i.e. companies and mass media) support this annual event which has an overall budget of around €60,000. The number of visitors has increased from around 1,500 in 1999 to more than 3,000 for the most recent festivals, with ticket prices of around €5–6.

The comics festival is one of the most prominent events in Angers cultural programming. It has grown rapidly and is the most important comic event in the Pays de la Loire region in terms of number of visitors, is ranked first in the Pays de la Loire region for number of paid entries and is well known in the comic world.

The originality of this event is to link the universal passion for comics to the local viticulture tradition of Anjou. As mentioned above, its novelty is based on the link between comic authors and local wine producers.[7] The meeting between Angers' wine growers and comics' designers give birth to wine stickers during every edition of the Festival since its very first one. The festival founders wanted to create something different and an event that was anchored in the local culture of Angers. Therefore, the association between wine and comics is one of the main differentiation factors of the Angers Festival in the overall market of comics' Festivals.[8] "*Wine and comics are synonymous with good taste and joy of life: it makes sense that they unite*"[9] (Le Courrier de l'ouest, 1999). It also increases the visibility of the festival beyond the city's borders based on sales of bottles of wine with customized labels.

The festival offers opportunities for dedication sessions that are used to be crowded with a long queue of "*passionate comics' hunters*" to obtain signed copies of certain comics, dedicated to themselves and seen as an artwork. Since the first edition of the festival, these dedication opportunities and auctions of comics have taken place during the two days of the festival. This festival also hosts several bookshops which specialize in new and used comics, as well as collection books, exhibitions, and sponsors village. Dedications are a phenomenon of the comics sector and consist of a personalized drawing usually on the first page of the book. These can be more or less accurate representations and be more or less original but are valued by their buyers. Some visitors collect dedications from certain authors and visit the festival every year to collect additional dedications. However, the festival organizers' main aim is for visitors to discover the comics world.

Over the years, the comics festival has included additional attractions. For example, the third edition in 2001 included a comics' competition for young people aged between 14 and 24 years. The competition consisted of submitting a comic cartoon that carried a road safety message. This proved so successful that the competition has been repeated in all succeeding festivals including displays of the previous year's cartoons. Another characteristic of the Angers comics festival is the involvement of volunteer college students. The tenth edition (2010) of the festival for the first time included manga which are Japanese comics or graphic novels.

These annual festivals are organized around a specific topic[10] that is investigated by an artistic, playful, didactic, and pedagogical approach. The festival provides entertainment for comics buffs and people interested to experience and discover the world of comics through attending exhibitions, conferences, and animations. Each edition of the festival is in partnership with another local actor such as Angers castle,[11] the Angers mediatheque, or local libraries which host exhibitions before, during, and after the festival. Other partners in addition to the local wine growers include institutions such as the town council, companies (Librairie Richer, Anjou Cola, Game cash, Hotel Mercure, Angers congress center), media (Ouest-France, radio NRJ). The festivals include quizzes and games with comics as prizes. The 18th edition (2016) for the first time partnered with a sports club, and 5,000 flyers advertising the festival were distributed at a football match between Angers and Nantes on the day before the festival opened. Match attendees were offered a €1 reduction on the entry ticket price. It is advertised also on the radio and in the local press, and on comics' websites.

Organization and management

Festivals are temporary and cyclical events, and their organization evolves throughout the year. The preparation phase relies on a core group of permanent staff (around 20 persons) who are all volunteers. In the peak festival period, additional volunteers are recruited to manage the event and the partnerships and public relations. Between these two periods, the organization gradually increases and then declines after the end of the festival. The festival organization involves around 30–40 volunteers.

The festival founders were seven comic shop customers living in Angers of various ages and socio-professional origins. They meet once a month throughout the year and exchange e-mails and telephone calls between meetings. The Angers festival is a non-profit organization characterized by a small number of permanent staff who plan these annual events on a voluntary basis. As the time of the festival approaches, the meetings become more frequent. Abfalter et al. (2012: 13) argue in the case of the Colorado music Festival that *"information technology infrastructure would enhance the sharing of knowledge outside the season, when the staff are dispersed"* but this is not required for the Angers comics' festival.

The interviews with some of the festival organizers showed that the main motivation for joining the organization was to *"create the event that he wanted to see when he was a child"*. The fact of *"creating something and meet at a regular basis other persons sharing the same interests"* is a strong motivation for the organizers. A surprising finding was that not all the organizers are passionate or comics readers: some contribute specific competences such as accounting. All share an interest in organizing a friendly, safe, and welcoming event (Abfalter et al., 2012). One interviewee emphasized the *"conviviality"* of the event and referred to seeing the same visitors every year and sharing a sort of *"human warmth"*. This conviviality has had a snowball effect on attracting more visitors. Also, *"the other strong point is the way the organizers "cocoon" the authors. No red carpet, but a relaxed atmosphere where everyone takes pleasure to exchange on the projects of one and the other"*.[12] Table 9.2 summarizes the relevant characteristics of the Angers festival.

Table 9.2 The Comics festival in Angers

Focus	*Promoting the comics' culture of Maine-et-Loire and around Maine-et-Loire. The aim was to promote local comics' authors and the city of Angers*
Organization	A non-profit organization called "Angers-BD". 20–40 people of different ages and socio-professional origins. The organization is standardized but at a level of conviviality: the organizers are all volunteers
Activities	Each festival focuses on a specific topic that is investigated by an artistic, playful, didactic, and pedagogical approach Dedication sessions Partnerships with local actors for exhibitions
Originalities	Link between a traditional aspect of the culture of Angers – wine growers – and comics' authors: original wine stickers
Location advantage	Angers has the most comics' shops in France and several comics' designers live in Angers

Source: Authors.

Avilés international comics journeys, Spain

Main focus and objectives

The *Jornadas Internacionales del Cómic Villa de Avilés* (Avilés International Comics Journeys) has been held in mid-September each year since 1996. The festival events take place in various locations in this small Spanish city which is located on the Northern coast of Asturias.

Avilés is medium sized city, is very open and includes several cultural aspects and provides an excellent location for the festival. It is home to several different types of artists. From the beginning, the city bet on the comics' festival and now comics fill the city. The success of the comics festival is due to its size and high quality. Writing and drawing comics tends to be a solitary activity and the Avilés festival enables interactions with readers, a development of a comics network. It attracts comics authors from various countries.

The festival started in 1996 as an initiative of the festival's current director, Jorge Iván Argiz, in collaboration with others interested in the comics world, who, in 1995, presented the project to the City Council of Avilés. The project was approved and the festival has been held annually in mid-September over a period of five days (Journeys). The organizers want to increase awareness of comics all year round, not just during the festival.

The aim of this festival is to offer a panoramic view of the comics world and its evolution; each edition emphasizes a specific topic (e.g. historical comics, Japanese manga, etc.). One of its most interesting aspects is the interaction that takes place between comics authors and the public – in bars, parks, and other public places in this small city. These face to face contacts are valued by the participating authors.

The organizers do not have an explicit strategy to link the festival with other local activities. In some years, there has been a carnival related to the comics' festival, and in the latest editions, the festival's promoters organized an initiative called "comics at school" which involved twice-yearly visits to schools by some Spanish comics authors to interact with students. In August 2018, it was decided to make a permanent space for the comics' festival in an old, converted ceramics factory.

The popularity of comics is undeniable, and the comics sector is one of the most dynamic publishing industry sectors in terms of sales and volume of work produced (Salvador, Benghozi, 2021). This has resulted in multiple events organized around comics around the world, often aimed at promoting sales. However, the Aviles festival is not part of this commercial festival network; the organizers are keen to maintain it as an "interaction space" based on the idea of culture as a public good that is available to everyone.

The distinctive character of this festival is linked to the strength of the relationships between comics authors and their audiences, and the festival attendees are all fans of comics and this form of artistic expression. The festival attendees are part of the festival; there are few restrictions imposed on interactions between the public and the comics authors. The Avilés comics festival is conceived as comprising "journeys" taking in different places in this small city.

Organization and management

The Avilés International Comics Journeys are organized by the non-profit cultural association "Friends of the Comic Strip of Asturias". The association benefits from support from the Asturias city council. Up to 2014, the city council provided all the funding needed, since then it has received sponsorship from Asturiana de Zinc of up to 30% of the funding required to run the festival.

The festival's activities and exhibitions take place in various locations in the city including the cultural center, the Atrium Shopping Center, the municipal art center, the Palace of Valdecarzana, the Aviles City Council and a marquee. Each year, four or five exhibitions are held in the city's exhibition center. At the end of 2018, a permanent space for comics exhibitions was made available in a converted ceramics factory.

The organizers hold twice monthly meetings, exchange some 200 e-mails a month and engage in frequent telephone calls. Also, since the three promoters are friends, they meet frequently which provides additional occasions to discuss the festival. In the days immediately preceding the festival and throughout the festival, the promoters work full time for the event. The festival also recruits volunteers to help during the event but there is no organized form of recruitment; interested persons use face-to-face meetings, e-mails, and social networks to signal their availability and willingness. The festival does not have a website (because the organizers do not have enough time to maintain or improve it) but its Facebook page[13] has more than 2,900 followers and is the main mechanism for disseminating festival news. The organizers advertise activities on this Facebook page and via Twitter, and on programs on the municipality's website (culture section), local radio, TV and press, comics magazines, and comics shops in the city. ICTs are used regularly by both comics authors and potential festival participants. The festival organizers offer opportunities for interaction via e-mail, blogs, forums, social networks, and SMS.

The organizers are motivated by the love of comics and their keenness to cultivate interactions between comics authors and the public. This is why this festival described in terms of "journeys". This is interesting and emblematic of the local dynamics at work. The term "Salon" refers to a static situation where the festival is confined to an autonomous space to which visitors go. The term journey implies that festival visitors follow a path around the entire area of the festival. The organizers are keen also to keep the festival focused on its mission – avoiding a huge commercial approach – and involving "journeys" to enable meetings between comics creators and comics lovers.

Table 9.3 The Avilés international comics journeys

Focus	The aim of this festival is to offer a panoramic view of the comics' world and its evolution, and to focus on a different topic every year
Organization	The non-profit cultural association "Friends of the Comic Strip of Asturias" organizes the Avilés International Comics Journeys
Activities	Several activities take place in various places throughout this small Spanish city
Originalities	Interactions take place between the authors and the public in bars, parks, and other public places around the small city
Location	Avilés is home to several different kinds of artists
advantage	Comics authors are usually solitary people and Avilés provides them with a natural space for interaction with their readers

Source: Authors.

The three festival promoters are decisive to the success, growth, and survival of the festival. All have a deep knowledge of the world of comics which are their passion, and their enthusiasm is inexhaustible. The festival is distinguished by the possibilities it provides for interactions between comics authors and the public which is an attraction for comics authors to participate without any financial reward. Some of the world's best-known comics authors attend the annual Avilés festival. Among the 100 best-selling comics in the world, 23 are from Spanish authors who attend the Avilés' Festival. Finally, the continued support of the city council is important: its leaders and political parties with responsibility for culture have changed over the years but the festival has never lost municipal support. On the first day of the festival, there is a reception which all parties attend, and the final report of the festival is sent to city council members. Although there is no strategic cultural plan due to time constraints, the comics festival is aligned to the general view of the council that culture is for everyone. This strengthens the links between the festival and the city. So far, political changes have not had an effect; however, should this change, since the festival depends on the city council for most of its funding, this is a potential weakness. Table 9.3 summarizes the main characteristics of this festival.

Discussion and concluding remarks

The focus on the creation and organization of festivals in the development strategies of many cities offers a new vision of the creative city. Organization of festivals can be considered a regional development policy (Crossick, 2006; UNCTAD, 2010) which provides brand identity for the city hosting the event. Specific events such as festivals enable visibility which might otherwise be difficult. They can be seen as complementing the city's identity constructed over time through architecture (Jones and Svejenova, 2017).

The annual designation of European Capital of Culture which was introduced by the European Union in 1985 gives prominence to the organization of cultural events to increase the city's visibility and attractiveness and achievement of a unique image. It provides an attractiveness linked to the temporary, unique, and media-related dimension of the events rather than a distinction based on cultural heritage. Cultural, social, and economic spillovers from these events increase the cities' reputation.

The peculiarities of individual festivals provide value for the city. This identity and place branding help to ensure the survival and economic success of small cities perhaps not rich in architecture, culture, tourist attractions or digital technologies. The organizers believed the Angouleme festival was the international reference for the comics sectors similar to Cannes, Berlin, and Venice for movies, and Salzburg for classic music. The Angers festival aims at fostering the comics' sector in Angers through attracting authors in this sector that otherwise would not come to this small city. As suggested in the introduction, we were interested in the dynamics at work in 'small' festivals such as the two we have studied, different from the strengths and success of big international festivals, in terms of conception, programming, and economic model.

Benghozi and Nénert (1995: 66) conducted a detailed analysis of the Cannes Film Festival and showed that a major success factor was the ability to simultaneously pursue economic/commercial and cultural/artistic objectives that might at first sight be seen as antagonistic. It is famed for the quality of the works shown and also has a central position among the professional film community and has become the decisive platform for film distribution.

Concern over providing public access to various artifacts combined with serving the interests of the community of professionals and economic partners is not specific only to the Cannes festival or other major festivals. It relates also to various exhibitions, festivals, fairs, and biennales, and influences the programming of their activities.

Many festivals are accompanied by parallel events which cater for different audiences, are based on specific development strategies and extend the festival environment. In the case of the two festivals analyzed, the focus is on the location – similar to the Cannes Film Festival – which is enriched by the festival which in turn is enhanced by the various exhibitions and conferences organized alongside them. The aim of both festivals is to promote a specific culture. Visitors include both local audiences and international participants. The authors' participation is usually not revealed until immediately before the festival in order to keep potential visitors in suspense.

Our analysis highlights the specificity of the small cities that host the events. They have adopted a culture valorization strategy and have become culture clusters which attract various types of artists. The period of the festival reaffirms the cities' cultural identity and enables conviviality and acts as a tourist attraction. The unique characteristics of the festivals studied (e.g. the link between wine and comics in the case of the Angers festival) are enhanced by the attention given by their organizing teams to the ambience and locations of the events. A welcoming environment is the goal of all local festivals, demonstrated by good customer service. Dantas and Colbert (2016: 81) suggest that this makes a difference for customers: "*attention to the level of service is particularly important in the cultural events sector, where supply exceeds demand*". The festival and the city hosting become a single entity: they identify with one another, and they share the same attractive influence. The link with schools and students is further evidence of this. The quality of the hospitality and the exchanges between participants, authors, and exhibitors in the cultural ecosystem are important. The absence of a commercial approach is also important. The persons involved in the event organization, including volunteers, are passionate about comics and keen to support this local event. The cities are involved in the festivals and host complementary activities such as exhibitions and concerts. This point is particularly important because it is through it that the paradox that we pointed out at the beginning of this chapter regarding the creation of event dynamics in the book publishing sector is finally resolved. In this case, the organization of the festival involves the whole city, including various volunteers and partnerships with other economic actors including those not involved in comics such as wine producers. This suggests some substitution or complementarity between the novelty of the event and its embeddedness in a traditional territory.

These festivals have been supported by the emergence of new ICTs which have increased their attractiveness and diffusion. These ICTs represent new resources and new development opportunities. The digital revolution and diffusion of ICTs have affected the whole business world and are leading to a new business landscape. Their impact is particularly noticeable in the cultural sector, which to an extent foreshadowed the transformations and disruptions currently affecting economies in terms of business models, configuration of offers, and consumer practices. Digital technologies are having a disruptive effect on traditional CCIs' models: the book publishing and music and cinema industries are among the most representative examples (Moreau, 2013; Salvador et al., 2019). Innovation processes and outcomes are being impacted by pervasive digitization, which is questioning traditional theories and innovation management processes, and leading to the idea of "digital entrepreneurship" which emphasizes the profound effects of digital technologies (Nambisan et al., 2017).

However, their effects on activities such as festivals are less well documented and appear more equivocal. It cannot be assumed that digital technologies have had a disruptive effect on small festivals linked to the local territory and the unique experience they assure visitors. Neither of these aspects can be substituted by digital tools. The festival setting, and their organization are characterized by temporality and a focus which involves well motivated workforce and intensive short-term collaborations and leadership by one or a few persons (Abfalter et al., 2012).

So, how is the digital revolution influencing the organization and management of small festivals? According to our case studies and the data derived from the interviews, it seems that the new dynamics are adding to the success of these festivals and consolidating the image of the cities hosting these events. ICTs are complementing the physical proximity necessary for the organization and management of these events. We would like to highlight the following dimensions. The analysis shows first that the business models of these events (Rajaobelina et al., 2019) are supported by the experience economy (Pine, Gilmore, 1998). In the case of the Angers festival personal dedications from comics' authors ensure a memorable experience. The link to the experience economy allows the economic model of these small festivals to be part of a form of permanence and reinforcement, avoiding the Red Queen effect (Kauffman, 1995; Voelpel et al., 2005; Barnett, 2008; Benghozi, 2015) of continuous search for alternative models. These small-scale festivals have no need to try "to run faster". They need only to ensure a memorable experience. Commoditization of goods and services demands a business differentiation strategy (Pine, Gilmore, 1998). Consumers desire memorable experiences: *"no two people can have the same experience, because each experience derives from the interaction between the staged event (like a theatrical play) and the individual's state of mind"* (Pine, Gilmore, 1998: 99). Visitors who recall the festival as special will become regular participants: the interviews confirmed fidelity among visitors over the years. However, the Internet and ICTs could enable new genres of interactive experiences (Pine, Gilmore, 1998).

While digital technology has profoundly changed all CCIs, we currently do not observe disruption on the scale of their effect on the economy, and no huge reconfiguration of their offers. We found no evidence of attempts to switch to online or remote festivals. Some music and film festivals have tried to offer an online experience sometimes with limited availability as in the case of live screenings. Others are using digital technologies to duplicate performances originally conceived in festival venues to provide access for a wider audience. However, most digital innovations related to festivals have been incremental and focused on improving the administrative functions (administration, ticketing, etc.) and interactions among existing audiences, rather than on exploring alternative forms. Innovation and ICTs have a specific place in festival organizations. Visitors want the memorable and "specific" experience offered by these small festivals and this enables to argue about the empowerment of a proper economic model related to the festivals themselves. Innovation and ICTs are essential to social networks which are used to diffuse information about the festivals along with traditional channels like radio and local press which are still important in small cities. Standardization combined with creativity results in an original and personalized experience and interactions rather than innovative products or services.

Research on some major festivals – Avignon for theatre, Cannes and Venice for cinema, Salzburg for music (Frey, 1994) – shows that to ensure growth and sustainable development, attractiveness and reputation, these events also require a professional marketing structure where producers and diffusers meet for commercial purposes. On the contrary, even if on a smaller scale, the case studies analyzed have maintained their original mission.

The lack of changes to the festivals studied is interesting and could be explained by lack of means to ensure their growth and development and expand and include an online presence. However, it could be argued also that it is their successful event dynamics and territorial anchoring that ensure their sustainability and identity. These aspects are part of a particular dynamic that is different from the forces at work in big festivals where sustainability and success depend on programming and professional marketing activity (cf. Benghozi, Nénert, 1995).

In all the editions of the comics festivals in Angers and Avilés, the aim has been to ensure a cultural focus. This is accomplished through the participation of both local and international authors, parallel exhibitions, visits to schools, and partnerships with institutional and business actors. The survival, affirmation, and originality of these small events may be linked mostly to respect for and maintenance of their nature and mission. The stability of these events is ensured by coherence and a friendly atmosphere.

Acknowledgments

The authors thank the organizers of the Angers Comics Festival (France) and the Avilés Comics Festival (Spain) for agreeing to interviews. A preliminary version of this article was presented at the 15th International Conference on Arts and Cultural Management (AIMAC), held in Ca' Foscari University of Venice, Italy, June 23–26, 2019. The authors thank two anonymous reviewers for constructive comments.

Notes

1 Author translation: *"l'étude des manifestations temporaires telles que Festivals, marchés, foires et autres événements éphémères reste finalement relativement limitée"*.
2 http://angersbd.fr/
3 https://www.avilescomarca.info/agenda/jornadas-del-comic-aviles/
4 For a review of the literature, see Vecco and Srakar (2017).
5 Due to the pandemic and the health directives in force, the board of directors of the Angers BD association decided to cancel the 2020 edition of the comics festival initially scheduled for December 5 and 6. The next edition is scheduled for December 4 and 5, 2021.
6 Vini Bandes Dessinées premiere cuvée: Vini Comics first vintage.
7 *"12ème Angers BD : un Festival grand cru"*, by Yannick Sourisseau, Angers, 06/12/2010.
8 Nonetheless, the association between wine and comics attracted contradictory reactions from the public: some liked it, others judged the link between alcoholic drinks and books often enjoyed by very young readers, inappropriate.

9 Author translation: "Vin et bande dessinée sont synonymes de bon gout et de joie de vivre : il est bien logique qu'ils s'unissent".

10 Medieval times in 2004; nature and environment in 2006; comics and cinema in 2007; comics and rock in 2016; and so on.

11 *"Le Château sort de sa bulle, dernier week-end pour profiter de l'expo"*, Angers Mag Info - Angers, 03/01/2014.

12 Author translation: *"L'autre point fort c'est la façon dont les organisateurs « cocoonent » les auteurs. Pas de tapis rouge, mais une ambiance détendue où chacun prend plaisir, à échanger sur les projets de uns et des autres"*, *"Festival BD d'Angers : toujours très convivial"*, by Yannick Sourisseau, Angers, 07/12/2009.

13 https://www.facebook.com/Jornadas-del-C%C3%B3mic-de-Avil%C3%A9s-195832180457638/

References

Abfalter, D., Stadler, R., Muller, J. (2012), "The organization of knowledge sharing at the Colorado music festival", *International Journal of Arts Management*, vol. 14, n. 3, pp. 4–15.

Baez-Montenegro, A., Devesa-Fernandez, M. (2017), "Motivation, satisfaction and loyalty in the case of a film festival: Differences between local and non-local participants", *Journal of Cultural Economics*, vol. 41, pp. 173–195.

Barnett, W.P. (2008), *The Red Queen among organization: How competitiveness evolves*. Princeton, NJ: Princeton University Press.

Benghozi, P.-J. (2015), "Culture and the red queen", *Tafter Journal*, n° 84 (September/October).

Benghozi, P.-J., Nénert, C. (1995), "Création de valeur artistique ou économique: du Festival International du film de Cannes au marché du film", *Recherche et Applications en Marketing*, vol. X, n. 4, pp. 65–76.

Benghozi, P.-J., Salvador, E. (2015), "Technological competition: A path towards commoditization or differentiation? Some evidence from a comparison of e-book readers", *Systèmes d'Information et Management (SIM)*, vol. 20, n. 3, pp. 97–135.

Benghozi, P.-J., Salvador, E. (2016), "Investment strategies in the value chain of the book publishing sector: How and where the R&D someway matter in creative industries?", *Technology Analysis & Strategic Management*, vol. 28, n. 5, pp. 568–582.

Benghozi, P.-J., Salvador, E., Simon, J.-P. (2018), "The race for innovation in the media and content industries: Legacy players and newcomers. Lessons from the music and newspaper industries", in P. Bouquillion and F. Moreau (eds.), *Digital platforms and cultural industries*. ICCA-Cultural industries, artistic creation, digital technology, vol. 6, pp. 21–40, Peter Lang editions.

Blichfeldt, B. S., Halkier, H. (2014), "Mussels, tourism and community development: A case study of place branding through food festivals in Rural North Jutland, Denmark", *European Planning Studies*, vol. 22, n. 8, pp. 1587–1603.

Caves, R. 2000. *Creative industries: Contracts between art and commerce*. Cambridge, MA: Harvard University Press.

Crossick, G. (2006), *Knowledge transfer without widgets: The challenge of the creative economy*. London: Goldsmiths, University of London, A lecture to the Royal Society of Arts in Leeds on 31 May 2006.

Dantas, D. C., Colbert, F. (2016), « Festival de Lanaudière : Differentiation in customer experience », *International Journal of Arts Management*, vol. 18, n. 3, pp. 79–85.

Del Barrio, M. J., Devesa, M., Herrero, L. C. (2012), "Evaluating intangible cultural heritage: The case of cultural Festivals", *City, Culture and Society*, vol. 3, pp. 235–244.

Frey, B. (1986), "The Salzburg festival: An economic point of view", *Journal of Cultural Economics*, vol. 10, pp. 27–44.

Frey, B. (1994), "The economics of music festivals", *Journal of Cultural Economics*, vol. 18, pp. 29–39.

Jones, C., Svejenova, S. (2017), "The architecture of city identities: A multimodal study of Barcelona and Boston", in M. A. Höllerer, T. Daudigeos, D. Jancsary (eds.) *Multimodality, meaning, and institutions* (Research in the Sociology of Organizations, Volume 54B) Emerald Publishing Limited, pp. 203–234.

Kauffman, S. A. (1995) "Technology and evolution: Escaping the Red Queen Effect", *McKinsey Quarterly*, vol. 1, pp. 118–129.

Luonila, M., Johansson, T. (2016), "Reasons for networking in institutionalized music productions: Case studies of an opera house and a music festival ", *International Journal of Arts Management*, vol. 18, n. 3, pp. 50–66.

Mayfield, M., Mayfield, J., Genestre, A. D. (2001), "Strategic insights from the international comic book industry: A comparison of France, Italy, Japan, Mexico and the USA", *American Business Review*, June, pp. 82–92.

Moeran, B., Strandgaard Pedersen, J. (2011), eds., *Negotiating values in the creative industries. Fairs, festivals and competitive events* . Cambridge: Cambridge University Press.

Moreau, F. (2013), "The disruptive nature of digitization: The case of the recorded music industry", *The International Journal of Arts Management*, vol. 15, n. 2, pp. 18–31.

Nambisan, S., Lyytinen, K., Majchrzak, A., Song, M. 2017. Digital innovation management: Reinventing innovation management research in a digital world. *Mis Quarterly*, vol. 41, n. 1, pp. 223–238.

Pine, B. J., Gilmore, J. H. (1998), "Welcome to the experience economy", *Harvard Business Review*, July-August, pp. 97–105.

Rajaobelina, L., Dusseault, P., Ricard, L. (2019), "The mediating role of place attachment in experience and word of mouth: The case of music and film festivals", *International Journal of Arts Management*, vol. 21, n. 2, pp. 43–54.

Salvador, E., Benghozi, P.-J. (2021), "The digital strategies of publishing houses: a matter of book content?", *International Journal of Arts Management*, vol. 23, n. 2, pp. 56–74, Winter.

Salvador, E., Simon, J.-P, Benghozi, P.-J. (2019), "Facing disruption: The cinema value chain in the digital age", *International Journal of Arts Management*, vol. 22, n. 1, pp. 25–40.

Snowball, J. D. (2013), "Are arts events a good way of augmenting the economic impact of sport? The case of the 2010 FIFA World Cup and the national arts festival in South Africa", *International Journal of Arts Management*, vol. 16, n. 1, pp. 49–61.

Suomi, K., Luonila, M., Tähtinen, J. (2020), "Ironic festival brand co-creation", *Journal of Business Research*, vol. 106, pp. 211–220.

UNCTAD (2010), Creative Economy Report 2010. Creative economy: A feasible development option.

Vecco, M., Srakar, A. (2017), "Blue notes: Slovenian jazz festivals and their contribution to the economic resilience of the host cities", *European Planning Studies*, vol. 25, n. 1, pp. 107–126.

Vestrum, I. (2014), "The embedding process of community ventures: Creating a music festival in a rural community", *Entrepreneurship & Regional Development*, vol. 26, n. 7–8, pp. 619–644.

Voelpel, S., Leibold, M. Tekie, E., Von Krogh, G. (2005), "Escaping the red queen effect in competitive strategy: Sense-testing business models", *European Management Journal*, vol. 23, n. 1, pp. 37–49.

Wong, J., Wu, H.-C., Cheng, C.-C. (2015), "An empirical analysis of synthesizing the effects of festival quality, emotion, festival image and festival satisfaction on festival loyalty: A case study of Macau food festival", *International Journal of Tourism Research*, vol. 17, pp. 521–536.

10 Beyond Economic Impact

The Cultural and Social Effects of Arts Festivals

María Devesa and Ana Roitvan

Introduction

Arts festivals have become a part of the cultural fabric of society and of places (Davies, 2021). They have increased enormously in number in recent years and constitute one of the most dynamic and attractive phenomena in the current cultural scene (Devesa et al., 2015). The COVID-19 pandemic, however, meant that many festivals in 2020 were either cancelled, reduced or postponed, which has led to substantial financial losses for the sector, in addition to the negative repercussion this has had from the social and cultural standpoint.

Yet, apart from the economic impact they have in terms of production, income, and employment that is closely related to the tourism impact, cultural festivals also generate a number of other effects which, although often intangible in nature, are equally important, if indeed not more so, than the former (Liu, 2014). These include (Devesa et al., 2012): cultural effects, linked to the increase in the cultural supply, opportunities for audiences, or cultural innovation (Black, 2016; Viviers and Slabbert, 2012); social effects, related to creativity, citizen well-being, social cohesion, learning or the creation of a positive atmosphere (Derret, 2003; Dwyer et al., 2000; Moscardo, 2008; Wood, 2008); physical impacts, such as the creation of permanent infrastructures, the transformation of the urban fabric, or the use of underutilized public and private spaces (Evans, 2005; Richards and Wilson, 2004); and environmental impacts, such as the generation of noise, pollution or congestion in some areas of the city (Fredline et al., 2005; Pavlukovic et al., 2017).

Measuring and evaluating the socio-cultural impact of festivals allows for a wider and more multidimensional approach to events, and also helps festival managers, cultural authorities, and sponsors to devise strategies that can ensure an event's success as well as its viability and long-term sustainability (Brown et al., 2015). It also provides food for thought on the role played by festivals and offers the chance to analyse how these events, from the standpoint of cultural tradition, often make a commitment to what is culturally avant-garde and, as meeting places and spaces for interaction, allow for artistic innovation.

DOI: 10.4324/9781003127185-14

Therefore, the main goal of this chapter is to examine what social and cultural impact arts events and festivals have on the areas where they are held. Specifically, we pursue two related goals. Firstly, we aim to develop a theoretical proposal to systematise how the socio-cultural impact is measured, focusing particular attention on puppet theatre festivals. Secondly, we apply the set of indicators created to a specific case study: the Segovia International Puppet Festival (*Titirimundi*), one of the most important and prestigious puppet festivals in Spain and Europe.

The chapter is organised in five sections. In addition to the introduction that sets out the goal of the research, Section 2 establishes the theoretical framework for measuring the socio-cultural impact of festivals. Section 3 develops the methodology, and Section 4 sets out the empirical analysis applied to the specific case study. Section 5 presents the conclusions, and the chapter closes with the references.

Theoretical framework: measuring the socio-cultural impact of arts festivals

In recent years, there has been general recognition of the need to analyse the socio-cultural impact of arts events and festivals (Black, 2016; Luonila et al., 2020; Robertson et al., 2009; Wood, 2008). These socio-cultural effects are extremely complex given that they are intangible, shifting, and differ for each type of stakeholder; they are often specific to a particular artistic expression or certain event; and they are in turn related to the goals pursued by the festival (UNESCO, 2015). As a result, they are hard to measure, to quantify, and to value (Dwyer et al., 2000; Fredline et al., 2003; Wood, 2005). However, these effects "are often more durable than economic impacts because they tend to be rooted well locally" (Liu, 2014, p. 984), so their importance demands they be examined.

The academic literature evidences two main blocks of analysis for the socio-cultural effects of arts festivals: a qualitative approach, focusing mainly on interviews, focus groups, etc. in which various stakeholders are asked about the event's socio-cultural impact; and a quantitative approach, in which an attempt is made to quantify said effects as far as possible. Here, we find two main measuring systems: impact perception scales (through surveys in which various stakeholders are asked about how they see the event's impact), and systems of objective indicators through data obtained from the festival organisers or surveys carried out amongst attendees. On occasions, quantitative measuring systems are in turn based on qualitative approaches, such that we focus on the former.

Perception scales

In the case of PERCEPTION SCALES, we should cite some pioneering works both for their definition of the effects analysed and for the measuring systems used: items considered and systems for evaluating these items.

Delamere (Delamere, 2001; Delamere et al., 2001) focuses on measuring the social impact of community-based festivals through an attitude scale: *Festival Social Impact Attitude Scale (FSIAS)*. In the former study (Delamere et al., 2001), the author develops the theoretical model, defining the items to be evaluated (a total of 47 items identified) and refining the scales. In the second study, Delamere (2001) applies FSIAS to the Edmonton Folk Music Festival (Canada). To do this, a survey is carried out among a representative sample of residents who are asked to value (i) whether they consider it has had the impact indicated, and (ii) how much importance they attach to the impact. The subsequent factorial analysis reveals two main types of impact, social benefits and social costs and, within the former, benefits for the community as well as cultural and educational benefits. Amongst the specific aspects pinpointed, prominent are image, community identity, well-being, pride and recognition, quality of life, variety of cultural experiences, disruption of normal life, and noise or traffic problems. This has been the most widely used scale in the few applied works to have been carried out to date (see Begiran and Kurgun, 2016; Pavlukovic et al., 2017; Van Winkle and Woosnam, 2014; Woosnam et al., 2013; Yolal et al., 2016).

Small et al. (2005) developed an alternative method within the framework of evaluating the social and cultural impact of events based on residents' perceptions: the *Social Impact Perception (SIP) Scale*. Small (2007) later carried out a practical application (based on 41 items) which distinguishes between six socio-cultural dimensions or effects: inconvenience caused by the festival, identity and social cohesion, personal frustration, entertainment and socialisation opportunities, growth, and development of the community and behavioural consequences. These six groups include such aspects as increased traffic and noise levels, community identity, pride, positive cultural impact, entertainment opportunities, the image created, job opportunities, the chance to get to know new people, or developing new skills.

Fredline et al. (2003) also develop their own scale to measure residents' perceptions of the social impact of cultural festivals. They use 45 items that reflect different social effects (positive and negative), both in the personal and the collective aspect. The factorial analysis carried out allows them to distinguish five dimensions or effects of festivals: social and economic development impacts (pride, meeting new people, entertainment opportunities...); inconveniences (noise level, traffic congestion...); impact on public facilities (local facilities available for local residents); behaviour and environment (litter, crime...); impact on prices.

Pasanen et al. (2009) develop a different scale to measure the effects of festivals: *Finnish Event Evaluation Tool (FEET)*. With it, they analyse the economic, social, and cultural effects of festivals by conducting surveys amongst different stakeholders: festival organisers, visitors, local entrepreneurs, residents, and policymakers. They apply the scale to 12 cultural and sports festivals and events. Amongst the socio-cultural impacts, they highlight the impact on local infrastructure and services, the environment, the image of the municipality, regional cohesion or the identity of the local people. The most outstanding feature of their model is that it is possible to examine at the same time various groups of people affected and to merge the evaluation of different effects into a single study (Colombo, 2016).

Another proposal for a perception scale focusing on the cultural impact of events and festivals is that of Colombo (2013, 2016). The author develops her own perception scale for the cultural impact of festivals (*Cultural Impact Perception, CIP*) based on five kinds of effects which, in turn, display a twin positive and negative dimension: information about culture (shared experience, negative community image...); preservation of cultural tradition (revitalisation of traditions, loss of heritage, etc.) constructing cultural identity (community pride, celebration of the community, cultural profanation...); integration of cultural effects (cultural integration, community alienation...); social cohesion (opportunity for intercultural contact or cultural offence).

Finally, there are also applications of perception scales of social and cultural effects on the part of the event organisers. In this case, the impact is extended to include economic effects (Gursoy et al., 2004), tourist aspects (González and Morales, 2017) and even repercussions of a political nature (Robertson et al., 2009).

Set of indicators

The second quantitative system for measuring the socio-cultural effects of arts festivals is to create SYSTEMS OF INDICATORS (*set of indicators*) that allow said effects to be explored and evaluated. These have been used far less, such that there are few academic papers, and those that do exist display major differences not only in the kind of indicators created (management, process, impact indicators...) but also in terms of the definitions used.

Prominent among the applied works is the article by Rogers and Anastasiadou (2011) focusing on creating and proposing a set of indicators to measure community involvement in festivals, since "community involvement through participation, sponsorship, and attendance is important for the long-term viability of festivals and their economic and social sustainability" (p. 388). It is not, therefore, an analysis of socio-cultural impact directly, but does offer a systematic proposal for creating indicators of a socio-cultural nature, and is one of the few carried out to date. It is based on local interviews with festival organizers and focus group discussion. The authors thus develop a set of community involvement indicators that approach the idea of social impact, organised into five major blocks: involvement of schools, volunteering opportunities, participation in decision making, accessibility, and business cooperation. The specific indicators include: number of shows/schools visited; number of trips/children attending; breakdown of local and nonlocal volunteers/total number of local volunteers; membership of liaison committee/number of meetings attended; number of shows/community venues used; amount of financial and in kind support provided (Rogers and Anastasiadou, 2011). The study is a theoretical proposal and the authors recommend testing it so as to fine-tune the proposed instruments and assess their relevance and practical advantages.

In a similar line, albeit without proposing specific indicators, also prominent are the works of Lade and Jackson (2004) and Carlsen et al. (2007). The former is based on in-depth interviews and the latter conducts an exhaustive review of the literature, in addition to some interviews in order to establish the categories of impact. In their analyses and reflections, they posit a number of ideas that might prove to be of great interest and help in creating and proposing socio-cultural impact indicators: benefits on arts, community, society, culture, etc.

Also, SACO (2016) proposes a framework for the monitoring and evaluation of publically funded arts, culture, and heritage projects, including festivals and events. Three kinds of cultural values are identified—intrinsic, economic, and social values—and different indicators are proposed by the researchers in the five main cultural themes: audience development; human capital and professional capacity building; inclusive economic growth; social cohesion and community development; and reflective an engaged citizens.

In sum, there is no single method or single classification for the socio-cultural impact of festivals and events (Viviers and Slabbert, 2012), with each author and each study using a different approach, even when the principal ideas concur (Woosnam et al., 2013). What is more,

> an effective framework needs to be adaptable enough to take into account the different goals and characteristics of events and projects, while at the same time giving guidance on the kinds of indicators that can be used to demonstrate the cultural values being targeted.
>
> (SACO, 2016, p. 15)

In any case, many of the ideas on socio-cultural impacts are repeated in these studies: opportunities for entertainment, opportunities for socialising, identity, sense of community, volunteering, extending the cultural offer, use of infrastructure, creating new audiences, image of the place or negative repercussions such as traffic, noise or litter.

These categories of impacts are gradually consolidated and thus create an ever-growing body of robust literature within which many of the works are case studies. Moreover, they gradually adapt to various situations (type of festival, aims of the event, link to the place, ...), thereby furthering the study of the socio-cultural impact of festivals and events. In this regard, studies of perception are perhaps more advanced, whereas studies of indicators may lag slightly behind and may depend to a certain extent on the former. Nevertheless, the two approaches feed into and complement each other and enable the situation of festivals to be explored as well as ideas and action strategies to be generated.

One weakness of perception studies is that they evidence certain subjectivity, whilst on the other hand, one of their strengths is that they provide an insight into the opinions and feelings—in sum, the perceptions—of the various stakeholders (residents, visitors, event managers, sponsors, ...). Studies based on systems of indicators are more complicated: to a certain degree, they are more objective (strength) but are of limited scope (weakness). In any case, they generate a need for systematising data, provide a detailed understanding of the festival and favour a very interesting reflection that can help with the festival's long-term sustainability.

As a result, and after having reviewed the literature on measuring the socio-cultural impact of festivals and arts events, we now focus on the chosen method, setting out in greater detail the concept, features, and types of cultural indicators, as well as on the theoretical proposal for the case study: puppet festivals.

Methodology

Socio-cultural impact indicators

An indicator is the conversion of a theoretical variable, obtained by observing a phenomenon, into a practical variable after applying empirical measurements. From a theoretical perspective, indicators should provide "a summary of information, a barometer which, without necessarily saying everything, allows us to know where we stand and, if possible, perceive trends" (Carrasco, 1999, p. 6). The basic functions of an indicator would therefore be simplification, quantification, and communication.

Indicators can be simpler or more complex, and in turn require various sources of information, ranging from primary sources such as surveys conducted among attendees or local residents, to secondary sources, such as programming data and festival budgets, analysis of Internet data (metrics of social network use) or tourism data from the area.

From the methodological standpoint, there are three main kinds of socio-cultural indicators (Carrasco and Coll, 2013), although there are other systems for classifying them:

> - Individual indicators: these are a function or an algorithm constructed on the basis of a single variable. There are proportions, percentages and reasons, frequency distributions, central trend measures, dispersion measures, variation rates, and so on.

- Composite indicators: these are the result of aggregating the dimensions, objectives, individual indicators and/or variables available that sum up a set of properties underlying the construct, with the aim being to explain and interpret said construct.

- Synthetic indicators: these are made up of multiple variables. The resulting indicator from the algorithm that concentrates the multiple dimensionality of the construct sums up, in a single latent or underlying variable, all the information from the set of variables, leaving part of the information unexplained.

Indicators should fulfil a series of characteristics such as being reliable, allowing for comparisons to be made in space and time, being compatible with foreign indicators, and being understandable to non-specialists (Carrasco, 1999; Pfenniger, 2004). Developing socio-cultural indicators is, however, complex for a number of reasons: the wide-ranging notion of what culture is, the lack of theoretical models, the intangible nature of many of the effects they seek to measure, lack of data and resources, existing methodological difficulties, or even the wide range of indicators that can be proposed (Bonet, 2004; Carrasco, 1999; Colombo, 2013).

Cultural or socio-cultural indicators have mainly been used for the cultural sector as a whole and, in particular, to evaluate public cultural policy (Bonet, 2004; Carrasco, 1999; Serrano, 1995). As pointed out, fewer applications are to be found for cultural festivals and events, and more specifically for measuring the impact or the effects generated where they are held, a field of study in which perception scales have held sway.

The proposals put forward for festivals are based on interviews, focus groups, panels of experts, and on a review of the literature, a literature which, although scarce in specific proposals for indicators, is growing in the general area of analysis and reflection on the socio-cultural effects of culture as a whole and on festivals in particular (Black, 2016; Dwyer et al., 2000; Dwyer and Jago, 2019; Getz et al., 2019; Moscardo, 2008; Robertson et al., 2009; Wood, 2008).

A proposal for measuring the socio-cultural impact of puppet festivals

The proposal for indicators put forward here focuses on theatre festivals, and specifically puppet theatre, whilst remaining aware that it must adapt to each particular case study. The theoretical approach is based on the literature reviewed and highlighted in the previous section and on our knowledge of puppet festivals; festivals which tend to be small, community based and which are closely linked to the place where they are held and which encompass an important educational component although there are also performances for adults. They also act as a showcase for this kind of theatre, which is quite minority in nature, such that they tend to opt for quality and avant-garde performances.

The proposal is based on three main impact categories, which are by no means either absolute or exclusive, but which are inter-related: (i) cultural impact indicators, whose objective is to measure the increase in the area's cultural capital; (ii) social impact indicators, which aim to reflect the increase in the area's social capital; (iii) urban impact indicators, which seek to capture the impact on the area's infrastructures, facilities, and image.

The specific indicators are generally simple, although more elaborate and complex indices might be based on them. Some indicators deal with aspects related to supply and others to demand. Likewise, some are individual and others collective. The main categories together with their meaning are shown in Table 10.1, whilst details concerning the proposed indicators may be consulted in Tables A1, A2 and A3 of the Appendix.

Having established the set of possible indicators, the following section develops an application for the Segovia International Puppet Festival (Spain).

Table 10.1 Categories and areas of socio-cultural impact indicators

Category	Areas	Meaning
Cultural impact indicators	Enrichment and diversity	Opportunities the festival generates from the standpoint of cultural programming
	Training and education	Opportunities the festival generates to learn and to acquire knowledge
	New audiences	The festival's role in attracting new audiences
	Cultural identity	The festival's contribution to the sense of community
	Quality of cultural supply	The increase in the quality of the area's scheduled activities thanks to the festival
	Developing cultural and creative industries	Contribution to the local productive fabric
	Satisfaction	Satisfaction
Social impact indicators	Social cohesion	The festival's impact on participation
	Social inclusion	The festival's capacity to provide access to culture
	Well-being and quality of life	The festival's influence on participants' well-being
Urban impact indicators	Infrastructure and facilities	The festival's influence on the use or creation of cultural infrastructure
	Communication, image and tourism	Impact in terms of image and tourism
	Local identity	The festival's role in the creation of the area and its social identity

Source: Author's own.

Empirical analysis

Case study: Segovia International Puppet Festival

Titirimundi, the Segovia International Puppet Festival, was created in 1985 and is celebrating its 35th edition in 2021. It is a project aimed at disseminating, promoting, and developing puppet arts. Over the 34 editions held to date, around 970 companies from 52 countries have come, putting on their shows at almost 50 different venues throughout the city, as well as in other areas in the province and the country. Over the years, Titirimundi has not only opened up to new spaces and locations but also to new audiences, new forms of puppet theatre and even to new times of the year by extending the programme to the autumn and winter months.

The festival arranges a series of puppet performances or shows in addition to other activities such as workshops, courses or talks (see Table 10.2). It is aimed at young audiences, families, and adults. School audiences have their own schedule, with a star programme, *Titiricole*, where children put on their own puppet shows, as well as the *School Performances*, festival shows specifically for schools.

Performances are held at indoor venues (theatres, churches, patios, …) or in open spaces (streets, squares, gardens), many of which have a historical backdrop. In 2019, around 42,000 attendees enjoyed these performances. In addition to the staff members, the festival also draws on the support of 140 volunteers without whose help it could not go ahead. The main data on the festival, which will serve to create certain indicators, are shown in Table 10.2.

Application of the system of socio-cultural indicators to Titirimundi

The application of the socio-cultural impact indicators to the case study focuses on the categories highlighted in the theory: cultural, social, and urban impact. Indicators have been developed in those aspects in which it has proved possible based on the data provided by the event organisers: the festival programme and the festival's accounts. Indicators correspond to the last three years, which also allows us to analyse how they have progressed.

Cultural impact

As regards the cultural impact, a certain effect in terms of cultural enrichment and diversity can be seen (Table 10.3), since foreign companies accounted for 57% of the total in 2019 (70% in 2018), with 9% of the total coming from "distant origins", in other words, from countries whose companies do not usually come to Spain (Russia, Argentina or Chile, for example).

Table 10.2 Titirimundi. Programme and attendance (2017–2019)

	2017	2018	2019
No. of days	6	6	6
No. of companies	37	33	35
International	19	23	20
National	18	10	15
No. of countries participating	11	14	14
No. of shows	40	35	36
No. of performances	425	382	316
No. of venues	29	32	29
Theatres	7	11	11
Patios	9	9	8
Street	9	8	6
Peripheral districts	4	4	4
Other activities	8	10	11
Workshops	6	7	7
Others	2	3	4
No. of spectators	48,018	46,462	41,861
Indoor venues	26,818	23,337	19,061
Street	21,200	23,125	22,800

Source: Own elaboration based on the festival programme and accounts.

Table 10.3 Enrichment and cultural diversity indicators

	2017	2018	2019
Number of different shows scheduled	40	35	36
Number of performances	425	382	316
Number of parallel activities	8	10	11
% of foreign companies out of the total	43.2	69.7	57.1
% companies of "distant origins" (*)	10.8	12.1	8.6
Number of countries taking part (including Spain)	11	14	14

(*) Countries such as Argentina, Russia, Taiwan, Israel or Peru, amongst others.
Source: Own elaboration based on festival data.

In terms of the educational and training impact, we see—through different variables and indicators—the key role played by specific festival programmes for schools: *Titiricole* and *School Performances*. This led to almost 5,000 schoolchildren taking part in the festival in 2019, meaning that 26% of all those attending at indoor venues were schoolchildren (Table 10.4). In addition, 34.8% of schools in the city were involved in the festival.

Therefore, the festival's involvement in educational terms and its impact in the formative sense is evident. The number of schoolchildren watching shows, together with the schoolchildren and teachers involved in the programme—acting in and directing performances, respectively— (Table 10.4), coupled with specific workshops for children and youngsters (see

Table 10.4 Training and education indicators

	2017	*2018*	*2019*
WORKSHOPS			
Number of workshops and courses	6	7	7
Number of participants	n.a.	1.000	600
TITIRICOLE PROGRAMME			
Number of schools taking part	10	12	14
Number of children involved (acting in shows)	296	n.a.	396
Number of performances	17	20	22
Number of spectators (schoolchildren) (a)	3,750	2,707	1,976
% of schools in the city of Segovia involved out of the total number of schools in the city	37.5	34.8	34.8
SCHOOL PERFORMANCES PROGRAMME			
Number of sessions	28	28	30
Number of spectators (schoolchildren) (b)	4,200	2,693	3,000
TOTAL (Titiricole + School Performances)			
Total number of spectators (schoolchildren) (a + b)	7,950	5,400	4,976
% of schoolchildren out of the total number of spectators in indoor venues	29.6	23.1	26.1

Source: Own elaboration based on festival data. n.a. = Not available.

Table 10.5), means that new audiences are being nurtured for the future, which is another effect posited in the literature.

The festival's success and its impact on satisfaction are measured by way of a proxy through ticket sales, or more specifically through the occupation of indoor venues, which averaged 96% between 2017 and 2019 (Table 10.6).

Social impact

From the social perspective, we distinguish between three dimensions, although these are inter-related. Firstly, the social cohesion indicators (Table 10.7) show the extent of social involvement through volunteering: 140 volunteers in 2019 (an average of 123 between 2017 and 2019), 60.7% being young people and 56% repeating the experience in 2018.

Secondly, social inclusion indicators evidence different aspects. The festival's involvement, and therefore its impact on children, has already been shown. Moreover, the festival schedules various sessions (five in 2019) with

Table 10.5 New audience indicators

	2017	2018	2019
Number of specific workshops for children and youngsters	3	3	2
% of workshops for children and youngsters out of the total	50.0	42.9	28.6
Number of Titiricole sessions	12	15	17
Number of sessions of School Performances	28	28	30
% of sessions for children out of the total number of sessions in the festival	9.4	11.2	14.9
Number of children in sessions for schoolchildren	7,950	5,400	4,976
% of schoolchildren out of the total number of spectators in indoor venues	29.6	23.1	26.1

Source: Own elaboration based on festival data.

Table 10.6 Satisfaction indicators

	2017	2018	2019
% of occupancy of indoor venues	100.0	90.0	98.0

Source: Own elaboration based on festival data.

Table 10.7 Social cohesion indicators

	2017	2018	2019
VOLUNTEERING			
Number of volunteers	123	107	140
% of volunteers repeating from the previous year	55.0	56.1	n.a.
% of younger volunteers (<25 years)	83.7	60.7	n.a.
% of older volunteers (>55 years)	7.3	3.7	n.a.

Source: Own elaboration based on festival data.

other social groups (Table 10.8), thereby providing important cooperation, since puppets offer a therapeutic contribution to improving the quality of life of those affected, such as the sick, the disabled or the elderly.

In the case of the peripheral districts (Table 10.8), and what this means in terms of access to culture, the number of venues and performances has remained stable in absolute terms. In 2019, these venues accounted for 40% of all the open-air venues used for the festival, although performances

Table 10.8 Social inclusion indicators

	2017	2018	2019
SCHOOLCHILDREN			
Number of children in sessions for schoolchildren	7,950	5,400	4,976
% of schoolchildren out of the total number of spectators in indoor venues	29.6	23.1	26.1
OTHER SOCIAL GROUPS			
Number of performances for other social groups	3	4	5
PERIPHERAL DISTRICTS			
Number of venues in peripheral districts	4	4	4
% of venues in peripheral districts out of the total number of outdoor venues	30.8	33.3	40.0
Number of performances in peripheral districts	4	4	4
% of performances in peripheral districts out of the total outdoor performances	4.0	9.1	3.5
STREET PERFORMANCES *(free shows)*			
Number street performances	100	44	114
% of street performances out of the total	23.5	11.5	36.1
% of street spectators out of the total	53.0	49.8	54.5

Source: Own elaboration based on festival data.

represented only 3.5% of all those held outdoors. In addition, the festival programmed 36% outdoor performances (more than in previous years), which meant that 54% of spectators who watched the performances did not have to pay, thereby opening the festival out to a broader audience.

Thirdly, taking the festival to towns and villages in the province and staging the performances at other times of the year has spread the supply of culture to more places and expanded the possibility of consumption to various audiences, which we interpret as an improvement in citizens' well-being and quality of life (Table 10.9).

Urban impact

Finally, and linking the involvement that Titirimundi has with the city where it is held, we see that two of the 19 indoor venues were opened up specifically for the festival, affording local as well as other spectators visiting from elsewhere the chance to get to know places that are usually not

Table 10.9 Well-being and quality of life impact indicators

	2017	2018	2019
PERFORMANCES IN THE PROVINCE			
Performances	15	31	43
Locations	15	31	43
Companies	10	10	11
PERFORMANCES THE REST OF THE YEAR			
Number of companies	14	13	9
Number of performances	17	23	17

Source: Own elaboration based on festival data.

Table 10.10 Use of public spaces indicators

	2017	2018	2019
Total number of venues used for the festival	29	32	29
Outdoor venues	13	12	10
Indoor venues	16	20	19
% of outdoor venues out of the total number of venues	44.8	37.5	34.5
Number of venues opened specifically for the audiences at the festival	3	3	2
% of venues normally closed but made available for the festival out of the total number of indoor venues	18.8	15.0	10.5
Number of historical venues (outdoor and indoor)	22	19	20
% of historical venues out of the total number of venues	75.9	59.4	69.0

Source: Own elaboration based on festival data.

open to the public. In addition, almost 70% of the festival venues are historical sites. Although this might seem logical in a historical city declared World Heritage by UNESCO, it still reflects the use made of the urban fabric. This might affect the use to which heritage is put, the perception created thereof, and the relation attendees have with said historical heritage (Table 10.10).

Conclusions

The aim of this chapter is to explore the cultural and social impact of cultural festivals, particularly for the case of puppet festivals, both from a theoretical perspective—with a systematic proposal of impacts and indicators—as well as from a practical standpoint, with an application to the Segovia International Puppet Festival (Spain).

Results point to the existence of certain socio-cultural implications. In this regard, Titirimundi—like so many other festivals—would be contributing to cultural enrichment, since it is seen to expand the possibilities of cultural consumption and offers a programme that is hard to find outside the festival. It also contributes to the formation of tastes and to the creation of new spectators, particularly through its programmes for schoolchildren as well as the specific workshops and activities for the young, where the latter learn and can enjoy puppet theatre, which helps to form future spectators, a role now played by many arts festivals.

From a social perspective, data point to substantial support from society through the number of volunteers, the role the festival plays in providing access to culture by staging performances throughout the city and thanks to its improving the quality of life by extending the programme throughout the year and spreading it to the rest of the province. These beneficial effects create a satisfaction which is reflected by the large numbers of spectators who attend.

The event's link to the city is seen through urban impact indicators. The festival's scope, its opening out to specific areas and the use of historical backdrops might be seen to be shaping the relationship which (both local and visiting) spectators have with the city, their appreciation of the heritage and the fondness for the people. Indeed, the city becomes one big stage during the festival; a festival which cannot be understood without the city itself. Again, this is common in cultural festivals, particularly in community-based as well as small and medium scale festivals.

From the perspective of tradition and the essence of puppet theatre, the festival thus contributes to cultural innovation, to what is artistically avant-garde and to social progress.

Managerial implications

The results to emerge should, however, be analysed with a certain degree of caution and always within the framework of the case study in question. The indicators obtained should be interpreted by the event's managers in terms of the aims and objectives of the festival itself. The data are not absolute and nor would all of the indicators make sense in all case studies. Nevertheless, the present proposal might serve as a guide for decision making and might help to ensure the viability of the event and its long-term sustainability.

The information created is vital to festival managers. Simply compiling, organising, and analysing the information is already helping in the day to day running of such festivals. Analysing this kind of data also helps to determine whether the festival's aims are being met, and serves to gain an understanding of what contribution is being made to society, in addition to justifying public and private support for the event. Gaining an insight into the socio-cultural impact helps to further the benefits generated by the festival and to reduce possible costs. It also facilitates the planning of the event, and serves to enhance relations with the local community, thereby promoting the festival's success.

Through this type of indicator, the public authorities charged with cultural, tourist or educational policy may find support for analysing, discussing, and designing their policies and actions, which are at times hard to explain and justify to society. Despite its limits, these indicators can help to visualise the impact which such policies have for citizens. This can also help to understand the link between the festival and the place it is held as well as assist with urban and local development strategies.

This kind of data can also be used by private sponsors for decision making and to justify their actions: in other words, to see whether they are reaching the types of groups they are trying to reach, and to see what is being achieved from a socio-cultural standpoint; in sum, to ascertain what impact they are having on society. Through impact indicator systems, society itself, together with its organisations, can better understand what role festivals play and can engage more actively in their development and organisation, which would again help them to succeed.

Contributions, limitations, and future research

This work makes a twofold contribution. First, it offers a specific proposal for indicators to measure the socio-cultural impact of arts festivals, an issue which has virtually been non-existent in academic literature. In this regard, the chapter offers both a theoretical reflection on how to measure such effects as well as a practical application showing their evaluation. This not only contributes to theory but also serves as an example to event and festival managers in their everyday practice. Second, the analysis focuses on a puppet festival, a cultural object hitherto relatively unexplored. This might help to encourage studies to be carried out on other minority arts, or on those that have failed to receive much attention thus far, with a view to continue contributing, with everybody's help, to the creation of a powerful corpus of research on the topic.

Amongst the limitations of this study, mention should first be made of the lack of data, since we only have data available on supply provided by the organisers but have no data on demand, or data from other secondary sources such as the city's tourist services or data from the use of social networks and Internet. Secondly, it should be pointed out that individual indicators have been created. These can be improved with other more complex indicators or, in future, with synthetic indicators. The third limitation is that we have only created positive indicators, indicators of benefits, leaving to one side the costs the festival might entail (noise, congestion in the streets, parking problems, disrupting daily life, …). Finally, we opted to use impact indicators when other very interesting kinds of indicators, such as indicators of innovation, might also be analysed.

Future inquiry should therefore seek to improve our system of objective indicators but, in particular, should aim to further our proposal by evaluating the perception of impact, in other words developing and applying an impact perception scale through surveys and their subsequent analysis, both amongst residents as well as amongst festival spectators. This would allow us to explore in greater depth those qualitative impacts which systems of indicators such as ours can only partially reflect.

References

Báez, A. and Devesa, M. (2017) 'Motivation, satisfaction and loyalty in the case of a film festival: Differences between local and non-local participants', *Journal of Cultural Economics*, 41(2), pp. 173–195.

Begiran, D. and Kurgun, H. (2016) 'A research on social impacts of the Foca Rock Festival: The validity of the festival social attitude scale', *Current Issues in Tourism*, 19(8), pp. 930–948.

Black, N. (2016) 'Festival connections. How consistent and innovative connections enable small-scale rural festivals to contribute socially sustainable communities', *International Journal of Event and Festival Management*, 7(3), pp. 172–187.

Bonet, L. (2004) 'Reflexiones a propósito de indicadores y estadísticas culturales', *Boletín GC: Gestión Cultural*, No. 7. http://www.gestioncultural.org/boletin/pdf/Indicadores/LBonet-Indicadores.pdf

Brown, S., Getz, D. Petterson, R. and Wallstam, M. (2015) 'Event evaluation: Definitions, concepts and a state of the art review', *International Journal of Event and Festival Management*, 6(2), pp. 135–157.

Carlsen, J., Ali-Knight, J. and Robertson, M. (2007) 'ACCESS—A research agenda for Edinburgh festivals', *Event Management*, 11(1–2), pp. 3–11.

Carrasco, S. (1999) 'Indicadores culturales: Una reflexión', *Econcult*, pp. 1–20.

Carrasco, S. and Coll, V. (2013) 'Observare-Laborare', *Periférica Internacional*, 14, pp. 91–118.

Colombo, A. (2013) 'Efectos, impactos y outcomes: Variantes tipológicas versus metodologías de análisis' in Martinelli, A. (coord.) *Impactos de la dimensión cultural del desarrollo*. Documenta Universitaria: Girona, pp. 201–216.

Colombo, A. (2016) 'How to evaluate cultural impacts of events? A model and methodology proposal', *Scandinavian Journal of Hospitality and Tourism*, 16(4), pp. 500–511.

Davies, K. (2021) 'Festivals post Covid-19', *Leisure Sciences*, 43(1–2), pp. 184–189.

Delamere, T.A. (2001) 'Development of a scale to measure resident attitudes toward the social impacts of community festivals, Part II: Verification of the scale', *Event Management*, 7(1), pp. 25–38.

Delamere, T.A., Wankel, L.M. and Hinch, T.D. (2001) 'Development of a scale to measure resident attitudes toward the social impacts of community festivals, Part I: Item generation and purification of the measure', *Event Management*, 7(1), pp. 11–24.

Derret, R. (2003) 'Making sense of how festivals demonstrate a community's sense of place', *Event Management*, 8(1), pp. 49–58.

Devesa, M., Báez, A. Figueroa, V. and Herrero, L.C. (2012) 'Repercusiones económicas y sociales de los festivales culturales', *Eure. Revista Latinoamericana de Estudios Urbano Regionales*, 38(115), pp. 95–115.

Devesa, M., Báez, A., Figueroa, V. and Herrero, L.C. (2015) 'Factors determining attendance at a film festival', *Event Management*, 19(3), pp. 317–330.

Dwyer, L. and Jago, L. (2019) 'Valuing the impacts of festivals', in Mair, J. (ed.) *The Routledge Handbook of Festivals*. Routledge: Abigdon, Oxon, pp. 43–52.

Dwyer, L., Mellor, R. Mistilis, N. and Mules, T. (2000) 'A framework for assessing 'tangible' and 'intangible' impacts of events and conventions', *Event Management*, 6(3), pp. 175–189.

Evans, G. (2005) 'Measure for measure: Evaluating the evidence of culture's contribution to regeneration', *Urban Studies*, 42(5/6), pp. 959–983.

Fredline, L., Jago, L. and Deery, M. (2003) 'The development of a generic scale to measure the social impacts of events', *Event Management*, 8(1), pp. 23–37.

Fredline, L., Raybould, M., Jago, L. and Deery, M. (2005) 'Triple Bottom Line Event Evaluation: A proposed framework for holistic event evaluation'. Paper presented at the Third International Event Management Research Conference, Sydney University of Technology, Sydney.

Getz, D., Andersson, T.D., Armbrecht, J. and Lundberg, E. (2019) 'The value of festivals', in Mair, J. (ed.) *The Routledge Handbook of Festivals*. Routledge: Abigdon, Oxon, pp. 22–30.

González, F. and Morales, S. (2017) 'El impacto cultural y social de los eventos celebrados en destinos turísticos. La percepción desde el punto de vista de los organizadores', *Cuadernos de turismo*, 40, pp. 339–362.

Gursoy, D., Kim, K. and Uysal, M. (2004) 'Perceived impacts of festivals and special events by organizers: An extension and validation', *Tourism Management*, 25(2), pp. 171–181.

Lade, C. and Jackson, J. (2004) 'Key success factors in regional festivals: Some Australian experiences', *Event Management*, 9(1–2), pp. 1–11.

Liu, Y.D. (2014) 'Socio-cultural impacts of major event: Evidence from the 2008 European capital of culture, Liverpool', *Social Indicators Research*, 115(3), pp. 983–998.

Luonila, M., Kurli, A. and Karttunen, S. (2020) 'Capturing societal impact: The case of state-funded festivals in Finland', *Journal of Policy Research in Tourism, Leisure and Events*, Published online: 03 Nov 2020, https://doi.org/10.1080/19407963.2020.1839474

Moscardo, G. (2008) 'Analyzing the role of festivals and events in regional development', *Event Management*, 11(1–2), pp. 23–32.

Pasanen, K., Taskinen, H. and Mikkonen, J. (2009) 'Impacts of cultural events in eastern Finland – Development of a Finnish Event Evaluation Tool', *Scandinavian Journal of Hospitality and Tourism*, 9(2–3), pp. 112–129.

Pavlukovic, V., Armenski, T. and Alcántara-Pilar, J.M. (2017) 'Social impacts of music festivals: Does culture impact locals' attitude toward events in Serbia and Hungary?', *Tourism Management*, 63, pp. 42–53.

Pfenniger, M. (2004) 'Indicadores y estadísticas culturales. Un breve repaso conceptual' *Boletín GC: Gestión Cultural*, No. 7. http://www.gestioncultural.org/boletin/pdf/Indicadores/MPfenniger.pdf

Richards, G. and Wilson, J. (2004) 'The impact of cultural events on city image: Rotterdam, cultural capital of Europe 2001', *Urban Studies*, 41(10), pp. 1931–1951.

Robertson, M., Rogers, P. and Leask, A. (2009) 'Progressing socio-cultural impact evaluation for festivals', *Journal of Policy Research in Tourism, Leisure and Events*, 1(2), pp. 156–169.

Rogers, P. and Anastasiadou, C. (2011) 'Community involvement in festivals: Exploring ways of increasing local participation', *Event Management*, 15(4), pp. 387–399.

SACO (2016) 'A framework for the monitoring and evaluation of publically funded arts, culture and heritage'. South African Cultural Observatory.

Serrano, I. (1995) 'Indicadores culturales y fuentes estadísticas', in Linde Paniagua, E. (coord.) *Cultura y desarrollo*. Ministerio de Cultura: Madrid, pp. 51–76.

Small, K. (2007) 'Social dimensions of community festivals: An application of factor analysis on the development of the Social Impact Perception (SIP) Scale', *Event Management*, 11(1–2), pp. 45–55.

Small, K., Edwards D. and Sheridan, L. (2005) 'A flexible framework for evaluating the socio-cultural impacts of a (small) festival', *International Journal of Event Management Research*, 1(1), pp. 66–76.

UNESCO (2015) 'Festival Statistics. Key concepts and current practices'. UNESCO Institute for Statistics: Montreal.

Van Winkle, C.M. and Woosnam, K.M. (2014) 'Sense of community and perceptions of festival social impacts', *International Journal of Event and Festival Management*, 5(1), pp. 22–38.

Viviers, P.A. and Slabbert, E. (2012) 'Towards an instrument measuring community perceptions of the impacts of festivals', *Journal of Human Ecology*, 40(3), pp. 197–212.

Wood, E.H. (2005) 'Measuring the economic and social impacts of local authority events', *International Journal of Public Sector Management*, 18(1), pp. 37–53.

Wood, E.H. (2008) 'An impact evaluation framework: Local government community festivals', *Event Management*, 2(3–4), pp. 171–185.

Woosnam, K.M., Van Winkle, C.M. and An, S. (2013) 'Confirming the festival social impact attitude scale in the context of a rural Texas cultural festival', *Event Management*, 17(3), pp. 257–270.

Yolal, M., Gursoy, D., Uysal, M., Kim, H. and Karacaoglu, S. (2016) 'Impacts of festivals and events on residents' well-being', *Annals of Tourism Research*, 61, pp. 1–18.

Appendix 10.1

Socio-cultural impact indicators proposed by categories and areas

Table A1 Cultural impact indicators

Areas	Indicators proposed
Enrichment and diversity	Percentage of local, national, and international artists/companies; percentage of artists/companies of nationalities and/or origins that are "distant, minority and/or unknown"; number of works presented/representations (and progression over time); number of national/international premières; number of parallel activities; percentage of people from elsewhere motivated mainly because of the festival
Training and education	Number of training courses and workshops organised by the festival; number of participants in the workshops (and progression over time); number of children/youngsters taking part in the courses; number of activities undertaken in conjunction with educational institutions; number of educational institutions involved; percentage of educational institutions involved out of the total
New audiences	Percentage of people taking part for the first time out of the total; number of courses, workshops, and activities for children and youngsters; number of courses, workshops, and activities for specific groups
Cultural identity	Percentage of local spectators out of the total; percentage of local spectators taking part in the parallel activities; percentage of local spectators taking part in the training activities; percentage of people who feel the festival boosts their cultural identity (survey)
Quality of cultural supply	Awards given to the festival; festival associations and/or festival networks the festival is a member of; public financial support awarded through open public calls; attendee satisfaction; percentage of attendees who return out of the total (repetition rate); number of companies with cultural awards
Developing cultural and creative industries	Percentage of services hired from local firms; percentage of local artists/companies; number of cultural jobs created in the area; number of local cultural infrastructures created, improved, renovated as a result of the festival
Satisfaction	Overall satisfaction with the festival (mean); evaluation of the festival's overall cultural quality (mean); evaluation of the various aspects of the festival (tickets, information, venues, …)

Source: Author's own.

Table A2 Social impact indicators

Areas	Indicators proposed
Social cohesion	Percentage of local public out of the total; percentage of public by ages (children, youngsters, adults, the elderly); origin of those collaborating with the festival; origin of the suppliers of the festival; number and type of complementary activities; number and progression over time of volunteers
Social inclusion	Percentage of children attending; percentage of adults attending; percentage of public per district of origin (social distribution); percentage of attendees from minority groups (the disabled, unemployed, ...); festival activities for minority groups (number and progression over time); specific activities for children (number and progression)
Well-being and quality of life	Festival activities throughout the year (extension and development of the festival); level of attendee satisfaction (mean) (survey); evaluation of the festival's quality (mean) (survey)

Source: Author's own.

Table A3 Urban impact indicators

Areas	Indicators proposed
Infrastructure and facilities	Number of cultural infrastructures created, improved or renovated as a result of the festival; percentage of services provided by local suppliers out of the total; number of "new spaces" used by the festival
Communication, image, and tourism	Presence in the media (number of news items in the written press, length and number of reports on television, minutes of radio time, ...); website visits; followers in social networks; percentage of non-local spectators drawn mainly by the festival; repetition rate of spectators from elsewhere; creation/adhesion of festival "brands"
Local identity	Whether the festival increases the pride felt for the city (% of positive answers in a survey); whether the festival forms part of what makes the city a special place (% of positive answers); evaluation of the importance attributed to the festival for the city (mean)

Source: Author's own.

11 Cultural Value of a Festival

The Quality Evaluator for Assessing Impact

*Arjo Klamer, Ludmilla Petrova and
Dorottya Eva Kiss*

Introduction

Since the beginning of 2000, *festivalization* is a fast-growing phenomenon across Europe (Frey, 2000), as shows in the rapid increase in the number of festivals and their institutionalization (Mulder, Hitters & Rutten, 2020). Increasingly, cultural and creative sectors, including cultural festivals, are perceived as a source for economic growth, urban development, also as identity anchor for cities or local territories, and drivers for creativity, social cohesion, and solidarity (Higgs, Cunningham & Bakhshi, 2008; KEA, 2009, 2015). Studies on creative and cultural industries, creative cities, clusters, and creative workers highlight how the richness of the content of culture-led practices generates and transfers new ideas and content to different territories, clusters and sectors (Currid, 2007; Florida, 2002; Jacobs, 1969; Jaaniste, 2009; Throsby, 2008). The key factor in the initiation of such knowledge transfers within certain localities, is the diffusion of new ideas arising from the circulation of creative workers (Florida, 2002). Further, Cooke and Lazzeretti (2008) argue that this shift towards the 'cultural enhancement' of the economy also profoundly affects the creative millennium within cities. Hence, creativity that originates from cultural and creative sectors is considered to be a pivotal factor for the qualitative changes that take place within a geographically specific area. These qualitative changes are often linked to new practices which aim at enriching the physical environment, creating a different social and cultural milieu or/and flux of knowledge in the territory (Currid, 2007; Landry, 2000; Pratt, 2004; Scott, 2010). As part of this context and due to their specific time-spatial nature, cultural festivals yield economic, cultural, and social values which define them as an important factor in city or local territory identity creation (Jakob, 2013; Quinn, 2005), respectively, in local tourism development (Bennett, Taylor & Woodward, 2014; Uriarte et al., 2020), and are important for the dynamic of the creative industries specific sectors (Mulder, Hitters & Rutten, 2020).

Acknowledging the multiplicity of effects that cultural festivals can produce, the challenge is still how to determine whether a cultural festival

DOI: 10.4324/9781003127185-15

is doing well in achieving its purposes. How to determine that financial sources are well spent and/or invested? What can the director of festival organization, its artistic leader, or a group of collaborators do better? This chapter is arguing that all stakeholders of a cultural festival are striving to realize certain economic, cultural and social values. These values lay the foundation of a festival's vision, mission, and impact while reflecting the festival's concrete context. The question remains: How to measure, assess or in general make sense of this myriad of values?

The values of cultural goods are focus of study for cultural economists[1] (Ginsburgh, 2003; Hutter & Shusterman, 2006; Hutter & Throsby, 2008; Klamer, 2002, 2017; Throsby, 2001; Snowball, 2011). While the economic value of cultural goods has been extensively studied and measured (Maas & Liket, 2011; O'Hagan, 2016; Throsby, 2001) and has got the attention in policy debates (DCMS, 1998; European Commission, 2010; KEA, 2006; OECD, 2014; UNCTAD, 2008), there are limited attempts to grasp the complexity of cultural and social values of a cultural good.[2] One of the obvious reasons is that the latter are difficult to be objectively defined, determined, assessed, and verified (Frey, 1994; Throsby, 2010). Nevertheless, despite these challenges, this chapter argues that in the process of valuing cultural goods, including a cultural festival, it is essential to acknowledge the importance of value (quality) versus merely measuring of quantities (Bell, Gillespie & Wilding, 2016).

The traditional quantitative assessments such as size of revenues, number of visitors, profits, number of citations, social media scores provide insufficient information. The reason is that organizers and visitors care most about the qualitative outcomes such as the quality of the performances, the atmosphere, the social interaction during an event, or the reputation of the festival. The numbers do not tell enough about such qualities. The often-applied satisfaction surveys might result in useful feedback but usually reveal little to nothing about the relevant qualitative characteristics of a festival. These surveys also suffer from a positive evaluation bias (Johanson & Glow 2015).

All kinds of alternative evaluation procedures are floating around. The British council and Goethe-Institut (2018), the Arts Council England[3] and the Department of Culture and the Arts of Western Australia (2014) have launched projects to measure cultural values. There are different applications of so-called impact studies that are intended to determine the social and cultural impact of cultural programing within different sectors like on health, social cohesion, or the strength of neighborhoods (i.e. Belfiore & Bennet, 2007, 2009; Klamer 2004, 2013; Maas & Liket, 2011; Newman, 2013; Rizzo & Mignosa, 2013; Young, Camic & Tischler, 2016). Most cultural institutions traditionally use the customary satisfaction surveys, economic impact studies, and report the numbers of critical reviews, visitors, and other quantifiable outcomes (Belfiore & Bennett, 2010; Bell, Gillespie & Wilding, 2016; Colombo, 2016; Evans, 2005; Galloway, 2009). But none of these methods tell the organizers whether they are achieving their qualitative purposes. For example, if the purpose is to make people more appreciative of a certain art form, none of these methods can tell whether people actually change in this direction (Johanson & Glow, 2015).

Existing qualitative approaches have usually the drawback that they are often done with the intention to show positive outcomes and run the risk for 'a biased research design' embedded in the relationships between the researcher and respondents (Johanson & Glow, 2015). The bias shows in the approach, like in the selection of factors and characteristics worthy of evaluation. Say that the evaluation establishes that certain cultural values are being realized, what follows from that? Is that a good sign? When are the changes satisfactory? Does the organizer need to adjust the strategy?

Acknowledging the challenges brought from the previous approaches, a quality evaluator (QE) is designed to capture in a systemic way the wide myriad of values (qualities) that a cultural event can generate. The QE that this chapter proposes is an innovative tool to evaluate the realization of the important cultural and social values or qualities of a cultural festival. It provides feedback to the initiators, owners or other stakeholders on how well they are doing, and what they could do different in order to realize their purposes. A distinctive feature of the QE is its ability to make a clear distinction between the qualities that visitors are seeking or expecting and the qualities they are experiencing. It also charts changes in the qualities or values that visitors are seeking. The latter feature is the crux. The organizers of a cultural festival want to know whether the type of program, the set-up, additional features, and the promotion has had an impact. When visitors and other stakeholders are not only satisfied but also changed some values of theirs, the festival apparently had an impact. The change is that counts. Say the aim of the organizers of a contemporary dance festival is to make young people more appreciative of contemporary dance, they want to know whether young visitors indeed became more appreciative of contemporary dance and, for example, want to start dancing themselves and wish to attend more performances. The QE is designed to provide that feedback. As the following sections will argue, the QE is context sensitive and can capture the diversity of audience experiences as attributes or proxies for different values. In this way, it overcomes the limited scope provided by the standardized metrics of evaluation (Belfiore & Bennett, 2010) and accounts for different cultural capital that people can acquire in different contexts (Bourdieu, 1977).

The QE is theoretically rooted in the so-called value-based approach (Klamer, 2017). Although it may get support from other theoretical and conceptual perspectives, this chapter elaborates the connection of the quality evaluator with the value-based approach, while evaluating Rotterdam Unlimited Festivals as the case. The following Section 2 introduces the conceptual framework of the QE while drawing on the theoretical origin of the vale-based approach. Section 3 addresses the stages and methods used by the QE and Section 4 is discussing the findings of the QE assessment of the Rotterdam Unlimited Festival's impact. The final Section 5, draws some conclusions on the application of the QE in a concrete context.

Quality evolution framework: a value-based approach

The premise of the value-based approach is that people value and evaluate all the time (Klamer, 2017; Lamont, 2012). The values of individuals, groups of people, or organizations answer to the question what is important to them. Values are qualitative. The qualities that people seek in activities reflect their values. The evaluation focuses on the question to what extent the relevant values or qualities are realized with certain activities, such as the organization of a cultural festival.

Accordingly, any evaluation needs to start with the question to the organizers, initiators or others responsible, or so-called protagonists—which values or qualities they seek to realize. These values constitute the purpose of the cultural festival, or its mission. They may say that they want to contribute to the social cohesion in a local community, or make people appreciate music of different cultures. Such purposes are non-quantitative. They are about good community and the diversity of music, thus, about qualities. The challenge remains to develop a conclusive method that measures or better said assesses the effects (impact) of values. "(E)valuation models have proliferated but they are often narrowed to crude measures of impact and performance" (Bell, Gillespie & Wilding, 2016, p. 2) wherein personal, societal, political "interests of transparency and economic efficiency with little respect afforded to the multiple perspectives and divergent goals of the actors involved" (p. 1).

In the value-based approach (VBA) the distinction of purposes from instrumental goals is crucial (Klamer, 2017). In daily practice, the two often get confused. The number of visitors is an instrumental goal but is usually not the substantive goal, or purpose that an artistic organization is seeking. The artistic director (the protagonist in this case) has the lead in determining that purpose. If (s)he is seeking to entertain people and maximize the revenue in order to survive with her organization, (s)he clearly will await different outcomes than the director who wants to make an artistic difference and seeks to get the appreciation of well-informed attendees. The evaluation in both cases should differ. In the first case, the evaluation needs to establish to what extent the visitors were entertained and how much revenue was generated. In the latter case, the evaluation needs to make clear with which expectations, which capabilities visitors attend the performance in order to assess how well informed their judgments are. When the protagonist seeks to change people's values and appreciations, the method needs to establish those before and after the performance or event.

In the end, purposes are always substantive and qualitative, and thus their measurement often brings the question of "a lack of clarity about *what* is being evaluated and from *whose* perspective" (Bell, Gillespie & Wilding, 2016, p.

1). Acknowledging this, the definition and articulation of social and cultural values are essential, and is the first challenge while implementing QE. The experience is that the protagonists often do not know what exactly values are important, or articulate goals that can mean anything and therefore mean not very much ("making a better world and/or art", "making people happy").

The VBA method assists the participants in the evaluation to agree on a clear articulation of the most important cultural and social values. It does so by having them focus on four clusters of possible values or qualities to pursue (Figure 11.1). They are:

- **The personal sphere** for their personal values and qualities (such as good, meaningful work, autonomy, "being entrepreneurial", being a good craftsperson, being a good parent, being a good friend, being a good citizen, being a social, knowledgeable, well-educated person, as well as behavioral values or virtues such as being honest, ambitious, loving, compassionate, responsible—all these qualities concern the protagonists themselves),
- **The social sphere** for social values and qualities (such as a good team, social status, a good family, good friendships, good communities, collegiality—these qualities characterize the activities that the protagonists share with more or less familiar people).
- **The societal sphere** for societal values and qualities (such as justice, liberty, democracy, social cohesion, diversity, a sustainable environment, human rights, nationalism, a shared identity—that is, values and qualities that characterize practices in general, with often unknown people).
- **The transcendental sphere** for transcendental qualities and values (such as beauty, truth, artistic meaning, faith, historical relevance, to celebrate the mysteries of life).

In reality, most of these values and qualities require practices or activities to realize. Following Dewey (1939), Klamer argues that values evolve around the "way in which values function" and "the action that comes with experiencing a value" (2003, p. 198). This invites us to examine the values of a cultural

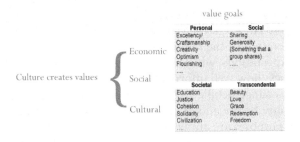

Figure 11.1 Values clusters.
Source: authors' adaptations of Klamer (2017).

good by experiencing them, "without which the sorting through, evaluation, revaluation and devaluation processes have no basis" (Klamer, 2003, p. 200). Similarly, Crossick and Kaszynska bring into focus personal experience as a "fundamental dimension of cultural value" (2016, p. 21). In this line, qualities or values are characteristics of a practice (Eliassen, Hovden & Prytz, 2018; Klamer, 2017). The quality of good friendship presumes a practice that we call "friendship"—it is a quality of what friends do with each other. Great art—a transcendental quality—comes about in the practice that artists call art. The quality of work comes about in the activity of people. An important point here is, that even if it seems that our practices are motivated by personal values, it often might be a matter of realization of a social and societal or even transcendental value we are not aware of. This suggests that the realization of these values is context related and cannot be standardized, as suggested by some other methods (for example, the Manchester Metrics Pilot[4] and the Public Value Measurement Framework of Western Australia).[5]

The QE is designed, in a way to evaluate all these values or qualities (intentional and unintentional) of what an event, a program, a policy or an organization contributes to those practices they are aiming at. In addition, besides the challenge of defining and operationalizing values, another important factor while assessing artistic, social, societal values of a cultural festival for instance, relates to the question: From 'whose' perspective does the evaluation takes place? It is argued that "(t)hose who initiate the evaluation often have a stake in advocating for the programs and projects evaluated" (Johanson & Glow, 2015, p. 255). Consequently, a well-defined scientifically reliable and valid framework of relevance is necessary when assessing impact, which leads us to another important aspect of the value-based approach that the QE makes use of. Namely, its emphasis on the role of (internal and external) stakeholders in the realization of the relevant values. Accordingly, when protagonists articulate their values and the practices to which they want to contribute, they also should identify the stakeholders who can assess a specific quality of the contribution. A general audience may assess the emotional and/or social impact of a performance, but could lack the expertise to appreciate the innovativeness of the performance. To assess the latter, experts are more relevant stakeholders. For the assessment of each quality appropriate, stakeholders need to be identified.

Qualitative evaluator: stages and methods

Stages

The QE consists of three stages (Figure 11.2) The first focuses on the diagnosis of shared values and identification of stakeholders; and the second registers changes, if any, in the previously defined shared values as experiences and observed by the relevant stakeholders. The third stage is the actual evaluation (stage 3, Figure 11.2).

Figure 11.2 Quality evaluator stages.
Source: authors' depiction.

Stage 1. Diagnosis and articulation of goal values

The determination of the values that the protagonists of a festival want to realize is a challenge. As noted before they may offer grandiose ambitions— like making the world better, or being different—which cannot be evaluated. It usually requires several sessions in which the organizers are asked to reflect on best practices (as they have experienced them and as they observe them in other festivals), on the qualities of those and to imagine their ideal cultural festival, respectively, the ideal practices. From what they identify as best or ideal practices, the researcher usually is able to extract the values or qualities they are seeking.

Stage 2. Realization of values: identification of stakeholders and strategies

After the protagonists have stipulated their values and the qualities that they strive for, they are asked to identify the relevant stakeholders. The protagonist needs to indicate which values or qualities can be evaluated by each stakeholder. Incidental visitors may express their emotional responses to the festival ("I really enjoyed it") but probably lack the knowledge to evaluate the substantive qualities of the performances. For the evaluation of those, more expert and/or frequent visitors need to be consulted.

At this stage of the QE, before the beginning of the festival, the relevant values of the stakeholders (in terms of expectations) are assessed (usually by means of a survey or panel). It is commendable to ask them to weigh various values, to determine an ordering for relevance. Then, the festival takes place. Various stakeholders contribute, participate (like the organizers and their employees, the volunteers, the performers), and observe the events (like the supporters, the financiers, the local community).

Stage 3. Evaluation

After the festival, stakeholders are asked basically two types of questions: (1) how did they experience various qualities of the festival and (2) their weighing of the relevant values for them on a scale of 1 (the less important) to 5 (the most important). The evaluation shows two outcomes: (1) the discrepancy between what values stakeholders find important (their expectations thus) and their experiences during the festival and (2) the change in their values, if any, or their weighing of them.

Say stakeholders were seeking a fun time (in stage 1 recorded as very important) and they tell afterwards that their experience was less fun than expected, that can sound unsatisfactory for the organizer, but it is not a negative outcome in case the organizers were seeking to realize the experience of new and different music. When stakeholders expressed little interest in new and different music before the beginning of the festival (i.e. a value which they weighted low), and afterwards confess that their appreciation of new and different music increased so much that they value that music more now, the organizers can be pleased and so can their supporters and financiers. A change in values is what impact is about. This way, the design of the QE "improves our understanding of how cultural value is constituted and captured, seeking to understand better the experiences or effects associated with arts and culture" (Crossick & Kaszynska, 2016, p. 3).

Methods

QE combines qualitative and quantitative methods including surveys, focus groups, panels, narratives, and visitation committees. The qualitative aspects of the research (focus groups, interviews, narratives, etc.) involve explorations of the experience of stakeholders to enhance awareness while defining their values and to 'bring[...] those experiences to being' (Johanson & Glow, 2015, p. 260). By asking respondents to rate their values on a Likert scale, we can assess the statistical relevance of various measures of qualities, make comparisons, and record changes.

Assessing the impact of Rotterdam Unlimited Festival

The Netherlands is a country where the festival sector is fast growing. Music festivals alone already amount to between 613 and 1123 in 2019 (Hitters & Mulder, 2020). This section provides an analysis of one of the largest Dutch festivals: Rotterdam Unlimited. Compared to the other festivals in Dutch cities (like Amsterdam and Utrecht), the Rotterdam government has a long tradition to support development and expansion of its festival culture (Hitters & Mulder, 2020). Accordingly,

> [t]he Rotterdam Model is a complex and interconnected system of urban music programming which emerged bottom up and not so much relies on the physical infrastructure, but much more on the network of trust between the people who are part of it.
>
> (Hitters & Mulder, 2020, p. 49)

Context of Rotterdam Unlimited Festival

Rotterdam Unlimited Festival (RU) is a five-day festival in Rotterdam presenting a wide range of dance, music, film, and poetry genres from acknowledged and upcoming artists. It started in 2013 as a merger of two festivals that had been held for three decades: the *DUNYA Festival* and *Zomercarnaval (Summer Carnival)*. The festival revolves around the diverse identities of Rotterdam and tries to do justice to those with an international programming. The cross-cultural character makes this festival unique in the Netherlands. The festival attracts more than 900,000 visitors from the Netherlands and abroad, with different social, cultural, ethnical, and educational backgrounds. It includes approximately 50% Western Europeans and 50% non-Western Europeans. Social and educational backgrounds vary a great deal, too.

Besides the festival director, who is responsible for the overall management, and the artistic director, responsible for the programming and the preservation of the artistic quality in relation to the mission and goals of the festival, there are four other people involved in the daily operations of the organization: (1) a financial manager who is simultaneously responsible for the coordination of production management; (2) an internal affairs coordinator who is also responsible for the coordination of the *Zomercarnaval*; (3) a PR-marketing coordinator; and (4) a coordinator who is responsible for the financial coordination of the sponsors and partners of the festival. Apart from these six people, several project-based volunteers and short-term employees contribute to the festival for a limited period each year. In addition, there are several committee and foundation members (in total fifteen) who on a voluntary basis advise and control the directors of the festival.

The festival is financed with public and private funding. It receives direct public funding from the Regional/Provincial Government, Rotterdam Municipality, as well as subsidies from Dutch public funds. The festival generates about 14.5% of the total budget by realizing own income and 24.5% by sponsoring. It also receives private donations.

Data collection

For the purposes of the evaluation, data is collected by way of a range of quantitative and qualitative methods: surveys, interviews, focus groups as well as an analysis of RU reports. The data concern the 2015 and 2016 editions of the festival. The data collection is based on 15 online surveys among the members of the organization, one focus group with the management team and two semi-structured interviews with the artistic and foundation director. The data for the audience (visitors, peers, and local politicians) of the festival are based on 20 interviews with visitors, 348 surveys (online and face-to-face) with visitors, 27 interviews with peers, and 8 interviews with local politicians. The survey questionnaires included close- and open-ended questions. In the close-ended questions, the respondents were asked to weigh on the scale from 1 (not important) to 5 (the most important) the importance of different aspects of their experience of different value dimensions (proxies).

Findings

In accordance with the phases of the VBA, this section presents the results of the analysis as follows: (1) Shared values of the protagonists and the values of relevant stakeholders and (2) assessment of the changes that RU generated for visitors and peers.

Shared values and related stakeholders of Rotterdam Unlimited Festival

The findings suggest that besides having strong artistic and cultural objectives, the protagonists of the festival have a societal objective that were articulated as a contribution to social cohesion. They consider it important that people with diverse backgrounds gather during the festival and gain an increased appreciation for other cultures and their music. They presume that such increased appreciation contributes to social cohesion in the city of Rotterdam and its surroundings. Prior the evaluation, different proxies for social cohesion were defined, that is values, that internal and external stakeholders agreed upon. The protagonists identified "solidarity" and "diversity" as key attributes for the qualities of the social practices that bring about social cohesion (Figure 11.3). The proxies for these attributes, that were decided together with the researcher, are "a sense of belonging", "togetherness", "social diversity", and "artistic diversity". Questions in the surveys were designed to ask for a valuation of these values and, in stage 2, the degree to which stakeholders experienced these qualities during the cultural festival.

Figure 11.3 Values map related to core stakeholders of RU festival.

Assessment of changes

After the festival, a survey and a series of interviews were conducted to determine how stakeholders had experienced the qualities of the festival and how they valued the same qualities. We basically posed two kinds of questions: (1) to what extent did you experience a sense of belonging/artistic diversity, etc. during the festival? and (2) How important is a sense of belonging/artistic diversity, etc. for you? The following section discusses the findings of the QE evaluation of RU. The analysis here focuses on the responses of visitors and peers.

Visitors' perspectives

A great majority of the visitors (87%) indicate before going to the festival *having fun with friends* as most important. This *social* quality of their intended visit was valued more highly than any other quality (4.3 out of 5). When asked after the visit, a slightly smaller majority (81%) values their experience of *having had fun with friends* a little lower. The conclusion is warranted that visitors were slightly disappointed on this count. Yet, because the protagonists did not identify this quality as important for their festival, this outcome is not a reason for concern and there is no need to adjust their strategy to increase the quality of *having fun with friends*. More relevant for the protagonists is the quality *communications among people with different cultural backgrounds, from different generations and diverse social groups*, as they address their purpose of contributing to social cohesion (Figure 11.3). More than half the visitors considered this quality important for their visit, and encouraging for the organizers, visitors indicated that they experienced this quality on an average 8% more, than they expected. The biggest gap between the initial valuation and the actual experience, thus the greatest (positive) impact, occurred with respect to quality *multicultural communication*, followed by *intergenerational communication* and *communication among diverse social groups*.

The quality *artistic diversity*, expressed by the valuation and experience of the *broad range of art forms* and *a broad range of genres*, was experienced less than initially valued (Figure 11.4). Although a large share of the visitors, respectively, 71% and 65%, valued these artistic dimensions as important before coming, a smaller share of the visitors, 60% and 51%, experienced them as important. This outcome is a cause of concern for the protagonists as artistic diversity is an important proxy for their contribution to social cohesion (Figure 11.3). However, most of the visitors experienced the programming of the *culturally and ethnically diverse art* (64%, Figure 11.5), and the participation of *different generations of artists*, both *emerging and well-known* (71%, Figure 11.5), as significantly important (Figure 11.4). These experiences met the valuation of diversity in the artistic programming. Accordingly, visitors were satisfied about this quality of the festival.

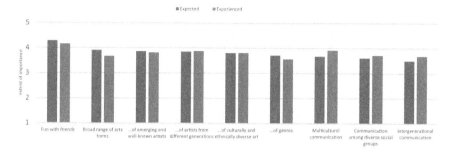

Figure 11.4 Visitors' perspective on RU social and cultural impact: expected vs. experienced by extent of importance, 2015/2016.

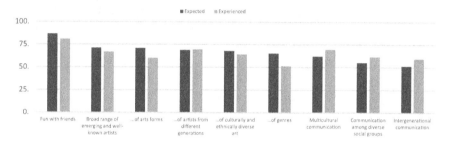

Figure 11.5 Visitors' perspective on RU social and cultural impact: expected vs. experienced by share of visitors (%) with positive attitude, 2015/2016.

Figure 11.6 Sharing, solidarity and belonging experienced during the festival by extent of importance, 2016.

In addition, in 2016, the visitors were asked to rate their actual experience of social qualities as *sharing*, *belonging*, and *solidarity*. Their responses indicate that they valued their experience of the qualities of *sharing*, *belonging*, and *solidarity* higher than before participating in the RU (Figure 11.6). This indicates a positive impact in respect to these values.

The interviews with visitors shed light on the possible reasons for visitors' strong experience of the *togetherness/sense of belonging* (Figure 11.7).

Figure 11.7 Visitors' description of their experience of RU, 2016.

They associated this with the *"energy of the group"*, *"enthusiasm and diversity of the crowd"*, *"openness among diverse people"*, or *"happiness, joy, group feeling"*. A smaller part of the respondents experienced the event as *"too messy"* and *"busy"*; for these visitors, the festival did not meet their expectation. Then again, the organizers had not aimed to realize a structured and quiet festival, so they do not need to change their organizational strategies because of this outcome.

Peer perspectives

The cohort of peers gave a positive assessment of both the social and artistic impact of RU (Figures 11.8 and 11.9). In general, peers have lower expectations than the visitors—valued on average about 3 out of 5—but in their experience of the actual event the peers encountered more social and program benefits than expected (on average up to 3.8). The biggest gap, and thus the greatest (positive) impact, was registered regarding *communication among different generations* and the *culturally and ethnically diverse programing* (Figure 11.8).

As far as the artistic dimensions of the festival are concerned, the peers valued the expected artistic quality of the festival quite low (about 3), but they experienced those qualities more positively. This was especially the case for *the cultural and ethnic programing* and *the diversity of artists from different generations*. This is an encouraging outcome for the protagonists.

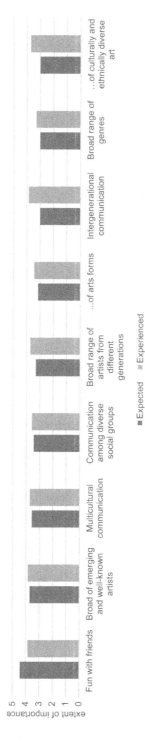

Figure 11.8 Peers' perspective on RU social and cultural impact: expected *vs.* experienced by extent of importance, 2015/2016.

Figure 11.9 Peers' description of their experience of RU, 2016.

What peers appreciate the most were the festive atmosphere of the cultural festival, the diversity of art forms and genres and the diversity of visitors that reflect the multicultural society of the city of Rotterdam (Figure 11.9).

Key dimensions of RU impact, 2016: visitors' perspectives

The evaluation of the festival in 2016 included additional qualities to be assessed: *awareness of diversity* and *sense of belonging* (Figure 11.10). They are qualities that the protagonists care about and that turned out to be relevant in the responses of the visitors. Almost half of the respondents (48%) report that by attending the festival they increased their *awareness and understanding of the people from a different social and cultural background*. Fifty-three percent indicates that because of the festival they increased their *sense of belonging*.

Notwithstanding this positive result, the visitors who were interviewed also note that even though the festival actually might increase the awareness of the diversity in the city, it does not necessarily add to the understanding of those diverse groups. At least half of the respondents were explicit about the differences between "*awareness*" and "*understanding*". The respondents made remarks like:

- "Yes, it [the festival] gives everyone the opportunity to taste and experience the atmosphere and the traditions of other cultures, but it is too short to influence the understanding".

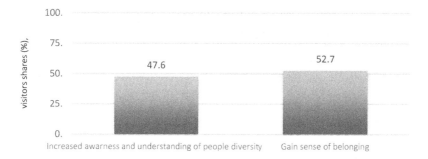

Figure 11.10 Key qualities that show a positive change in the expectations and experiences of visitors (% of visitors that signal a positive change), 2016.

- "We were definitely aware of the diversity of cultures of the people at the festival, both in the public and in the performances, but I wouldn't say that my understanding of them has increased. I would say that the festival increased our awareness of the diversity of Rotterdam".
- "In part, it [the festival] makes it clear that you live in a city with people with many cultures. I sincerely hope that for other people it matters and makes them want to see who other people are. But does it work this way? That is the question".

Getting to understand other people with different cultural backgrounds apparently takes more time and diverse forms of engagement. Even so, the protagonists may be encouraged by this outcome. They should also derive support for their efforts from the positive impact with the qualities, *diversity of the artistic offer in the city* and *social cohesion* that both the visitors and the peers register (Figure 11.11). The visitors consider the impact of RU on the *artistic diversity in the city* important (with an average score of 4) and the peers had an even higher appreciation of this quality (4.6). The caveat is that the evaluation should be extended over time and broaden the sample to be confident of a sustainable impact on the social cohesion in the city of Rotterdam. Given the limitations of this evaluation, this outcome is more an illustration of the potential impact of the cultural festival than its long run impact on the city.

Conclusions

The quality evaluator (QE) is a concrete answer to calls of cultural organizations, social corporations, foundations, and governments for an assessment of qualitative outcomes over and beyond the customary quantitative assessments. It is a method that can account for changes in values of their

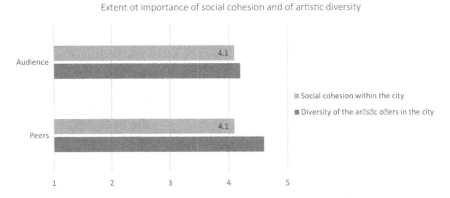

Figure 11.11 Visitor and peer perspectives on RU impact on the social cohesion and artistic diversity in the city by extent of importance, 2016.

audience or visitors and with that can function as an indicator of impact. QE's mixed method approach is thus another added value to quality (value) measurement techniques, wherein consistent procedures (e.g. demarcation and operationalization procedures for defining values and the related quantitative methods of setting up surveys), leave room for qualitative research (focus groups, interviews), to find the nuances that a standardized metrics for benchmarking would miss to include. This way, QE's mixed data collection techniques, addressing clearly operationalized values in relation to experiences, can function: As "an extension of the artistic event itself because their experience is inherently social, and so post-performance research can heighten their experience of that event" (Johanson & Glow, 2015, p. 260).

The quality evaluator is in development. It should be applied annually over an extended period to prove its merits. Its methods need to be refined. For example, a weighing of the qualities included is necessary to know which qualities are most relevant. In addition, some respondents (some stakeholders) might be more relevant than others in certain cases, or with regard to certain values. That gives an index problem that needs to be addressed. A distinction between incidental and regular visitors is also desirable in the future. The voice of internal stakeholders (the volunteers and employees) needs to count too, while the values of the funders need to be weighed in.

Despite these limitations—as a result of budget and time limitation from the festival's side—the quality evaluator has proven to be a promising device for the evaluation of qualitative impact. It is a reliable alternative to the impact studies, the surveys, the professional reviews, and the anecdotal evidence that cultural organizations and funders use now to evaluate qualitative outcomes or qualitative impact.

A critical element of the quality evaluator is the requirement that the protagonists (the organizers, the initiators) clearly articulate the qualities that they seek to realize with their cultural event or organization, and indicate which quality should be evaluated by each stakeholder. In the case of the Rotterdam Unlimited festival, and also in other cases where the quality evaluator was applied, defining concrete values and the qualities to strive for turned out to be a real challenge, and ended up being a revelation for the protagonists. It raised their awareness of what is most important to them. In many cases, the protagonists were not used to focus enough on the realization of those qualities, as they were to counting numbers of visitors and registering their satisfaction. They realized that the outcomes of the quality evaluator would be an important test of the effectiveness of their programming and other features of the festival.

The RU festival also realized that the outcomes gave them material to present to their funders, among whom is the city council. For the first time, the festival organizers were able to show how the festival contributes to the social cohesion in the city, which is a quality that members of the city council care about. Their only concern was how to communicate these results to a broader audience. After all, the quality evaluator is new and still in an experimental state. An additional positive factor was that the research was executed by scholars of the university, which made the evaluation reliable and more valid.

An important feature of the quality evaluator is the recognition that the qualities that the visitors or other stakeholders' value may be different from the qualities that the protagonists strive to realize. Vagueness remains if there is no clarity on how values are defined and assessed, when the definition of a certain value (social cohesion for instance in case of the RU festival) is as vague as it differs from stakeholder to stakeholder. There is thus a need for a clear reference point. Using quality evaluator, there is a strong emphasis on not only the research and the establishment of internal (e.g. managerial level) value definitions but also on the identification of clear specification of *proxies* that the internal stakeholders and the research team aims to measure and investigate.

In this way, the quality evaluator does justice to the ambition that most people in the cultural world appear to have: to change people, to raise awareness, to get them appreciate certain qualities (like artistic qualities) more, to overcome resistance (against new artistic genres and cultures, for example). This is certainly the case for the protagonists of the RU festival. In the literature, this feature shows in the theory of change, the aspiration to change values. The theory of change underlies the movement to stress the importance of impact as impact is actual change in the appreciation of relevant qualities. The quality evaluator has the potential to register such a change, or impact.

Another important feature of the quality evaluator is also that it provides relevant feedback to the protagonists. Certainly, when it includes panels and interviews, the protagonists gain insight into which strategies of theirs were effective, that is, brought about the desired changes, and which did not. They can take measures to improve the desired outcomes. At the same time, funders finally get the kind of evaluation that indicates whether the reasons for funding the project were correct, or not. Although the protagonists stand to gain from applying the quality evaluator, they may be reluctant from adopting it because the effectiveness of their activities will become more transparent.

In short, the application of the quality evaluator reported here confirms that:

- The protagonists become more aware of what is important to them when organizing a cultural festival;
- They also become aware of the composition of their stakeholders;
- They get as a feedback whether the visitors changed their valuation on the relevant qualities of their participation;
- This gives them additional leverage in communication with their funders and with their audiences.

The quality evaluator is a useful device to contribute to the cultural and social impact of cultural activities. It raises awareness of the qualities that really matter, and provides a rationale for sidestepping the tendency to stress economic impact.

Notes

1 These studies form so-called valuation approach tradition within the cultural economics (Dekker, 2014).
2 Klamer (2004) explicitly separates between social and cultural value of a cultural good, while delineating the differences between "culture as expression" and "culture as identity" (p. 32).
3 The report of Arts Council England is published at https://www.artscouncil. org.uk/measuring-outcomes.
4 The Manchester Matrix Pilot is explained in details in Knell (2017).
5 The Public Value Measurement Framework of Western Australia is presented at Department of Culture and the Arts WA (2014).

References

Belfiore, E., & Bennett, O. (2007). Rethinking the social impacts of the arts, *International Journal of Cultural Policy, 13*(2), 135–151.
Belfiore, E., & Bennett, O. (2009). Researching the social impact of the arts: Literature, fiction and the novel, *International Journal of Cultural Policy, 15*(1), 17–33.
Belfiore, E., & Bennett, O. (2010). Beyond the "toolkit approach": Arts impact evaluation research and the realities of cultural policy-making, *Journal for Cultural Research, 14*(2), 121–142.

Bell, S., Gillespie, M., & Wilding, C. (2016). *Rethinking Models of Evaluation: Sustainability as the Goal of International Cultural Organisations*, in International Sustainable Development Research Conference, 13–15 Jul 2016, Lisbon, Portugal.

Bennett, A., Taylor, J., & Woodward, I. (2014). *The Festivalization of Culture*. Ashgate: Burlington.

Bourdieu, P., & Passeron, J. (1977). Cultural reproduction and social reproduction. In R. Brown (ed.), *Knowledge, Education and Cultural Change*. London: Tavistock, pp. 71–112.

British Council (2018). *Cultural Value Project: A Literature Review*. Retrieved from https://www.britishcouncil.org/sites/default/files/lit_review_short_working_paper_final_final.pdf

Colombo, A. (2016). How to evaluate cultural impacts of events? A model and methodology proposal, *Scandinavian Journal of Hospitality and Tourism, 16*(4), 500–511.

Cooke, P., & Lazzeretti, L. (2008). *Creative Cities, Cultural Clusters and Local Economic Development*. Cheltenham: Edward Elgar.

Crossick, G., & P. Kaszynska (2016). *Understanding the Value of Arts and Culture*. The AHRC Cultural Value Project. Arts and Humanities Research Council. Retrieved from http://www.ahrc.ac.uk/documents/publications/cultural-value-project-final-report/

Currid, E. (2007). How art and culture happen in New York, *Journal of the American Planning Association, 73*(4), 454–467.

DCMS (1998). *Creative Industries Mapping Document*. London: Creative Task Force.

Dekker, E. (2014). Two approaches to study the value of art and culture, and the emergence of a third, *Journal of Cultural Economics, 39*(4), 309–326.

Department of Culture and the Arts WA (2014). *Public Value Measurement Framework: Measuring the Quality of the Arts*. Department of Culture and the Arts WA.

Dewey J. (1939). Theory of valuation, *International Encyclopedia of Unified Science, 2*(4), 67.

Eliassen, K., Hovden, J. F., & Prytz, O. (eds.) (2018). *Contested Qualities: Negotiating Value in Arts and Culture*. Fagbokforlaget.

European Commission (2010). *DG Education and Culture. Green Paper: Unlocking the Potential of Cultural and Creative Industries*, COM (2010) 183. Brussels: European Commission.

Evans, G. (2005). Measure for measure: Evaluating the evidence of culture's contribution to regeneration, *Urban Studies, 42*(5–6), 959–983.

Florida, R. (2002). *The Rise of the Creative Class*. New York: Basic Books.

Frey, B. (1994). The economics of music festivals, *Journal of Cultural Economics, 18*(1), 29–39.

Frey, B. S. (2000). The rise and fall of festivals—reflections on the Salzburg festival. *SSRN Electronic Journal*. Retrieved from https://ideas.repec.org/p/zur/iewwpx/048.html

Galloway, S. (2009). Theory-based evaluation and the social impact of the arts, *Cultural Trends, 18*(2), 125–148.

Ginsburgh, V. A. (2003). Awards, success and aesthetic quality in the arts, *Journal of Economic Perspectives, 17*(2), 99–111.

Higgs, P., Cunningham, S., & Bakhshi, H. (2008). *Beyond the Creative Industries: Mapping the Creative Economy in the United Kingdom.* NESTA.

Hitters, E., & Mulder, M. (2020). Live music ecologies and festivalisation: The role of urban live music policies, *International Journal of Music Business Research,* 9(2), 38–57.

Hutter, M., & Shusterman, R. (2006). Value and the valuation of art in economic and aesthetic theory. In V. A. Ginsburgh & D. Throsby (eds.), *Handbook of the Economics of Art and Culture,* Vol. 1, Amsterdam: Elsevier, pp. 169–208.

Hutter, M., & Throsby, D. (2008). *Beyond Price: Value in Culture, Economics, and the Arts.* Cambridge: Cambridge University Press.

Jaaniste, L. (2009). Placing the creative sector within innovation: The full gamut. Innovation: management, *Policy & Practice, 11,* 215–229.

Jacobs, J. (1969). *The Economy of Cities.* London: Penguin Books.

Jakob, D. (2013). The eventification of place: Urban development and experience consumption in Berlin and New York City, *European Urban and Regional Studies, 20*(4), 447–459.

Johanson, K., & Glow, H. (2015). A virtuous circle: The positive evaluation phenomenon in arts audience research, *Participations, 12*(1), 254–270.

KEA (2006). *The Economy of Culture in Europe.* Brussels: European Commission. Retrieved from https://ec.europa.eu/assets/eac/culture/library/studies/cultural-economy_en.pdf

KEA (2009). *The Impact of Culture on Creativity.* Brussels: DG EAC.

KEA (2015). *The Smart Guide to Creative Spillovers to Assist Cities Implementing Creative Spillovers.* EU: URBACT.

Klamer, A. (2002). Accounting for social and cultural values. *De Economist, 150,* 453–473.

Klamer, A. (2003). A pragmatic view on values in economics, *Journal of Economic Methodology, 10*(2), 191–212.

Klamer, A. (2004). Cultural goods are good for more than their economic value. In V. Rao & M. Walton (eds.), *Culture and Public Action.* Stanford, CA: Stanford University Press, pp. 138–162.

Klamer, A. (2013). The values of cultural heritage. In I. Rizzo and A. Mignosa (eds.), *Handbook on the Economics of Cultural Heritage.* Cheltenham/Northampton. Edward Elgar Publishing, pp. 421–437.

Klamer, A. (2017). *Doing the Right Thing: A Value Based Economy.* London: Ubiquity Press.

Knell, J. (2017). *Manchester Metrics Pilot.* Arts Council England. Retrieved from https://www.artscouncil.org.uk/sites/default/files/download-file/Manchester_Metrics_Pilot_Final_Report_of_Stage_One.pdf

Lamont, M. (2012). Toward a comparative sociology of evaluation. *The Annual Review of Sociology, 38,* 201–221.

Landry, C. (2000). *The Creative City.* London: Earthscan.

Maas, K., & Liket, K. (2011). Social impact measurement: Classification of methods. In R. Burrit (ed.), *Environmental Management Accounting and Supply Chain Management.* Dordrecht: Springer Netherlands, pp. 171–202.

Mulder, M., Hitters, E., & Rutten, P. (2020). The impact of festivalization on the Dutch live music action field: A thematic analysis, *Creative Industries Journal.* Retrieved from https://www.tandfonline.com/doi/full/10.1080/17510694.2020.1815396

Newman, A. (2013). Imagining the social impact of museums and galleries: Interrogating cultural policy through an empirical study, *International Journal of Cultural Policy, 19*(1), 120–137.

OECD (2014). Creative industries in the knowledge economy In *Tourism and the Creative Economy*. Paris: OECD Publishing, pp. 31–50.

O'Hagan, J. (2016). Objectives of arts funding agencies often do not map well on to societal benefits, *Cultural Trends, 25*(4), 249–262.

Pratt, A. C. (2004). Mapping the cultural industries: Regionalization, the example of south-east England. In D. Power & A. J. Scott (eds.), *Cultural Industries and the Production of Culture*. Abingdon: Routledge.

Quinn, B. (2005). Arts festivals and the city. *Urban studies, 42*(5–6), 927–943.

Rizzo, I., & Mignosa, A. (2013). *Handbook on the Economics of Cultural Heritage*. Cheltenham/Northampton: Edward Elgar Publishing.

Scott, A. J. (2010). Cultural economy and the creative field of the city, *Geografiska Annaler: Series B, Human Geography, 92*(2), 115–130.

Snowball, J. D. (2011), Cultural value. In R. Towse (ed.), *A Handbook of Cultural Economics,* Cheltenham: Edward Elgar, pp. 172–176.

Snowball, J. D. (2013). The economic, social and cultural impact of cultural heritage: Methods and examples. In I. Rizzo and A. Mignosa (eds.), *Handbook on the Economics of Cultural Heritage*. Cheltenham/Northampton: Edward Elgar Publishing, pp. 421–437.

Throsby, D. (2001). *Economics and Culture*. Cambridge: Cambridge university press.

Throsby, D. (2008). The concentric circles model of the cultural industries, *Cultural Trends, 17*(3), 147–164.

Throsby, D. (2010). *The Economics of Cultural Policy*. Cambridge: Cambridge University Press.

UNCTAD (2008). *Creative Economy Report*. UNCTAD. Retrieved from https://unctad.org/system/files/official-document/ditc20082cer_en.pdf

Uriarte, Y., Petrocchi, M., Catoni, M., Cresci, S., Nicola, R., Tesconi, M., & Uriarte, R. (2020). Exploring the relation between festivals and host cities on Twitter: A study on the impacts of Lucca Comics & Games, *Information Technology & Tourism, 22*(2), 625–648.

Young, R., Camic, P. M., & Tischler, V. (2016). The impact of community-based arts and health interventions on cognition in people with dementia: A systematic literature review, *Aging & Mental Health, 20*(4), 337–351.

12 Cultural Events and Japanese Pop Culture in Europe

The Case of the Japan Expo in France

Norio Tajima, Keiko Kawamata, Shoetsuro Nakagawa and Toshihiko Miura

Introduction

What is Japanese pop culture?

In recent years, Japanese pop culture (JPC), as represented by manga (Japanese comic strips) and anime (Japanese animation), has gained popularity among young people worldwide. For example, WIRED reported that the most widely searched word on Lycos in 2002 was 'Dragon Ball', the name of a Japanese anime (Wired News, 2002). Pop culture is entertainment that the masses can casually enjoy. As intuitive and emotional enjoyment are important for mass casual enjoyment, pop culture can be viewed as an entertainment with a low degree of required prior knowledge. Meanwhile, some entertainment can be enjoyed cognitively. To enjoy entertainment cognitively, it is important for consumers to have some basic prior knowledge. Pop culture, such as manga and anime, can certainly be enjoyed cognitively with prior knowledge, but the way we enjoy them is mainly intuitive and emotional. By defining pop culture in terms of the degree of prior knowledge required, it is possible to view it as entertainment that can easily be enjoyed by many consumers, especially young people who do not have some prior knowledge.

Generally, it is not easy to produce entertainment that attracts consumers intuitively or emotionally because an implicit element is necessary to do so. In this respect, the Japanese pop culture industry has accumulated the know-how to create works that include these implicit elements, which has been cultivated over many years of history. For example, JPC producers know a lot about setting up character personalities and storylines that consumers can easily relate to.

Furthermore, the environment surrounding the Japanese pop culture industry is very competitive, in terms of the number of works released each year and a distribution system that reflects the popularity of the works. The products that survive in such a production system and competitive environment have enough appeal to attract not only Japanese consumers but

DOI: 10.4324/9781003127185-16

also consumers from all over the world. Therefore, we define JPC as 'pop culture created by the unique production process of the modern Japanese pop culture industry'.

Purpose of this chapter

JPC events (JPCEs), in this chapter, refer to events that attract fans and/or consumers to JPC. JPCEs have been held worldwide, and their number and attendance size are rising. We are aware that the proliferation of JPC overseas is not the result of Japanese publishers' intentional expansion strategies. From a marketing perspective, the driving forces behind the rapid expansion of JPCEs outside Japan are not fully known.

This chapter, therefore, aims to examine how JPCEs as a category of 'cultural festivals' have influenced the acceptance of JPC in Europe especially in France. We focus specifically on the Japan Expo, held in Paris since 2000, with approximately 250,000 attendees annually. We use the megamarketing framework to analyse the development of JPCEs as a social legitimation process of JPC. Some JPC have characteristics including stigmatised cultural products that must overcome numerous barriers to be accepted in Europe. Thus, JPC is an innovation in the sense that it expresses values that are new to European traditions, and its diffusion in Europe is not easy. However, our basic argument in this chapter is that JPCE as a cultural festival plays an important role in JPC being accepted as an innovation within European tradition. For example, acknowledgement by the mainstream media and the involvement of government and companies facilitate legitimation, and JPCEs serve as publicly available spaces to visualise JPC. We also show three stages of the expansion process—(1) individual, (2) user community, and (3) non-user community—to indicate the role of JPCEs in promoting JPC.

In the following sections, first, the authors present the results of several years of visits to JPCEs and interviews with those involved, as well as theoretical considerations related to the event from a marketing perspective. On projecting the JPCEs' role in legitimising the JPC, we present a hypothetical model about the social acceptance process, called the three-step model. Next, based on this model, a case study of Japan Expo, which is held annually in Paris, is analysed; a detailed discussion of how Japan Expo has developed from 1999 to 2019 and its contribution to the social acceptance of JPC in France is provided. Finally, according to the findings in this chapter, managerial implications for the various actors involved in JPCEs are delineated from a marketing perspective.

Methodology

The data include document analysis, site observation, and interviews with event organisers, exhibitors, and attendees. Thus, the data for this chapter were obtained through the case study method. Each interview lasted approximately 1 to 2 hours, and interviews were conducted either in English or Japanese. In addition to JPCE organizers, exhibitors, and participants, interviews were also conducted with government-related organizations and Japanese residents to understand how they view the JPC and JPCEs. JPCE organisers and exhibitors were asked about the local acceptance of the JPC, the success factors of the JPCE and future strategy. Participants were asked about their personal experience of attending the event.

The survey in Europe had to be carried out during short business trips from Japan, so in some cases, it spanned several years. The authors visited 12 JPCEs and conducted 32 interviews. One of the authors visited Japan Expo in 2008, which led to the 2015 survey. In this chapter, Japan Expo is taken as the case study because it is one of the largest in terms of the number of visitors and a prototype for later JPCEs.

The proliferation of JPC and JPCE

How did JPC spread overseas in the first place? As mentioned in the Introduction, the JPC is created in Japan, but it has not been disseminated worldwide by a corporate initiative. Japanese cultural anthropologist Shiraishi (2013) examined how and why a JPC, such as anime and manga, proliferated abroad without intervention by JPC publishers, as they were not targeting overseas markets in their expansion strategies. She located four expansion channels: (1) personal relationships; (2) television broadcasts of anime programmes; (3) the development of information and communication technologies (ICT); and (4) consumers who actively consume, produce (translate), and distribute (introduce, publish) anime or manga. Active consumers were primarily people of Japanese ancestry and students who studied in Japan and majored in computer science (Shiraishi, 2013). Hence, the proliferation of JPC began to a large extent as a grassroot movement, and the development of ICT has been instrumental in the diffusion of JPC around the world. The number of overseas JPCEs is increasing in line with the rising popularity of JPC (Kawamata et al., 2017) from 191 events in FY2015 to 239 in FY 2019. (Chief Cabinet Office, 2015, 2019)

Theoretical framework

This study primarily aims to examine how JPCEs have influenced the acceptance of JPC in France. In marketing, events are classified as marketing communications tools, and such tools are gaining importance and popularity in this digital age. This chapter focuses, among other things, on grassroots, which are consumer-generated marketing events not planned by publishers or promoters—how these have evolved and developed in terms of consumer behaviour and marketing, and how they have influenced the formation of the new market for JPC.

Event consumption from participants perspective

Attractiveness of JPC

The reason JPCEs fascinate so many participants is attributed to the attractiveness of JPC itself. As mentioned in the introduction to this chapter, the JPCs that have been accepted around the world are those that survived the fierce competition in the Japanese market. Specifically, JPC has a long history of expertise in setting up character profiles and worldview; works that are created with this expertise and meet the strict aesthetic standards of Japanese consumers have the universality to succeed worldwide.

In general, the factors that lead consumers to be fascinated with pop culture such as manga and anime are closely related to fan identity, and Williams (2016) sees the relationship with fan objects as a way for fans to alleviate difficulties and anxiety in life and maintain a stable self. Sandvoss (2005) considers the experience of creating a sense of self through the objects provided by the media as an important aspect of being a fan; Sandvoss sees fan identity as one of the various selves in daily life. While normal viewers exit their role as an audience when they stop watching a work, fans continue with it as an everyday identity even after they leave media consumption (Cavicchi, 1998).

There are various elements embedded in JPCs that allow consumers to project their identities. For example, there are a large number and variety of characters that appear in a single work. The personalities of each character and the relationships between them are meticulously designed, and the psychological descriptions are detailed. The stories are not simply good and punishing, and even characters who appear to be opponents of the protagonist may have beliefs that consumers can fully sympathize with. By having a variety of characters, including opponents, it is possible for any consumer to find a character that fits his or her values enough to commit.

Therefore, JPC has the know-how to embed elements to attract consumers during the production process, and as a result, it has enough attractiveness to lure not only Japanese consumers but also global consumers.

Participants/fans of JPCEs

While some consumers enjoy the work in relation to the subject, others enjoy JPC in interaction with other consumers. In particular, for consumers that are fans, one of the factors that defines their identity is 'relationships and communication among fans' (Ross and Nightingale, 2003). Sugiyama (2020) states that relationships with other fans are important in maintaining their long-term fan identity. While much of what we do today may take place online, the events which we focus on can still be a particularly important place for fans to interact. Booth and Kelly (2013) state that face-to-face interactions such as conventions, are important places that support fan identity.

JPCs have a universality that strongly attracts consumers around the world, but at the same time, JPCs are scalable to be developed in various media formats. For example, a successful manga work can be developed into a variety of media, including TV anime, movies, merchandise, events, and stage performances. Fans then try to get involved with the work across the media formats. Among these, events, in particular, have the aspect of defining identity through events as media and interaction with other fans. In other words, events are the place to experience and enjoy interaction with other fans and enhance their own identities. Hence, JPC fans are inevitably highly motivated to participate in JPCE. In fact, the Japan Expo attracts 250,000 attendees each year, and the annual JPCE in Japan, Comic Market, attracts 750,000 attendees each time.

The event from marketing perspective

The event as marketing communication tool

In the previous section, we discussed the reasons why JPC fans gather at JPCE. In this section, we will discuss JPCE from a marketing perspective.

While some event studies define events as 'an occurrence at a given place and time; a special set of circumstances; a noteworthy occurrence' (Getz and Page, 2020, p. 51), a standard marketing textbook includes events and experiences as part of the marketing communications mix, and explain their function as to deepen the relationship between the target market and the company's brand experience (Kotler and Keller, 2015). Kotler and Keller (2015) also mention that many firms create their own events and a large part of local, grassroots marketing is experiential marketing (Pine and Gilmore, 1999). Experiential marketing not only communicates the features and benefits of a product or service but also links the product or service to the unique and interesting experiences of the participants/fans. In other words, events and experiences are a means to become part of a special and more personally relevant moment in participants/fans' lives (Kotler and Keller, 2015). JPCE is not only a show case of JPC but also the place to experience and enjoy interactions with other fans and enhance their own identities. Then, how do JPCEs evolve and develop as a place to enjoy JPC itself, and interaction with other fans?

Event evolution and legitimacy

Beverland, Hoffman, and Rasmussen (2001) studied some Australasian wineries and examined the evolution of the Australasian wine sector events. They presented an event life-cycle model, drawing on the life-cycle model in the fields of organization and marketing theory. Their description of the early stages is of particular interest to us since this chapter focuses on evolution and development of consumer-generated, unplanned events.

Their preliminary findings suggest that the early stages of the event life-cycle model show that awareness and subsequent support from stakeholders is necessary. Their model raises the need for legitimacy in order to gain support from stakeholders. Croidieu, Rüling, and Boutinot (2016) analysed the generation of the fine wine genre in the Australian wine industry and referred to the roles of stakeholders.

Professional management is necessary for grassroots, amateur-led fandoms to grow into large, ongoing events (Getz and Page, 2020). In addition to the information spread over social networking sites, mass media coverage is also considered to be effective in obtaining awareness in the early stages of an event. What then, should companies bear in mind when considering JPCE as a marketing communication tool?

Matsui (2019) pointed out that some cultural products, especially JPCs such as manga and anime, carry a 'stigma' (Goffman, 1963), which can hinder diffusion. JPCs are considered a stigmatized product, which is attributable in part to their nature and their fans. Jenson (1992) pointed out that the word, 'fan' as the term's origin refers, is characterized as a potential fanatic. In particular, fans of the JPC are likely to be associated with a deviant image. Coping with that image, Jenkins (1992a) describes fans as those who produce, write, and participate, and Jenkins (1992b) sees the characteristics of fandom as a participatory culture. He also refers to the grassroots aspect of the fans (Jenkins, Ito, and Boyd, 2018).

As described in the previous section, JPC fans are highly motivated to participate in all aspects. For JPCE organisers, cognitive legitimation for stakeholders is necessary in order to grow from a small fandom to a JPCE. For companies that use JPCE as a means of marketing communications mix, legitimation to lower the hurdle to participate in JPCE is indispensable unless their target market is the core JPC fans.

Megamarketing

Kotler (1986) offers the framework, megamarketing, a marketing strategy to enter a blocked or protected market, aiming at multiple stakeholders, including competitors, suppliers, retailers, regulators, the media, critics, certification bodies, and associations. He defines megamarketing as 'the strategically coordinated application of economic, psychological, political, and public relations skills to gain the cooperation of a number of parties in order to enter and/or operate in a given market' (Kotler, 1986, pp. 117–118).

Drawing on the concept of megamarketing, Humphreys (2010), Chaney, Slimane, and Humphreys (2016), and Humphreys, Chaney, and Slimane (2017) argue that the creation of new markets is a cultural, political, and social process, requiring stakeholder-framing to achieve legitimation; this is a key construct of her work. Humphreys (2010) offers alternatives to the strictly firm-driven market development approach, acknowledging the importance of other stakeholders, including media and public policy actors, who play important roles in the legitimisation of the industry. Her institutional approach shows how firms need to build the cognitive, normative, and regulative conditions required to establish a market. She selected the US casino industry to demonstrate the process of legitimation, because it experienced a noticeable shift of regulatory, normative, and cultural–cognitive barriers over time (Humphreys, 2010).

Evolution of the Japan Expo: the three-stage model

By definition, legitimation is the process of acknowledgement of JPC as accepted by the non-user community utilising JPCEs. As events necessitate awareness, recognition, and legitimation to grow, following the megamarketing approach, we examine the evolution of JPCEs as a process of legitimation and analyse it by setting the three stages in Figure 12.1. In our three-stage model, Stage 1 is where fans enjoy JPC personally and in Stage 2, gather with people sharing the same interest. The legitimation is required at Stage 3, where people gather at a JPCE, which presumably serves as a publicly available venue to help JPC gain non-users' acceptance (i.e. other stakeholders and society at large).

Stage 1: Enjoying JPC personally. JPC fans enjoyed JPC at home through television, comic books, magazines, and the internet, as a personal activity. At this stage, there is no JPC fandom or fan culture; 'culture' here is defined as shared values and symbols. Moreover, JPC is not yet influential in the larger communities.

Stage 2: Grassroots gathering with people sharing the same interest. Fans enjoyed voluntarily attending community and web gatherings. This can be seen as the transition from individual behaviour to social gathering (Stage 1 to Stage 2) and in some cases, JPC is shared as a symbol of the community, where fans confirm their identity. However, JPC is still only a grassroots user community culture at best, and not yet visible or accepted in society. At this stage, JPC has the power to influence fans but is not yet influential in the larger communities.

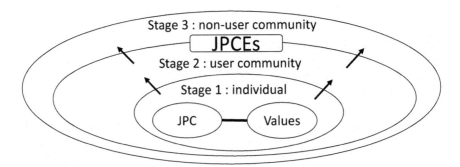

Figure 12.1 Stages of evolution of JPCEs.

Stage 3: Gathering at JPCEs. The mainstream media, the Government of Japan, large corporations, and well-known guests get involved. A JPCE such as Japan Expo serves as a forum for visualising JPC, thereby helping JPC to be recognised and legitimated by the society. JPC now has some impact on society (non-user communities). A JPCE is considered as playing an important role in transferring JPC from the culture of the user community, to the culture of the expanded or non-user community. This means that JPCEs play an important role in the process of society accepting JPC innovation in harmony with traditions of society. At this stage, the awareness of fan community is likely to shift from a grassroots fan gathering to JPCE.

The process of development and evolution of the Japan Expo

What is the Japan Expo?

The Japan Expo is one of the largest and most well-known JPCEs in the world. It began in 2000 with only 3,200 attendees. The exact origins of the event are controversial, but the primary elements are agreed upon (Sabré, 2013).

According to the materials distributed at the Japan Expo briefing in Tokyo on 17 December 2019, the profile of visitors is slightly higher for women (53%), with two-thirds of attendees aged between 15 and 22 years. The materials claim that social networking services (SNS) have been used to access the Expo by over 317,000 Facebook fans, over 57,000 Twitter followers, over 42,000 Instagram subscribers, and over 2.5 million video viewers, and their app has received over 2 million views with over 32,500 actual app downloads. What drew our attention was that 40% of the visitors are newcomers every year.

Sabré (2013) depicts the Japan Expo as a large commercial convention with a mix of events: from commercial entities such as shops and professional editors, to amateur illustrators and fanzines (magazines written by fans). Sabré (2013) states that the combination of JPC elements with more traditional aspects of Japanese culture and everyday life is the most striking characteristic of the event. 'Stands are held not only by shops but also fanzine illustrators' non-profit associations, tourism agencies, Japanese television channels, Japanese language schools, among many other examples. The visitors can find Japanese food, enjoy cosplay competitions, fashion shows, concerts, and conferences' (Sabré, 2013, p. 98).

Prehistory and the dawn of the Japan Expo: 1999–2001

In the 1980s and 1990s, Japanese anime was so popular among French children that their parents were concerned about its influence on them. After a long debate, le Club Drothée, the most popular TV youth programme featuring anime, was cancelled in 1997 (Brunet, 2015).

However, anime fandom was far from over in France. The internet facilitated communication between fans across fan sites and helped write the next chapter, which was the Japan Expo. The first stage of the Japan Expo began in 1999; then, three students—Jean-François Dufour, Sandrine Dufour, and Thomas Sirdey—from Institut Supérieur du Commerce de Paris hosted the first convention in 2000 in their school basement. They founded the grassroots convention out of a great love for anime, rather than as a school project or assignment, and the attendance increased steadily every year (Brunet, 2015; Sabré, 2012, 2013; Tajima, 2016; Kawamata et al., 2017).

One epoch-making issue for JPC (manga) to be acknowledged in France, is that a Japanese mangaka (cartoonists), Taniguchi Jiro, won Best Screenplay Award for 'Chichi no koyomi [Le Journal de Mon Père (Father's calendar)]' in the 2001 Festival International de la Bande dessinée Angoulême.

From the introductory stage to take-off: 2002–2006

After the first two editions, in 2002, the Japan Expo started a 'copyright-matching event', and business orientation spurred. As the Japan Expo had grown considerably, it moved from the school building to the Centre des Nouvelles Industries et Technologies in 2003. After an intermission in 2005, the event once again relocated in 2006, this time to Parc des Expositions de Paris-Nord Villepinte, where it took its current form (Sabré, 2013). Figure 12.2 displays the number of visitors to the Japan Expo from 1999 to 2019.

Brunet (2015) discusses the Japan Expo's transformation from an anime and manga fan convention, to a standardised Japanese fan event. He quotes Alexi, an anime fan who served as a staff member at the Japan Expo in 2006. Alexi could not relate to the 'bleached' (Brunet, 2015, p. 170) (more standardised, homogenised, and popular) geek culture; Japan Expo's atmosphere suggested that it was reserved for privileged fans. However, these more commercialised orientations provoked criticism of the Japan Expo from veteran anime fans; this is unlike Epitanime, a French Anime convention, which is still considered core anime fan oriented. Japan Expo has ceased to be a place to enhance fan identity or deepen experiences with JPC. Despite the criticism, Japan Expo grew and the expansion of Japan Expo's new fan base continued.

Attracting more people leads to legitimation. In parallel, Brunet (2015) describes the change in the tone of the French journals which had played a central role in criticising Japanese anime since the 1980s, that is, 'La folie manga, art ou japoniaiserie?' in Télama (n.2745, 24–30 aout 2002, pp. 12–18). In 2006, Le monde covered Japan Expo for the first time, 'Mangas: "Goldorak", vers l'âge adulte'.

For the Japan Expo, participants from the 'home' country of Japan also contribute to the legitimacy of the event. When TV crews from a Japanese local Television, TV Aichi, Nagoya, Japan came to cover the event, they were enthusiastically welcome (Oguri, 2016). The Japan Expo organisers

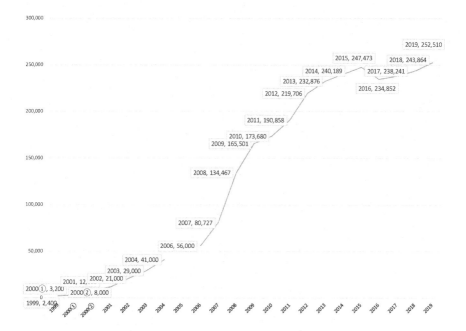

Figure 12.2 Numbers of visitors: Japan Expo (Paris) 1999–2019.

Source: Compiled from https://www.japan-expo-paris.com/fr/ and https://fr.wikipedia.org/wiki/Japan Expo

Note: 1 Day (1999–2001), 2 Days (2002–2004), 3 Days (2006–2007), 4 Days (2008–2013, 2015–2019), 5 Days (2014).

started inviting more JPC creators to the convention and the scope of invited guests was expanded from anime and manga to music and games.

In the meantime, three famous Japanese mangaka received awards from the Festival International de la Bande dessinée Angoulême. In 2003, Taniguchi Jiro again won the Best Screenplay Award for '*Harukana machi he* [Quartier Lointiain (Far District)]'. In 2004, Urasawa Naoki won the Best Feature Award for '*20th Century Boys*', and Nakazawa Keiji won the Tournesol Award for 'Hadashi no Gen' [Gen d'Hiroshima I & II (Barefoot Gen)] (Casterman 2020).

Growth stage for market expansion: 2007–2013

SEFA Event, a private company, was created to professionally manage the Expo in 2007. Starting in 2008, the Japan Expo tried to enter new markets: Chibi Japan Expo (2007 in Paris, 2008–2010 in Montreuil, France), Japan Expo Sud, Marseilles, France (2009–); Japan Expo Centre, Orleans, France (2011–2012); Japan Expo Belgique (2011–2012); and Japan Expo USA, San Francisco (2013–2014). Apart from Japan Expo Sud, Marseilles, all of these events have been discontinued.

During this period, two very important factors are considered contributing to legitimation: participation of Japanese large corporations and acknowledgement from the Japanese government. As for the latter, the Japan Expo was granted several awards from the Japanese government: the 2009 Foreign Minister's Award (2009) from Ministry of Foreign Affairs; the 16th AMD Award for meritorious service sponsored by the Ministry of Public Management, Home Affairs, Posts and Telecommunications (2011); and the Commissioner's Award from the Agency for Cultural Affairs (2013).

Changes in the Japanese tourism policy provided the Japan Expo with opportunities to grow. The Japanese government launched the Visit Japan Campaign in 2003 with the goal of doubling inbound tourism by 2010. *Kanko Rikkoku*, the political initiative for building a tourism nation, reflected the new economic priorities of Japan as reflected in the Visit Japan Campaign, the 2007 Building a Tourism Nation, the 2008 Japan Tourism Agency campaign, the 2009 Roadmap to 30 million campaign, and the 2012 Tourism Nation Promotion Basic Plan. When the authors visited the Japan Expo in 2019, its ability to attract tourists had expanded accordingly.

As of 2020, there are 19 Japanese award winners in Festival International de la Bande dessinée Angoulême, and Mizuki Shigeru became the first Japanese mangaka who won the Best Manga Award for '*Nonnon baa to Ore [Non-NonBâ]*'. In 2013, Toriyama, Akira won the 40th Anniversary Award at the Festival International de la Bande dessinée Angoulême. In 2015, Katsuhiro Otomo became the first Japanese Grand Prix winner (Comics and Cola 2015).

From maturity stage to present: 2014–2019

Figure 12.2 demonstrates that the Japan Expo reached its maturity stage with around 240,000 attendees. When the authors interviewed SEFA in July 2015, they revealed that they expected a maximum of 250,000 visitors. They voiced intentions to expand the market by attracting attendees' families, new fans, and non-fans. To that end, in looking for something new to attract attendees, for example, they introduced the Japanese cuisine, *washoku* in 2015. In 2018, in honour of the 160th anniversary of the establishment of diplomatic relations between France and Japan, the tourism section was opened. SEFA established Japan Expo G.K. in Tokyo in 2019 as a base for the Japan Expo.

Participation of famous Japanese guests, and of major Japanese companies continued. In 2018, the Award for the 50th anniversary of the establishment of the Agency for Cultural Affairs was granted. Brunet (2015) referred to very interesting news about the French journalist who used to critique Japanese anime; he and his daughter stayed in Kyoto, Japan to explore the world of *NARUTO* (a popular Japanese manga/anime) for their project (Villa Kujoyama, 2016). In 2019, Takahashi Rumiko became the first Japanese woman to be awarded the Grand Prix, one of the two female winners in history of the Festival International de la Bande dessinée Angoulême. (Festival d'Angoulême, 2019). Table 12.1 provides a summary of the growth of Japan Expo.

Table 12.1 Timeline of events

1999–2001: THE DAWN OF THE JAPAN EXPO

2001   Festival International de la Bande dessinée Angoulême, France, Best Screenplay Award, Taniguchi Jiro, 'Chichi no koyomi [Le Journal de Mon Père (Father's calendar)]'

2002–2006: FROM THE INTRODUCTORY STAGE TO TAKE-OFF

Emerging business orientation. New inbound tourism initiative in Japan. Guests from Japan started to join: manga and music. Five Japanese mangaka won prizes at Festival International de la Bande dessinée Angoulême.

2002   Télama*, <La folie manga, art out japoniaiserie?>, n.2745, 24–30 aout 2002, pp. 12–18. * Changes in the tone of journal essays played a central role in Japanese anime criticism since the 1980s

2003   Festival International de la Bande dessinée Angoulême, France, Best Screenplay Award, Taniguchi Jiro, '*Harukana machi he [Quartier Lointiain (Far District)]*'

2004   Festival International de la Bande dessinée Angoulême, France, Best Feature Award, Urasawa Naoki, '*20th Century Boys*', Prix Tournesol, '*Hadashi no Gen [Gen d'Hiroshima I & II (Barefoot Gen)*', Nakazawa Keiji.

2006   *le monde*, <Mangas: 'Goldorak', vers l'âge adulte>, keyword: 'Japan Expo' for the first time.

2007–2013: GROWTH STAGE FOR MARKET EXPANSION

Market expansion challenges: Chibi Japan (2007–2010), Japan Expo Sud (2009 to date), Japan Expo Centre, Japan Expo Belgiu(2011–2012), Japan Expo USA(2013–2014). Entry of major Japanese firms. Guests from Japan varied.: manga, music and games. The 150th anniversary of the establishment of diplomatic relations between France and Japan. Six Japanese mangaka won prizes at Festival International de la Bande dessinée Angoulême.

2007   SEFA event, a private company established.
       Festival International de la Bande dessinée Angoulême, France, Best Manga Award, Mizuki Shigeru, '*Nonnon baa to Ore [NonNonBâ]*'

2009   Foreign Minister's Award from the Ministry of Foreign Affairs of Japan

2011   The 16th AMD meritorious service award sponsored by the Ministry of Internal Affairs and Communications

2013   Festival International de la Bande dessinée Angoulême, France, the 40th Anniversary Award, Toriyama Akira
       Commissioner's Award from the Agency for Cultural Affairs

2014–2019: FROM MATURITY STAGE TO PRESENT

Guests varied.: manga, music, games, cosplay and sports. (Not necessarily only from Japan) The 160th anniversary of the establishment of diplomatic relations between France and Japan. Seven Japanese mangaka won prizes at Festival International de la Bande dessinée Angoulême. (2014–2020)

2015   Festival International de la Bande dessinée Angoulême, France, Grand Prix, Otomo Katsuhiro

2016   Emanuel Carröre of Télamak, the representative who used to criticise Japanese anime was in Kyoto Japan to explore the world of *NARUTO* with his daughter.

2018   Award for the 50th anniversary of the establishment of the Agency for Cultural Affairs 2018

2019   Representative Office converted to Tokyo Office (Japan Expo GK)

2019   Festival International de la Bande dessinée Angoulême, France, Grand Prix, Rumiko Takahashi

Discussion

The Japan Expo began as a grassroots gathering of anime and manga enthusiasts with a volunteer spirit. As the event grew, the transition from Stage 2 to Stage 3 of the three-staged model (Figure 12.1) occurred; the characteristics of the gathering changed from a grassroots fan gathering to a professionally managed JPCE with commercial orientation.

At Stage 3 (Figure 12.1), legitimation to be accepted by the society is needed. The factors which contributed to the legitimation of the Japan Expo include (1) articles in quality newspapers such as *Le Monde* (Figure 12.3), (2) awards from the Japanese government, (3) the participation of major companies, and (4) the growing number and type of guests such as popular mangaka, anime directors and producers, game producers, and entertainers from Japan.

The direct impact of (1) and (2) on the younger generation, the primary group of visitors, is questionable, but these do affect the willingness of exhibitors to participate. For example, a representative of the World Cosplay Summit (Nagoya, Japan)—a similar JPCE for cosplay, a partly stigmatised JPC—stated that 'government endorsement' contributed to the acquisition of sponsors (Oguri, 2016). JPC such as manga and anime have often faced

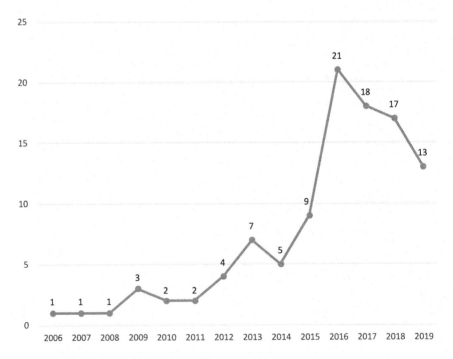

Figure 12.3 Results of keyword-search 'Japan Expo' in *Le Monde*.
Source: https://www.lemonde.fr/.

similar issues in its status among Japanese people who may view it as inferior to more traditional art forms. Some examples of mixed feelings of Japanese people exist(ed).[1] This contrasts with the French fans who embrace JPC in Japan Expo. Government recognition and other legitimising factors are useful for internal communication with exhibitors and may make it easier for them when applying for funds from their superiors.

As for (3) and (4), the participation of major companies and high-profile guests also increases the credibility of the Japan Expo and leads to legitimation, which would induce other companies and guests to become exhibitors or attend the Expo. This could result in increased attractiveness of the exhibition to attendees and fans. Especially in a society like Japan, where the sense of legitimation provided by large and established company brands is likely to increase willingness to attend and lower barriers to participation.

Implications for management

First, to develop their events, JPCE organizers can implement a marketing strategy that induces interaction not only among the participants, such as anime fans, but also among various actors involved in the event as a platform. Second, if the Japanese government supports the hosting and development of JPCE in Japan, it can attract a large number of tourists from abroad for the purpose of anime tourism, which can be expected to have various economic effects. In addition, by supporting JPCEs overseas, the government can contribute to the acceptance of JPC locally, and as a result, provide the basis for JPC's global expansion. Third, supporting JPCEs by the local governments and industries in respective regions can generate large economic effects on the regions both in Japan and overseas. In JPCE, the JPC itself is a tourism resource—any region can hold a JPCE without any specific tourism resource. Fourth, JPC copyright holders can utilise JPCE to facilitate acceptance of JPC in the regions and countries where JPCEs are held. This measure will help gain long-term revenues from JPC. Finally, companies collaborating with JPC can also expect some economic impact. In recent years, many Japanese companies have launched products in collaboration with anime. Participating in JPCE as an exhibitor can help these firms reach young people and easily enter the local market. Table 12.2 provides a summary of the managerial implications for each subject.

Assuming JPCEs are platforms where products and services bring together groups of users in two-sided networks and provide infrastructure and rules that facilitate both groups' transactions (Parker and Van Alstyne, 2006), legitimations should catalyse both cross-side network effects (participation of major companies causes rise in visitors) and same-side network effects (participation of major companies induce other companies' participation).

According to Kotler (1986), some effective megamarketing strategies for JPCE organisers to facilitate legitimation include gaining coverage from

Table 12.2 Summary of managerial implications for each subject

Subjects	Managerial implications
JPCE organizer	- Marketing for evolution and development of JPCEs
Japanese government	- Marketing to use JPCEs for attracting people from abroad - Marketing to use JPCEs for the global expansion of JPC
Local government and industry	- Marketing to use JPCEs for attracting people to revitalize not depending on regional resource
JPC/Content publisher and content producer	- Marketing to use JPCEs for improving the status of JPC as a culture - Marketing to use JPCEs for global expansion of their own JPC
Companies collaborating with JPC	- Marketing to use JPCEs for introducing their own products to JPC fan as promising market

mass media, developing relations with Japanese governments, and soliciting major companies and celebrities. A megamarketing strategy requires organisers to create a foundation for the acceptance of a different culture, namely the JPC. To achieve success, organisers must reach beyond traditional dyadic transactional relationships that focus on marketing to direct customers such as visitors and exhibitors; marketing efforts must be extended to building relationships with all stakeholders involved in creating, encouraging, and legitimating the demand for JPCs and JPCEs.

In the digital age, it is crucial for event organisers to manage both online and offline channels. Diffusion of JPC via the internet played an important role for JPC fans—they found each other easily online and formed communities for exchange of views. Japan Expo now serves as a major JPC platform. We researched the online search behaviour of British, French, and German JPC fans who are potential tourists to Japan. We found that they preferred to access JPC through video streaming sites such as YouTube, and events are one of the most preferred and trusted offline sources of media of French JPC fans. Although the use of offline sources is relatively low, it was found that in France particularly, JPCEs are highly valued as a source of information for JPC.

Limitations and future research

This research may have limited generalisability, because it focuses on a single case, the Japan Expo. Nonetheless, the historical context provided and the examination of Japan Expo's marketing strategy to identify factors that facilitated its legitimation should be of great use to all parties involved in the production, distribution, and promotion of JPC materials, especially JPCEs. Although the authors did not elaborate on Japan Expo participants and consumer behaviour at the microlevel, exploring the emotional aspects of these actors is important (Martin and Schouten, 2014) to reach a deeper understanding of their interactions with JPC and of what might drive their continued participation in JPCEs. This research suggests that a macro–micro integration model is needed in terms of future research. Additionally, follow-up studies should address various other patterns of JPCE development and additional factors that contribute to legitimation.

Acknowledgements

This work was supported by JSPS KAKENHI Grant Numbers, JP17K02123, JP18K11875, JP20K12435, and JP21K12486. We would like to acknowledge Editage (www.editage.com) for English language editing.

Note

1 When one of the authors visited Japan Expo for the first time in 2008, she was struck by the exhibitions, interpretations, and expressions of Japan and was unable to find the appropriate words to express her mixed feelings. Many people who visited the 2008 Expo at that time reported similar impressions. One journalist commented in July 2008 that the rapid increase in the number of young people interested in Japan that was triggered by manga and anime should be considered a major opportunity to expand international exchanges. He ended his article by saying, 'After the cosplay competition, the participants went back home to Paris on a train in cosplay. It was a strange sight' (Fukui 2008). In another case, a Japanese woman, whose husband was French and lived in Marseilles, made some harsh comments in her blog on Japan Expo Sud in Marseilles when her French nephew brought her family there. Apparently, she could not stand it, and said that in the first place, the name should not be English, but French: 'L'Expo Japonaise'.

References

Beverland, M., Hoffman, D. and Rasmussen, M. (2001). The Evolution of Events in the Australasian Wine Sector. *Tourism Recreation Research*, 26(2), pp. 35–44.

Booth, P. and Kelly, P. (2013). The Changing Faces of Doctor Who Fandom: New Fans, New Technologies, Old Practices? *Participations: Journal of Audience & Reception Studies*, 10(1), pp. 56–72.

Brunet, T. (2015). *Suiyo bi no anime ga machidoushii* [Vivement les dessins animés du mercredi!]. Tokyo, Japan: Seibundo-shinkosha.

Casterman official site (2020). *Jirô Taniguchi*, [online] Available at: https://www.casterman.com/Bande-dessinee/Auteurs/taniguchi-jiro [Accessed 17 June 2021].

Cavicchi, D. (1998). *Tramps Like Us: Music & Meaning Among Springsteen Fans*. Oxford: Oxford University Press.

Chaney, D., Slimanem K. B. and Humphreys, A. (2016). Megamarketing Expanded by Neo-institutional Theory. *Journal of Strategic Marketing*, 24(6), pp. 470–483.

Chief Cabinet Office. (2015). *Cool Japan Event Calendar*. [online] Available at: http://www.cao.go.jp/cool_japan/event/pdf/siryou_2015.pdf [Accessed 20 April 2020].

Chief Cabinet Office. (2019). *Cool Japan Event Calendar.* [online] Available at: https://www.cao.go.jp/cool_japan/event/pdf/siryou_2019_all.pdf [Accessed 17 June 2020].

Comics and Cola. (2015). Katsuhiro Otomo to attend Angouleme 2016 as Festival President, with Conference, Tribute Exhibition and Book. [online] Available at: http://www.comicsandcola.com/2015/11/katsuhiro-otomo-to-attend-angouleme.html [Accessed 17 June 2021].

Croidieu, G., Rüling, C. and Boutinot, A. (2016). How Do Creative Genres Emerge? The Case of the Australian Wine Industry. *Journal of Business Research,* 69, pp. 2334–2342.

Eisenmann, T., Parker, G. and Van Alstyne, M. W. (2006). Strategies for Two-sided Markets. *Harvard Business Review,* 84(10), pp. 92–101.

Festival d'Angoulême. (2019) CEREMONIE, [online] Available at: https://twitter.com/bdangouleme/status/1088133871772860417 [Accessed 17 June 2021].

Fukui, S. (2008). *Japan Expo Furansu no wakamono ni nihon bumu* [Japan Expo: Boom About Japan Among Young French People]. *The Mainichi Shimbun,* 20 July 2008.

Getz, D. and Page, S. J. (2020). *Event Studies: Theory, Research and Policy for Planned Events.* 4th ed. London: Routledge.

Goffman, E. (1963). *Stigma: Notes on Management of Spoiled Identity.* Englewood Cliffs, NJ: Prentice-Hall.

Humphreys, A. (2010). Megamarketing: The Creation of Markets as a Social Process. *Journal of Marketing,* 74(20), pp. 1–19.

Humphreys, A., Chaney, D. and Slimane K. B. (2017). Megamarketing in Contested Markets: The Struggle between Maintaining and Disrupting Institutions. *Thunderbird International Business Review,* 59(5), pp. 613–622.

Jenkins, H. (1992a). 'Strangers No More, We Sing': Filking and the Social Construction of the Science Fiction Fan Community. In: Lewis L.A (ed.) *The Adoring Audience: Fan Culture and Popular Media.* London: Routledge, pp. 208–236.

Jenkins, H. (1992b). *Textual Poachers: Television Fans and Participatory Culture.* London: Routledge.

Jenkins, H., Ito, M. and Boyd, d. (2016. *Participatory Culture in a Networked Era.* Cambridge: Polity Press.

Jenson, J. (1992). Fandom as Pathology: The Consequences of Characterization. In: Lewis L.A (ed.) *The Adoring Audience: Fan Culture and Popular Media.* London: Routledge, pp. 9–29.

Kawamata, K, Tajima, N., Kuroiwa, K. and Miura, T. (2017). Some Preliminary Notes on the Evolution and Development Process of Japanese Pop Culture Events. *Aoyama Journal of Cultural and Creative Studies,* 9(2), pp. 73–94.

Kotler, P. (1986). Megamarketing. *Harvard Business Review,* 64, pp. 117–124.

Kotler, P. and Keller, K. L. (2015). *Marketing Management.* New York: Pearson.

Martin, D. M. and Schouten, J. W. (2014). Consumption-driven Market Emergence. *Journal of Consumer Research,* 40(5), pp. 855–870.

Matsui, T. (2019). *Amerika ni Nihon no Anime wo yushutsu suru* [Exporting Japanese Manga to the USA]. Tokyo, Japan: Yuhikaku.

Oguri, T. (2016). The Scope of Contents Tourism Studies. In: Proceedings of the Symposium: International Comparative Research on the Spreading and Reception of Culture through Contents Tourism, held at Hokkaido University (15–16 March 2015), *CATS,* 8, pp. 17–64.

Pine II, B. J. and Gilmore, J. H. (1999). *The Experience Economy: Work is Theatre and Every Business a Stage*. Cambridge, MA: Harvard Business School Press.

Ross, K. and Nightingale, V. (2003). *Media and Audiences: New Perspectives*. Maidenhead, Berkshire: Open University Press.

Sabré, C. (2012). Neojaponism and Pop Culture New Japanese Exoticism in France. *Regioninės Studijos*, 6, pp. 67–88.

Sabré, C. (2013). New Images of Japan in France: A Survey to Japan Expo. *Regioninės Studijos*, 7, pp. 95–122.

Sandvoss, C. (2005). *Fans: The Mirror of Consumption*. Cambridge, MA: Polity Press.

Shiraishi, S. (2013). *Gro-barukashitanihon no manga to anime* [Globalized Japanese Manga and Anime]. Tokyo, Japan: Gakujutsu Shuppankai.

Sugiyama, R. (2020). *Anime no Shakaigaku* [The Life Course of Being a Fan, Sociology of Anime]. Nakanishiya, pp. 39–52.

Tajima, N. (2016). *Shohisha Kodo Kenkyu no Rekishi to Shukeika no Patan* [History of Consumer Behaviour Research: Focusing on Aggregation Patterns]. *The Research in Management and Accounting*, 106, pp. 495–518.

Villa Kujoyama. (2016). EMMANUEL CARRÈRE *LITTÉRATURE*. Available at: https://www.villakujoyama.jp/resident/emmanuel-carrere/ [Accessed 17 June 2020].

Williams, R. (2016). *Post-object Fandom: Television, Identity and Self-narrative*. New York: Bloomsbury Publishing.

WIRED. (2002). *2002nen Lycos de mottomo kensaku-sareta kotoba wa nihon anime Dragonball* [The Most Widely Searched Word for Lycos was the Japanese Animation "Dragonball"]. Available at: https://wired.jp/2002/12/19 [Accessed 20 April 2020].

13 Facts about Music Festivals

What We Know and What We Would Like to Know[1]

Jean-Paul Simon

Introduction

When one starts taking a closer look at cultural festivals, the first striking point it that it is both a global activity and a fast developing one. It has even been described as *"one of our most ubiquitous cultural phenomena"* (Maughan, 2015: p. XII).[2] Travel agencies (some specialized) are even now proposing catalogues of "cultural festivals" around the world: in India, Diwali (Festival of Lights),[3] in Ethiopia, Timket Festival,[4] in New Orleans, Mardi Gras, ... The wording "cultural" festivals seems a bit all-encompassing or flexible, blending religious events (like Diwali or Timket), traditional events like carnivals (Nizza, Rio, Venice...), new year's eve (China's Lantern Festival, Hogmanay in Scotland), or Northern Europe's Oktoberfest. Some of the quoted festivals have been around for quite some time. China's Lantern Festival[5] has over 2,000 years of history.

Newbold et al. (2015: p. XVI) state, *"there are as many different festivals taking place in Europe as there are definitions of what a festival is"*. A vagueness already noted 20 years agon by Frey (2000: p. 1): *"exactly what a music festival is, is ill-defined"*. The Unesco report on festivals statistics (Unesco, 2015: p. 9) stressed *"the varied perspectives on the meaning of festivals"* as they may have several different objectives and functions. Indeed, the scope of festivals is rather wide, Newbold et al. add that some are primarily civic in nature, with values that prioritize community self-celebration; other festivals place artistic promotion and development at their core; and others exist principally for profit. Festivals are indeed blending tradition and innovation.

As for music festivals, it seems that more people than ever are flocking to watch live music, with attendance at concerts and festivals at an all-time high. De Cossio (2018) deems that these events find themselves in an unprecedented stage of growth and popularity among audiences, which has been facilitated by new tourism, business and leisure trends and has led them to become the most popular cultural events in Europe. She considers it became key points in cultural and tourism strategies throughout Europe, employing thousands of people and working as economic stimulators in the regions where they are held.

DOI: 10.4324/9781003127185-17

Frey (2000: p. 1) stressed that, already at the end of the 1990s: "*Festivals became a significant part of the serious music and opera scene in the 1920s but the real boom took place within the last 20 years*". Around that period, the number of "serious" music festivals in Europe fluctuated between 1,000 and 2,000 according to sources quoted by the same author. The continuing growth of this phenomenon, mostly in western countries but also in other regions, this mushrooming of festivals has been characterized as "festivalomania", or "festivalisation"[6] (Boogaarts, 1993; Jordan, 2016: p. 6; Maughan, 2013: p. 265, Négrier, 2011, 2015: p. 19), or "festival fever" as they often take place during summer.

The chapter aims at marshalling and analyses which kind of facts and data about music festivals, documenting the trend and taking a closer view at some of the current assumptions about their economic impact. The first section opens with an overview of music festivals, indicating some elements of the economics of music festivals, displaying some of their main features (type of music, attendance, budget...). This section relies mostly on the pioneering work of Négrier and Jourda (2007) and Négrier (2011, 2013).[7] The second section accounts for music festivals in a sample of European countries: France, Italy, Spain, and the UK. Reviewing elements of the sociology and demographics of festival goers, it allows to further flesh out the broad overview of the first section, hinting at some of the motivations of festival goers.[8] The chapter concludes with questions about the economic impact of music festivals, and beyond the economic dimension stresses the multidimensional nature of music festivals.

The chapter is based on desk research and an analysis of the available scientific and grey literature, the former often consisting in reports from consultancies commissioned by festivals organizers.

What can we learn from pioneering studies?

The economics of music festivals

In the 1980s and 1990s, Frey (1986, 1994, 2000) initiated a series of studies of music festivals from a cultural economics viewpoint. In its 2000 paper, he described the determinants of both the demand side and the supply side.[9] On the demand side, he noted the following features:

- A high income effect with consumers willing to spend more of the disposable income on performing arts.
- Attracting new groups of visitors.
- Focusing attention by presenting some "extraordinary" cultural experience.
- Newsworthiness as festivals are news, and attract the attention of the media.
- Low cost to visitors as it may be a marginal cost of tourism.

- Low price elasticity of demand as tourists tend to compare the ticket price to expenditures for their trip as a whole.

On the supply side, he considered five major determinants:

- Low production cost: the absolute cost of many festivals may be high, but only marginal (additional) costs are covered by the festival (venues can be free). Festivals do not have to support any fixed costs of employment.
- More scope for artistic creativity as opposed to permanent opera houses and orchestras that are strongly bound by the (often) conservative tastes of their regular clientele, or required to play the standard repertoire.
- Evading government and trade union regulations.
- More sponsoring.
- Career enhancement.

All these determinants contrast with the conditions faced by the permanent venues (high fixed costs) and did *"contribute to the festival boom"* according to him. Although this analysis dates back from 2000, it seems that most of the points raised then are still valid.

The main features of music festivals

Since this pioneering work, the most comprehensive overview of music festivals is to be found in a 2013 seminal study by Négrier et al. (2013), based on a survey, conducted over the course of 2012 and using a sample of 390 festivals, from 15 different countries.[10] The study focused on western countries and did not include any country from Asia of Africa.[11] The lack of availability of data is, indeed, a major issue, making it difficult to get a better view of the global geography of music festivals. Some indications are to be found though, in the 2015 Unesco report, for instance.[12] Data and academic studies about festivals in Asia are hard to find, although one can compile a few elements. Box 13.1 is an attempt to give a quick glimpse of music festivals in China.

Box 13.1 Music festivals in China in a nutshell

China: a recent but loss-making activity

As of 2016, the live music sector in China was worth 15 billion yuan (US$ 2.18 billion) and it covered: concerts (65.25%), musicals (25.72%), music festivals (7.64%) and live house (1.39%). Large-scale open space music festivals in particular emerged in the late 2000s as a new form of entertainment in the developing sector of Chinese cultural and creative industries. Over the past ten years, live performance was deemed to be the fastest growing and the most successful market in China's music industry. According to the National Business Daily (2019), there were 269 music festivals in 2017 in China: an increase of 33.8% over the previous year.

The overall ticket sales of all these music festivals reached 580 million yuan (US$ 84 million) in the year, representing a growth rate of 20%. Around 80% of them suffered huge deficits.

Tickets are priced cheaply usually at 150 yuan ($20) to 400 yuan ($53). Besides, giant music carnivals housing more than 100,000 audiences are not allowed in China, making it difficult to break even.

A key player: Modern Sky

Modern Sky, the largest independent record label in China, became the key player in China's live music sector, especially music festivals. It started with the Modern Sky Music Festival in 2007, and a few years later under the banner of Strawberry Festival, it became the most famous Chinese brand of music festival. For example, in 2015, the Strawberry Festivals were held in 20 cities across China including Beijing, Shanghai, Xi'an, Zhejiang, Chengdu, and Shenzhen.

The case of the Midi Music Festival

Midi Music Festival is a three-day outdoor live rock music festival, run by Beijing Midi Music School (private) and Beijing Midi Performance Company (private). In 2007, it was reported that there were more than 350,000 people counted by entry times. Midi, launched in 1997, is the longest running and largest non-government music festival in mainland China. Although there are no official published statistics, Li and Wood found that 98% of the attendees are under 35 years. The festival currently is held annually in four Chinese cities: Beijing, Shanghai, Suzhou and Shenzhen.

To the motivations for festival attendance in western contexts (socialization, family togetherness, novelty, excitement and thrills, general relaxation, entertainment, learning, and music), Li and Wood add two unique Chinese ones: "spiritual escape" and "spiritual pursuit" grounded in the cultural and social context.

Source: Compiled by author from, Yu (2019), National Business Daily of China, http://m.nbdpress.com/articles/2019-05-14/6705.html, Music Business China (2019), http://chinamusicbusinessnews.com/?p=2548, Um (2019: p. 444, 447), Li and Wood (2014).

Négrier et al. (2013) examine the following seven key variables: country (nation); dominant musical genre; age of the festival (the number of seasons a festival has had since it was established); size of audience; size of the budget; number of days in its program; and the season of the year.

Building on these variables, the study unveils the main features of music festivals: the distribution of festivals according to the dominant musical style (World-Trad, Rock-Pop, Multi Style, Jaz-Blues, and Classical), the dominant musical genre by country in the EU, the size of the audience, and the size of the budget. One may be tempted linking (too quickly) musical festivals with rock-pop music, since say Woodstock (1969) and other rock festivals that followed (Isle of Wight, 1968,[13] Glastonbury, 1971). Music festivals[14] are often associated *"with hippie-inspired clothing and ideals of the counterculture in 1960s"* (Rudolph, 2016, p. 9). However, Négrier et al. (2013: p. 48) reveal that the classical music genre was leading in 2012, accounting for 36.2% of the musical style, ahead of the Rock-Pop genre with 26.7%.

The genres are unevenly spread across countries: classical music is clearly dominant in Sweden, and Norway but represents a rather small share in Switzerland. The Rock-Pop category leads in the Wallonia-Brussels Federation. However, the sample does not include the UK.[15]

Regarding the size of the audience there are five sections: more than 80,000 participants, between 20,000 and 79,999, between 6,000 and 19,999, between 3,000 and 5,999 and less than 2,999, with a fairly homogeneous distribution among all of them, except for the upper section, where the proportion is significantly lower (Négrier et al., 2013: p. 49). As for the budget, it varies, but audience and budget are highly spread among the sample studied, the latter nearly evenly distributed across sizes of budget (Négrier et al., 2013: p. 49). This illustrates the diversity of festivals. Négrier et al. stress its heterogeneity. In spite of this, in terms of size of the audience, the study adds that 50% of the festivals studied do not attract more than 8,000 participants, with an average number of festival goers situated at 28,455, but a much lower median: 7,888 participants.

Nevertheless, diversity can be encapsulated in one figure: regardless of musical genre, the median of the total budget is inferior to the average. Rock/pop festivals display a significantly higher proportion of festivals with budgets in excess of 900,000 euros: 31%. This aspect does impact the average budget of the genre (near 1.200 million euros). However, median budgets are almost similar across musical genres, hovering around 273 000 euros (Négrier et al., 2013: p. 45), three times less than the average.

Half of the expenses are allocated to artists "fees" (Négrier et al., 2013). The entities in charge of setting up festivals are hybrid entities (SMEs) relying strongly on voluntary work. Volunteers account for over 50% of the number of jobs.

The study remains cautious about any generalization, stressing instead the diversity of festivals. The authors note that larger audience are most often found within rock/pop, while classical music festivals tend to attract smaller audiences. These audiences are mostly drawn from the locality or neighbouring areas: 48% of the participants for all musical genres, participants from elsewhere in the country represent 19%, while non-national participants represent 8% (Négrier et al.: p. 103). Within the audiences, upper categories and people with college degrees are better represented even in rock festivals (Négrier, 2013).

About the funding of festivals, the study reveals that festival incomes are particularly sensitive to national traditions, while at the same time differing according to the musical genre: for classical music festivals, subsidies represent more than half of their total resources, and for rock/pop festivals, they remain below one third of the total, with ticketing accounting for 35% of the revenue. Rock-Pop festivals seem to have more ability to generate other income. However, public funding is an important contribution across all genres with an average of 45%, even if it fluctuates between 54% for classical music festivals and 31% for Rock-Pop festivals (Négrier et al., 2013: p. 62).

Public funding differs according to the musical genre but the public entities involved are not the same across countries. For instance, local funding is important in France, and Spain, around a third of the income, above the average of 20%. Regional funding is a major source of income in the Wallonia-Brussels Federation (FWB), and national support takes the lead in smaller countries like Ireland or Norway (Négrier et al., 2013: p. 63).

Even though the summer is considered to be the season par excellence[16] for festival activity, it contains only half of the festivals. The length of festivals is closely linked to the dominant musical genre with classical music festivals having the longest duration.

The authors conclude the first section of their book, stating that they *"have been unable to find any features that are exclusive to particular nations, musical styles, or funding levels"* (Négrier et al.: p. 164).

Music festivals in some EU countries: France, Italy, Spain, and the UK

Information about music festivals in Europe is highly heterogeneous and varies in time and space.[17] Therefore, we concentrate in this section, on countries[18] where some data or studies were available.

France

A study by Négrier and Jourda (2007) concentrated on a sample of 76 music festivals in France[19] but was limited to classical music in a very loose sense,[20] to which they added a sample of 10 dance festivals. Their findings for 2005, are broadly in line with the 2013 study. The average audience was 9 902 participants, and the median of 5001 participants. This gap shows, again, the impact of big festivals. Half of the income is coming from subsidies, and half of the budget is spent to pay the artists. Nearly 61% of the people involved are working on a voluntary basis. The average price was 64.12 euros and the median, 59.52 euros.

The study that followed (Négrier et al., 2010) further documented the sociology of audience, based on a smaller sample of 49 music festivals. They find that upper class account for over 58% of the audience, and that people with college degrees dominate, even if middle-class attendees stand for 29%. Working class are doing a little bit better in the current and world music categories, where together with middle-class attendees they provide the majority of spectators. The level of income is a little less pervasive even if the average income of festivals goers is above the average. In terms of gender, there are more women attending than men: a 59.7% ratio (for 51.6% within the French population). Some festivals, like dance festivals, are more feminine than others. The audience is mostly built out of active people rather than students or retired people. They state that contrary to some common wisdom about the audience being made of the same group of people, of "habitués", the renewing of the audience is a strong element of the very dynamic of music festivals: 39% of spectators came for the first time in 2008. But they add that it does not necessarily equate to a broadening of the social base as these new spectators may come from the same social groups.

Négrier and Djakouane (2020) released in 2020, a new study, SoFest commissioned by France Festivals,[21] based on survey of a sample of 184 festivals. The results show a stability across surveys: dominant musical style (classical: 32%, and rock/pop/world: 34%),[22] distribution of resources (on average, a lower level of subsidies: 44%, and an increase of other income: 54%)[23] budget (average: 1.10 million euros in 2011, 1.16 in 2018; median: 324 million in 2011, 360 in 2018)[24] (see Table 13.1), prices (19 euros on average),[25] season, ratio of volunteers, ratio of new attendees (38%). The study adds that, on average, a festival lasts 11 days in 10 locations, offering 40 shows with 178 artists, out of which 54 are coming from abroad.

Table 13.1 Distribution of budgets according to the style of music (2018)

	20–269 k€	270–1399 k€	1400 k€ and over
Songs ("chansons")	59%	18%	24%
Classical ("Musiques savantes")	40%	40%	21%
Live shows (dance, theatres, circuses)	24%	57%	19%
Jazz Blues	50%	42%	8%
Rock, pop, world	34%	38%	28%
Total	38%	39%	22%

Source: Négrier and Djakouane, « Indicateurs d'activités » (2020: p. 11).

About the demographics and sociology of festival goers in France, Djak-ouane (2014) provided a first overview of the main features of the audience that complements the earlier studies. It is based on a secondary analysis of the previous 49 festivals to which he added another sample of 6 world music festivals.[26] Table 13.2 presents these main features as of 2008 and 2018, based on a sample of 91 festivals. The findings are in line with the earlier study about the prevalence of upper class and higher income attendees, but higher for upper class and lower for income. He stressed a link between the price level and the shrinking of the social base: in other words, there is a link between rates, aesthetic and social origin. The 2020 study confirms the lack of diversification of the audience and the continuing domination of the upper class. Worse, it reveals a sharp decline of the working class. Participants are not the same every year: they are mostly local (2008: 30%) or regional (2008: 24%), with only 30% out of region participants as of 2008, 44% as of 2018.

Babé (2012: p. 10) indicated that the percentage of the French population (ages 15 and older) that attended cultural festivals was of 16%, higher for some genres like rock and pop (33%) and "music of the world" (27%), lower for other such as classical-lyrical-jazz (14%). This percentage has been increasing, it reached 19% in 2018 (Négrier and Djakouane, "festival annulés", 2020: p. 7). A recently released "panorama of festivals"[27] (2020) mapped 1710 festivals of "current music" ("musiques actuelles")[28] and 218 of classical music. The document stressed how difficult it was to track festivals given they have both a high birth rate... and a high mortality rate.

A 2016 study[29] by Barofest gives data on 1,887 music festivals for the year 2015, classified under this rather loose label of "current music". The study stresses the diversity of the festivals. These festivals are spread out

Table 13.2 A sociology of festival goers in France (2008, 2018)

Variables	2008	2018
Age	51 years	48 years
Women	60%	61%
College degree	72%	72%
Upper income	58%	60%
Active	54%	51%
Retired	32%	31%
Local spectators	30%	52% (local and regional)
Regional spectators ("département")	24%	
Out of region spectators	30%	44% and 4% from abroad
Average number of concerts	1.5	NA
Average number of past concerts	5.5	NA
Attendance in couple	40%	34%
Attendance with friends	28%	35%

Source: Compiled from Djakouane (2014), Négrier and Djakouane, « Publics» (2020).

all across France, even if from a regional viewpoint, some musical genres appear to dominate, like jazz and improvised music on the French riviera area. The distribution of the musical genres is the following: 32% for electronic music, 24% jazz-blues and improvised music, 22% with two kinds of musical genre, 15% for world or traditional music, and 7% for songs ("chansons" not very precise either). Barofest differentiates three kinds of festivals according to the size: the small ones with a budget under 10 000 euros, the medium ones between 10 000 and 100 000 euros, and the big ones with budgets over 100 000 euros. The big ones accounted for only 14% of the festivals but drew 88% of the box office, the medium one stood for 47% of the festivals and 10% of the box office. These festivals generated 155 million euros of revenue in 2015, accounting for 30% of all tickets sold for today's music that year in France.

On average, festivals cover a rather short time span: 54% of the festivals last between one and three days, with jazz festivals having a tendency to last longer, over a week for a significant amount of them (162 out of 458). 47% of the festivals take place during summer. Nearly half of them are charging for admission (49%), but some 20% are entirely free. Pay entries are dominant for electronic music (61%) and "songs" (52%), and free ones more numerous among the two "current" music genres category (30%). If one breaks down the festivals according to their size (big, medium, and small), the small festival category accounts for 52% of the free festivals (v. 5% for the big ones). 70% of festivals are set up by NGOs ("associations"), 16% by public bodies, and only 6% by private entities. According to Négrier and Djakouane ("Indicateurs", 2020: p. 26), the number of free festivals has been decreasing steadily: 7% in 2018.

Italy

The Italian collecting society SIAE (2019: p. 40) supplies data about concerts, but without differentiating permanent venues and festivals. The report breaks the data into three types of music only: rock-pop[30] music, classical music, and jazz. As of 2018, "pop music" accounted for 44.75% of the number of concerts, but 86.29% of revenue out of a total of 513.72 million of euros with 3.62% of the sector's revenue generated by various streams of revenues (sponsorships, advertising, public and private contributions, etc.). Classical music accounted for a close number of concerts, 43.56% but a much lower share of revenues, 11.2%. Jazz concerts stood for 11.69% of concerts and 2.5% of revenues but reached a higher percentage of audience than classical concerts: 11.77% of the total (937 837) v. 3.96%.

The SIAE report complements these data with another set on "outdoor events" ("Manifestazioni all'aperto") which is also an all-encompassing category. In 2018, SIAE registered 51,714 shows noting a monthly distribution with a significant concentration in the summer months, and a turnover of 179 million euros with a higher contribution of "other streams" of revenues,

10.9%. The turnover has been growing quickly over the last decade. These two sets of data certainly overlap but it is difficult to allocate any number to music festivals only, the quoted figures can only provide a ceiling. However, the list of the top ten lyrical concerts reveals that Verona accounted for 5 in the list, with an attendance of 121 000 for the number one, "Aida" (2019: pp. 75–76). This may signal a trend similar to the one noticed in the French case with big festivals providing the largest share of revenue.

Dal Pozzolo and Carnelli (2013: p. 224) state that over 1,600 events and more than 1,200 festivals are organized each year.[31] However, the data they provide are very limited in scope, only dealing with festivals in Piedmont Region, financed by the Department of Culture of the Piedmont Region: 94 festivals with a wide range of legal statuses (associations, foundations, cooperatives, local institutions, etc.), in 2010. The aggregate budget reached approximately 14 million euros. The main streams of income are the following: public contributions (mostly regional), 43%, private contributions (20%), earnings (20%), and festival generated income (17%; Pozzolo and Carnelli, 2013: p. 230). The overall expenses for Piedmont festivals during the 2010 season amounted to 17 million euros, 87.3% of which was allocated to artistic expenses. The low contribution of direct income (festival generated income and earnings) has to do with a parameter, stressed by the authors, that characterizes Italian festivals: free admissions policies or reduced ticket prices.

Spain

Bonet and Carreño (2013: p. 183) estimated that the number of music and dance festivals grew from 438 in 1985 to 989 in 2011, an increase of 70%, mostly within the field of music. However, they use a sample of 409 festivals for 2011.

In Spain as well, the distribution by musical genres shows that classical music festivals predominate[32] (40% of the total), followed by rock-pop (27%), world/traditional music (15%), jazz/blues (11%) and multistyle (6%). Classical music festivals are usually much older (30 years); the rock-pop festivals appeared more recently, mostly over the last decade. Over a third (35%) are operated by private companies; they benefit from larger and more diversified budgets (sponsoring by brands may be significant).

On the opposite, this anteriority/"seniority" of classical music festivals may account for the fact that Spanish festivals rely on a high degree of economic and institutional dependency on local and regional governments. None of the classical music festivals are operated by private companies (Bonet and Carreño, 2013: p. 186). These festivals are either publicly owned or operated by non-profit organizations. Indeed, classical music festivals obtain 62% of their income from governments. On top of that characteristic, the authors add that a quarter of non-profit festival organizations and 11% of for-profit festival enterprises are owned directly by the government. Public funding takes the form either of direct contribution (for public entities), or subsidies (for non-profit entities). As stressed by the authors, this feature is linked to the political history of Spain. On the opposite, private companies accounted for 35% of the Pop-rock festivals.

43% of Spanish festivals have budgets below the 80,000 € mark, and volunteers represent 21% of the workforce. For the authors, this relatively slow level of involvement of volunteers, could be explained by the fact that government authorities supporting the festival would assign part of their personnel to staff festival events. The average turnover generated by Spanish festivals in 2011, was 583 064 euros, with ticketing only accounting for 36.6% of the total income,[33] but ticketing accounts for over 50% of the private festivals (with an average turnover of 1 397 657 euros). The second largest source of income comes from public funding (34.8%). Private sponsorship and the other sources of income (catering, merchandising, rentals, fees for educational programs, etc.) are trailing far behind. However, sponsorship is the second source of income for the private festivals: 18.4%. The percentage of very small festivals (those having fewer than 3,000 participants) seems high. However, the average size of audience in Spain is of 18,300 participants (with a median of 5,500).

Pérez-Gálvez et al. (2017) released a study of the audience of the Cordoba Guitar Festival.[34] With 24,236[35] spectators attending the 2015 edition of the Cordoba Guitar Festival,[36] the festival stands somewhat above the mentioned average. As of 2018, its budget reached 1.135.912 euros (Arjona, 2018). Among the participants, 53.3% were men, 46.7% women, more than two-third of the sample were under 50 years of age. 72.5% declared being university graduates or postgraduates (Table 13.3). The authors characterize the attendees as having medium-high purchasing power, with 44.9% declaring income over €1,500, and 30.9% with a monthly income of less than €1,000. With 61.2% of local spectators, the distribution of the origin of the attendees is aligned with the data of our overview, national participants stand for 30.3%, and foreigners 8.5% (Pérez-Gálvez et al., 2017: p. 351).

Table 13.3 A sociology of the audience of the Cordoba Guitar Festival (2016)

Variables	
Age	2/3 under 50 years
Women	46.7%
College degree	72.5%
Monthly income	30.9%
- below 1000 euros	44.9%
- over 1500 euros	
Local spectators	61.2%
National spectators	30%
Foreign spectators	8.5%

Source: Pérez-Gálvez et al. (2017: p. 351).

Among the motives that stand out in attracting spectators, cultural reasons rank first: listening to favourite artist and/or group live, the search for new musical experiences and the fame and reputation of the festival. Six out of ten persons surveyed indicated listening to their favourite artist(s) and/or group(s) live as the most relevant reason for going to the festival. Motivations of a social type and of convenience seem of lesser importance. The spectators indicate a high satisfaction with their experience at the festival, but it fluctuates according to the musical preferences of the spectators. *"The more heterogeneous the musical preferences of the spectators, the more positive the image perceived of the festival"* (Pérez-Gálvez et al., 2017: p. 357).

United Kingdom

As of 2017, according to Statista, the UK hosted the highest number of festivals within the EU (Kienast, 2018). Maughan (2013: p. 265) notes that the first festivals that established a presence, in what was then an emerging sector, were predominantly those that related to a classical form: for example, Cheltenham Music Festival (1945). It was not until 1955 that other genre of music festivals began to appear with the Sidmouth Folk Festival (1955) and, a decade later, Cambridge and Towersey Folk festivals (1965). Commercial music festivals in the UK came later with the first Isle of Wight Festival in 1968.

The Glastonbury Festival, held annually in the month of June in Somerset, England, is the best known. The pre-sales of tickets for the 50th year of Glastonbury in 2020, reached a record number of people: 2.4 million had registered to be eligible for the sale within 37 minutes, 135,000 tickets had been sold (Bakare, 2019). As the tickets are sold on line for £248 plus a fee, a quick calculation shows box office revenue of £34.15 million. The 2016 budget was of £22 million (Tremethick, 2016), but of 40 million in 2019 (47.60 million euros, O'Connell, 2019).

The festival sector experienced a tremendous growth period between 2000 and 2011 (Webster, 2014: p. 9). Although the same author was expecting the attendance to plateau after a predicted peak in 2014, the attendance at festivals in the United Kingdom has been growing steadily: from 2.79 million £ as of 2012, to 3.9 million as of 2016 (Statista, 2019). The data refer to both local attendants and music tourists from abroad. A 2017 UK Music's study provided a higher number, stating that, in 2016, audience numbers had hit 30.9 million, up from 27.7 million in 2015, with 4 million people attending a growing number of British music festivals. According to the "Measuring Music 2018 report", in 2017, music festivals generated a contribution to the UK's economy of around £1 billion. The sub-sector of live music employed 28 659 people out of a total of 145 815 for the UK (UK Music, 2018).

In 2019, it reached the £1.3 billion mark and was expected to grow another 11% in 2020, but the pandemic brought a slump of as much as

85% (Sweeney, 2020). Big festivals, like Glastonbury, may be on the verge of bankruptcy if the festivals cannot take place on 2021 (Lopez-Palacio, 2020). A parliamentary inquiry found that *"the vast majority of British music festivals will disappear if faced with a second consecutive barren year"* (Snapes, 2021).

Most of these UK reports are not characterized by understatements or by being overcautious, they stand on the verge of advocacy: e.g., *"Festivals make a huge contribution to the UK economy"* (Oxford Economics, 2013). Several other reports are stressing the positive impact of music festivals, considered as cultural tourism. There were 6.5 million music tourists to the UK in 2012: £2.2 billion was the total direct and indirect spending generated by music tourism[37] in 2012 (Oxford Economics, 2013). In 2014, the total direct and indirect spending went up to £ 3.1 billion, and they were 9.5 million music tourists, out of which 546 000 were coming from abroad, shelling out an average £751 while in the UK (Oxford Economics, 2015: p. 7), a figure that is nevertheless lower to the spending of UK tourists (around £900). However, as noted by the 2013 Oxford Economics report, for 2012, music festivals accounted for only 17% of all live music attendances, as concerts and gigs accounted for 83%. The impact is less impressive although significant (£374 million), but in line with the data we found for other countries (e.g. 155 million euros for France).

These statistics do not allow any comparison with the situation found for other countries and are summarized in the first section: a mostly local/regional audience. As the Négrier et al. (2013) study did not include the UK in their sample, we may presume it could be a specificity of the country linked to the strength of its music culture, but without further evidence.

Webster (2014: p. 19) in her report for the UK Association of Independent Festivals (AIF), based on a survey of its member festivals, notes that *'The general atmosphere and overall vibe, character and quality of the event'* has been by far the most important motivation for attending a festival" with a 53.2% average). The music (i.e. 'The music generally' as a motivation) itself comes second: a 27.7% average. As since the AIF started, there have been 66 member festivals in total, the sample may not be representative. This motivation may describe the formation of what Laing and Mair (2015: p. 25) call *"a portable community"*, with the drawback of focusing more on the people attendance, rather than those living nearby, thereby potentially reducing some forms of social inclusion. This emphasis on the *"general atmosphere"* and the creation of such *"a portable community"* is a possible explanation of lower local audience, but this hypothesis would need some stronger evidence. Webster and McKay (2016: p. 10) refer to a number of studies dealing with festivals as *"places for being with like-minded people and for engendering feelings of belonging, 'communitas', and community"*.

Main lessons

Webster and McKay (2016: p. 7) are rather assertive about the economic impact:

> Much work has shown that music festivals have the capacity to generate positive economic impacts, to varying degrees, including employment and increased revenues from locals and visitors, as well as providing focal points for marketing, attracting visitors and growing the tourism sector of the local economy.

They do quote an array of studies[38] to back their view, but this may reflect the specificity of the UK scene. However, they do stress that: "*There is no generally agreed view as to what, or how much, cultural festivals contribute to the respective local economy...*" (Webster and McKay, 2016: p. 23).

The authors we have been leaning on so far, are cautious. Maugham (2015) notes that the development of festivals in post-war Europe does provide an illustration of the growing importance of the cultural economy and of the widespread belief among policy makers that festivals have a major role to play in the tourism industry. Indeed, local authorities became increasingly interested in festivals as vehicles for urban regeneration, to respond to the process of de-industrialization and economic restructuring in cities including. Obviously, festivals, during this phase became increasingly part of tourism promotion and city marketing strategies. A positive move in itself; however, Maugham reminds us that "*perhaps because this is a nascent field, a lot of the effects of festivals are presumed*". Besides, the validity of economic impact assessments is often questioned, for instance because of a number of methodological problems (Unesco, 2009: p. 20).[39] Already in 1986, Frey (1986: p. 30) deemed that neither impact studies nor welfare analysis was convincing. For the latter, "*the externality and merit good arguments do not differ from those given as a general reason for supporting any other professional activity and the arts in general*".

By the same token, Bonet and Carreño (2013) highlight that the arguments of policy makers are indeed economic in nature, referring to job creation or tourism, or associated with strengthening local identity or image. But they deem that "*This rhetoric does not always correspond to reality: very few festivals are truly tourist attractions, though they may in fact complement the leisure activities already offered in the locality*". Nevertheless, these arguments could have been useful in reinforcing the importance of these sectors for policymakers and others including would-be sponsors.

Measuring the spill-overs of an event, or a sector on the rest of the economy is always a complex task. Stressing the presumed existence of positive externalities is one thing, measuring them precisely is another one. Nevertheless, Négrier (2013) considers that on average, one euro of subsidies can generate six euros. However, he warns than these data have to be handled with care. On the one hand, the economic impact is likely to yield lower returns than other forms of investments, other events may have a stronger leveraging effect (Frey, for instance, suggested that car races or other sport events may have a higher multiplier effect: 1986: p. 30). On the other hand, from his point of view, there is no obvious overlapping between the economic impact and the artistic impact: the "best" festivals from an artistic viewpoint are not necessarily the most profitable. In other words, a debate about the impact of music festivals will have to take into account various dimensions including the "democratization" of culture, the educational dimension, the creative dimension, the role of public support. As festivals are of multidimensional nature, non-economic indicators must be factored in.

However, as noted in the Unesco report: *"despite the multidimensional character of festivals, assessments often follow a one-dimensional, economic approach"* (UNESCO, 2015: p. 47). The report suggests *"the need for 'all-inclusive' approaches"* (p. 25) and indicates some possible *"alternative models for festival assessment"* (p. 28). Neither this report, nor the "Culture statistics" from Eurostat (2019) provide detailed data. With the exception of Négrier et al., there is a lack of information on the organization of the festivals (type of entity, promoters and employees, volunteers, funding sources, etc.) as illustrated by the case of the UK where most of the reports identified concentrate on the size of the phenomenon (number, revenue, audience).

The quick overview we went through, does reveal some significant features: the relative prevalence of classical music (number of festivals), the local dimension of audiences, ..., as well as, less surprisingly, the relatively privileged social position of festival goers which is in line with research on cultural participation by educational attainment and income.[40] Public funding appears to play a significant role if not a major one in certain cases. Although some private festivals came up with some innovative approach and business models, there is still room for some public intervention and public policies, even if some more evidence could help better substantiating their main objectives. Frey (1986, 1994) called for caution about public funding. He stated that *"The government subsidies must be given with great care"* (2000: p. 13). Subsidies may reduce or destroy the incentives of the organizers on the one hand. On the other hand, increased subsidies may bring (logically) increased regulation and control, raising the fixed costs, eventually festivals end up being "captured". However, Frey's analysis focused on "serious" music festivals in the 1980s and specifically the case of Salzburg. This may have changed.

Besides, it can and is usually mitigated by the involvement of communities and the role of voluntary work, an important contribution as we have noted. Though, as stressed by Getz and Frisby (1988: p. 37) in their pioneering study of community run festivals (including music),[41] this involvement varies according to the category of festivals. Each festival blends its own parameters creating its specific dynamic: incentives of organizers, commitment of the community and volunteers, public and private support and engagement of festival goers. Therefore, taking into account the multidimensional character of festivals makes it difficult to draw any strong conclusions about the management of festivals that have different objectives and functions. Whatever the parameters and the hierarchy adopted, the stakeholders (artists, organizers, communities, policy makers and sponsors, and festival goers) need building an ad hoc consensus and working relationships between them as they may have conflicting goals. Further research on these relationships between stakeholders is needed.

One should add on a final note, that perhaps the most obvious economic impact of music festivals that often remains under the radar, has to do with the evolution of the main streams of resources of the artists in the music industry. Since the turn of this century (Simon, 2019), revenues are again coming from performances and related rights rather than from royalties redistributed by music recording companies. Artists were enabled to capture a larger share of the music ecosystem's revenues through these continued shifts in revenue towards concerts, as so far according to a CITI report (CITI, 2018: p. 87), as of 2017, only 12% of total revenue were flowing back to the artists ($5.0 billion out of $43 billion in estimated potential revenue). In other words, live music became crucial for artists.

Unfortunately, the COVID-19 pandemic is disrupting the entire music economy, hitting hard especially live events like music festivals as most of the events were postponed or cancelled. New business models and additional streams of revenue are still a question mark. The role of public funding is likely to be critical as ever. As emphasized by Négrier and Djakouane ("festival annulés", 2020: p. 13) about the French case, the sub-sector is not in a position to deal with such a challenge by itself. At the same time, the segment of recorded music revenues grew 7% in 2020 (Mulligan, 2021), mostly due to a 20% growth of streaming revenue now accounting for 61% of the global revenue. 2019 and 2020 revealed the continued rise of independent artists: the artists direct segment outperformed the market. This is a positive signal for an emerging generation[42] of artists as stressed by Mulligan (2021, a, b): *"direct to consumer became a lifeline for many smaller labels and independent artists"*. It is too early to predict if this growing stream of revenue may or may not mitigate the losses from the live music segment. However, it will not compensate for the lack of training and experience gained from live events and touring.[43]

Notes

1 This paper has been prepared to answer to the invitation to speak at the conference that took place in Valencia: "Cultural Festivals' Organization and Management: new challenges in the digital age?", University of Valencia, 26–27 November 2019, https://cfest.webs.upv.es/. The author would like to thank the organisers for giving this opportunity to work on a topic that was, so far, an unchartered continent for him. However, as a festival-goer, the author attended

his first festival in 1970: the US Ann Arbor Blues Festival. https://sunday-blues.org/wp-content/uploads/2019/07/1970-Ann-Arbor-Blues-Festival-Program-ABBYY.pdf

2 The website Music Festival Wizard provides practical information (ticket prices, current line-ups, and venue) and ranking of music festivals, but no data, and only for western countries: https://www.musicfestivalwizard.com/about/

3 The festival of lights is celebrated by Hindus, Jains, Sikhs and some Buddhists every autumn in the northern hemisphere.

4 Timkat is the Orthodox Tewahedo celebration of Epiphany. It is celebrated on January 19th, corresponding to the 10th day of Terr in the Ethiopian calendar.

5 China's Lantern Festival sends lit paper lanterns into the sky to call for hope in the new year.

6 The French academic journal "Cahiers d'ethnomusicologie" released a special issue on "Festivalisation(s)" in 2014.

7 The author would like to thank the authors of these studies for allowing him to use their data.

8 Motivation studies of festival goers as such are out of the scope of this paper. For a review of motivation studies, see Li and Wood (2014: pp. 3–10). For festival studies, Getz (2010) provides a comprehensive (and impressive review) of the nature and scope of festival studies based on a large-scale literature review of 423 research articles published in the English-language scholarly press.

9 The study concentrates on the example of the Salzburg Festival, which was also the focus of the 1986 paper.

10 While stressing that an agreement on a definition is hard to find, they nevertheless state that "*It is not difficult to establish a broad definition of a festival: an event limited in time and space which develops a specific artistic project and takes place at regular intervals*" (Négrier et al., 2013: p. 35).

11 There is a network of festivals focusing on global music and local cultures, the Forum of Worldwide Music Festivals (FWMF) with over 50 members, from Oslo/Norway to Ulsan/ South Korea, from Douala/Cameroon to Ljubljana/ Slovenia: the FWMF-festivals reach more than 3 million people. http://www.fwmf.world/about/

12 The report notes festivals in Australia and South Africa: see section 3 of the report: "Best practice in measuring festivals: The case of Australia and South Africa", pp. 36–46. The report provides a box on festivals in New Zealand (p. 23). The report acknowledges some studies of festivals in the Caribbean but does not quote any on Latin America but it does stress that: "*There is an urgent need to document a wider spectrum of the academic and consultancy-based literature from the developing world*" (2009: p. 18).

13 The original Isle of Wight festivals held between 1968 and 1970. The 1970 event was at the time one of the largest human gatherings in the world, with an estimated 600,000 people in attendance.

14 Rudolph (2016: pp. 10–21) provides a short history of music festivals but concentrates mostly on rock-pop festivals.

15 Ireland and the United Kingdom are studied through a case study in the second part of the book: Maughan, C. "Festivals, a journey from here to where a British perspective" pp. 262–277. However, the chapter does not provide any similar statistics.

16 They are often called "estivals"!

17 The European Festivals Association (EFA) connects about 100 festivals (music, dance, theatre and multidisciplinary arts festivals) and festival associations in 40 countries since 1952. The association does not provide any data. One can find a list of papers and publications related to festivals but it has not been

updated since 2015 and the links do no work. The association publishes Festival Bytes Booklets giving the views of players. https://www.efa-aef.eu/en/about/

18 For Germany, we only found a table displaying the interests towards music festivals, for the period 2006–2009, broken down into three categories: rock-pop, jazz and classical (Music in Germany, 2019). The same source gives an aggregate figure of 1.42 billion euros for theatres and concerts as of 2008, out of a total of 6.23 billion euros for the German music industry.

19 Most of them belonging to the organisation, France Festivals, member of EFA.

20 I.e., medieval, baroque, classical per se, contemporary and lyrical music.

21 One should stress that not only this last study but also the series of studies initiated in 2006, are the output of a fruitful cooperation between the researchers and France Festivals.

22 Figure 13.1 gives 36.2% for classical, and 45.2% for rock-pop-world, but the percentages do not include live events.

23 Strong growth of the revenues coming from ticketing: up 54% from 2011.

24 Nominal values which means the average budget slightly decreased.

25 As noted, the 2005 study concentrated on classical music with higher rates.

26 Détours du monde (Chanac, Lozère), Fiesta Sète (Sète, Hérault), Ida y Vuelta (Perpignan, Pyrénées Orientales), Les Internationales de la guitare (Montpellier, Hérault), Le Festival de Thau (Mèze, Hérault), and Les Voix de la Méditerranée (Lodève, Hérault).

27 An Open Data interactive website: https://www.culture.gouv.fr/Sites-thematiques/Culture-et-territoires/La-Culture-en-region/Panorama-des-festivals

28 We translate by "current" music rather than contemporary music as the latter often refers to trends in modern music.

29 Commissioned by CNV, IRMA, and SACEM.

30 Our translation of "musica leggera" as the report gives the names of artists such as Eminem, Beyonce, and "Gun n' Roses" in the list of the top ten of "musica leggera" (p. 75).

31 Melley in his introduction to Guerzoni's book (2008: p. 4), gave the same amount. The author would like to thank Costanza Sartoris for forwarding a pdf copy of the work of Guerzoni.

32 Mostly classical music from the 18th century to 1950.

33 The authors do not give any data bout the total turnover of the festivals; however, if one multiplies the number of festivals (409) by this average amount of income (582 064 euros), one reaches almost 239 million euros.

34 Based on a sample of 612 interviews completed during the 2016 Festival.

35 24.618 in 2019, (Velasco, 2019). For a history of the 25 years, see Priego (2009).

36 The festival offers a wide range of genres of music: blues, classical, flamenco, jazz, and rock-pop.

37 The report classified domestic tourists as resident in the UK but travelling a significant distance for the event (more than 3 times the average commuting distance of that region). Foreign music tourists were those that travelled to the UK from overseas.

38 These studies are summarized in a table: pp. 23–25. The report provides a very comprehensive bibliography: pp. 27–30.

39 For a review of the criticisms, see "2.3.2. The validity of economic impact assessment", pp. 20–23.

40 See for the EU Eurostat, *Culture statistics 2019*, pp. 134–139.

41 21 music festivals out of a sample of 52 festivals in Ontario, with five more events offering concerts.

42 This new generation is most likely to use the new DIY tools such as Native Instruments, according to Mulligan.

43 This learning curve is very well explained by Elton John, "I learned by touring Europe in the 60s. Young artists need the same chance". https://www.theguardian. com/commentisfree/2021/feb/07/elton-john-touring-europe-young-art-ists-brexit-negotiators-musicians-support

References

Arjona, A.R. (2018), «El festival de la guitarra destina 560.000 euros a nueve artistas". https://www.diariocordoba.com/noticias/cultura/festival-guitarra-destina-560-000-euros-nueve-artistas_1216992.html

Babé, L. (2012), « Les publics de la musique classique. Exploitation de la base d'enquête du DEPS ». Paris, Ministry of Culture. https://www.culture.gouv.fr/content/download/94843/852552/version/1/file/6-05_Rep%C3%A8res%20Musique%20classique.pdf

Bakare, L. (2019), « Glastonbury tickets sell out in 34 minutes ». https://www.theguardian.com/music/2019/oct/06/glastonbury-tickets-sell-out-in-34-minutes

Barofest (2016a), "Baromètre des festivals de musiques actuelles. France. 2015 ». http://www.francefestivals.com/fichier/p_download/2051/download_fichier_fr_barofest_20160412.pdf

Barofest (2016b), « Les genres les plus représentés ». http://www.francefestivals.com/fichier/p_download/2050/download_fichier_fr_infographie_festival_2016.pdf

Bonet, L., Carreño, T. (2013), "The context of music festivals in Spain", in Négrier, E., Bonet, L., Guérin, M. (eds.), *Music festivals, a changing world*, Paris, Michel de Maule, pp. 182–192. https://hal.archives-ouvertes.fr/hal-01439617

Boogaarts, I. (1993), « La festivalomanie. À la recherche du public marchand », *Les Annales de la Recherche Urbaine*, n°57–58, pp. 114–119.

CITI (2018), *Putting the band back together, remastering the world of music.* https://ir.citi.com/QnhL09FARMDbvMhnCWFtjkqYOlPmgXqWS5Wrjts%2B6usU7suR9o7uUEFwZNjmUfyrAn10iZxCkYc%3D

Colomer, J., Carreño, T. (2012), "El paisaje de los festivales escénicos en España", in Bonet, L., Schargorodsky, H. (eds.), *La gestión de festivales: miradas comparadas*, Barcelona: Gescénic, pp. 127–149. http://www.ub.edu/cultural/wp-content/uploads/2018/10/La-gestion-de-festivales-esc%C3%A9nicos-conceptos-miradas-y-debates.pdf

Culture Open Data (2020), "Panorama des festivals: entre source d'information et invitation à la découverte ». Paris, Ministry of Culture. https://www.culture.gouv.fr/Sites-thematiques/Culture-et-territoires/La-Culture-en-region/Panorama-des-festivals

Dal Pozzolo, L., Carnelli, L. (2013), "For a taxonomy of festivals in Italy. The five W's of festivals: Who, what, when, where, and why", in Négrier, E., Bonet, L., Guérin, M. (eds.), *Music festivals, a changing world*, Paris, Michel de Maule, pp. 224–234. https://hal.archives-ouvertes.fr/hal-01439617

DCMS (1998), *Creative industry task force report*, London, Department for Culture, Media and Sport.

DCMS (2001), *Green paper: Culture and creativity: The next 10 years.* http//www.culture.gov.uk/reference_library/publications/4634.aspx/

De Cossio, M.R. (2018), *Music festivals in Catalonia in a European context. Factors of competitiveness of a dynamic creative industry.* http://diposit.ub.edu/dspace/bitstream/2445/125878/1/TFG-GEI-De%20Cossio-%20Maria-Jun18.pdf

Djakouane, A., Négrier, E., Jourda, M.J., (2010), *Les publics des festivals,* Paris: Michel de Maule. https://hal.archives-ouvertes.fr/hal-01439297/document

Djakouane, A., (2014), « Les publics des festivals de musiques du monde. Entre ouverture et conformisme », *Festivalisation(s), Cahiers d'ethonomusicologie,* n°27, pp. 133–153. https://journals.openedition.org/ethnomusicologie/2170

Eurostat, *Culture statistics 2019 edition.* https://ec.europa.eu/eurostat/documents/3217494/10177894/KS-01-19-712-EN-N.pdf/915f828b-daae-1cca-ba54-a87e90d6b68b

Frey, B.S. (1986), "The Salzburg festival – from the economic point of view". *Journal of Cultural Economics,* 10: 27–44.

Frey, B.S. (1994), "The economics of music festivals". *Journal of Cultural Economics,* 18(1): 29–39. https://www.bsfrey.ch/articles/C_244_1994.pdf

Frey, B.S. (2000), "The rise and fall of festivals. Reflections on the salzburg Festspiele". Zurigo, Institute for Empirical Research in Economics. *Working Paper* No. 48. http://www.econ.uzh.ch/static/wp_iew/iewwp048.pdf

Getz, D., Frisby, W. (1988). "Evaluating management effectiveness in community-run festivals". *Journal of Travel Research,* 27: 22–27. https://www.researchgate.net/publication/249700730_Evaluating_Management_Effectiveness_In_Community-Run_Festivals

Getz, D. (2010). "The nature and scope of festival studies". *International Journal of Event Management,* 5(1): 1–47. http://ijemr.org/wp-content/uploads/2014/10/Getz.pdf

Guerzoni, G. (2008), *Effetto festival. L'impatto económico dei festival di approfondimento culturale.* Milano, Fondazione Eventi – Fondazione Carispe.

Jordan, J. (2016), "Introduction: focusing on festivals", in Newbold, C., Jordan, J. (eds.), *Focus on festivals: Contemporary European case studies and perspectives,* Oxford: Goodfellow Publishers Limited, pp. 6–18.

Kienast, K., Statista (2018), "Countries with the most major music festivals in the European Union (EU) in 2017". https://www.statista.com/statistics/756238/music-festivals-eu/

Kienast, K., Statista (2019), "Music concert and festival attendance in the United Kingdom (UK) from 2012 to 2016". https://www.statista.com/statistics/282032/music-concert-and-festival-attendance-in-the-uk-by-attendee-type/

Laing, J., Mair, J. (2015). "Music festivals and social inclusion: The festival organizers' perspective". *Leisure Sciences, An Interdisciplinary Journal,* 37(3): 252–268. https://www.researchgate.net/publication/276425266_Music_Festivals_and_Social_Inclusion_-_The_Festival_Organizers'_Perspective

Li, Y.N., Wood, E. (2014), "Music festival motivation in China: Free the mind". *Leisure Studies,* 35, 2016- Issue 3, pp. 332–351. https://www.researchgate.net/profile/Emma_Wood12/publication/277971666_Music_festival_motivation_in_China_free_the_mind/links/562fa6e108ae8e1256876f86/Music-festival-motivation-in-China-free-the-mind

Lopez-Palacio, I. (2020), "Medio siglo de Glastonbury, el festival que cambió el pop británico". https://elpais.com/cultura/2020/07/02/babelia/1593710095_195328.html

Maughan, C. (2013), "Festivals, a journey from here to where a British perspective", in Négrier, E., Bonet, L., Guérin, M. (eds.), *Music festivals, a changing world,* Paris, Michel de Maule pp. 262–277. https://hal.archives-ouvertes.fr/hal-01439617

Maughan, C. (2015), "Preface", in Newbold, C., Maughan, C., Jordan, J., Bianchini, F. (eds.), *Focus on festivals: Contemporary European case studies and perspectives*, Oxford, Goodfellow Publishers Limited, pp. XII–XIV.

Mulligan, M. (2021a), "Recorded music revenues hit $23.1 billion in 2020, with artists direct the winners – again". https://www.midiaresearch.com/blog/recorded-music-revenues-hit-231-billion-in-2020-with-artists-direct-the-winners-again?utm_source=MIDiA+Research+Newsletter&utm_campaign=0cc5a95cbc-EMAIL_CAMPAIGN_2019_01_14_12_03_COPY_01&utm_medium=email&utm_term=0_8602b921cd-0cc5a95cbc-523297657

Mulligan, M., (2021b), "IFPI confirms global recorded music revenue growth". https://midiaresearch.com/blog/ifpi-confirms-global-recorded-music-revenue-growth?utm_source=MIDiA+Research+Newsletter&utm_campaign=3a6f74d-4bf-EMAIL_CAMPAIGN_2019_01_14_12_03_COPY_01&utm_medium=email&utm_term=0_8602b921cd-3a6f74d4bf-523297657

Musical life in Germany, "Interest in music festivals". https://www.miz.org/musical-life-in-germany/download/statistics/1001_Interest_in_music_festivals.pdf

Newbold, C., Maughan, C., Jordan, J., Bianchini, F. (2015), "Introduction: Focusing on festivals", in Newbold, C., Maughan, C., Jordan, J., Bianchini, F. (eds.), *Focus on festivals: Contemporary European case studies and perspectives*, Oxford, Goodfellow Publishers Limited, pp. XV–XXVI.

Négrier, E., Jourda, M.J. (2007), *Les nouveaux territoires des festivals*, Paris, Michel de Maule. Ffhal-01439256f

Négrier, E. (2011), «La festivalización de la Cultura. Una dialéctica de los cambios de paradigma», in Bonet, L., Schargorodsky, H. (eds.), *La gestion de festivales: miradas comparadas*, Barcelona, Gescénic 2012, pp. 17–32.

Négrier, E. (2013), « *Intervention devant la commission des affaires culturelles et de l'éducation de l'Assemblée Nationale* », Mercredi 11 septembre 2013. http://www.assemblee-nationale.fr/14/pdf/cr-cedu/12-13/c1213066.pdf

Négrier, E. (2015), "Festivalisation: Patterns and limits", in Newbold, C., Maughan, C., Jordan, J., Franco Bianchini, F. (eds.), *Focus on festivals: Contemporary European case studies and perspectives*, Oxford, Goodfellow Publishers Limited, pp. 18–27.

Négrier, E., Bonet, L., Guérin, M., (2013), *Music festivals, a changing world*, Paris, Michel de Maule. https://hal.archives-ouvertes.fr/hal-01439617

Négrier, E., Djakouane, A., (2020), *L'empreinte sociale et territoriale des festivals*. Six reports. https://www.francefestivals.com/:
- Les publics des festivals,
- Les indicateurs socio-économiques des festivals,
- Les bénévoles,
- Festivals annulés,
- Les partenariats d'intérêt général des festivals, forthcoming,
- La communication sociale des festivals, forthcoming.

O'Connell, D. (2019), "Why Glastonbury has £10m in the bank". https://www.bbc.com/news/business-48750501

Oxford Economics (2013), *Wish you were here - Music tourism's contribution to the UK economy*. http://eventandconference.co.uk/economic-impact-music-festivals/

Oxford Economics (2015), *Wish you were here - Music tourism's contribution to the UK economy.* https://www.oxfordeconomics.com/my-oxford/projects/307897

Pérez-Gálvez, J., Lopez-Guzman, T., Gomez-Casero, G., Fruet Cardozo, J. (2017), "Segmentation of the spectators attending a festival based on musical preferences", *International Journal of Event and Festival Management*, 8(3): 346–360. https://www.emerald.com/insight/content/doi/10.1108/IJEFM-03-2017-0021/full/pdf?title=segmentation-of-the-spectators-attending-a-festival-based-on-musical-preferences

Priego, J.L. (2009), *1981-2005. 25 años del Festival de la Guitarra de Córdoba.* https://issuu.com/jopren/docs/25_a_os_de_guitarra

Rudolph, K.F. (2016), *The importance of music festivals: An unanticipated and underappreciated path to identity formation.* https://digitalcommons.georgiasouthern.edu/cgi/viewcontent.cgi?article=1209&context=honors-theses

Simon, J.P. (2019), "New players in the music industry: Lifeboats or killer whales? The role of streaming platforms", *Digital Policy, Regulation and Governance*, 21(4). https://www.emerald.com/insight/content/doi/10.1108/DPRG-06-2019-0041/full/pdf?title=new-players-in-the-music-industry-lifeboats-or-killer-whales-the-role-of-streaming-platforms

Snapes, L., (2021), "Music festivals call for new government scheme as sector faces ruin". https://www.theguardian.com/music/2021/jan/05/music-festivals-call-for-new-government-insurance-scheme-as-sector-faces-ruin?utm_term=3137d-b91f5b0a6a19fb030de7fc90458&utm_campaign=BusinessToday&utm_source=esp&utm_medium=Email&CMP=bustoday_email

Società italiana degli Autori ed Editori (SIAE) (2019), *Annuario dello Spettacolo 2018.* https://www.siae.it/sites/default/files/SIAE_Annuario_dello_Spettacolo_2018.pdf

Sweney, M. (2020), "UK music industry will halve in size due to Covid, says report". https://www.theguardian.com/business/2020/nov/18/uk-music-industry-will-halve-in-size-due-to-covid-says-report?utm_term=cf3be567091c7c89b727e3f7f-77c966a&utm_campaign=BusinessToday&utm_source=esp&utm_medium=Email&CMP=bustoday_email

Tremethick, R. (2016), "Glastonbury 2016 – Money facts from the world's largest festival". https://blog.torfx.com/general-interest/glastonbury-2016-money-facts-from-the-worlds-largest-festival/

UK Music (2018), *Measuring music 2018.* https://www.ukmusic.org/assets/general/UK_Music_Measuring_Music_2018.pdf

Um, H., (2019), "UK–Asia music business collaborations: Liverpool sound city, modern sky and Zandari Festa", *Global Media and China*, 4(4): 437–461. https://www.researchgate.net/publication/337795697_UK-Asia_music_business_collaborations_Liverpool_Sound_City_Modern_Sky_and_Zandari_Festa

Unesco (2015), *Festival statistics: Key concepts and current practices*, 2009 Framework for Cultural Statistics Handbook n° 3. http://uis.unesco.org/sites/default/files/documents/festival-statistics-key-concepts-and-current-practices-handbook-3-2015-en.pdf

Velasco, J. (2019), "El Festival de la Guitarra se cierra con 24.618 espectadores, en la media de la última década". https://cordopolis.es/2019/07/17/el-festival-de-la-guitarra-se-cierra-con-24-618-espectadores-en-la-media-de-la-ultima-decada/

Webster, E. (2014), *Association of independent festivals six-year report 2014.* London: Association of Independent Festivals. https://aiforg.com/wp-content/uploads/AIF-Six-Year-Report-2014.pdf

Webster, E. and McKay, G. (2016). *From Glyndebourne to Glastonbury: The impact of British music festivals.* Norwich: University of East Anglia. https://ueae-prints.uea.ac.uk/59132/1/Festival_Report_online.pdf

Working Group European Statistical System Network on Culture (ESSnet-Culture) (2012), *ESSnet culture final report.* https://ec.europa.eu/assets/eac/culture/library/reports/ess-net-report_en.pdf

Index

Note: **Bold** page numbers refer to tables; *italic* page numbers refer to figures and page numbers followed by "n" denote endnotes.

Printed in the United States
by Baker & Taylor Publisher Services